The Hero's Trail

ALSO BY PETER C. MOWREY

Award Winning Films: A Viewer's Reference
to 2700 Acclaimed Motion Pictures
(McFarland, 1994)

The Hero's Trail

*Myth and Art
in the American Western,
1903–1953*

PETER C. MOWREY

McFarland & Company, Inc., Publishers
Jefferson, North Carolina

LIBRARY OF CONGRESS CATALOGUING-IN-PUBLICATION DATA

Names: Mowrey, Peter C., 1967– author.
Title: The hero's trail : myth and art in the American western, 1903–1953 / Peter C. Mowrey.
Description: Jefferson, North Carolina : McFarland & Company, Inc., Publishers, 2022 |
Includes bibliographical references and index.
Identifiers: LCCN 2022021491 | ISBN 9781476682389 (paperback : acid free paper) ∞
ISBN 9781476644271 (ebook)
Subjects: LCSH: Western films—Encyclopedias. | Myth in motion pictures. | National characteristics,
American, in motion pictures. | West (U.S.)—In motion pictures—Encyclopedias. | BISAC:
PERFORMING ARTS / Film / Genres / Westerns
Classification: LCC PN1995.9.W4 M63 2022 | DDC 791.43/6587803—dc23/eng/20220523
LC record available at https://lccn.loc.gov/2022021491

BRITISH LIBRARY CATALOGUING DATA ARE AVAILABLE

ISBN (print) 978-1-4766-8238-9
ISBN (ebook) 978-1-4766-4427-1

Front cover photograph by Bob Wick (Bureau of Land Management)

Printed in the United States of America

*McFarland & Company, Inc., Publishers
Box 611, Jefferson, North Carolina 28640
www.mcfarlandpub.com*

For Stephen and Ingrid,

who bring love, joy, laughter,
and the wonder of childhood
to every single day,

and give me hope.

Acknowledgments

I am grateful for all the support I have gotten from so many quarters as I have researched and written this book. There is not space to thank everyone here, but I would like to single out a few people without whom I don't think this book would have happened. My sincere thanks go out to:

My wife Melissa and my children, Stephen and Ingrid, for being patient and supportive and helping me to make space for this work among all the other insanities of life—school and work and coronavirus and academia and everything else;

My parents, Jim and Judy, for being so loving and encouraging, and for taking me as an eight-year-old to see my very first Western at the drive-in so many years ago (*Rooster Cogburn*)—it all started there;

My siblings, Jim and Andrea, for their cheerleading and feedback—the best big brother and sister a person could ask for.

My brilliant colleague Jonathan Guez, who read early drafts of the beginning chapters back when I was even wondering if there was a book in all this—without his encouragement at that crucial point, I doubt I would have proceeded any further;

All of the folks at McFarland, who have been so kind, and especially Dré Person, who has been unfailingly helpful and patient with my millions of questions along the way;

The greats in film criticism, commentary, and scholarship who have helped me to think about cinema as an art form (and a mythology) in so many new ways—particularly Richard Slotkin and three who are tragically no longer with us: Pauline Kael, Roger Ebert, and William Goldman;

And of course, Joseph Campbell, whose writings I first encountered as a college student and who forever changed the way I thought about art, music, literature, film, philosophy, religion, life, and love.

Table of Contents

Table of Contents

Preface:
On the Ethics of Writing
a Book About Westerns

In early August of 2019, I almost stopped writing this book. At that point, I had finished drafts of most of the essays in the section on silent Westerns and was eager to plunge ahead into the world of sound. A full year of sabbatical lay ahead, and there was nothing holding me back.

Then the American people went through a long, long weekend. On Friday, August 3, a man walked into a Walmart in El Paso carrying a semi-automatic rifle and opened fire, killing twenty-three people and wounding twenty-three more. It was one of the deadliest anti–Latino attacks in American history. Then, the following day, another gunman, this time carrying a modified semi-automatic pistol and wearing body armor, shot forty-one rounds into a crowd outside a bar in Dayton, killing nine (including his own sister) and injuring seventeen. In the space of just thirteen hours, two of the three deadliest mass shootings of 2019 had occurred—this in a year that saw more than one such event per day on average.

Gun violence in American life, in both its individual and mass-killing forms, has become an everyday phenomenon—commonplace, business-as-usual. Even as I write this, in the midst of a pandemic, mass shootings continue to happen. The year of coronavirus, 2020, has also averaged over fifty American mass shootings per month; in fact, their frequency only increased after the nation entered lockdown. Every single month, thousands of Americans are killed by firearms, whether by murder, suicide, or accident. No other country on earth experiences gun violence to the degree that we do, even though many of the usual culprits cited—mental illness, video games, violent movies, etc.—are prevalent throughout the world. Furthermore, the events that sparked the Black Lives Matter movement and the protests still going on across this nation have highlighted the disproportionate impact that gun violence inflicts upon American communities of color.

Now, I should make it clear right up front: ***this book is not about politics.*** I have strong opinions about political issues, including guns, but that has nothing to do with my project here. Considering the interactions between Western movies and American politics is a worthy topic indeed, but one that has already been explored in a number of excellent books. I would refer the interested reader particularly to Stanley Corkin's *Cowboys as Cold Warriors* (2004), Michael Coyne's *The Crowded Prairie* (1997), Patrick McGee's *From Shane to Kill Bill* (2007), Robert B. Pippin's *Hollywood Westerns and*

American Myth (2010), Jane Tompkins's *West of Everything* (1992), and most especially Richard Slotkin's *Gunfighter Nation* (1992). In contrast to these wonderful works, however, *The Hero's Trail* is intended to be as apolitical as possible. Politics is simply not my primary interest here, and my hope is that this book may be enjoyed by anyone who loves movies—liberal or conservative, socialist or libertarian. Beyond this preface I will not dwell directly on political matters in any significant way.

Nevertheless, the events of last August precipitated a crisis for me. Even though a little book about Westerns seemed pretty trivial next to everything else that was happening, the mass shootings in El Paso and Dayton still raised questions about my project that I could not ignore.

What are the ethics of writing a book about Western movies—a genre largely populated by plots that are "resolved" through gun violence—during a time when the real-world culture of gun violence is spiraling so far out of control? I would never want to do anything that supports or contributes in any way to the fetishization of lethal weaponry in this country.

Nevertheless, after a great deal of difficult reflection that August, I decided to proceed—and here's the essential reason why. Whatever one's feelings about guns and gun control, my hope is that this book will encourage all of us to read Westerns *metaphorically* rather than literally. Fortunately, that is where the real richness comes, where the genre opens up to reveal its true treasures—insights about the human condition that often, paradoxically, speak quite powerfully *against* the fear and weakness of character that can so often lead to violence.

None of us will ever have to walk down a dusty frontier street like Will Kane, six-shooter at our side, in order to literally "gunfight" our problems away—just as (with regard to other genres) none of us will ever have to slay a dragon, confront a Gorgon, or fight hostile aliens with laser weaponry. But all of us will have to engage in confrontations, showdowns; we all have our *metaphorical* dragons to slay. And, like Will Kane, each one of us will experience moments in our lives when we are called upon to stride down that street all alone, jaw set, deserted by others who might have helped us, but doing our best to walk tall and win through, nonetheless.

That's what Westerns are about, among many other things! That's why the best of them—and the best Arthurian romances, and the best myths, and the best science fiction—speak to us on a deeper level, a symbolic level, about those universal truths that are the essence of our humanity.

At their core, Westerns are no more about guns than tales of the Round Table are about lances. They are about courage and cowardice; solitude and community; nature and culture; selfishness and sacrifice; honor and ignominy; love and death.

That is why they matter.

Notes on Language
and Cast/Credit Charts

It is impossible to write about classic-period Westerns without confronting problems of language, especially with regard to the differences between the contemporary era and the early twentieth century in how people refer to human beings generically (by pronoun) and Native Americans particularly (by proper noun). In each of these cases, I have had to make some stylistic decisions; overall, I've tried to favor clarity and readability, but I also wish to avoid jarring instances where the language being used doesn't fit with the time context of the passage, whether classic or contemporary. The result is inevitably a compromise; each choice gains something and loses something, and I hope the reader will be charitably disposed to these imperfect solutions and understand that my intention is always to treat all people with respect. Indeed, engaging with and celebrating human universals is one of the primary purposes of this book.

To take the most prevalent case first: the term "Indian" is unquestionably loaded and problematic. However, while writing these essays, I was continually struck at how awkward and inappropriate it seemed, for example, to talk about "Native Americans" within the action of *The Battle of Elderbush Gulch* or *Stagecoach*, whose characters (and writers) would not have been expected to use that term themselves. In general, then, I have tended to favor the world-consistent "Indian" when speaking within the imaginary perspective of the movie itself, but to use today's more respectful term "Native Americans" when referring to actual humans and cultures. Thus, the essay on *Elderbush Gulch* describes a settler within the fictional narrative "whose own body lies next to that of a slain **Indian**," but also refers to a real-world actress who lived "nearly her entire life during a time when clashes between government forces and **Native Americans** were occurring."

I have tried to take a similar approach to gendered pronouns when applied to universal human principles, letting the context help shape my choice of words. For example, because so much of the mythic content of Westerns relates to the archetypal Hero Cycle, there are many instances in this text where I talk about the *hero* as a universal human concept, and in fact I hope it will become clear that I believe each one of us to be the hero of our own life story. However, in almost all of these Westerns, the actual specific hero of the story is male, and so I frequently find myself writing sentences like this one, from the essay on *The Big Trail*: "Perhaps all orthodox Westerns feature the same eternal, archetypal hero at various points in **his** life, moving slowly but inexorably from sunrise to sunset." Again, when discussing heroes (or other universally human concepts) in a more general context, including that of our own era, I will strive to use

3

appropriate gender-neutral language (his or her, their), but in sentences like the one above about orthodox Westerns, it would be both cumbersome and misleading to use a gender-neutral term. Again I ask for charity on the part of the reader, for whom I hope this book will make clear my deep belief that the mythic elements present in these Westerns are relevant to *all* of us, across identity categories.

Throughout this volume, then, I will favor inclusive language when writing in a contemporary context but will favor the idioms of the earlier era when that context is predominant. In more ambiguous situations, as a musician I will be guided by my ear. In all cases, the reader may take it as a given that my interest in the ways these films can speak to human beings is a universally inclusive one.

Cast/Credit Charts

The essays in this book are organized around individual movies, chronologically. At the beginning of each essay, I list some basic cast and credit information for the film being discussed, in the following format:

AKA: *Titles*
Premiere Date (Location)
Country—Language(s)
Production Company
Runtime—Sound—Color—Aspect Ratio

Direction: Names
Screenplay: Names
Principal Cast: Names
Production: Names
Cinematography: Names
Editing: Names
Art Direction: Names
Music: Names
Awards: Names
Nominations: Names

Notes on the Categories

AKA: Any alternate English-language titles under which the film has been released are listed.

Premiere Date (Location): Date and place of the film's initial premiere.

Country—Language(s): The country or countries of production, and the language(s) spoken (or shown on titles) in the original version.

Production Company: The primary production company for the film. Subsequent distributors are not listed.

Runtime: The length of the film in minutes. If different versions exist, the longer time is preferred.

Sound: The sound mix of the movie—for this volume, Silent or Mono.

Color: The color process—"BW" for Black and White; Technicolor; etc.

Aspect Ratio: The aspect ratio of the image as width to height, with height equal to 1.

Direction, Screenplay, Production, Cinematography, Editing, Art Direction, Music: The crew members responsible for each of these categories are listed, whether or not they appear in the film's credits. If they are not credited in the film, that is also indicated here. Names of individuals often changed throughout the course of their careers or were listed in different ways; here, for consistency's sake, I have always used the person's name as listed in the Internet Movie Database, even when this conflicts with the way the name is given in the movie's credits. If a film was based on a preexisting work, I have included the author under "Screenplay" and provided the title of the original work if it differs from the movie's title. For the production credit, I have favored the title of *producer* over *executive producer* (where applicable) because of the former's more direct involvement (typically) with the creation of the film. For the music credit, I have listed the actual composer(s) of the film score rather than the musical director.

Principal Cast: Primary members of the cast are listed, again using the IMDB standard; and character names are given in parentheses as they are listed in the film's credits (when provided). As a way of keeping these lists to a reasonable length, I have generally included only actors listed in the film's opening credits, in order of appearance, omitting uncredited actors or those who appear only in end credits. The first few entries contain some uncredited actors in their cast lists, since credits tended to be quite incomplete in the early days.

Awards: Major film awards won (with persons winning them, where appropriate).

Nominations: Major award nominations received but not won.

Unless otherwise noted, illustrations are taken directly from the screen image and not from studio promotional materials. Production information about each movie (e.g. running time, sound mix, premiere date and location, cast and crew), if not specifically credited, is taken from the Internet Movie Database.

Introduction

It is always a surprise to the people who know me when they learn of my love for the American Western movie. Why on earth would a peace-loving, Prius-driving college professor with an aversion to guns be so ardently drawn to this genre?

In all honesty, I was puzzled by this too, until I realized that Westerns seemed to be lighting up the same parts of my brain as some of the other things I have always loved: Greek myths; Arthurian romances; science fiction. As a child in the 1970s, I could not get enough of *Star Trek* or Edith Hamilton or *Le Morte d'Arthur*; and as an adult, I began to find that Western movies struck a similar chord.

But what do classical myths, tales of knights-errant, fantastic fiction, and Westerns share in common?

- They all have radically different settings, in time and/or place, from the environment in which they were created—and yet also offer penetrating snapshots of the contemporary cultures that produced them;
- They feature heroes venturing forth into unknown frontiers on the edge of knowledge and encountering beings strange or exotic to them: gods, dragons, aliens, or native inhabitants;
- By placing ordinary human beings into supernormal, idealized, or magical circumstances outside everyday experience, these genres are ripe for testing boundaries and exploring questions about the human condition—ethics, psychology, society, family, and the individual's pathway through life;
- When done well, they can be poetic, lyrical, beautiful, and profoundly moving;
- The best examples of each are all deeply metaphorical, and—while certainly attracting their share of literal-minded followers who obsess over surface-level details—are best read and understood symbolically rather than as merely linear, quasi-historical narratives.

In short: all of these genres have the potential to be *mythic*—and as such, the Western, at its most potent, is *bona fide* American mythology.

Like art, myth has the potential to imbue our lives with beauty and meaning. It helps us experience and explore more fully what it means to be human: the awe we feel before the wonder of existence, as well as how we move through the stages of life, how we come together in community, and how we make sense of the world around us. In this sense, mythology—working metaphorically—is critically important to human psychology, society, and culture. In the past century and more, we have seen the effects of the draining of mythic vitality from our lives, and for that I blame the death of metaphor amid the growth of an obsessive, unhealthy literalism in our culture. On one side, people have been abandoning religion in droves because they can no longer accept its claims as literal truth in the light of what science has revealed to us about the origins of life and the universe. On the other side, there has been a reactionary retrenchment of some religious communities into closed, dogmatic, pre–Enlightenment echo chambers. In each case, metaphor has been devalued in the face of an all-pervasive literalism. The result of this draining is visible in our culture every day: a retreat from both the aesthetic and the rational; larger proportions of our population less and less equipped to deal with the stresses and challenges of life; the dominance of mindless escapism— whether through vapid entertainment or mind-altering substances—over deeper and more meaningful pursuits; the growth of polarization, absolutism, and distrust; and the loss of a sense of community, shared humanity, and shared purpose.

No one in the public discourse has articulated the relevance of mythology and mythic thinking to human culture, psychology, and the arts more clearly and impactfully than the comparative mythologist Joseph Campbell (1904–1987). I will be drawing on his ideas frequently throughout the essays that follow—in fact, Campbell's concept of the monomyth ("The Hero's Journey") inspired the title of this book, which refers to the myriad occurrences of the trail as a metaphor for an individual's life-quest in Western pictures.

Obviously, there is a great deal to say about mythology and the American Western; this major theme will be explored and expanded upon in detail in the essays that follow. For now, I will simply note that, according to Campbell, myths serve four critical functions within a culture:

- A **metaphysical** (or **mystical**) function, evoking a sense of awe before the beauty and mystery of being;
- A **cosmological** function, helping to situate human beings within the reality of the world around them;
- A **sociological** function, reinforcing social mores and drawing the culture together through a shared literature;
- A **psychological** (or **pedagogical**) function, guiding individuals through the stages of life and helping them cope with those challenges we all share as human beings.[1]

Notice that all but one of these functions do not rely in any way on whether the myth in question is actually "true." The cosmological function can, but in today's world we rightly turn to science rather than myth to understand the nature and origins of our universe. For the mystical, sociological, and psychological services that myth renders to human beings, literal truth is irrelevant, and in fact there is the ever-present danger that reading the myths as historical fact will actually rob them of their deeper meaning and suck them dry of their transformational power. Joseph Campbell compared the literalization of myths to a diner eating the menu rather than the meal.

It is unfortunate that the word *myth* has taken on negative associations in our language today. We speak of myths as "lies," setting them up as an opposite pole to truth. This, I believe, is a mistake. It is much more appropriate to see myths as an art form, like poetry, literature, painting, dance, music, or film. No one derides or dismisses poetry for being untrue; no one criticizes a symphony for lying to them. There may have been an actual flesh-and-blood woman posing for the *Mona Lisa*—but if there weren't, or if the person being depicted was Leonardo himself (as some scholars suspect), the impact on our aesthetic appreciation of the work is relatively trivial. We don't devalue an Impressionist painting for not providing a photorealistic view of a landscape, nor do we criticize operas and musicals on the basis that, in real life, no one breaks into song and dance like that. Why, then, do we treat myths this way? Why do some people who organize their lives around myths think that they must be literally true in order to value them? And, conversely: why do others think that myths are of no value simply because, taken literally, they are demonstrably false? In my view, both the Christian fundamentalists who literally believe that light did not refract prismatically into a spectrum prior to Noah's rainbow and the atheists who believe that in disproving the biblical timeline they have rendered all mythic systems irrelevant are guilty of the same logical fallacy. Both think that literal truth is all that matters—whether defending or attacking mythic beliefs. Both argue from unstable ground, a perilous quicksand upon which the myths were never intended to stand. The dogmatic believer's "My sacred scriptures are valuable because they are the literal truth" is actually the equivalent statement to the militant atheist's "Because your sacred scriptures are not literally true, they are worthless"—in syllogistic terms, both argue from the same flawed major premise.

To be clear, and in the interests of full disclosure, I am very much pro-science and anti-dogmatism. As a result, I would maintain that we as human beings don't need to believe nonsense; we don't need to subscribe to ridiculous superstitions and pseudoscience; nor should we sign on to any systems that foster further divisions between segments of the human race. But it also seems clear that we need metaphor in addition to truth; we need emotion as well as logic; we need both art and science. And we have shown throughout our history as a species that we need myth too.

The American existential psychologist Rollo May summed this up very neatly in the opening lines of his aptly titled book *The Cry for Myth*:

> A myth is a way of making sense in a senseless world. Myths are narrative patterns that give significance to our existence. Whether the meaning of existence is only what we put into life by our own individual fortitude, as Sartre would hold, or whether there is a meaning we need to discover, as Kierkegaard would state, the result is the same: myths are our way of finding this meaning and significance. Myths are like the beams in a house: not exposed to outside view, they are the structure which holds the house together so people can live in it.[2]

May links the decline of myths in our society to rising rates of suicide, drug addiction, social disconnection, and mental illness, among other problems. We need myths, and we suffer from their absence in our lives.

Picasso once described art as "a lie that makes us realize truth."[3] Mythology, as a human-created art form, does the same: like the Buddhist image of the finger pointing beyond itself to the moon, it points past literality to deeper truths that cannot be expressed in words. There are of course facts about the physical world and its history that can be captured very well verbally: the motions of planetary bodies; the mechanisms of photosynthesis; the date and events of the Battle of Hastings. But for the elusive truths about what it means to be human, for insights about the human experience and the things that connect us despite our differences, and for a sense of oneness and reconciliation with the beauty of nature, we often (and more properly) turn to poetry, art, music, literature, film—and myth.

In my own lifetime, I have seen a number of books, television shows, and movies rushing to fill the vacuum of metaphorical relevance left by the dwindling of the old mythologies. The fifties gave us Tolkien, inspired in part by Norse and Germanic myths; the sixties gave us *Star Trek*, a direct descendant of classical Greek humanism; and the seventies gave us *Star Wars*, structured quite deliberately by George Lucas after Campbell's monomyth. (Interestingly, each of these has also inspired legions of "fundamentalists" who perform literal-minded exegeses on the original "texts"—leading to, for example, scholarly dissertations arguing the true identity of Tom Bombadil; books classifying all of the starships in Starfleet and organizing *Enterprise* adventures chronologically by "stardate"; and extensive encyclopedias of the alien races and technologies within a certain galaxy far, far away. This obsessive dissection of metaphorical stories as if they were historical fact runs counter to their purpose and completely misses the original point of these creations. All one needs to do is study the evolution of Trekkies or *Star Wars* fanboys to see, in microcosm, how religious orthodoxies are created.)

But new attempts at mythmaking didn't stop after the seventies. Even in recent years, when postmodernism seemed to have triumphed totally over metaphor, we saw the birth of a myth for a new generation of children in the *Harry Potter* books—at the same time resuscitating, not incidentally, a phenomenon even more astonishing than that of the Boy Who Lived, namely, the Child Who Reads! J.K. Rowling has certainly garnered her share of criticism recently, but I would not want to overlook the fact that she helped to bring an entire generation of children back to books, no mean accomplishment. (More on the phenomenon of creative heroes with feet of clay in a moment, and throughout the book.)

Science fiction and fantasy aside, however, the steadiest, most pervasive, and most universally experienced source of modern and specifically American mythological motifs for more than a hundred years has been the Western movie. For most of the twentieth century, and with reverberations extending to the present day, few American cultural products have served mythic functions for the mainstream culture to the extent that this genre has. Whether acknowledged or not, Westerns have had profound effects upon our society and the ways in which Americans live in the world. Many of these effects have been problematic, to be sure; and yet there are still rich treasures here for those who can find them.

Let's get this part out of the way right now, acknowledging the elephant in the room so we don't need to address it in every single essay that follows. John Wayne, Walter Brennan, William S. Hart, and other Western stars expressed views we would consider racist today; Wayne, Brennan, Ward Bond, Gary Cooper, John Ford, Borden Chase, and other significant Western figures became members of the Motion Picture Alliance for the Preservation of American Ideals, which provided numerous friendly witnesses for HUAC; John Ford could be bullying and cruel on his movie sets, even punching some of his actors like Henry Fonda and Maureen O'Hara; and on and on. The people who helped shape the development of the Western were often flawed, mean, reactionary, or bigoted. What's more, for the first half of the history of the Western, most of the movies gave at least tacit and often overt approval to the idea that America's genocidal war against Native Americans was not only morally acceptable but even glorious, a part of the nation's Manifest Destiny and perhaps the will of God. Even afterward, when revisionist Westerns of the sixties and seventies tore apart this idea and presented the Native Americans as the oppressed and the U.S. government as the oppressors, the movies still continued to glorify guns and gun violence as the solution to most problems.

For many people today, that settles it. Why care about these movies made by people who were less than admirable, and espousing or at least accepting political viewpoints now deemed deplorable? Why spend any time at all trying to find gold within this troubled, ideologically tainted genre? This is a perfectly understandable viewpoint, and to the people who hold it and cannot be persuaded otherwise (but would nevertheless like to read more about the frontier mythos and its effects on culture), I would eagerly recommend Richard Slotkin's magnificent trilogy on the history of American frontier mythology: *Regeneration Through Violence* (1973), *The Fatal Environment* (1985), and *Gunfighter Nation* (1992). To my mind, no one has done a better, more thorough, or more engaging job exploring the development of the myth of the frontier and its frequently disastrous consequences. It is worth noting, however, that even Slotkin—after spending nearly two thousand pages across three volumes explaining, in often harrowing detail, the impact of frontier mythology on American culture over four centuries—ends his trilogy on a note of reconciliation with our mythology rather than outright rejection of it:

> There is no reason why a myth of national solidarity and progress should not be claimed and used by Americans who envision the nation as polyglot, multicultural, and egalitarian and whose concept of "progress" is not defined by the imperatives of the commercial corporation or the preferences of a managerial or proprietary elite. The history of the Frontier did not "give" Roosevelt or Kennedy or Reagan the political scripts they followed. What they did—what any user of cultural mythology does—was to selectively read and rewrite the myth according to their own needs, desires, and political projects. It follows that our mythology has been and is available, at every moment of our history, to the claims of other constituencies…. The traditions we inherit, for all their seeming coherence, are a registry of old conflicts, rich in internal contradictions and alternative political visions, to which we ourselves continually make additions.[4]

The internally contradictory tradition of the Western movie is a seminal part of American mythology, not only revealing a great deal about our own history and national character but also offering much of relevance to the psyches of the people who still, for better or worse, are a part of the same culture that birthed the Western.

Although I will certainly deal in this book with how the Western grew and changed in its approach to its literal content—in terms of gender, race, history, and politics— it will serve no one's interests, neither mine nor the reader's, for me to be apologizing every other sentence for the political and moral sins of the Western and its architects. For this to be a worthwhile endeavor, we need to take it as read that we acknowledge the problematic nature of the genre and some of its creators but, nevertheless, are committed to journeying further through this difficult terrain in order to find the treasures hidden within it. And there are many. There is a reason why these pictures survive—the best of them, at any rate.

With all its faults, the American Western is the most significant new mythology that emerged from our national consciousness during the last century. Uncovering both the human universals that lie at the core of the genre and then the ways in which those universals were filtered through a societal lens and articulated in specific times and places is key to understanding ourselves as a culture. It also affords us the opportunity to encounter a richly rewarding art form with genuine (and positive!) things to teach us about the human experience and the human psyche. I am reminded of the Arthurian legends: it is so commonplace to note the pervasive influence of Arthurian literature on Western culture, and we tend to focus on the knightly virtues of courage, courtesy, self-sacrifice, determination, loyalty, honesty, and modesty that works such as Malory's *Le Morte d'Arthur* uphold, to the point that we often forget little details like the fact that Arthur commits mass infanticide, Herod-style, in order to protect his throne; that the exemplar of chivalric virtue, Sir Tristram, once beheads a lady for the sin of not being as beautiful as the glorious Iseult; that the noble Sir Gawain indulges in murderous familial blood feuds for decades; and that non–Christians are consistently treated as subhuman. But with medieval chivalric romance, it's easier for us to be inspired by the deeper, nobler human truths that the legends exalt while skimming over the more horrific surface elements that, after all, were just reflections of the savageries of the time. We tend to do this with the Bible as well, spending far more time with the lovely bits—David and Jonathan, "love your enemies," and the Twenty-Third Psalm—than we do with the divinely-sanctioned, wholesale slaughter of men, women, and children that is so common in the Good Book. (See, for example, Hosea 13:16: "They will fall by the sword; their little ones will be dashed to the ground, their pregnant women ripped open.") But it may be easier for us to find the gold among the dross with the Bible or with Malory: we are further removed in time (and, for most of us, in place) from the writers of these texts. The painful history of our own country, in contrast, with its exploitation and persecution of non-white races, is too close to us in both time and place—too raw, too tender—for us to ignore the troubling aspects of the traditional Western narrative (nor do I propose that we should do so). We might not wish to miss out on all that the Western mythology can provide us—after all, it is a foundational art form from our own culture, and one with so much to offer—but how can we get past our initial discomfort to reap these psychological and artistic rewards? Do we have to become callous? Must we set aside our sympathy and horror at the sufferings of vast swaths of humanity brought about by, for example, the bizarre doctrine of Manifest Destiny?

As I suggested earlier, one possible way forward for many of us (myself included) is to learn to read all of these things—religious texts, knightly legends, classical myths, and Western movies—metaphorically rather than literally. This helps greatly with the content problem: Arthur's attempt to kill his son via mass infanticide is not a literal historical event, but a symbol of the fears that all of us have that the work that we do will be rendered irrelevant by a younger, fresher, more capable generation. Likewise, although the U.S. campaigns against Native Americans were actual historical fact, the battles in *Fort Apache* weren't—and none of us are fighting such literal battles today. Henry Fonda's last stand in *Fort Apache* must have some other significant meaning for us; and exploring the ways in which we can discover it is one of the things I hope to do in this book. However, even if metaphor offers us a way to get past the problematic historical content of Westerns, how do we address the loathsome attitudes (by today's standards) held by so many of the genre's creators?

As a classical musician, questions like this are not exactly foreign territory to me. Even setting aside the troubling issues of class, privilege, and elitism that classical music raises, the fact remains that many composers and performers were horrible people. This was certainly true in the past, but—as the growing number of classical performers called out by the #MeToo movement shows—the problem still persists. I have albums in my collection by conductors and performers who have been accused of harassment, including those that contain some of the most beautiful musical moments I have ever heard. How does—or should—this affect how I experience the music performed by these people?

My answer—although this may seem overly facile to some—is that in our interactions with each other in life, it is the people that matter, but when an individual experiences art, it is the art itself that matters, not the performer or the creator. We should not conflate the art and the artist, for they are two different things. Richard Wagner was in many ways a horrible human being, and I can (and do) rightly condemn his behavior to others in his own life, but that doesn't change the fact that the "Liebestod" from *Tristan und Isolde* feels like a blast of pure, golden light touching the noblest parts of my soul. Should I deny myself this intensely human and beautiful experience simply as a sacrifice to the gods of moral superiority and judgmentalism? And would I be willing to subject myself to the same scrutiny by future generations, who might well be appalled by, let's say, my carbon footprint or my occasional eating of animals, just as I am appalled by Wagner's anti–Semitism? Isn't it possible that Wagner, despite all his flaws as a human being, still created something worthwhile? Can't we dislike Wagner as a person and still love the "Liebestod"? Personally, I do not find this difficult. With apologies to William Cowper, perhaps Beauty also moves in a mysterious way, and expresses itself through art made by human vehicles who are not necessarily the ones that we might expect or even choose.

We can "cancel" art all we wish, of course, and the decision about what art to allow into our lives and what to exclude is up to each one of us. I will note, however, that ruling out works of art on the basis of the morality of their creators (especially art of past periods with different mores than ours) or by the ways in which they fail to conform with our modern political sensibilities can, if applied stringently enough, eliminate virtually the entirety of our artistic tradition—a tragic impoverishment that I for one am not willing to bear. And here's why: I believe that art has the capability of transcending its roots, of moving past its ignoble origins and speaking to something fully and deeply human in each of us, saying things that perhaps even its creators never intended. Indeed, one of the most rewarding aspects of the artistic experience to me (beyond the obvious primary aesthetic one) is finding new meaning, new relevance, new humanity in a work of art from a previous age. All art is made by flawed people, products not only of their times but also of their own human idiosyncratic weaknesses. Most art is equally flawed, and doesn't survive, nor does it deserve to. (We must always remember Sturgeon's Law: ninety percent of everything is crap.) But some art does stand the test of time, usually because it resonates with something universal inside all of us. The best artworks—paintings, sculptures, poems, novels, plays, pieces of music, films—speak across time and space, and they do so not because of their surface-level content but because of the deeper wells of the human psyche from which they spring. They also do so irrespective of the defects of their creators. ***Flawed human beings can still be vehicles through which true Beauty can express itself in art—in fact, that is the only way it has ever been done.***

For these reasons, and others which will become clearer over the course of these essays, I am not ready to wash my hands of the Western genre. Quite the contrary: I think the Western mythos is exceedingly rich and capable of speaking to the best parts of our humanity rather than the worst, once one looks past the inevitable fallibility of the creators and reads the content of the films metaphorically rather than literally, as all effective art is meant to be read. Certainly, Westerns still make sense if one reads the guns simply as guns, the Native Americans simply as the indigenes of a particular place at a particular time, and the events as unfolding during a specific historical moment rather than inside the human imagination. In fact, this is how Westerns are treated all too frequently—and that's a true shame. Yes, the frontier can be, prosaically, the Western portion of the North American continent during the nineteenth century; or it can be, poetically, the unexplored potentialities of the future and the human spirit, both frightening and brimming with adventurous possibility. When the latter perspective is favored, and the greatest Westerns, as works of mythic art, are allowed to speak to us on a symbolic, metaphorical level—beyond the surface elements of cowboys and Indians, settlers and ranchers, horses and guns—the walls can open up, and our vision can become as vast and expansive as the magnificent vistas that fill the Western movie screen.

The preceding is the best brief case that I can make for the Western as both a mythologically relevant and potentially beautiful artistic genre on a general level; the rest of my argument lies in the specifics, the individual movies that I intend to explore in the essays that follow.

Are you still with me? If so, let's forge ahead!

There is a great deal of wonderful writing about Westerns out there—please see the references in the back for some excellent examples—but I think that this book fits into a niche of its own. I'm not aware of any resource that approaches the Western in quite this way, and so I hope that this will serve as a positive addition to the literature.

But what exactly is this book?

First, it is a **series of essays** about individual Western movies appearing during the first fifty years of the genre—between 1903 and 1953—organized chronologically by release date. These essays explore: the ways in which Western movies created gradually, through accretion, a genuine, homegrown American **mythology**, one which performs the critical functions that myths do within a culture; how these movies incorporated and developed **universal mythic themes** also present in other cultures and other times; and how, running beneath the dominant culture, there were also a handful of movies which, overtly or covertly, managed to **subvert** the prevailing mythic orthodoxy and reinterpret Western tropes in more heretical ways. (These subversive elements would finally come to predominate in the Westerns of the latter half of the twentieth century and beyond; I plan to examine the period from 1954 to the present in the second volume of this study—at this point tentatively titled *The Wild Frontier*.)

Second, this book is deeply concerned with the **aesthetic qualities** of the Westerns discussed within; it seeks to explore the Western movie as an **art form** of powerful potential. The **evolution of style** and connections to other **arts and literatures** will be examined. Reading Westerns—especially the greatest of them—through an aesthetic lens, and with an eye toward **metaphor**, can be vastly rewarding, yielding rich benefits to those who are willing to dig a little deeper beneath the surfaces of these often surprisingly complex and nuanced films.

Third, this book is a **film guide**—but, to be quite clear, nowhere near an exhaustive one. I have tried to include the movies generally regarded as **the greatest and most important Westerns** from the genre's first fifty years (as well as some "lesser" works that

I have chosen because of their mythic, stylistic, or historical interest). Given the thousands of American Westerns that were made during this time period, the ones discussed here necessarily represent only a tiny fraction of the vast Hollywood Western catalog. Nevertheless, my hope is that the reader will finish this book having spent some time with the very best that the genre has to offer, perhaps equivalent to the experience that a visitor to an art museum has when encountering many great, canonical works—alongside some more unusual, idiosyncratic pieces—even while understanding that for every painting or sculpture on view in this curated collection, there are uncounted thousands more that space cannot accommodate or that history has forgotten.

Fourth, this book uses the Western movie genre as a window through which to examine the diverse array of **extra-cinematic topics and themes** that inform these films, and upon which they in turn cast light. As with all art, Westerns have relevance to things beyond their own materials and stories, speaking to human universals that are deeper and more ancient than the mere idiosyncrasies of the time and place in which they were made. As a result, our explorations of the Western genre will also lead us to a variety of topics beyond film and mythology; these essays will not be afraid to explore some of these side paths as they appear. So, for example, within these pages we will touch upon:

- The paradox of time in *The Battle of Elderbush Gulch* (1913)
- The consequences of violence in *Keno Bates, Liar* (1915)
- The persona of the hero in *The Covered Wagon* (1923)
- The fall of civilizations in *The Vanishing American* (1925)
- Compassion and redemption in *3 Bad Men* (1926)
- The shadow within us all in *Viva Villa!* (1934)
- Embracing ambiguity in *The Plainsman* (1936)
- The qualities of American art in *Stagecoach* (1939)
- The significance of metaphor in *Dodge City* (1939)
- Creating art within constraints in *Union Pacific* (1939)
- Taoist philosophy in *Destry Rides Again* (1939)
- Aristotelian friendship and judgmentalism in *The Westerner* (1940)
- The union of opposites in *The Ox-Bow Incident* (1942)
- The poetics of emptiness in *My Darling Clementine* (1946)
- Operatic Love-Death in *Duel in the Sun* (1946)
- The nobility and heroism of enemies in *Fort Apache* (1948)
- The integration of the Jungian psyche in *Red River* (1948)
- The inscrutability of fate in *Yellow Sky* (1948)
- Aging in *She Wore a Yellow Ribbon* (1949)
- Community and democracy in *Wagon Master* (1950)
- Greek tragedy in *The Gunfighter* (1950)
- Anthropology and human universals in *Winchester '73* (1950)
- The interaction of art and politics in *Broken Arrow* (1950)
- The arc of the moral universe in *Devil's Doorway* (1950)
- The mythic heroism of the ordinary individual in *Rawhide* (1951)
- Thomas Mann's erotic irony in *Along the Great Divide* (1951)
- Nature and change in *Bend of the River* (1952)
- Isolation and alienation in *High Noon* (1952)

- Human motivation and Kuṇḍalinī yoga in *The Naked Spur* (1953)
- The bittersweet passing of generations in *Shane* (1953)

Finally, this book is a **personal, reflective journey** through the first five decades of the American Western. Although I have been as scrupulous as possible with regard to the facts, when it comes to interpreting the mythic or aesthetic value of these films, I make no claim of objectivity. I have spent my life immersed in both art and mythology, and this—along with my own history as a creative artist—undoubtedly colors the way I approach Western movies. Thus, among other things, I hope that this book serves as a work of **film criticism**, but one from a particular point of view that prioritizes both artistic and mythic elements.

A note on inclusion: the films I have chosen to discuss certainly incorporate the lion's share of the canon; my guess is that film buffs or critics compiling their lists of the "All-Time Greatest Westerns" would find most if not all of their picks (from 1903 to 1953) discussed here. Included movies generally meet the following two criteria: (a) they are easily obtainable for viewing; and (b) they have aesthetic and/or mythological significance that, in my view, merits a closer look. But as I mentioned, there are some little-known, offbeat inclusions as well, and I believe that the essays themselves will make clear why I chose to discuss them. The final list of films, then, is a combination of canon and cult classics. Inspired perhaps by my Western heroes (as well as the questing knights-errant), I will not be afraid, at least sometimes, to find my own less-traveled path, one which may lead to surprising places.

Each essay focuses on one or two significant aspects of the film as they relate to the overarching themes of the book (though some will also feature a final section of interesting "tidbits and trivia"). This means, however, that no essay is an exhaustive study of its movie; there will always be aspects left unexplored, especially those which have already been covered in great detail elsewhere. One upside to this approach is that even connoisseurs intimately familiar with a particular film may find things within its essay that surprise them, enhance (or challenge) their understanding, and suggest new perspectives on the movie.

Another advantage, I hope, to this book's structure is that the essays could be read individually and in any order. Each, to a certain extent at least, stands on its own. Having said this, however, I do believe that a subterranean current wends its way through these pages, and that, when taken together as a whole, the essays reveal a larger picture emerging from the sum of the parts.

I should now take a moment to say what this book is *not*. It is not intended to be a scholarly history of the Western, even though it does proceed chronologically through the movies discussed. Historical context is present throughout, of course, but I am not a historian, and my chosen areas of focus (and the scope of this study) mean that I must ignore or just lightly touch on large portions of the Western repertoire—television Westerns, serials, B-movies, "singing cowboy" movies, and Western musicals, for example—either because they yield fewer fruits from an aesthetic or mythological point of view, or because I simply must place some boundaries around what could become an unmanageably vast project.

Also, this book is not intended to provide a thorough exploration of the treatment of race, gender, and identity in Western movies. Obviously, that is an enormously meaningful and relevant topic. There are great studies that have been written about, for example, the portrayal of Native Americans or the propagation of gender-role stereotypes in Westerns—but this is not one of them. Clearly, it is important to consider how films of this genre and from earlier eras treat (often problematically) issues of identity, and I will certainly touch on those themes throughout the book where appropriate. However, with the exception of cases where gender, race, sexuality, or identity are directly relevant to the film's aesthetic or mythological status, these instances will only serve as grace notes within the larger discussion.

Again, I hope it is clear that my decision to foreground other aspects of the American Western is not to diminish the importance of the subject of identity in film, but instead is simply an acknowledgment of two realities: first, that there exist experts in gender, race, and sexuality studies who are far better equipped to address these questions than I am; and second, that my primary purpose here is a different one, seeking to look beyond the surface literality of the Western narratives in hopes of finding a broader and more metaphorical engagement with the universals of human nature—those things which transcend all identity categories and have the potential to speak across all human boundaries—and while doing so, to say something about the Western as a mythology and an art form.

The major themes of this book will emerge gradually, as each essay examines a different instance of the American Western and its possibilities, but there are some conclusions that I have reached that I would like to share right now, at the beginning of our journey together, in order to help contextualize the discussions that are to follow. Here, then, are what I would frame as the Four Laws of Western Movies. These apply both to classic-era Westerns, as covered in this volume, as well as to the revisionist, neoclassical, and postmodern movies of the second half of the Western's history to date.

- **The Law of Time:** As with science fiction or medieval romances, *at their heart Western movies are far more about the era in which they are made than they are about the time in which they are set.* The true history of American Westerns is a history of the twentieth and twenty-first centuries, not the nineteenth.
- **The Law of Craft:** Contrary to the common idea that classic Hollywood Westerns are merely simplistic morality plays featuring white hats and black hats, *the most successful Westerns* (and even many "ordinary" ones) *are far more sophisticated, nuanced, and perceptive than we typically give them credit for.* In fact, there is a lot that modern filmmakers could learn from these works about artistic subtlety, emotional realism, psychological complexity, and the effective portrayal of the ambiguities of human life.
- **The Law of Variation:** Like the Blues, another distinctly American creation, Westerns are constructed upon patterns and tropes quite familiar to their audiences and easily recognized as such, and yet there is a stunningly varied range of ways in which these patterns are realized in the final product. In both cases, *what's interesting is not the patterns themselves, but how the creators build upon them, interpret them, combine them, and sometimes subvert them, in order to fashion ever-varying works of art.* As Roger Ebert said about filmmaking in general: "A movie is not about what it is about. It is about *how* it is about it."[5] This certainly applies to Westerns. In short: *Western* is an adverb!

- **The Law of Metaphor:** Like other myths, *Westerns can be wonderful when read metaphorically, horrible when read literally.* I would never suggest looking to the literal, narrative content of Westerns to tell us how we should think about (for example) the settling of the frontier, or the treatment of Native Americans, or the roles of men and women, or the instrumental value of an actual "good man with a gun." But if we let the rich, metaphorical, archetypal language of the Western work on us—on a deeper mythic and symbolic level, where a horse is not merely a horse, but Nature; a gun not a gun, but the individual Will; and an "Indian" not merely a specific representative of a native tribe, but rather the undiscovered natural potentialities within us all—then we have moved a little closer to the realm of myth. This is the best way to engage with the Western movie, as it is with art, literature, and other mythologies; to do otherwise is indeed to eat the menu instead of the meal.

Extending the meal image further than I should: the heritage of Western movies is a great feast, and I certainly hope this book will encourage you to partake of many of these films, whether for the first time or the twenty-first. Having said that, however, I do not believe that one must see all of these movies to follow (and hopefully enjoy) the discussions about them. (On the other hand, as mentioned above, they are all easily obtainable, usually inexpensively and sometimes even freely.) These essays are meant to be read as one might explore a review of a film not yet seen, but which one might consider seeking out if the review is tantalizing enough. May it be so!

The first half-century of the Western, from *The Great Train Robbery* in 1903 to *Shane* in 1953, is a kaleidoscope of artistry and myth. The fifty-two Westerns examined in this volume, and countless others from the early days through the Golden Age, contain a myriad of visions that, taken together, provide a fully realized mythos with much to say about the human experience, the adventure of life, and the boundless possibilities that lie beyond the next horizon. These movies present a wide, wild, free world, one in which we find ourselves wanting to live. We want to play in it, like kids playing cowboys.

Despite the common territory generally explored by the genre, however, each single movie vision is different, carving out a special place for itself in its own particular ways. Just as individual human beings, varied and unique, come together to form coherent societies, so the thousands of Western films from the classic era combine to form a consistent and perceivable whole, with each movie contributing its own special bit—its own little thread in the grand Western tapestry. Together these films provide a priceless window into the American experience and the human experience, one rarely available to us outside of the arts.

As we know, and as *High Noon* (1952) would eventually underscore in powerful fashion, we are all alone, trapped inside of our own heads. Everyone experiences life differently, and it's hard to know how we can even begin to encounter the world as others encounter it. Art and myth, though, are capable of providing a path forward, a bridge across this seemingly unbridgeable gulf, especially when numerous artists and storytellers approach the same inherited cultural material in their own peculiar ways. The body of work that results from this, taken as a whole, can uncover both human universals and cultural particulars, all measured against a common frame of reference—in this case, the stylistic coherences of the classical Western story.

Watching the great Westerns, we experience varying human imaginings of the same essential myth projected onto a screen, each shot from a specific point of view (literally and figuratively) and each different from all the rest. It is as if we were climbing into someone else's head, seeing what they see, hearing what they hear, feeling what they feel as they engage with a vibrant and active mythic landscape. This is the true power of cinema—and the true power of the Western.

Done right, the Western broadens our experiences, thrills us, moves us, sometimes outrages us, connects us to that which is universally human, and occasionally allows us to apprehend Beauty; in short, it does all of the things that art is supposed to do. And, like myth, it also yields genuine insights, feeds our sense of awe and wonder, accompanies us through the stages of life, and helps to knit our society together by appealing to at least some measure of commonly accepted cultural values.

Most enjoyably, the Western also provides an enormous stage for our imagination. The real Old West was nothing like filmmakers presented it, of course; it was just a few years in a few places, confined in space and time and unfolding in prose rather than poetry. But the Old West of film (and literature) is something entirely different, a mythic landscape that is boundless and somehow eternal. We feel like we could roam its vast tracks forever, a new adventure always waiting just over the next rise.

PART ONE

The Silents

The Great Train Robbery (1903)

December 1903 (USA)
USA—English
Edison Manufacturing Company
12m—Silent—BW—1.33:1

Direction: Edwin S. Porter (uncredited)

Screenplay: Edwin S. Porter (uncredited), Scott Marble (story; uncredited)

Principal Cast: A.C. Abadie (Sheriff; uncredited), Gilbert M. "Broncho Billy" Anderson (Bandit / Shot Passenger / Tenderfoot Dancer; uncredited), Justus D. Barnes (Bandit Who Fires at Camera; uncredited), Walter Cameron (Sheriff; uncredited), John Manus Dougherty, Sr. (Bandit; uncredited), Donald Gallaher (Little Boy; uncredited), Shadrack E. Graham (Child; uncredited), Frank Hanaway (Bandit; uncredited), Adam Charles Hayman (Bandit; uncredited), Tom London (Locomotive Engineer; uncredited), Robert Milasch (Trainman / Bandit; uncredited), Marie Murray (Dance-Hall Dancer; uncredited), Mary Snow (Little Girl; uncredited)

Production: Edwin S. Porter (uncredited)

Cinematography: Blair Smith (uncredited), Edwin S. Porter (uncredited)

Awards: National Film Registry

We see a weathered bandit (played by Justus D. Barnes) in close-up and watch in disbelief as he stares straight into the camera and slowly aims his pistol directly at us, the audience. He then coldly fires six shots into our faces, point-blank, in a steady, deliberate rhythm. Clouds of smoke form around him. Even after his gun is empty, we see him continue to pull the trigger repeatedly; and despite this being a silent film, we can almost hear the clicks on the empty chambers.

This iconic moment is the final image from the first real Western, a twelve-minute short from 1903 called *The Great Train Robbery*, directed by Edwin S. Porter. Audiences at the time were bowled over by this groundbreaking film, particularly by its startling coda—they gasped, screamed, and some may have even fainted, if reports are to be believed. Then they clamored for more.

Given that this film anticipated so many things in so many ways, it is hard not to think that its last indelible scene was prescient as well—as if saying, "Hold on tight, folks; the history of the Western movie is just beginning, and you are all in for a *wild ride*."

And so, the mythmaking begins. The journey will be a long and circuitous one, but it all starts here, and so many of the elements that will later become stock parts of the Western are already present: a train robbery; a posse chase; a fight on top of a moving train; a villain shooting a man in the back; a saloon dance; men falling from horses in the midst of a shootout; a bully firing at the ground to make a poor tenderfoot dance; and—perhaps most significantly—the automatic assumption that the "good guys" in a Western are nevertheless willing and able to kill.

The Great Train Robbery is often erroneously credited as both the first narrative film and the first Western. In point of fact it is neither. As of this writing, the earliest known narrative Western is a short

A bandit (Justus D. Barnes) fires his pistol directly at the audience in the film's final moments. Nothing would ever be the same. *The Great Train Robbery* (Edison, 1903).

from 1899, *Kidnapping by Indians*, made—incredibly—by the British film company Mitchell & Kenyon in Blackburn, Lancashire. Calling it either "narrative" or a "Western" is a bit of a stretch, however. The film, shot in one continuous take from one stationary camera, is hilariously incompetent. In order not to spoil the Ed Wood–like delights of *Kidnapping by Indians*, I will resist the temptation to describe it further; it must be seen to be believed. The short is available in its full two-minute glory on YouTube.

Mitchell & Kenyon's opus notwithstanding, *The Great Train Robbery* is the first *true* Western, and the first important and well-crafted example of narrative moviemaking, a leap beyond any of its predecessors. In addition, it is no exaggeration to say that *The Great Train Robbery* launched the American film industry. As Jay Hyams writes: "The birth of Westerns was the birth of movies."[1]

The beginning of the Western movie was as mythic, in its own way, as the subject matter which would inhabit the genre for more than a century. Among other things, *The Great Train Robbery* was inspired by the exploits of Butch Cassidy's Wild Bunch, whose last train robbery had occurred just a few months prior to filming! The movie was shot in New Jersey over just two days in November of 1903, on a budget that was certainly no more than two thousand dollars and may have been as little as $150. Within a month it had premiered in New York, and audiences couldn't get enough. They shouted, they cheered, they rooted on the posse as audiences would do for decades to come. Hyams writes:

> Porter's twelve-minute film changed movies forever. It also changed America, for it brought to life the American West in a way that outdid the antics of Wild West shows. It was as though what had been lost had been rediscovered—the real West was over, but another, even more exciting West was just beginning.[2]

The creation of this "new West"—the unreal one, the mythic one—would be the primary driving force in the shaping of the American Western movie.

The Great Train Robbery features no credits and no title cards. The story is told entirely visually, without recourse to dialogue (anticipating the lasting importance of the visual element in Western filmmaking). And the visuals are *exciting*, making use of cinematic techniques that were revolutionary at the time: cross-cutting between simultaneous scenes in different locations (which Porter, as both writer and director, feared would confuse his audiences); motion toward and away from the camera; panning and camera movement; hand-tinting of some scenes (in some prints); a mix of interior and location shooting; and the strategic use of editing to create the dramatic shape, pace, and form of the narrative.

Porter had notes distributed with the film indicating that the famous final shot (or, more accurately, shots!) could alternatively be placed at the beginning of the movie if desired. However, all surviving prints have this scene at the end, and that is where it belongs, dramatically and aesthetically. In fact, the moment is made even more powerful by the fact that this very bandit, within the narrative, has been shot down and killed a few moments before. The bad guys have been routed and good has triumphed, yet there he still stands, outside of time and space: the archetype of chaos, disorder, sociopathy, and violence, firing his gun into our eyes—an apt metaphor for the dawn of the twentieth century if ever there were one.

Barnes's close-up is unforgettable, but *The Great Train Robbery* is packed with other memorable moments as well. The kinetic action scenes on top of the moving train are exciting (despite a rather noticeable cut, by which a live actor is exchanged for an obvious dummy before the character is brutally clubbed and thrown off the top of the train). The gunning down of a fleeing passenger, shot in the back, is gripping and horrifying. The climactic gun battle in the woods, with puffs of smoke erupting everywhere, is a stunning foretaste of things to come.

But for me the most striking scene (within the narrative) is inside the moving express car, in which the poor soul tasked with guarding the mail and the strong box meets his fate. We first see him by himself in the car, as scenery flits by the open door—another great visual touch. Soon, though, he hears the telltale sounds of the robbery, then heroically locks the strongbox and throws the key quickly out the door. As two bandits burst in, he engages in gunfire with them in close quarters—only feet away—but soon is shot down. Even more horribly, the bandits then proceed to dynamite the box right by the feet of the corpse. The actor doesn't even flinch, and there is no cut to allow for the substitution of a fake body. I'm not sure how they managed this one, but the special effect is gasp-inducing.

And so, this poor guard becomes the first fatality in an American Western—a Cain and Abel moment that will forever mark the genre. (It is perhaps mythically appropriate that the film debuted, among other places, at the Eden Musée.) From here onward, violence will be a major thematic element in nearly all Westerns, and how movies choose to address it, employ it, and explore it will become a significant aspect of the genre's continual examination of ethical questions.

Here at the start, what is the ethical position of *The Great Train Robbery* toward violence? I would maintain that it has none, even though its characters clearly do. Both bandits and posse, simply by behaving as they do, seem implicitly to accept the

The "Cain and Abel" moment of the movie Western, its first murder, as a mail messenger (possibly Robert Milasch) is gunned down aboard the train. *The Great Train Robbery* (Edison, 1903).

soon-to-be standard Western movie code of rough justice, with gunfire the final arbiter and courts of law nowhere in sight.

It may be due to the lack of dialogue, or perhaps the fact that nearly all the movie is presented in long shots (thereby keeping us at a certain objective distance), but *The Great Train Robbery* comes across to me as if I were simply watching a filmed record of events. There is a reason why, ninety years later, the movie *Tombstone* (1993) used sequences from *The Great Train Robbery* in its introduction, presented with Robert Mitchum's voice-over narration as if the scenes were newsreel footage.

Even though the actions depicted in *The Great Train Robbery* are frequently horrific—the awful bludgeoning of the man (or dummy) on top of the train, the murder of the fleeing passenger—none of the characters are presented as stand-ins for the audience, nor do they comment in any way on the action. The posse may be the "good guys" in the narrative sense, but before they run off to gun down the bandits, they are bullying the Easterner into dancing by shooting at his feet. For me, then, the film comes off as essentially amoral. Everyone simply does what they do—the outlaws steal and murder, the posse gives chase, the pursuers hunt down and eventually kill the bandits—but we are offered no commentary, either explicit or implicit, about the events. We simply watch things unfold, and project our own judgments.

It's unfortunate that we can only watch *The Great Train Robbery* in retrospect, with our inescapable knowledge of what will follow. We can stretch our imaginations, but there is no way that we can truly experience this film as its 1903 audiences would have. How incredible it is to think of all the things that were in store for the American Western that had not yet come to be when this was made. When *The Great Train Robbery* was filmed, cinema knew no such thing as a climactic quick-draw showdown in the center of a town; or on-screen singing cowboys; or swinging saloon doors. There was no Gene Autry, or Roy Rogers, or Hopalong Cassidy. John Wayne, the greatest star in Western history and the man most identified with the genre, would not even be born for another four years. Furthermore, *Stagecoach* (1939)—Wayne's breakthrough movie and the point at which the modern adult Western truly began—was still more than a third of a century away. There was roughly as much time between *The Great Train Robbery* and *Stagecoach* as there was between *Stagecoach* and Wayne's final film, *The Shootist* (1976). Or between *The Shootist* and today. That is, the thirty-seven-year heyday of Wayne's career only spans the middle third of the history of the Western to date.

One cannot help but think about the nature of time and causality in this case; how easy it might have been, had the right people not done the right things at the right times, for the entire genre to vanish like a puff of smoke, and for *The Great Train Robbery* to go down in history as just a cul-de-sac, an eccentric fluke, the like of which would never be seen again. But thankfully, not only for the cinematic arts but also for American mythology, history would take a very different course.

We may be startled by the timeline, and by the roughly equal spans between the benchmarks mentioned above—*The Great Train Robbery* to *Stagecoach* to *The Shootist* to the present day—but these same benchmarks can also provide us with a relatively simple and useful way to conceptualize the history of the American Western to date. Using them as our guides, we can divide this history into thirds, into three great periods, each in the neighborhood of forty years long (at this writing). Each of these larger style periods divides further into two subsections. (These boundaries, of course, are organizing conveniences, and so are necessarily fuzzy and permeable; they should be taken as transitional moments rather than as hard-and-fast stylistic breaks.)

This rough framework yields six subperiods in all, plus a long enough transition between the two halves of the High Western to justify a seventh; the present book will focus on the first three, from the birth of the movie Western in 1903 until the beginning of the transitional period from Golden Age to Silver Age in the mid–1950s. The subsequent volume will pick up where this one ends, addressing the growing dominance of the subversive Western—which came fully into its own in the 1960s and 1970s—and the ensuing disintegration, reconstruction, and postmodern reinterpretation of the classical Western mythos.

Given the caveat above about blurry boundary lines, here is a summary of these style periods as we might conceive them:

- **The Early Period:** from *The Great Train Robbery* until *Stagecoach*
    o **The Silent Western** (1903–28)
    o **The Early Talkies** (1928–39)
- **The High Western:** the age of the classic Western, from *Stagecoach* to *The Shootist*, with a lengthy transitional period separating its two subsections
    o **The Golden Age** (1939–53, the full flowering of the mythos)
    o **Transition** (1953–1962, as the old and new styles coexist and interact)

    o **The Silver Age** (1962–76, when mythic subversion and deconstruction begin to predominate)
- **The Postmodern Western:** the more eclectic (and erratic) output of Westerns since John Wayne's final film
    - o **Reconstruction** of the Western from its deconstructed parts in the late twentieth century (1977–2000)
    - o **The 21st-Century Western** (2001 to the present)

A vast, grand history indeed, and it all started here with the first true Western. When *The Great Train Robbery* was made, the airplane had not yet been invented, most Americans died before the age of fifty, indoor plumbing was rare, and no one knew what a world war was. The expanse of the twentieth century, unparalleled both in its beauty and its horror, was still to unfold.

The Western would be there, every step of the way, illuminating and reflecting its time as only art and myth can do. In the essays to come, we will have many opportunities to ponder how the great Westerns are both timely and timeless; how they shape their era and are shaped by it in turn; and, just as importantly, how this quintessential American creation grew and evolved as an art in its own right.

What an amazing experience it is to watch *The Great Train Robbery* today, in light of the long, winding, ever-surprising trail that lies ahead. From this modest seed will spring forth a rich, kaleidoscopic genre that will give us, in time, not only the great classical Western heroes like William S. Hart, John Wayne, Randolph Scott, Henry Fonda, and James Stewart; not only saloons, shootouts, and roundups; but also—in the second half of the century—subversive new icons like Clint Eastwood's Man with No Name, as well as the grim fatalism of *Lonely Are the Brave* (1962), the psychedelic insanity of *El Topo* (1970), the elegiac solemnity of *Ride the High Country* (1962), the terrible beauty of *The Searchers* (1956), the eclectic irreverence of *Little Big Man* (1970), the sophomoric hijinks of *Blazing Saddles* (1974), the apocalyptic violence of *The Wild Bunch* (1969), the delightful gender-bending camp of *Johnny Guitar* (1954), and the vast heart-breaking humanity of *Lonesome Dove* (1989).

The trail beckons—let's ride!

The Battle of Elderbush Gulch
(1913)

AKA: *The Battle at Elderbush Gulch*
December 1913 (USA)
USA—English
Biograph Company
29m—Silent—BW—1.33:1

Direction: D.W. Griffith
Screenplay: D.W. Griffith (uncredited), Henry Albert Phillips (uncredited)
Principal Cast: Mae Marsh (Sally Cameron, the First Waif), Leslie Loveridge (The Second Waif), Alfred Paget (The Waifs' Uncle), Robert Harron (The Young Father), Lillian Gish (Melissa Harlow), Charles Hill Mailes (The Ranch Owner), William A. Carroll (The Mexican), Frank Opperman (The Indian Chief), Henry B. Walthall (The Indian Chief's Son), Joseph McDermott (The Waifs' Guardian), Jennie Lee (The Waifs' Guardian)
Cinematography: G.W. Bitzer (uncredited)

We flash forward a decade to *The Battle of Elderbush Gulch* (1913), directed by D.W. Griffith, who would go on to release the seminal and controversial *Birth of a Nation* (also featuring Lillian Gish and Mae Marsh, and developing many of the same cinematic techniques) just over a year later. Ten years have passed since *The Great Train Robbery* (1903), but aesthetically and thematically the Western is still very much in its infancy.

But what an active and vibrant infancy! By this point Westerns were being produced by the bucketful; indeed, they represented the dominant genre in American cinema. Not only the subject matter but even the production of movies had moved west. Whereas *The Great Train Robbery* was filmed in New Jersey, *Elderbush Gulch* was shot on location near San Fernando, California.

At least two cuts of this early short still exist, one titled *The Battle at Elderbush Gulch* (the original title, it seems) and another called *The Battle of Elderbush Gulch*. The footage remains mostly the same, but the title cards are different—no doubt reflecting versions assembled for subsequent rereleases of the film in 1915 and 1916.

Although the original version's titles were terser, the rerelease of *Elderbush Gulch* stakes out the movie's moral position right away, with an initial card stating: "A tale of the sturdy Americans whose lifework was the conquest of the Great West." This is representative of the treatment of the American Indian Wars by the film industry at the time. At this point, there is little to no humanizing of the natives; they are portrayed as wild, dog-eating savages, where the white settlers are heroic, civilized, and pious. (Mae Marsh prays no fewer than three times over the course of this half-hour story.)

As with *The Great Train Robbery*, the plot is featherweight, serving mainly as a vehicle for the staging of suspenseful action sequences. Nevertheless, there are a couple

Sally (Mae Marsh, center) and her little sister (Leslie Loveridge) receive a cold farewell from their guardians (Jennie Lee, left, and Joseph McDermott, background). "Mommy's no help anymore." *The Battle of Elderbush Gulch* (Biograph, 1913).

moments that are striking from a mythological perspective. The first of these is at the very beginning of the film, in which orphaned teenager Sally (Marsh) and her little sister (Leslie Loveridge, Marsh's real-life niece) are "sent to join their uncles on the frontier." They are seen off by their guardians, a couple with grim and stoic demeanors anticipating Grant Wood's *American Gothic* by seventeen years. The distraught Sally moves in to hug the old woman but is stiffly rebuffed. She and her sister climb onto the wagon, weeping, and it rolls away.

Of course, this serves to set up the action to follow, and it helps bring us into the drama by encouraging our empathy with the characters. It also underscores a real historical truth, namely the staggering fortitude which it must have taken in those days for people to set out for the unknown frontier. (I say this setting aside my judgments about the rightness of this particular enterprise, the usurpation of the West from its native inhabitants.)

I believe this first scene serves another important function as well, a mythic one. After all, Griffith could just as easily have begun his film out on the frontier, introducing us to Sally and her sister upon their arrival by stagecoach. We still could have felt their sorrow and fear, and this would have provided the drama with an Aristotelian unity of place.

But Griffith's Western has the opportunity to touch on something deeper and more mythic here, an "elementary idea"[1] that has expressed itself in many other cultures. Here I will turn to Joseph Campbell for a relevant example, in which he discusses the circumcision rites for boys at puberty among the Australian Murngin tribe. In these rituals, the boys are first frightened and run to their mothers, who pretend to try and protect them, knowing all the while about the larger purpose. The men of the tribe appear dressed as supernatural figures in service of the Great Father Snake, who covets the foreskins of the young boys. The men then "kidnap" the boys and take them through a series of initiations that also serve to expose them to crucial elements of the tribal mythology. As Campbell writes: "In this way, 'within' the Great Father Snake as it were, [the boys] are introduced to an interesting new object world that compensates them for their loss of the mother; and the male phallus, instead of the female breast, is made the central point (*axis mundi*) of the imagination."[2]

Now obviously in *Elderbush Gulch* our young protagonist is female, not male, but she too is undergoing a rite of passage in her adolescence, one in which the "feminine" world of hearth and home—symbolized by the stern female guardian who is clearly the dominant force, while her husband opens the gate and stays in the background— is about to be replaced by the "man's world" of the frontier. Therefore, the old woman's stiff rebuff accomplishes something of the same sort as the pretense of the aboriginal mothers: "Mommy can't protect you anymore." Now Sally is off to the frontier where, in Campbell's terms, the male phallus (represented by the barrel of rifle and handgun) is the dominant image, not the female breast.

But *Elderbush Gulch* endows this mythic transformation with a surprisingly progressive character (for its time). Overall, as we know, the history of the Western movie will be dominated by the males, weathered and scarred individuals meting out frontier justice with the phalluses descending from their leather gun belts. But here is a film which, though already steeped in tropes that permeate the early Westerns—Indians on horseback circling embattled settlers, the cavalry riding to the rescue—also places its women front and center. The men are all relatively one-dimensional; their function is to protect and fight. The women, however, are the ones with whom we sympathize. They are more fully fleshed-out as characters—especially Sally, whom we follow from her tearful departure from "civilization" through her anxious arrival at the frontier, then finally to her act of courage in rescuing the baby of the settler Melissa (Lillian Gish). Over the brief twenty-nine minutes of this movie, we also see Sally's piety and her plucky side—e.g. coaxing the settler to provide a secret entrance into the cabin for her dogs. Sally is our stand-in here, and the true heroine of the drama.

This is not to claim that the film is not problematic from the point of view of gender, of course. In this world, it is still the role of the men to provide protection for the helpless women. It doesn't occur to any of the female characters to pick up a gun and assist in the fight; instead, they mainly cower inside and hope not to be raped. But Marsh's character shows glimmers of a counter-archetype that will also come into its own as the Western evolves, namely the spirited, strong woman who carves out a place for herself among all this testosterone, as would be found later with different inflections, for example, in *Union Pacific* (1939), *The Furies* (1950), *Rawhide* (1951), *Rancho Notorious* (1952), *Johnny Guitar* (1954), *Forty Guns* (1957), *Lonesome Dove* (1989), and *Meek's Cutoff* (2010). Marsh's Sally shows genuine courage, at one point even charging unarmed at two Indians to protect her little dogs. She is still a fresh-faced adolescent, of course, thereby representing the early days of this cinematic image, one which would continue to develop as the Western felt its way toward its own maturity.

One other moment stands out to me as particularly mythic and aesthetic: the shot of the live baby clutched in the dead arms of one of the settlers, whose own body (along with another settler's) lies next to that of a slain Indian. This film is unabashedly pro-white and anti–Indian, but there is something about this image that transcends the movie's unenlightened, surface-level point of view. Here lie bodies of different races, from this angle intertwined, brothers united in death. I cannot help but recall the wonderful medieval *Parzival* of Wolfram von Eschenbach, in which white-skinned Parzival

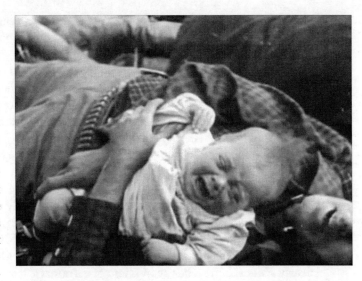

Life from the ashes, as a baby lies clutched in a dead settler's arms. *The Battle of Elderbush Gulch* (Biograph, 1913).

fights a mighty battle against the Muslim Feirefiz, with his magpie-like skin mixing black and white—and who will be revealed to be Parzival's half-brother. In acknowledging the brotherhood of these combatants, Wolfram says, "Whoever wishes to name them 'two' is entitled to say 'Thus did *they* fight.' Yet they were no more than one." The two knights will eventually reconcile, but before then, each does the other and himself "much hurt."[3]

Here in *Elderbush Gulch*, added to this already rich and potent imagery, we see also the living child cradled in the dead settler's arms, life seemingly springing forth from the ruins of the clash of opposites—who are themselves, in actuality, one. What a marvelous moment! It may not have been consciously intended by the filmmakers, but it resonates nonetheless, and one cannot help but wonder if, despite Griffith's overt intentions about his portrayal of whites and Indians, an unconscious part of him—on a more profound level—recognized a deeper truth.

A few other things I find interesting about this film:

- The male settlers on the frontier are all scruffy, not scrubbed and clean-cut as they would later become in the era of the homogenized Western hero. At the time of *Elderbush Gulch*, memories of the actual frontier may have been too fresh for audiences to buy clean-shaven men in white hats and sequined shirts. These settlers look pretty authentic, grizzled and unkempt—and yet they still have the capacity to light up and become playful at the sight of a child.
- In contrast to the settlers, we only ever see adult Indian men. Among the whites, we have unarmed, noncombatant women and children to evoke our sympathy, but the Indians are all savage male warriors. The audience's fear of them at the time was undoubtedly enhanced by the superimposition of flames over the scene of them gearing themselves up for war, and, later, by their "sneaky" tactics, posing as corpses on the battlefield before rising up in stealth to attack.
- *Elderbush Gulch* also contains an early example of a trope which will recur many

times throughout the history of the Western, namely the reserving of one bullet
for the heroine to be able to take the quick way out, should the prospect of "a
fate worse than death"—rape at the hands of a native—present itself. In some
later cases, it is the female lead herself who is prepared to suicide; in this film
a gun in the hand of an off-screen settler slowly obtrudes into the frame from
above, pointing at Melissa's head. She remains unaware of its presence, although
the expression on her face and the even clearer one on the elderly woman (Kate
Bruce) who holds Gish in her arms serve to let us know just what exactly it is that
they fear. After the cocking of the gun, we cut away to some of the battle action,
and the suspense builds until the cavalry arrives in the nick of time. The gun
is withdrawn, and the worst is averted. Even though this motif recurs so many
times in Westerns—and is even referenced in relatively recent movies like the
James Bond flick *Quantum of Solace* (2008)—I can recall only one instance (in
the brutal *Ulzana's Raid*, 1972) in which the last resort is actually employed. In
fact, the threat of the heroine's suicide, or her mercy killing by the hero, seems
nearly always to precede the moment of a dramatic last-minute rescue.

- As will continue to be the case in the American Western, the landscape is
  evocative and plays a major role in the aesthetic of the piece. Particularly
  memorable are the images of the plains, shot from on high, with puffs of gun
  smoke blooming everywhere.
- There is a moment during the battle when Sally prays, before rushing out
  through her escape hatch to save the baby. There is no title card here in the
  original version, but in the rerelease, we see the dialogue: "Dear God, help me
  not to be so scared!" This is an interesting take on her character, paradoxically
  underlining her essential fortitude. One might imagine a less courageous
  woman simply praying for a good outcome to be provided from above, but
  Sally prays for the bravery to be able to do the difficult task herself. A subtle
  distinction, but a meaningful one.

One cannot watch a film like *Elderbush Gulch* without pondering the passage of time.
The familiar Western clichés bring us deceptively closer to the time of this movie than
is warranted. In fact, the film is a relic of an era that virtually no one living today was
around to witness. Everyone on the screen here is long since gone; even the player who
survived the longest, another niece of Mae Marsh who appears briefly as a four-year-old
child in the settlement and who lived well into her eighties, has been dead for over two
decades. Ashes to ashes, dust to dust; once living people now just flickering, ghostly
images on century-old film.

Reaching back into time the opposite way: Jennie Lee, the old guardian woman who
refuses Sally's embrace at the beginning, lived nearly her entire life during a time when
clashes between government forces and Native Americans were occurring. She was in
her mid-sixties when *Elderbush Gulch* was filmed, meaning that she was twenty-seven
years old when Custer died at Little Bighorn. In fact, the last (relatively small) alterca-
tions of the American Indian Wars were still in the future when *Elderbush Gulch* was
made; these skirmishes continued, albeit rarely, until the early 1920s.

Our painful fraternal history as settlers and Native Americans (and as mythic
echoes of Parzival and Feirefiz) is, paradoxically, both further from and nearer to us in
time than we think.

The Squaw Man
(1914)

AKA: *The White Man*
February 15, 1914 (USA)
USA—English
Jesse L. Lasky Feature Play Company
74m—Silent—BW—1.33:1

Direction: Cecil B. DeMille, Oscar Apfel
Screenplay: Cecil B. DeMille, Oscar Apfel, Edwin Milton Royle (play)
Principal Cast: Dustin Farnum (Capt. James Wynnegate, aka Jim Carston), Monroe Salisbury (Sir Henry, Earl of Kerhill), Red Wing (Nat-U-Ritch), Winifred Kingston (Lady Diana, Countess of Kerhill), "Baby" Carmen De Rue (Hal), Joseph Singleton (Tabywana), William Elmer (Cash Hawkins), Mrs. A.W. Filson (The Dowager Lady Elizabeth Kerhill), Haidee Fuller (Lady Mabel Wynnegate), Foster Knox (Sir John), Dick La Reno (Big Bill), Richard L'Estrange (Grouchy), Fred Montague (Mr. Petrie), Art Acord (Townsman)
Production: Cecil B. DeMille (uncredited)
Cinematography: Alfred Gandolfini (uncredited)
Editing: Mamie Wagner (uncredited)
Art Direction: Wilfred Buckland (uncredited)

Cecil B. DeMille's *The Squaw Man* (1914) was the first feature-length movie shot in Hollywood, and it marked the moment at which filmmakers began to deal with the Western genre on a more ambitious scale. The story (set in contemporaneous times, with automobiles and telephones) stretched from east to west, from England to New York to Wyoming, although shot entirely in California.

Conventional wisdom is that, over the course of the history of the Western, Hollywood treated Native Americans unsympathetically and in caricature at first, and then progressively more sympathetically and three-dimensionally as the twentieth century unfolded. This is a largely true statement, of course, which is what makes *The Squaw Man* all the more surprising, because it is a movie that, relative to its time and taken as a whole, treats its Indian characters (and especially Nat-U-Ritch) with uncharacteristic respect and empathy. Yes, Nat-U-Ritch's father Tabywana (Joseph Singleton) is a drunken stereotype for much of the picture, but even he is shown to act nobly before the end. And Nat-U-Ritch herself (Native American actress Red Wing, also known as Lillian St. Cyr) emerges as the true heroine of the movie.

Clearly *The Squaw Man*, like the 1905 stage play upon which it is based, draws upon the idea of the Noble Savage, as passed down from Dryden to the eighteenth-century sentimentalists and the nineteenth-century Romantics. The Indians here are indeed noble, living close to Nature and at their best when uncorrupted by civilization. In one scene, the movie exploits the all-too-common trope of the white man taking advantage of the Indian by getting him drunk, but here it is the white character who is diminished by this action, not the native. The alcohol is a symbol of all of the encroachments of white culture without which the Indians would do far better. The crudity of so-called civilization taints the pure nobility of the natural way of life.

In tandem with this, the least sympathetic characters in *The Squaw Man*—the ones who come closest to being villains—are all white, and they share the common specific characteristic of dishonesty. In short, they are cheats—from the embezzler Sir Henry (Monroe Salisbury) to the crooked Cash Hawkins (William Elmer) to the pickpockets of New York. This is not to claim that the film is anti-white, or that it calls into question the application of Manifest Destiny and the white conquest of the West—although one cannot help but recall the hundreds of treaties between the U.S. and Native Americans which were all eventually broken by the government, clearly a large-scale example of the devastating effects of dishonesty. But here the movie's ethical interests are focused on the microcosm, not the macrocosm, and the impact of deceit plays itself out on the more intimate scale of individual human lives.

In his theory of the monomyth and the Hero Cycle, Joseph Campbell discusses two contrasting ways by which the Hero's Adventure can be set in motion: through deliberate choice, as when the protagonist sets out on a quest with a defined goal; or through serendipity, when an adventure unfolds that propels the hero along willy-nilly and, in Shakespeare's phrase, thrusts greatness upon him.

One of the striking things about *The Squaw Man* is that it is actually an amalgam of two simultaneous and contrasting Hero's Adventures: one which is serendipitous and ends relatively well for its hero, Jim (Dustin Farnum); and another featuring the Indian maiden Nat-U-Ritch, who takes deliberate charge of her narrative on three critical occasions and acts with incredible nobility and self-sacrifice, although her story ends in tragedy. Ironically, it is the "civilized" Englishman Jim who becomes the hero blown by the winds of chance, whereas the child of Nature is the one who most clearly takes events

into her own hands rather than letting them unfold spontaneously.

For the first half of the story, Jim's serendipitous adventure is what drives the plot. I am reminded again of Wolfram's *Parzival* here: its hero certainly acted deliberately from time to time, but that often ended badly. Most of the major advances in Parzival's quest happened when he let go of the reins of his horse and just allowed events to unfold according to Nature and his own inner character. It is the same way with

Nat U Ritch (Red Wing) just after killing Cash Hawkins. She has saved Jim Carston's life for the first time—but not the last. *The Squaw Man* (Jesse L. Lasky, 1914).

Jim: he seems to act effortlessly out of his own decent center, but his destiny is largely out of his own control. Left to his own devices, he would probably choose to remain firmly ensconced in British aristocracy, but throughout his story external forces drive him onward. The Dowager's urgings and his cousin Henry's embezzlement from the orphans' trust push Jim, now burdened with the blame for Henry's crimes, west to New York. The chance encounter with Big Bill (Dick La Reno)—in which Jim, acting instinctively, saves Bill from being pickpocketed—leads him further west. ("Come out West," says Bill, "where folks keep their hands in their own pockets.")

At this point we begin to see that Jim is following a trail which already seems laid out before him, but unwittingly. And so it continues: Jim spontaneously intervenes with Cash Hawkins on Nat-U-Ritch's behalf, out of his own innate chivalry, and Nat-U-Ritch soon responds by saving Jim's life from Hawkins's attempt on it. This entwines Jim's fate with that of the Indian girl, a situation furthered by perhaps the most nakedly mythological sequence yet, when, blinded by snow, he is rescued for the second time by Nat-U-Ritch. There is an obvious nod to *Parzival* in this scene as Jim's horse wanders freely—but here the result is opposite. Instead of being led to the Grail Castle, as Parzival was when he let go of the reins, Jim is led straight into Hell—in this case, "the poisonous fumes of Death Hole," a sulfurous pit in the earth belching forth noxious gas. Nat-U-Ritch rescues him by securing him with a rope to his own horse and pulling him free, anticipating a similar sequence in *True Grit* (1969) by over half a century. Here the Indian maiden leads Jim forth from the Underworld in a gender-reversed version of Orpheus and Eurydice. This cannot be by accident; the entire Death Hole sequence is not necessary to the plot, as Jim could just as easily have been rescued from exposure out in the snow. It is easy to believe that this extra scene was deliberately created to further mythologize the narrative.

Jim's entire story, including his ultimate salvation, is shaped by people and events seemingly outside of his control: his being saved by Nat-U-Ritch twice; her subsequent unplanned pregnancy; the letter from Henry confessing to his crime and thereby absolving Jim; and Nat-U-Ritch's ultimate sacrifice on behalf of Jim and their son. In the final analysis, Jim has less strength of character than Parzival, with whom I have compared him. Parzival eventually seizes control of his own destiny, and in fact even changes the laws of God through his own perseverance; but Jim, while still a man with a noble heart, never truly takes charge of his own life.

Nat-U-Ritch's story arc, in contrast, is driven by her deliberate intervention in the events of the drama. Unlike Jim, she is not swept along by the tides of fate; she consistently decides and acts. This is most obvious in her three great heroic deeds: saving Jim from Hawkins; saving him again from the snowstorm and the great pit; and saving him a third time (or at least saving his name, and that of her son) by her final selfless act.

Here then we encounter that relative rarity, a Hero's Adventure with two heroes, one of whom is on the serendipitous adventure and the other of whom is on her own deliberate version of the self-chosen quest. In the end, though, there is a tension created between these two radically different but intersecting life courses, a tension that demands a tragedy in order to achieve resolution.

As mentioned before, mythological elements abound in *The Squaw Man*, and it does not seem like too much of a stretch to draw relatively overt connections to European mythology, whether classical or Arthurian. We have already noted two versions of

Diana (Winifred Kingston) springs to life from the page. *The Squaw Man* (Jesse L. Lasky, 1914).

the Hero Quest, the Orphic imagery in Nat-U-Ritch's rescue of Jim from the bowels of the earth, and the resonances with *Parzival*, especially in the treatment of the symbol of the horse (as the spontaneity of Nature) and the hero's actions (as the spontaneity of the noble heart). There is also an amazing and beautiful moment in which the lonely Jim, sitting in his cabin in the middle of the wild frontier, reads a book with an illustration on one page of a classical female figure, robed and semi-reclined like a Greek goddess. As we watch, the image of Jim's British love, Henry's wife Diana (played by Winifred Kingston, Farnum's real-life wife), is superimposed upon the illustrated image and then moves, coming to life in Jim's imagination.

Throughout the narrative we see Jim's romantic devotion divided. Each of his loves is "forbidden"—Diana because she is already married to Jim's dissolute cousin Henry, and Nat-U-Ritch because she belongs to an alien race. I am reminded of the five levels of love as reckoned in ancient (East) Indian myth, the highest level of which is illicit love—that is, love which is so powerful that it breaks through all societal rules and taboos.

Jim's heart is torn between these two idealized and seemingly unattainable women, and of course between the cultural and archetypal traits that each represents: cultivated civilization on the one hand, wild Nature on the other. ("Nature" = "Nat-U-Ritch.") It is difficult to imagine him fully reconciling his divided loyalties or living completely comfortably within either realm. His problem is the same as that of contemporary human beings, who are torn between the order and comforts of modern life and the ancient evolutionary connection to the raw and untamed natural world. In this context, the choice of Diana as the name for the European Muse is both ironic and significant. In Roman mythology, Diana was the virgin huntress, living out in the wild and scorning the "civilized" life. Here, of course, it is Nat-U-Ritch and not the British Diana who exemplifies these qualities perfectly.

But this seems like more than just an ironic twist; I read it as a comment on the delusional nature of Jim's affections. He may think that he is captivated by his cousin's wife, but this false Diana is merely a stand-in for another woman altogether, a true virgin huntress. Jim originally believes that his soulmate is a woman from his own culture, but he is only projecting: his true Diana lives in a wilderness halfway around the world. Whether he is capable of truly recognizing her as such, rather than just passively relying on her services, is a question that the ending of the film leaves unresolved.

We can see Nat-U-Ritch as a mythic character, but one whose fate has reversed the outcomes of her mythological forebears. She is indeed the true Diana; but whereas in Roman mythology mortal men from civilization who beheld or desired Diana were struck dead, here it is the goddess who pays the price while the man lives on. Nat-U-Ritch is also an Orpheus figure in rescuing her mate from the Underworld, but again, she is the one who eventually incurs the tragic fate, not her beloved.

Although primitive in technique by today's standards, *The Squaw Man* is still a beautiful film in many ways. From our perspective and the benefit of more than a century of hindsight, the filming—whether on sets or in outdoor location shooting—seems oddly constricted, walled in by the frame, perhaps betraying the theatrical origins of the movie; yet there are genuinely aesthetic visual moments that still shine through. One striking and beautiful recurring feature is the way in which the symbolic images of the film let us inside Jim's thoughts. I have already mentioned the moment where Diana springs forth from the pages of Jim's book. Similarly, when Jim learns that his name has been cleared and he can come home, we see his thoughts made visible, as pictures from his former life dance before his eyes, superimposed on the local background through double exposure. But soon afterwards, as Jim is teaching his soon-to-be Anglicized son how to kneel and pray before bed, he is painfully struck by a vision of Nat-U-Ritch silhouetted against the sky—the fading sunset of his true Diana.

The acting is also particularly strong and heart-wrenching, especially in the final third of the movie. We have seen Jim's transformation as he has moved west, but it is not just his outer appearance that has changed; he has become more authentic, less stiff and more three-dimensional as the movie has progressed. But with this awakening as a human being has also come the capacity for great pain. We witness his internal emotional turmoil as he agonizes about sending his son back to England; he is truly torn between two worlds, two women, two lives. Farnum's portrayal of this tormented character is exceptionally powerful as the film draws toward its close, especially in his interactions with Little Hal (actually played by a six-year-old girl, Carmen De Rue).

The supporting cast also does an excellent job. The grizzled cowboys in particular are very touching, aided by a script which affords them the opportunity to surprise us with their compassion. I particularly love the moments in which they stand up for Jim and his taboo marriage; when they accept with great grace the tokens that he gives them because he cannot afford to pay them; and when they then return these tokens as gifts to the departing child. These are background characters who so easily could have been cheap stereotypes, but the movie refuses to waste them in that way.

The same is true of Diana, who is not given much to do for large spans of the film, but then gets a wonderful and redemptive moment at the end, when she asks Little Hal, "Whose child are you?" The boy points proudly to his father, and we see Diana's heart break before our eyes; but then, once again, the movie shows us the spontaneous act of a noble soul. It's a beautiful scene.

But in the end, the heart of the film belongs to Nat-U-Ritch. Her moment of apotheosis is both heartbreaking and beautiful; it stays with us. She is the real heroine of the drama, and yet she remains an enigma. Do we ever fully understand her? Does Jim? In the final image of the film, he carries Nat-U-Ritch's lifeless body and says, "Poor little mother!" This comment seems strikingly detached and condescending, the words of a man feeling pity as if for a dead animal, rather than the grief of a widowed husband for a lover who sacrificed herself on his behalf not once but three times.

What was Nat-U-Ritch finally to Jim? Did he see her as his true soulmate and salvation, or was she just his idealized fantasy of a Diana that could never be realized in flesh and blood? Or, less charitably, simply a woman who was on hand and available to Jim to provide him with what he needed at the time, whether rescue or companionship?

The movie ends in ambiguity—the uncertain future now faced by Jim, Diana, and Little Hal, and most especially the enigma of Nat-U-Ritch. She was heroine, savior, goddess, child of Nature—and yet somehow unknown, voiceless, anonymous, just like the thousands of Native Americans whose names we will never know, whose lives, loves, and deeds are forever lost in time while "civilization" marches on.

The Bargain
(1914)

AKA: *The Two-Gun Man in the Bargain*
December 3, 1914 (USA)
USA—English
New York Motion Picture
70m—Silent—BW—1.33:1

Direction: Reginald Barker (uncredited)
Screenplay: William H. Clifford (uncredited), Thomas H. Ince (uncredited)
Principal Cast: William S. Hart (Jim Stokes, the Two-Gun Man), J. Frank Burke (Bud Walsh, the Sheriff), Clara Williams (Nell Brent), J. Barney Sherry (Phil Brent, Nell's Father), James Dowling (Wilkes, the Minister)
Production: Thomas H. Ince
Cinematography: Robert Newhard (uncredited), Joseph H. August (uncredited)
Awards: National Film Registry

In 1888, a young William Surrey Hart began his stage career and enjoyed great success. As time went on, he performed Shakespeare in the United States and England, played Messala in the original theatrical production of *Ben-Hur*, and even originated the role of Cash Hawkins in the stage version of *The Squaw Man*. Then in 1914, at the age of forty-nine, he made the transition to film, right at the time when movies were becoming full-blown commercial ventures and classic Hollywood was being born. In spite of his age, Hart would go on to become the greatest and most beloved Western star of the silent era.

And it all started with *The Bargain* (1914).

Hart's first feature has one of the most wonderful beginnings of any Western I know, one that must be seen to be experienced, and the startling effect of which no amount of description on my part can adequately

William S. Hart, pre-transformation. *The Bargain* (New York Motion Picture, 1914).

convey. We see a title card
introducing us to Hart as
Jim Stokes; then we see
Hart the actor standing in
tuxedo, with stage curtains
drawing back on either side
of him. He surveys his audience, takes a very deliberate and formal bow, and at
the bow's lowest point there
is a slow (and amazingly
smooth!) dissolve. We gradually discern the outlines of
a Western hat and costume,
and as Hart lifts his head up
again, he is now the bandit
Stokes, staring directly at us
with steely, deadly eyes. His

The bandit Jim Stokes, post-transformation. *The Bargain* (New York Motion Picture, 1914).

right hand moves slowly to the butt of the pistol now hanging on his right hip. His left hand follows suit. It is an incredible, heart-pounding transformation; watching it, I can truly believe that he could draw those pistols in a flash and shoot me dead. In deference to the theatrical origins of some of its players, *The Bargain* introduces each of its five main characters in this way. It is a fabulous way to open a picture, and a fitting start to the meteoric film career of one of the Hollywood Western's greatest stars.

As the narrative opens, we are greeted with a title card that reads: "The West! The Land of Vast Golden Silences Where God Sits Enthroned on the Purple Peaks and Man Stands Face to Face with His Soul." A mythic beginning indeed, the West writ large, and underscored by the dramatic landscape, much of it in and around the Grand Canyon. However, the story itself is actually something more intimate and personal, concerned more with situational ethics and morality than it is with any grand epic themes. As in so many Hart Westerns, his character is an unwholesome outlaw who will eventually be redeemed through the love of a good woman.

The movie is filled with charming touches, starting with the "Wanted" sign that introduces us to the main character: "Eyes, Blue and very piercing…. Age, about 30." Hart, of course, was almost fifty at the time—but his eyes were certainly piercing. The opening holdup and subsequent chase are exciting and funny, as Stokes shows both his ruthlessness—shooting an old man in the shoulder as a part of the robbery—and his crafty wit—setting up a fake "gang" of dummies in the bushes to fool his pursuers. "Boys," he says loudly, "keep them covered for five minutes and if they make a move during that time, shoot to kill." The movie wisely shows us the follow-up to this after Stokes rides off, as the robbery victims wait and wait and wait, then finally make a break for their guns to engage in a thunderous (and very one-sided) battle with their life-less opponents. This endearing blend of action and humor will persist throughout *The Bargain*.

I have referred earlier to the idea that, in some myths and legends, horses repre-sent Nature—either the forces of the natural world, or the hero's own (perhaps uncon-scious) inner nature. It seems significant to me, then, that on the way to his fate, Stokes first comes to a literal crossroads and clearly hesitates before choosing the path that will lead to his own redemption; then, after doing so, he is ambushed by the posse in search of him and has his horse shot out from under him. In other words, after choosing his path he must die to his old nature and find a new way of being. Following this, the wounded Stokes literally wanders in the desert, like countless mythological figures before him, until being found by Phil the prospector (J. Barney Sherry), the father of Nell, the woman whose love will cure him of his wicked ways. (Clara Williams, who plays Nell, would become the director Reginald Barker's wife within a few years, retiring from pictures. Sadly, she would die of illness in 1928, at the age of forty.)

It is interesting to note that had Jim Stokes chosen the other path at the crossroads, he very likely would have escaped his pursuers, but by the same token would never have met Nell and, presumably, would have continued his banditry until coming to a bad end. This recalls a theme also present in *Parzival*, namely the notion that every action has both positive and negative results. One path holds violence and ambush, but also redemption; the other holds escape and freedom, but also the continuance of a wasted life.

The romance between Stokes and Nell is actually quite brief and happens offscreen; we simply get a title card stating, "Jim Stokes, recovered from his wound and in love with his pretty nurse, proposes marriage." Another knightly theme appears here, this time owing something to the legend of Tristan and Iseult.[1] In this timeless story, given perhaps its ultimate expression by Gottfried von Strassburg (but also set memorably by Malory in *Le Morte d'Arthur* and Wagner in the opera *Tristan und Isolde*), the noble knight Tristan is wounded and nursed back to health by Iseult, during which time love blossoms between them. But Tristan has a secret past that would threaten this fragile new love if Iseult were to find out about it.

So it is with Jim Stokes; he dares not reveal his banditry to the upright Nell, instead vowing to himself—after witnessing a tender scene between Nell and her father—to give up his life of crime and reform his ways. This will prove difficult; old habits are hard to break, as evidenced by a wonderful nuanced touch during the scene where Stokes marries Nell. Two strangers (to Stokes) attend as witnesses, and he senses the threat they pose. (His instincts prove true; they will later bring him to the attention of the sheriff.) Stokes tries to conceal his reaction, but sharp-eyed viewers will notice his hand slowly rising to the now empty spot on his hip where his gun used to hang.

Surprisingly, *The Bargain* is interested in more than one redemption. In fact, a great deal of attention in the storyline is devoted to the character of the sheriff (J. Frank Burke). After the sheriff captures Stokes, there is a wonderful sequence centered around a rough-and-tumble border-town saloon and gambling hall. The saloon is a very evocative environment, with numerous gaming tables, animal pelts on the wall, and a great deal of seedy atmosphere. We first get a true feel for the place when there is a slow 360-degree pan around its interior, as seen through the sheriff's eyes—a shot which lasts more than a minute! Soon after, Stokes is tied up in an upstairs room while the sheriff proceeds to gamble away all of the former bandit's ill-gotten gains at a crooked roulette table. Horrified at his own behavior, he confesses afterwards, "I'm a bigger thief than you are, Stokes." Stokes instinctively laughs heartlessly at this—the reaction of a man used to being on the other side of the law—but then the image of the woman he loves literally appears (through the magic of multiple exposure) over his shoulder, and at this moment he decides to ally himself with the poor sheriff and help him find his own redemption. This moment of truth will then propel the remaining bits of the narrative to their satisfying conclusion.

It is interesting to note that even though Hart as Jim Stokes is the star of the picture, the seventy-minute movie devotes over twelve minutes to Sheriff Walsh's fall from grace at the gambling tables. For this long span of time Hart's character is inert, tied up helplessly in the upstairs room. Now the movie is all the sheriff's, and only after we see him reduced to this pitiable state does the focus return to Stokes, who has the opportunity to save another person just as he has been saved. "Sheriff, I'll make a bargain with you. You turn me loose and I'll get the money back for you or they'll take me home in a box." Stokes's robbery of the crooked roulette boss is exciting and kinetic; we laugh in appreciation when he returns a wad of money to the sheriff afterwards, saying simply, "There may be a little more than you lost, but I was in a hurry."

The Bargain is a delight from start to finish, and its exploration of the hidden noble nature of its hero is reflected by the natural beauty of the exteriors. The movie takes full advantage of its gorgeous landscape, from the exciting opening scenes to the final shot of Stokes and Nell waving to the sheriff with the majestic Grand Canyon in the background. Throughout the history of the Western, the landscape will play a significant role, serving as a counterpoint to and commentary on the drama, and frequently becoming almost a character in its own right.

The last point I would like to make about *The Bargain* is actually a larger one about Westerns, and movies in general, made during the early years and the subsequent Golden Age of Hollywood. This observation is sparked by the final title card of the movie: "No star is lost we ever once have seen / We always may be what we might have been." This fitting close to a story about redemption is actually a slightly misquoted excerpt from the last section of a long poem called "A Legend of Provence," written by Adelaide Anne Procter (1825–1864), an English feminist, philanthropist, and favorite poet of Queen Victoria. The last lines of the poem:

> Have we not all, amid life's petty strife,
> Some pure ideal of a noble life
> That once seemed possible? Did we not hear
> The flutter of its wings, and feel it near,
> And just within our reach? It was. And yet
> We lost it in this daily jar and fret,
> And now live idle in a vague regret.
> But still our place is kept, and it will wait,
> Ready for us to fill it, soon or late:
> No star is ever lost we once have seen,
> We always may be what we might have been.
> Since Good, though only thought, has life and breath,
> God's life—can always be redeemed from death;
> And evil, in its nature, is decay,
> And any hour can blot it all away:
> The hopes that lost in some far distance seem,
> May be the truer life, and this the dream.[2]

So here we have a Western starring an actor trained to do Shakespeare on the stage, which opens with one of the most dazzling visuals of its day, presents an engaging storyline in which several characters undergo significant transformations, uses and references motifs that also occur in classic medieval literature (and earlier), and closes with an apt quotation from Victorian-era poetry.

This gives the lie to the conventional wisdom about the early Westerns, that they are merely simplistic and unsophisticated shoot-'em-ups. In fact, as I claimed in the Law of Craft and hope to demonstrate through these essays, there is far more to the American Western than many people realize; the best of them can be phenomenally well-done, aesthetic, sophisticated, meaningful, and moving. In their day, classic Westerns certainly fulfilled a public craving for enjoyable entertainment, but there are also depths to the genre that have not been sufficiently acknowledged. Indeed, the filmmakers of today could learn a lot about how to imbue their work with more depth, subtlety, visual power, and human meaning by studying the history of these supposedly simple movies.

Knight of the Trail
(1915)

AKA: *A Knight of the Trails; Prowlers of the Plains*
August 20, 1915 (USA)
USA—English
Kay-Bee Pictures; New York Motion Picture
24m—Silent—BW—1.33:1

Direction: William S. Hart (uncredited)
Screenplay: Thomas H. Ince (uncredited), Richard V. Spencer (uncredited)
Principal Cast: William S. Hart (Jim Treen), Frank Borzage (W. Sloane Carey; uncredited),
Leona Hutton (Molly Stewart; uncredited)
Production: Thomas H. Ince (uncredited)
Cinematography: Robert Doeran (uncredited)

Knight of the Trail (1915) features William S. Hart once again as a bad man made good in the hands of the right woman. Not only is it a thoroughly enjoyable short, but it also manages to unite the two most prominent metaphors of the early Westerns in its irresistible title.

I have already referred several times to medieval chivalric legends such as those of Parzival or Tristan. These stories were commonly known by early Western writers, and the majority of the audience would have known them as well, in an era where the tales one encountered growing up were experienced mainly through books rather than screens. The mythic function of the knights-errant was to venture out into the unknown frontier, a place removed from the comforts of home and civilization, filled with strange people and extraordinary occurrences. In fact, this device permeates the history of storytelling, from the *Odyssey* to medieval chivalric romances to the literature of science fiction.

Understanding this, it is not a difficult leap at all to connect the knights of romance to the Western heroes—men riding forth on horseback into unknown territory, armed and ready for battle or single combat, facing whatever adventures may come—and each, of course, representing certain facets or potentialities of the human character. Their stories, done properly, tell us something about ourselves and the ways in which we, in our everyday environments, also face up to challenge, adversity, and ethical dilemmas.

The second prominent Western metaphor, especially in the earlier days of the genre, is that of the trail, representing the life-course of the hero. In the early Westerns the heroes themselves use this image frequently in their own dialogue. For example, in *Hell's Hinges* (1916), the William S. Hart character says to the woman who, again, will redeem him: "When I look at you, I feel I been ridin' the wrong trail."

— Total Number of "Trail" Titles per Year (3-year rolling average)

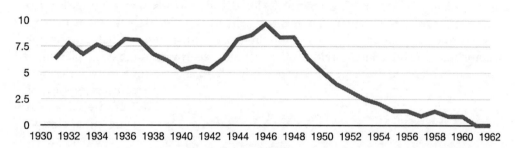

— "Trail" Titles per Year as Percentage of Total Westerns (3-year rolling average)

Figures compiled from information in *The BFI Companion to the Western* (Edward Buscombe, ed., 1988) and *The Western* (Phil Hardy, 1983).

One imprecise but interesting measure of the metaphorical importance of the trail to the Western genre is the frequency of the word itself in movie titles. It was certainly common during the silent era, from (at least) D.W. Griffith's *The Twisted Trail* (1910) until the aptly named *Silent Trail* (1928), but what is truly striking is the sheer volume of "trail" titles in the 1930s, 1940s, and 1950s. By my count, during these three decades there were at least 173 American Westerns with "trail" in the title, from *Trailing Trouble* (1930) to *The Oregon Trail* (1959). The 1930s titles are often wistful and elegiac—*The Lonesome Trail* (1930), *Near the Trail's End* (1931), *End of the Trail* (1932), *The Sunset Trail* (1932), *The Last Trail* (1933), *Trail's End* (1935)—perhaps reflecting the tenor of the Great Depression and the period of the Western's doldrums. Postwar "trail" titles tend to be more matter-of-fact—*On the Old Spanish Trail* (1947), *Navajo Trail Raiders* (1949)—or grimmer—*Trail to Vengeance* (1945), *Terror Trail* (1946), *Slaughter Trail* (1951), *Dead Man's Trail* (1952).

I wonder if one can roughly perceive the rise and fall of the trail as a dominant Western metaphor by counting the "trail" titles, year by year. The result is pretty suggestive, with a peak in the mid–1930s, a dip approaching World War II, a resurgence during and after the war, and a dramatic decline in the 1950s. After 1953, only a handful of Western titles would include the term, and it would all but vanish after 1959. With the death of the old mythologies and the subversive, anarchic Westerns that followed—for which the neat-and-tidy metaphor of the trail as a pathway through one's life seemed increasingly inappropriate—the potency of the image had faded, and it was time to move on. Silver Age antiheroes tended to ride their own ways through the Wild Frontier, rather than following trails already established by the older generation.

I should note, however, that in the late twentieth century, when Western filmmakers began to draw on both the countercultural subversion of the Silver Age and the epic myth-building of the Golden Age, the trail metaphor occasionally returned. For example, in Kevin Costner's *Dances with Wolves* (1990), there is a scene where the Sioux medicine man Kicking Bird (Graham Greene) speaks to his friend Lt. Dunbar, now called Dances with Wolves (Costner), and says: "I was just thinking that of all the trails in this life there is one that matters most. It is the trail of a true human being. I think you are on this trail, and it is good to see." And the word *trail* even appears once again in the title of a significant twenty-first-century Western, the 2006 miniseries *Broken Trail*, directed by Walter Hill and starring Robert Duvall.

As far as *Knight of the Trail* itself goes, it is a delightful short. Hart is in fine form as the bandit with the heart of gold. He also seems like a very educated thief; his letter to the sheriff, in very neat writing, reads: "Enclosed find proceeds of recent stage robberies committed by writer, except money spent, which writer will make good later. The writer has reformed and you need fear no more holdups at his hands." What a literate protagonist! Leona Hutton is adorable as the love interest—sweet, tomboyish, playful, and heartfelt—and Frank Borzage plays a good oily villain, a cigar-smoking wheeler-dealer

with connections in Chicago. Here we see an early prototype of a common Western love triangle (still present as late as *Tombstone* in 1993) between a plucky girl, a hero with a past, and a slick Eastern-style con artist.

This is the first movie in this book—although by no means the first ever—in which the villain meets his end in a one-on-one shootout with the hero. (Hart fires in self-defense, after being wounded by Borzage.) Obviously, this will become a staple of the Western movie; it would not be long before audiences could watch the opening of a standard Western, identify the hero and the bad guy early on, and know that an hour later they would see the villain gunned down by the protagonist in a

William S. Hart, the greatest of silent Western stars, circa 1918.

climactic showdown. The question then is how the movie gets from Point A to Point B, how it builds suspense and maintains interest until the moment that everyone in the theater knows is coming.

Of course, the showdown has its own mythic and psychological relevance. Consider *High Noon* (1952), for example, in which Will Kane is a stand-in for all of us as we face life's challenges largely alone, despite being ostensibly supported by friends, loved ones, and well-wishers. No matter how much magical assistance is given on the Hero's Journey, at some point the hero has to turn the trick by himself. This trope, then, provides the Western with something of real worth; we gain a metaphor about standing on one's own against the forces of chaos. But is there an element of nuance and depth that gets sacrificed? It may be exhilarating (if on a more obvious level) when we see the good guy give the bad guy his comeuppance at the end, but this rarely happens in real life; therefore, when this expectation is subverted, it can be even more effective—as we will see in some of the films to come.

Keno Bates, Liar
(1915)

AKA: *The Last Card*
August 27, 1915 (USA)
USA—English
Kay-Bee Pictures
27m—Silent—BW—1.37:1

Direction: William S. Hart (uncredited)
Screenplay: J.G. Hawks (uncredited), Thomas H. Ince (uncredited)
Principal Cast: William S. Hart (Keno Bates), Margaret Thompson (Doris Maitland), Herschel Mayall (Wind River), Louise Glaum (Anita), Gordon Mullen (Jim Maitland)
Production: Thomas H. Ince
Cinematography: Robert Doeran (uncredited)

The previous two William S. Hart Westerns have certainly shown that the writer/producer Thomas H. Ince (a major force in many areas of filmmaking, also dubbed the "Father of the Western") knew and enjoyed playing with themes from myths and legends. In the case of *Keno Bates, Liar* (1915), one primary influence on Ince seems to have been the tale of Tristan and Iseult. As mentioned in the essay on *The Bargain* (1914), the legend places its young lovers under the shadow of a dark secret—namely, that Tristan has previously killed Iseult's kinsman Morholt, something she discovers while nursing Tristan back to health after a dreadful wound. The question that arises, then, is whether romantic love is strong enough to overcome familial loyalty. This is the case in *Keno Bates* as well, only here it is not the heroine Doris's uncle that has been slain by the hero but rather her brother, the thief Jim Maitland (Gordon Mullen).

Although not the greatest of Hart's Western shorts, *Keno Bates* is an engrossing piece, featuring beautiful and evocative locations, and with Hart as compelling as ever. Here he is afforded the opportunity to show his considerable range, from tough and laconic to gentle and tender. Critics have often accused Hart's movies of being overly sentimental, but I do not believe this is a fair charge; one must remember that, prior to postmodernism, it was permissible for characters in films (and elsewhere) to experience deep feelings without ironical detachment. And this approach forces us, the audience, into a deeper and more meaningful engagement with the human experience than its alternative.

As one example, whereas most films today presuppose a certain desensitization to violence in the audience, *Keno Bates* is not afraid to confront the moral ambiguity even in a justified killing. Maitland is a crook and a thief—his last name literally means "bad disposition"—and when he attacks his pursuer Keno (Hart), Keno kills Maitland in

self-defense. It would have
been simple to present this
in a stereotypical manner:
good guy shoots bad guy,
pure and clean. But the film
will not take that easy path;
instead, Keno finds a locket
with a picture of Doris
(Margaret Thompson) in
it, accompanied by her letter to Maitland: "Dearest
Brother—Mother is dead. I
have no one to turn to but
you. I will arrive in Dry
Creek on Thursday's stage.
Meet me. Your loving sister,
Doris." We see the regret in
Keno's eyes and body as he
reads the letter, and he sags
a little over the dead man's

Keno Bates (William S. Hart) kneels over the body of Jim
Maitland (Gordon Mullen), whom he has just killed. In Hart
Westerns, violence—even when justifiable—always has con-
sequences. *Keno Bates, Liar* (Kay-Bee, 1915).

body. It is clear that killing is not a casual matter to him; he feels this one. In a William S. Hart Western, violence—even when committed by the hero—has consequences.
Today we are so used to movies in which violence, at the climax of the film, resolves
everything, but in many early Westerns—*The Squaw Man* and *The Bargain* from the previous year, for example—the narrative arc is focused upon the difficulties that arise in
the aftermath of violence. That is, violence is just as likely to launch a story arc as it is to
resolve it.

The situation Keno now finds himself in sets up the ethical difficulty alluded to by
the film's title, as he turns to his friend and says, "Wind River, you or me has got to do
a heap o' lyin'." Which he does; upon meeting Maitland's sister for the first time, Keno
tells her, "Yore brother is dead, Miss. Killed in a mine accident. He was my partner." It
goes without saying that Doris will eventually learn the truth, but her ultimate response
when this happens is shocking—a brutal attack upon the man she has grown to love,
again showing Ince's tendency to explore the ambiguities and consequences of violence.
There is a wonderful moment when the grievously wounded Keno returns to his saloon
and says to his partner, "Give me my saddle bags, Wind River, I'm going to take that
trail."

Keno Bates, Liar is a short film which, despite being enjoyable, also contains some
genuinely dark moments. In fact, in many ways the movie seems as if it is naturally
heading for a very different ending than the one that it gets, leading some writers to
speculate that the happy ending was tacked on after the fact, though I am unaware of
any direct evidence that this happened. Indeed, I suspect the opposite: the final images
of Doris nursing Keno back to health seem to complete the circle with the Tristan legend, but in this case the nursing is a redemptive act, coming after the dark secret's discovery rather than before.

The movie shares elements in common with another Hart/Ince short released earlier the same year, *The Taking of Luke McVane*, especially including the symbolic use of

flowers. But more flowery still is the language for the final title card: "The sun of love has dissolved the clouds of misunderstanding and shines through on the valley of peace." Fortunately, the early silent Westerns were generally more adept at conveying metaphor through visual means than they were on title cards.

Hell's Hinges
(1916)

March 5, 1916 (USA)
USA—English
Kay-Bee Pictures; New York Motion Picture
64m—Silent—BW (tinted)—1.33:1

Direction: William S. Hart, Charles Swickard (uncredited), Clifford Smith (uncredited)
Screenplay: C. Gardner Sullivan (uncredited)
Principal Cast: William S. Hart (Blaze Tracey), Clara Williams (Faith Henley), Jack Standing (the Rev. Robert Henley), Alfred Hollingsworth (Silk Miller), Robert McKim (A Clergyman), J. Frank Burke (Zeb Taylor), Louise Glaum (Dolly)
Production: Thomas H. Ince (uncredited)
Cinematography: Joseph H. August (uncredited)
Awards: National Film Registry

In Wolfram von Eschenbach's medieval Arthurian romance *Parzival*, there is a marvelous moment—one of a multitude in this incredible work—in which Parzival, his Eastern half-brother Feirifiz, and the wounded Grail King Anfortas are present in the Grail Castle when the Holy Grail itself is borne into the room, carried by the beautiful Grail Maiden Repanse de Schoye. Everyone in the hall is nourished by the Grail, but Feirifiz is unable to see it, only the Maiden who carries it. Feirifiz is immediately smitten with her, and begs Anfortas, her brother, to tell him how he might win her love.

Anfortas perceives that Feirifiz has not yet seen the Grail, and those present realize that this is because Feirifiz is not a Christian, so they implore him to be baptized. The exotic pagan Feirifiz then asks, "If I were baptized for your sakes, would Baptism help me to win love?" "If you want my aunt [the Grail Maiden]," Parzival replies, "you must forswear all your gods for her sake and be always ready to fight the Adversary of God on high, and faithfully observe God's Commandments."

"Whatever will assure me of winning that maiden shall be done and seen to be done, fully and faithfully," Feirifiz answers. "If it will soothe my anguish, I shall believe all you tell me. If her love rewards me, I shall gladly fulfill God's Commandments. Brother, if your aunt has God, I believe in Him and her—never was I in such need!"[1] And so Feirifiz converts. But what is truly motivating him? Wolfram presents us with a very secular conversion here: Feirifiz is overcome not by spiritual piety but by the love of a woman.

This one episode exemplifies well the subtle (and very modern!) psychological and ethical stances that permeate this thirteenth-century masterwork. Life happens in the gray areas, and every act has good and evil results. Thus, one major motif in *Parzival* is that of an almost Aristotelian (or even Taoist) moderation between pairs of extremes:

good and evil, light and dark, Christian and Saracen, sacred and profane. Feirifiz's skin is mottled with patches of black and white; and the name of Parzival, as Wolfram tells it, literally refers to "piercing the valley" between opposites.

Blaze Tracey (William S. Hart), the protagonist of *Hell's Hinges* (1916), also explores the valley between light and darkness during his own quest. In true Parzival fashion, Blaze is poised upon a moral knife edge; an early title card describes his character as "the embodiment of the best and worst of the early west."

A simple rendering of the plot would be one familiar to Hart fans: a wicked man turns to righteousness through the love of a good woman. At first blush, this is no secular ethical shift, but rather an overt conversion to Christianity. But here again we find echoes of *Parzival*, for our hero, like Feirifiz, is brought to Christ not through the ministrations of the clergy, who are corrupt or ineffectual, but through an earthly, aesthetic response to the beauty of a saintly woman. When the altar call happens, Blaze rises not because of the effect of the religious service, but because of his love for Faith Henley (Clara Williams). He catches sight of her—"one who is evil, looking for the first time on that which is good"—and is forever changed. "I reckon God ain't wantin' me much, ma'am," he says, "but when I look at you, I feel I've been ridin' the wrong trail."

To the film's credit, Blaze may have this transformative moment of aesthetic arrest, but his metamorphosis is still not instantaneous, nor is it presented without ambiguity. Even after being seized with his vision of the good (as represented by Faith, in both

Blaze Tracey (William S. Hart) in aesthetic arrest as he beholds Faith. "One who is evil, looking for the first time upon that which is good." *Hell's Hinges* **(Kay-Bee, 1916).**

senses), Blaze is at first willing to let the folly go on in the barn where the worshippers are being harassed. He smiles and starts to walk away, but then Faith prays, and we see an image of a cross standing in front of flowing water. At this moment, Blaze turns around and walks back.

When Blaze first stands up for the little church—when he draws his two guns and drives back the unruly crowd—he is clearly on the side of good now, but of course he is only able to do this because of his fearsome reputation, because of the fact that he's lived the wicked life he's lived. A lifelong straight arrow couldn't have pulled that off. Blaze needs redemption (in the film's worldview), but it could be argued that he also needs his checkered past, at least at this one critical moment. There is a wonderful shot after Blaze's conversion in which we see a Bible lying next to a whiskey bottle on his table. This underscores the fact that we typically find imperfect, "all too human" characters so much more interesting than spotless, squeaky clean ones. Launcelot is an indelible character; Galahad is a bore.

Hell's Hinges, which Hart both starred in and directed, is one of the most critically beloved of his Westerns. George Fenin and William Everson write: "The camera placement, the simple yet effective symbolism, and the flair for spectacle, plus the real 'feel' for the dusty, unglamorized West, should have earned Hart a reputation as one of the great directors."[2] On the film's rerelease in 1994, Michael Wilmington (*Chicago Tribune*) called it "perhaps the finest Western made before John Ford's 1939 *Stagecoach*" and "as emotionally powerful as any American film of the teens, except for the masterpieces of D.W. Griffith and Erich von Stroheim."[3]

However, I must confess that I find *Hell's Hinges* a second-tier Hart, and love it far less than, for example, *The Bargain* (1914) or the later *Tumbleweeds* (1925). Part of it is just my own contemporary sensibility; even though there are many films from this era that I find deeply affecting despite a century's difference in style, in the case of *Hell's Hinges* both the piety and the symbolism are a bit too heavy-handed for my taste. The movie starts with a sermon, and there is no shortage of sanctimony to come. Plus, our heroic couple are actually named "Blaze" and "Faith"—inspiring perhaps a bit of eye-rolling from today's viewer.

And yet one must give *Hell's Hinges* credit as an early Western which stakes out an ethical position with vigor, and for which ethical thinking is a substantially important part of the drama overall. It also explores terrain which is beyond a simplistic moral monochrome. Like so many of the Westerns from this era, the movie contains and indeed embodies contradictions. On the one hand, it's a devout morality tale extolling Christian virtue, with symbolism so obvious that we can feel bludgeoned by it. On the other hand, there is an ambiguity here. Blaze, as mentioned above, requires both his light and dark sides to advance the plot, and while the virtues of Christianity are upheld, Blaze seems to find them outside of the established church.

In some cases, simplistic stereotypes are avoided or explicitly denied: the man is morally adrift, but the woman is a solid rock of strength and fortitude who shows our hero the way. ("When women like her say there's a God, there *is* one, and He sure must be worth trailin' with.") The lay protagonists are the true Christians, whereas the clergy are weak hypocrites. Yet other stereotypes are gratingly present, unquestioned: for example, the antagonist Silk Miller (Alfred Hollingsworth) is described completely gratuitously as having "the oily craftiness of a Mexican." (We should note that Hart's next

Western, released later the same year, was *The Aryan*, which explicitly celebrated white culture over the perceived values of Mexicans and Indians. Enlightened attitudes have always come far too slowly—in the Western, in Hollywood, in America, and in the world.)

Paradoxes and contradictions within a film often lead to a sense of nuance and ambiguity that adds depth and resonance to its effect. However, when the ambiguity is actually between ambiguity itself on the one side and guity itself on the one side

Blaze (William S. Hart), enhaloed. *Hell's Hinges* (Kay-Bee, 1916).

and non-ambiguous heavy-handedness and clunky stereotyping on the other, the effect is compromised, and aesthetic potential is often thwarted by unevenness of tone. Still, great moments stand out, and there are more than a few here.

Tidbits and Trivia

- We see perhaps the earliest example of a modern Hollywood trope during the climactic biblical conflagration at the end—the hero standing unfazed with fire (or today, explosions) behind him. As Fenin and Everson write, "Hart, holstering his guns, walks out of the inferno, apparently oblivious to it all, a sudden burst of flame creating a halo-like effect behind his head seeming almost to identify him as an agent of divine vengeance."[4] It works far better here, resonant with mythic overtones, than it does in today's standard action flick, where the only point seems to be that the hero is so tough that he transcends the physics of shock waves.
- Hart is such a tremendous actor. Just as one example: the transformation of his face at the moment when he walks over to try to threaten the newcomers, but then sees "good" for the first time (in the person of Faith), is simply incredible. It calls to mind the opening of *The Bargain*—what Hart could do with just a look!
- *Hell's Hinges* exemplifies my claim in the Introduction ("The Law of Time") that Westerns are not about the time period in which they occur, but rather about the time in which they are made. It's hard to imagine any story like this one actually unfolding in the Old West, but its rock-ribbed portrayal of the values of mainline white Protestant Christianity fits perfectly with the America of 1916. Similarly, the character of Dolly (Louise Glaum, who played many a vamp in her time) does not look like anyone we would ever expect to meet in the nineteenth-century West; however, she looks exactly like a 1916 conception of a woman of

easy virtue, invoking the already-established flapper style which would reach its climax in the Roaring Twenties just around the corner.

- The Bible verse Blaze reads is Matthew 21:22, which, as it turns out, immediately follows a more familiar passage about faith moving mountains. Blaze then asks God for "Faith"—and he gets her!

- In true Gospel fashion, Blaze even tells a parable. "Boys, you all remember Arizona Frank, the best roper in the territory, don't you? Once I seen Arizona rope a steer with as pretty a throw as was ever made, but the rope broke and the steer got away. That wasn't Arizona's fault. It was the thing he was dependin' on that was no good." Then he leaves the story there, allowing his listeners to work out the allegory for themselves.

- This movie anticipates the "sick town" movie of the future—*High Noon* (1952), *Bad Day at Black Rock* (1955), *A Fistful of Dollars* (1964), and most especially *High Plains Drifter* (1973), which also features a town named after Hell and a climactic inferno.

- In contrast with today's mainstream movies, the resolution of the plot's traumas is not immediately followed by a feel-good ending; our heroes don't just shrug off their preceding ordeals and leap into each other's arms as if nothing happened. Faith's brother lies dead, and our pair rides off, sobered and scarred, into an uncertain future. There is something almost fatalistic in Blaze's final words: "Over yonder hills is the future—both yours and mine. It's callin', and I reckon we'd better go."

The Heart of Texas Ryan
(1917)

AKA: *Single Shot Parker*
February 12, 1917 (USA)
USA—English
Selig Polyscope Company
56m—Silent—BW—1.33:1

Direction: E.A. Martin (uncredited)
Screenplay: Gilson Willets (story), Zane Grey (novel *The Light of Western Stars*; uncredited)
Principal Cast: Tom Mix (Single-Shot Parker), Bessie Eyton (Texas Ryan), George Fawcett
   (Colonel Ryan), Frank Campeau (Dice McAllister), William Ryno (Mandero)
Production: William Nicholas Selig

If you ever wanted proof that striking moments strung together don't make a movie, you would be hard pressed to find a better argument than *The Heart of Texas Ryan*—released in 1917, but only available today in its 1923 reissue version.

Tom Mix's first feature-length film was also his last venture with William Selig's Polyscope Company before moving to Fox. The original intent was an adaptation of a Zane Grey novel, *The Light of Western Stars*, but there was difficulty securing the rights. Instead, Selig cobbled *Texas Ryan* together from several disparate bits and pieces, including scenes from previous Mix one- and two-reelers. The memorable saloon fight, for example, was lifted straight out of 1914's ten-minute short *The Telltale Knife*.

The result is a film full of moments, but with little plot coherence and wildly uneven tone. Scenes seem cut short; story elements and characters are launched and then disappear; critical events happen offscreen, only summarized on title cards; and the climax of the narrative is skipped in aid of an ending so abrupt that one can only stare in disbelief.

It is better to view this movie as a compilation of scenes, the way one might watch a clip show from a television sitcom, rather than to try and engage with the tacked-on narrative as any kind of aesthetic whole. So where can one take pleasure?

The dialogue and whimsical title cards. There is a delightful humor present in some of the scenes, reflected in both the dialogue and some of the title cards as they comment on the action. A few examples:

- Our hero confronts the threatening marshal. "Pard, when I shoots it's for a plumb good reason—and I seldom, if ever, emerges as a corpse."
- After Mix beats up the villainous lawman with his own boot in the saloon's poker room, some of the locals come rushing in to find the marshal sprawled upon the floor. Mix says, "He ain't hurt serious-like. It's mighty hard to kill a snake with a boot!"

- The title card before the Fourth of July sequence reads: "The spirit of independence— the more spirits he took the more independent he felt."
- Another card: "When the State Senator elected to ride a broncho he was defeated by an overwhelming majority."

Stunts and special effects. A coach rolls over and over down a hill, and then when it comes to a rest a man pops out of the top— and the shot is all in one take, no cuts. Gunshots pop realistically through doors, our hero tumbles head over heels down a steep cliff with his hands tied together, and there are plenty of fireworks and (small) explosions.

William Fox presents a new star—
Fox Special Features   TOM MIX

Scenery and striking shots. There are some lovely visual moments, includ-

Tom Mix in promotional material from 1917, when he made the move to Fox, not long after *The Heart of Texas Ryan*.

ing nighttime rain running off the top of the rustlers' shelter, a terrific shot of Texas Ryan (Bessie Eyton) reading a book on an open train section while the terrain flashes by behind her, and an occasionally breathtaking landscape.

Overall, though, *The Heart of Texas Ryan* does not succeed as a film. Aside from its general incoherence, its Frankenstein-like assemblage from scraps, and its wildly erratic tone, there are just too many missed opportunities. The most exciting parts of the narrative are summarized in title cards, such as the escape of Mandero (William Ryno). The action that does occur is often filmed in long shot, keeping us at a distance. And at the climax of the plot, when Mix's character is being held hostage by a brutal gang of rustlers and scheduled to be executed, his love interest, Texas Ryan, simply pays off the bandits with $2,000 and secures Mix's release—offscreen! "The End" appears within seconds, and the viewer is left wondering what in the world just happened. The last hour of narrative was all just leading to this?

So why would I bother to write about this relatively inconsequential little film? To me, *The Heart of Texas Ryan* is a fairly good metaphor for the condition of the Western genre as it existed from the latter days of the First World War and into the early twenties: a series of individual moments, some sparkling (as in the Hart Westerns discussed above), but many others more ordinary, tied loosely together by familiar, comfortable formulas, with little coherence and even less sense of overall direction. What we say watching *Texas Ryan*, we might also imagine contemporary audiences saying of the late-teens Western as a whole: there are some fine moments, to be sure, but what is all this in aid of? Will the payoff justify the journey? Or has this already given us all it can give? Are we, as a culture, outgrowing it?

The Heart of Texas Ryan ends with a whimper, not a bang—and for a time, it looked like that would be the fate of the Western as well. The late teens and early twenties saw a decline in popular interest in the genre, and as the Western movie approached its twentieth birthday, it seemed destined to fade into irrelevance.

As would be the case many times over the course of the Western's first century, a revitalizing blast of fresh air was needed to bring new spirit and new direction. And in 1923, it came.

The Covered Wagon
(1923)

March 16, 1923 (New York City)
USA—English
Paramount Pictures
98m—Silent—BW—1.33:1

Direction: James Cruze
Screenplay: Jack Cunningham, Emerson Hough (novel)
Principal Cast: J. Warren Kerrigan (Will Banion), Lois Wilson (Molly Wingate), Alan Hale (Sam Woodhull), Ernest Torrence (William Jackson), Tully Marshall (Jim Bridger), Ethel Wales (Mrs. Wingate), Charles Ogle (Jesse Wingate), Guy Oliver (Kit Carson), Johnny Fox (Jed Wingate)
Production: Jesse L. Lasky (uncredited)
Cinematography: Karl Brown
Editing: Dorothy Arzner (uncredited)
Awards: Kinema Junpo Award—Best Entertainment Film, Photoplay Medal of Honor

The Covered Wagon (1923) is not a great film, but it was exactly what was needed to reenergize the Western after the doldrums of the late teens and early twenties, for several reasons.

First, it was the earliest true Western epic, with its massive train of covered wagons cutting their course across two thousand miles of rugged country. Many of the wagons filmed were genuine articles from the pioneer days, often driven by the families that still owned them. The movie featured river crossings and buffalo hunts and Indian battles and treks through snowy wastes, all on a grand scale. The cost of filming *The Covered Wagon* was enormous for its day, nearly $800,000. Epic visions, after all, still have to be paid for.

Second, the movie was beautiful to behold, featuring magnificent vistas and excellent photography by Karl Brown. The Western landscape was coming into its own, and audiences would henceforth expect these films to provide them with awe-inspiring scenery—an appropriately majestic backdrop for the American mythos.

Third, *The Covered Wagon* was an attempt to frame a familiar, personal story within the context of great historical events in motion. Though not entirely artistically successful because of the relative banality of the small-scale plot (a B-movie love triangle between hero, heroine, and villain), it nevertheless blazed the trail for the great Western epics to come.

Finally, and perhaps most importantly, audiences loved it—so much so, in fact, that they made it both the box-office champion of 1923 and the highest-grossing silent Western ever made. This burst of enthusiasm almost single-handedly revitalized the Western as a genre; there were fifty Hollywood Westerns made in 1923, but in the following year, after *The Covered Wagon*, that number jumped to 125.[1]

It is inevitable that *The Covered Wagon* will always be compared with John Ford's *The Iron Horse* (1924). They are the two earliest important epic Westerns, released within eighteen months of one another, and each one combines an intimate storyline with the grand sweep of larger historical forces. While *The Iron Horse* is by far the better of the two films, *The Covered Wagon* has the distinction of being first, and of being the more popular of the two during its day.

The movie sets the stage from the very beginning, with a title card that proclaims: "The blood of America is the blood of pioneers—the blood of lion-hearted men and women who carved a splendid civilization out of an uncharted wilderness." Two great historical events from the late 1840s are referenced: the migration along the Oregon Trail and the California Gold Rush. The film sets these in opposition to one another, the path of virtue and the path of greed. As Jesse Wingate (Charles Ogle), the leader of the wagon train, puts it, "The pick and the shovel never built up a country—you've got to have a plow."

The film does not question the doctrine of Manifest Destiny in any way, of course, but neither does it demonize the natives. Although the Indians are certainly shown as enemy combatants, they are not depicted as inhuman or monstrous. In fact, the most brutal moment in the movie comes when the white villain (Alan Hale) shoots down an unarmed Indian ferryman in cold blood to get out of paying the fare. Meanwhile, the only Indian dialogue presented seems both understandably concerned and eerily prophetic. At a tribal gathering, one member says, "The Pale Face again crosses the River of Misty Water—always advancing towards the setting sun." An elder adds, "With him he brings this monster weapon [the plow] that will bury the buffalo—uproot the forest—and level the mountain. The Pale Face who comes with this evil medicine must be slain—or the Red Man perishes!"

For all of its epic sweep, *The Covered Wagon* comes across as curiously lacking in action. Portions have an almost documentary feel to them—as, for example, the river crossing, which lasts for about four minutes of screen time without any real incident. Immediately after-

Molly Wingate (Lois Wilson) watches as Will Banion (J. Warren Kerrigan) crafts a doll for a young pioneer girl (Barbara Brower). A metaphorical template for the epic Western: intimate drama in front and grand history in the background. *The Covered Wagon* (Paramount, 1923).

wards, however, a title card informs us that there was "a staggering loss of wagons and stock," something we never see dramatized.

The exception to this, however, is the climactic Indian battle, which packs the most powerful emotional punch in the movie. Here there are several gut-wrenching moments: our heroine, Molly Wingate (Lois Wilson), is suddenly impaled upon an Indian arrow just before her intended marriage to the film's villain; a horse falls off a steep cliff; a woman hides her baby in a barrel; and in the film's most poignant moment, our hero,

Bill Jackson (Ernest Torrence) watches in horror as our heroine, Molly Wingate (Lois Wilson), is suddenly pierced by an Indian arrow. This gasp-inducing phallic attack, with its overtones of rape, would become a Golden Age Western trope, reappearing (among other places) in *Red River* (1948) and *Bend of the River* (1952). *The Covered Wagon* (Paramount, 1923).

Will Banion (J. Warren Kerrigan), finds the doll he once made for a little girl pioneer lying alone in the dirt. The girl is gone.

The persona of the hero in the American Western can take many forms: William S. Hart's coiled intensity; George O'Brien's scrappy physicality; John Wayne's straight-shooting swagger; Jimmy Stewart's multi-layered, dark complexity; Randolph Scott's granite-jawed, laconic morality; Clint Eastwood's amoral anarchism; and so on. All of these have their mythic/legendary forebears, and I believe that Kerrigan's character Banion is no exception—indeed, he strikes me as a Western echo of Malory's Launcelot. I say this not because of Banion's position in a love triangle—the Arthurian triangle is of a different nature entirely—but rather because of his obvious gentleness and chivalry.

One reason why Launcelot springs from the pages of *Le Morte d'Arthur* as a three-dimensional character is the striking contrast between his unmatched excellence as a fighter and his equally unsurpassed courtesy, modesty, and gentility. Upon his death, his brother Sir Ector sings praises over his corpse for these dual aspects:

> Thou were the courteoust knight that ever bare shield. And thou were the truest friend to thy lover that ever bestrad horse. And thou were the truest lover of a sinful man that ever loved woman. And thou were the kindest man that ever struck with sword. And thou were the goodliest person that ever came among press of knights. And thou was the meekest man and the gentlest that ever ate in hall among ladies. And thou were the sternest knight to thy mortal foe that ever put spear in the rest.[2]

This combination of strength and gentleness is characteristic of Banion as well. From the beginning of *The Covered Wagon*, we see him as a strong hero: he's a leader of men, a veteran of the trail, and a tough fighter. And yet, when grizzled old Bill (Ernest Torrence) says quite baldly to Mr. Wingate that Banion should be the captain of the entire wagon train, Banion immediately defers to Wingate: "Mr. Wingate is captain over *all* of our trains, Bill." Banion then takes his assignment at the back of the train without complaint, even when his wagon group is put under the villain's (and his romantic rival's) command. He comforts the little girl who has broken her doll, unknowingly winning the heart of Molly Wingate, who watches from afar. After pinning his foe Woodhull (Alan Hale) in a fight, Banion shows mercy even though Woodhull has demanded a no-holds-barred contest and clearly would not have shown him the same courtesy. And though his name has been wrongfully stained by accusations of cattle theft, Banion endures it with dignity, just as Launcelot did as the "Knight of the Cart" when paraded through the streets like a criminal while people hurled food and garbage at him. The plot in which Banion plays a part is slight, but he is still a character who earns our affection—and in whom we dimly recognize reflections of greater characters from the chivalric past.

It's worth saying a word here about lead actor J. Warren Kerrigan's tragic life. Prior to *The Covered Wagon*, Kerrigan had appeared in over 370 films starting in 1910—mainly shorts, but gradually transitioning to features in the mid-teens. His career was going well until a disastrous interview in 1917, in which a *Denver Times* reporter asked him whether he would join the war effort, and Kerrigan responded:

> I am not going to war until I have to. I will go, of course, if my country needs me, but I think that first they should take the great mass of men who aren't good for anything else, or are good only for the lower grades of work. Actors, musicians, great writers, artists of every kind—isn't it a pity when people are sacrificed who are capable of such things—of adding to the beauty of the world?[3]

Once this statement was widely printed, Kerrigan's career was permanently damaged.

Nevertheless, Kerrigan had a chance at a renaissance with *The Covered Wagon* and his subsequent starring roles in *The Girl of the Golden West* (1923; now lost) and *Captain Blood* (1924). But in late 1924, he and his long-time lover James Carroll Vincent (also a silent film actor) were involved in an automobile accident in Dixon, Illinois, and Kerrigan's face was badly scarred, thus ending his acting career. At this point Kerrigan and Vincent had already lived together for about a decade (with Vincent explained as Kerrigan's secretary); their relationship would continue for over two decades more, until Kerrigan's death from pneumonia in 1947. Four months after Kerrigan died, Vincent married a woman named Mitty Lee Turner; five months after that, he committed suicide.

Tidbits and Trivia

- Emerson Hough, the writer of the novel on which *The Covered Wagon* was based, died a week after viewing its Chicago premiere.
- Charles Ogle, who played the captain of the wagon train (and our heroine's father), has the distinction of being cinema's first Frankenstein monster, in a 1910 version of the story produced by Thomas Edison.
- William S. Hart did not care for the film; in fact, he pointed out errors which, he said, "would make a Western man refuse to speak to his own brother." For example, no trail boss worth his salt would camp in a closed canyon, easy prey for attack, nor would he send cattle across a river with their yokes still on.[4]

The Iron Horse
(1924)

August 28, 1924 (New York City)
USA—English
Fox Film Corporation
150m—Silent—BW (tinted)—1.33:1

Direction: John Ford
Screenplay: Charles Kenyon, John Russell
Principal Cast: George O'Brien (Dave Brandon), Madge Bellamy (Miriam Marsh), Charles
  Edward Bull (Lincoln), Cyril Chadwick (Jesson), Will Walling (Thomas Marsh), Francis
  Powers (Sergeant Slattery), J. Farrell MacDonald (Corporal Casey), Jim Welch (Private
  Mackay), George Waggner (Buffalo Bill), Fred Kohler (Bauman), James A. Marcus (Judge
  Haller), Gladys Hulette (Ruby)
Production: John Ford
Cinematography: George Schneiderman
Awards: National Film Registry

He was born John Martin Feeney in 1894; as John Ford, he would become one of
history's preeminent filmmakers. Ford directed more than 140 movies over a period of
fifty-three years and became a master of the classic Hollywood drama, winning a record
four Best Director Oscars (*The Informer*, 1935; *The Grapes of Wrath*, 1940; *How Green
Was My Valley*, 1941; *The Quiet Man*, 1952).

He was also the greatest Western film director of all time.

In his first seven years as a director, Ford made around fifty films, from one- and
two-reelers to feature-length movies; unfortunately, only a handful of these early efforts
still survive. Then, in 1924, he released his first epic—*The Iron Horse*.

It exists in different cuts, but the full version is 150 minutes, making Ford's earliest major work his longest one as well. The film is grand in scope even by today's standards, more so in 1924. Costing around $280,000 to make, it was a massive undertaking,
requiring location shooting in the Sierra Nevada, the construction of two complete
towns, and the involvement of thousands of extras, thousands of animals (horses, cattle, and buffalo), and a regiment of cavalry. According to Jay Hyams, there were so many
people involved that the set had a daily newspaper that printed events such as births,
deaths, and marriages.[1]

When the National Film Registry selected *The Iron Horse* for its preservation list
of "culturally, historically, or aesthetically significant films" in 2011, they noted that it
"introduced to American and world audiences a reverential, elegiac mythology that has
influenced many subsequent Westerns."[2]

The plot of *The Iron Horse* is a mixture of the grandly historic and the intimately personal, which it pulls off far more successfully than its spiritual predecessor, *The Covered Wagon* (1923). On the one hand, this is the story of the building of the first transcontinental railroad, culminating in the driving of the Golden Spike at Promontory Summit on May 10, 1869. On the other, it is the story of a young boy whose father is brutally murdered, and who subsequently spends his life trying to help realize his dead father's dream. The integration of these two separate streams, large-scale and small, into a coherent whole is one of the great successes of this film, one to which many later Westerns have aspired.

The first title card reads: "Accurate and faithful in every particular of fact and atmosphere is this pictorial history of the building of the first transcontinental railroad." Pictorial, yes; accurate, not entirely. Much is fictionalized, including the movie's claim that the two engines used in the finale were the originals. The second title card, however, points us in a different direction, away from any sense that this film will unfold in an objective documentary style. "DEDICATION: To the ever-living memory of Abraham Lincoln, the Builder—and of those dauntless engineers and toilers who fulfilled his dream of a greater Nation."

The organizing myth of *The Iron Horse* is that of America's divinely sanctioned destiny as a continent-spanning nation, a new "Empire of the West." And so, we start with America's most mythic (yet actual) figure, Abraham Lincoln. He is there at the beginning of the narrative—not just as the marble bust that we see in the opening, but also as a flesh-and-blood character in the early scenes as the Brandons (father and young son) prepare to depart for the West. Here Lincoln is the embodied Spirit of America, personally overseeing the foreordained expansion of the United States. "He feels the momentum of a great nation pushing westward—he sees the inevitable." When Marsh the skeptic (Will Walling) sees the Brandons setting off to find a new passage to the West, he scoffs, "Poor dreamer—He's chasing a rainbow!" Lincoln responds, "Yes, Tom—and some day men like you will be laying rails along that rainbow." (Lincoln is played magnificently by an incredible lookalike, Charles Edward Bull, who was a justice of the peace in Reno.)

The ideal of Manifest Destiny—with all the inhumanity toward the native inhabitants that it conveniently ignored—was a common mythic theme from the time of *The Covered Wagon* and *The Iron Horse* onward. It was able to be sustained for a while, but humanity caught up, and by the 1950s this romantic and sanitized understanding of American history was already on the wane. Its last significant gasp was probably in the grand folly *How the West Was Won*, released in 1962, far too late for that picture to come across as anything other than musty and tone-deaf. At the same time, notably, Ford was working on his final Westerns, through which, among other things, he hoped to atone for his earlier cinematic treatment of Native Americans.

Myths can present a people with a romanticized history and a sense of shared destiny; they can also speak quite effectively to that which is truly human in all of us—the universal truths and questions that we hold in common by virtue of our shared humanity. One helpful way to examine these themes in a fictional context is to take very real human characters and place them out on the frontier, on the edge of what is known, and away from the restraints of civilized culture. This holds true from the *Odyssey* to

Parzival to *The Iron Horse* to *Star Trek*. All of these, and so many more, work because their authors have realized that if you want to engage in grand meditations on what it means to be human, there is no better laboratory in which to explore vast ethical questions than away from the stifling superstructures of society and out on the frontiers of experience—wherever they happen to be.

Lincoln (Charles Edward Bull) watches the Brandons depart for the West to fulfill America's destiny. The East and West are represented here by the right and left sides of the frame: the comforts of home on one side, the open frontier on the other. *The Iron Horse* (Fox, 1924).

There are many moments both mythical and supremely human in *The Iron Horse*; despite its imperfections, it still manages to resonate deeply at many points. Some of the most powerful moments are dialogue-free, purely visual. Among my favorites is the scene in which the railroad workers abandon North Platte, soon to become a ghost town, to continue their westward push. Before they leave there is a raucous Swedish wedding and much celebration; but as the train pulls away, we see the outline of an old cloaked woman in the foreground, watching the departure as she stands silently by a row of graves. Progress and the railroad both roll on, but the woman bears mute witness to those forgotten souls who were sacrificed along the way.

This moment echoes a similar scene in *The Covered Wagon*, in which a burial is immediately followed by a birth—once again the future emerges from among the ashes of death—but Ford's version handles the theme far more deftly and effectively. For one thing, in *The Covered Wagon* we first have the burial and then the birth comes next, in some sense countering whatever empathy may have been evoked by our learning of the death of a character we've never met. But Ford, with his incredible sense of both visual and narrative power, gives us death and rebirth simultaneously, within the same frame—and the death is not that of a specific, named character but rather something more universal, not "death" but Death. Likewise, the woman is not any particular woman; she is Age and Grief and Loneliness and Time contained in one figure.

Lead characters can also become stand-ins for larger ideas in Ford's cinematic world. A wonderful example of this is the moment when the hero, Dave Brandon (George O'Brien, in his first major role), rides off to join the Central Pacific railroad, while Miriam (Madge Bellamy), his love interest and the daughter of Marsh the railway magnate, stays behind. She watches him leave, then turns toward the camera, standing right in the middle of the tracks, with the distant mountains framed behind her. In this instant she *is* the railroad, and all of the dreams of pushing onward to the farthest shore surround her like a shining halo.

The trail as metaphor is ever-present as well; in fact, the crucial point in the plot is that Dave Brandon knows about the hidden short-cut through the mountains, the pass that will make the transcontinental railroad a possibility. This craggy pass is the Way of the Hero, but here it is not just an individual's trail—it is also the path of America. Our protagonist is the only one who knows the way; the fate of a nation, in this telling, rides upon his shoulders.

Death and destiny in one shot. *The Iron Horse* (Fox, 1924).

Despite some flaws, *The Iron Horse* succeeds on a narrative and aesthetic level in many ways. Here are a few of my favorites.

The visuals. In addition to his many other cinematic talents, Ford was a master of the use of landscape. Already in this early work, the vistas are stunning, and the land becomes a character in its own right. Also, Ford's ability to make the most of an allegorical image is in play from the very beginning of the movie. While Brandon and son prepare to take their leave of civilization, we see a long row of solid, regular houses fading into the distance on the right side of the frame, behind a fence that embodies the frontier waiting to be pushed westward; on the left side, just snowy, trackless emptiness. Here we are at the hard edge of civilization, with the beckoning West, in all its mystery, literally filling the left side of the screen.

In a Ford movie, it is normal to expect that virtually every shot will be aesthetically composed; pause on any frame and it is likely to look artistic. This certainly holds true for *The Iron Horse*. Furthermore, the camerawork is quite daring for its day—take, for example, the scenes when something massive (a locomotive, or a herd of cattle) comes barreling straight for the camera, running right over it and, by extension, the audience. Such shots became far more commonplace in the heyday of the Western, but they were pioneering in 1924.

Ford also shows an early mastery of the tracking shot. In the hands of lesser directors of the time (or even great ones, as in William Wyler's *Hell's Heroes* from 1929), shots involving camera movement can easily seem forced, gimmicky, or overused, but here Ford finds the sweet spot. Tracking shots are reserved for moments where they will have the most impact, and many of them are absolutely breathtaking—the shot along the North Platte rail, for example, or most especially the pulse-pounding shots when the Indians are chasing young Brandon alongside the moving train. (This scene also has one of the most memorable stationary shots, when the shadows of the Indians on their horses appear, writ large, on the sides of the railway cars.)

Ford's expert use of visuals extends to his treatment of the very human characters as well. Witness, for example, the scene where Miriam pleads with the railway workers not to abandon their jobs when the payroll is delayed. ("Make your Nation proud of you!") We cut back and forth between her flawless, radiant face and the grizzled, weathered faces of the weary workers. She addresses some by name, and we see their faces change, close up. It's a continuous study in contrasts, and very powerful, narratively and artistically. Our aesthetic arrest as viewers is mirrored in the responses of the workers: "For the beautiful signorina, Tony he build the beeg ra'lroad heemself—alone!"

The character of Dave Brandon. We first meet our hero as a young boy in the early scenes of the movie. It is easy for child actors to be cloying or annoying, but an uncredited Winston Miller does a phenomenal job playing our nascent protagonist. (Miller later became a producer and writer of many scripts, including those for television and movie Westerns. As a writer, he worked with John Ford again in 1946 on *My Darling Clementine*. Miller died in 1994, aged eighty-three.)

We are already drawn to "Davy" when we see his chivalric behavior toward young Miriam Marsh (Peggy Cartwright from the *Our Gang* series, also uncredited); their childhood romance is tender and sweet, and as we watch their tearful farewell—"Are you ever comin' back, Davy?"—we hope, and know, that they will meet again. Abraham Lincoln is present in this scene as well, tactfully turning his back as the two share their first innocent kiss.

But by far young Davy's most powerful scene comes after the horrific murder of his father (James Gordon, uncredited) at the hands of the villain Deroux (Fred Kohler) and his band of Indians. The elder Brandon's death by his own axe is gut-wrenching in its own right, but made even more dramatic by the clear, beautiful, unabashed love shown between father and son. The father kisses Davy's forehead and clutches him, knowing that death is closing in, and the lack of any faux-macho posturing makes the scene pack a genuine wallop.

After the killing, time stands still. Ford doesn't want to rush things along, or gloss over the raw emotionality of the moment. We linger with the boy for a full two minutes, just watching him grieve, and imagining what he must be feeling as a newly made orphan lost in a vast, unfriendly wilderness, hundreds of miles from home, all alone. It's a masterful scene, splendidly acted by Miller and superbly directed by Ford.

Dave Brandon as an adult is the role that put former stuntman George O'Brien on the Hollywood map—and yet it is striking that the actor doesn't make his first appearance until nearly an hour into the movie! When he arrives, though, he owns the character, imbuing Brandon with his own flavor of open, muscular physicality. O'Brien is strong and upright here, but also vulnerable and believable. And though Brandon's role in the plot of *The Iron Horse* is often described by reviewers as a man seeking vengeance for his father's death, that's an erroneous assumption colored after the fact by all of the "revenge Westerns" that populated the Silver Era. Taken on its own terms, *The Iron Horse* presents Brandon's primary motivation as that of fulfilling his father's dream of a transcontinental railroad, not avenging his father's murder. Brandon does eventually confront Deroux, but this is secondary.

The pacing. At 150 minutes long, *The Iron Horse* is a lot to take in, but Ford and his editorial department do a stunning job at holding our interest, while also being unafraid to pace scenes deliberately when they carry a deal of emotional weight (as in the scenes with young Davy mentioned above). The movie is in many ways an exercise in slow burn, both within scenes—such as the terrific barroom encounter between

Brandon and Jesson (Cyril Chadwick)—and as a whole. This makes the final joining of the rails and the driving of the Golden Spike a most satisfying culmination.

The treatment of violence. The overriding theme of the movie is about creation, not destruction, but Ford was not naïve enough to ignore the violence that went along with the "winning of the West." In the world of the film, violence is present, but it is never without grave consequence. Brandon may defeat the oily Jesson in hand-to-hand brawling, but in doing so he breaks faith with Miriam and must regain her trust. Even when he fights and kills Deroux, his father's murderer, there is nothing romanticized about it. The bare-handed battle is grim, brutal, realistic, and not stylized. In the end, Brandon beats Deroux to death with his bare hands, but then we see the impact of this through the expression on his face. It's a powerful, emotional moment, and the images speak for themselves.

Today's mainstream Hollywood film has lost touch with this more humanly real and nuanced understanding of violence. In today's typical action-movie fare, Brandon would spell out all of the emotional content, spoon-feeding it to the viewer. ("You—it was you—you killed my father!") Then he would proceed to dispatch the villain in some stylized, supercool way and go off to have celebratory sex with the heroine. But here, little is said before Deroux's death (just a quick verbalization of Brandon's realization, "Two fingers!"), and nothing is said afterwards. Deroux has been defeated, but Brandon has suffered a defeat as well.

The same nuanced view is a part of the final battle with the Indians. The last death we see is a random one, and then the railway folk return home saddened and spent, despite being the victors. Too many have died, too much blood has been spilled, for celebration—only weary continuance. Older films are often criticized by the unknowing as being emotionally unrealistic, when in fact that's not the case at all. Modern viewers often misinterpret a more visually and narratively metaphorical style as oversentimentality, when in fact it is closer to Picasso's "lie that tells the truth." Violence always has a cost, and acknowledging that—even by way of a more symbolic aesthetic—is true realism. This is something that has gotten lost along the way as our culture has succumbed to postmodernism (or even just escapism). We've gotten so completely used to seeing the good guys win the climactic battle and reading that as a happy ending (even after much suffering and death) that it has become a part of our movie-going DNA. In this sense, *The Iron Horse* and so many films of its era give us something far more emotionally true and powerfully real.

So where doesn't *The Iron Horse* succeed? Well, on an aesthetic level, it has to be said that while Ford was a master of epic drama, he did not possess a deft touch when it came to humor. As many have pointed out, the "comedic" slapstick scenes in Ford's Westerns tend to be their weakest points. For example, the whole business with the show trial of Ruby, the loose saloon girl who shoots a man for throwing a drink in her face, is meant to be comic, but comes across instead as contrived and ham-fisted. Other scenes are similarly out of place, including—it must be said—the framing titles and scenes with Lincoln, which seem tacked-on, despite Bull's excellent performance. (Apparently the producer, William Fox, had always wanted to make a Lincoln biopic, and these bits were included to help partially satisfy that urge.)

The other real liability is the script's overreliance on moldy stereotypes, resulting in both lazy storytelling and a degradation of human values in a film which is otherwise a celebration of the human spirit. The Indians here are nothing but brutal sadistic savages, without redeeming qualities, as demonstrated in the scene where the elder Brandon is killed as we see the onlookers, in close-up, leering and grinning in delight. (This was the starting position for which Ford eventually felt he had to apologize in late Westerns like 1964's *Cheyenne Autumn*.) We are also presented with Chinese, Mexican, Italian, and Swedish ("By jiminy!") caricatures, as well as Slattery and Casey, our pair of brawling Irish rogues—though Ford's lifelong affection for the Irish, deriving from his own heritage, is still very much in evidence here. Ruby, the vamp and proto-flapper, is problematic as well, representing as she does the woman of easy virtue whose sexual liberation was so threatening to the social conservatives of the day. Ford's movies would later abandon this prudery, of course; in fact, judgmental bluenoses would become targets of biting satire by the time of 1939's *Stagecoach*, a film in which the saloon girl scorned by the town prigs becomes the eventual love interest of our hero John Wayne!

There are also uncomfortable racial undertones present in the treatment of *The Iron Horse*'s villain Deroux. Early on, when the elder Brandon encounters Deroux and his band of Indians out in the wilderness, he exclaims in surprise, "You're white!" Deroux does look white in that scene; but later, when the character is with the railroad company and surrounded by whites, Fred Kohler (playing Deroux) seems to be in not-so-subtle blackface. I read this as implying that Deroux is of mixed race, and—in the view of the film—that he therefore belongs to neither culture. No matter how I might interpret this bit, it still makes me squirm.

Having leveled some criticisms against the use of stereotyping, I would be remiss if I did not point out some redeeming features of *The Iron Horse* in its attitudes toward race. First, we do still get touches of Ford the progressive—for example, when the Irishman shares his tobacco chaw with a Chinaman, or when, as the railroads meet, we are treated to some touching images of men from different nations and races embracing and joining together. There is also one humane moment regarding the Indians. In a battle, one Indian is shot and falls to the ground, dead. We see flies already settling on the body, and then the Indian's little dog comes over and lies down with his head cradled on top of his dead master. Moments like these are when the film transcends its less enlightened roots.

Tidbits and Trivia

- *The Iron Horse* was released just fifty-five years after the events it portrays, making it equivalent to a film of today set in the sixties!
- At around forty-six minutes into the movie, there is the earliest precursor I've seen to the "Not!" joke popularized by *Wayne's World* (1992) and the like. After Miriam persuades the railway workers not to abandon their jobs, one character (Casey, played by Ford favorite J. Farrell MacDonald) says, "'Twas me iligant Irish iloquence that did it—was it not?," to which Sergeant Slattery (Francis Powers) replies, "Yes, it was—[new title card]—not!"
- Aside from its (debunked) claims about using original transcontinental railroad locomotive engines, *The Iron Horse* supposedly also featured a derringer owned by Wild Bill Hickok and a stagecoach used by Horace Greeley.
- The movie posits the westward expansion as a means for healing the nation after

the Civil War. "From Omaha the following year come the Union Pacific crews—chiefly ex-soldiers of North and South, working peacefully side by side." If only it had been so easy. Here we are today, a century and a half after the driving of the Golden Spike, and we are still playing out the rift between North and South in our politics and in our own lives. Does a country ever recover from a civil war?

- The final scene of *The Iron Horse* is pure epic grandeur. ("With his own hands he has driven the last spike—the buckle in the girdle of America.") But this triumphant ending has been achieved only through very real sacrifice, which is what makes it resonate. There is a message here, I think, not only about the aesthetics of film but also about life itself, and the things that give our lives meaning.

The Vanishing American
(1925)

AKA: *The Vanishing Race*
October 15, 1925 (New York City)
USA—English
Paramount Pictures
110m—Silent—BW—1.33:1

Direction: George B. Seitz
Screenplay: Lucien Hubbard (adaptation), Ethel Doherty (screenplay), Zane Grey (novel)
Principal Cast: Richard Dix (Nophaie), Lois Wilson (Marion/Marian Warner), Noah Beery (Henry Booker), Malcolm MacGregor (Captain Earl Ramsdale/Ramsdell), George Magrill (Nophaie the Warrior, 16th Century), Guy Oliver (Kit Carson), Charles Crockett (Amos Halliday), Shannon Day (Gekin Yashi/Yasha), Charles Stevens (Shoie/Tolie), Bert Woodruff (Bart Wilson), Bernard Siegel (Do Etin)
Cinematography: Charles Edgar Schoenbaum, Harry Perry

It's no secret that Native Americans fared poorly in Western pictures for the first half century of the genre's history. In most cases, these movie "Indians" were faceless, disposable enemies, sometimes serving simply as plot devices or gun fodder for exciting battle sequences, at other times symbolizing the primal terrors lying hidden in our psychological lives—in either case, never fully human. There were exceptions to this, of course, sympathetic portraits rendered by films like Thomas H. Ince's *The Heart of an Indian* (1912), Cecil B. DeMille's *The Squaw Man* (1914), and Donald Crisp's *Ramona* (1916); but in general, indigenous people were viewed as subhuman obstacles to American progress—stiff, backward, inarticulate, essentially voiceless.

That all would change in the watershed year of 1950 with the release of two powerful pro–Indian films, *Broken Arrow* and *Devil's Doorway* (both discussed later in this book). These came at a time when America was ready to hear the message, and they resonated with the post–World War II audience. Others soon followed. From that point onward, movies which accepted uncritically the dogmas of Manifest Destiny and the stunted animalistic portrayals of Native Americans were rare indeed, and the ones that did appear were dismal failures. Humanity progresses; we can get better.

The most important waystation on the path toward a more enlightened treatment of indigenous people in American movies happened about midway between the birth of the Western and *Broken Arrow*: the groundbreaking silent epic *The Vanishing American* (1925), based on a novel from the same year by Zane Grey, which in turn was adapted from his earlier serial for *Ladies' Home Journal*. Grey's book was one of the earliest popular Western novels to offer a harsh take on the treatment of the Indians by the

71

United States government; it also viewed missionary attempts to foist Christianity on the natives with great contempt.

Whereas Grey's novel pulled no punches, the creators of its film adaptation took a safer, less courageous route. Instead of the U.S. government as the primary evil, the villain in the movie is a single corrupt white man, Indian Affairs agent Henry Booker (Noah Beery). Likewise, the great spiritual awakening of the hero Nophaie (Richard Dix) in the movie is his conversion to Christianity under the teaching of the saintly Marian Warner[1] (Lois Wilson). A title card reads: "Suddenly the simple faith of his fathers seemed a foolish thing. He thought of Marian … and of Bethlehem…." In contrast, the book has Nophaie, alone in the grandeur of Nature, undergoing an epic, syncretic, visionary experience in which he apprehends a mystical oneness underlying the disparate religions. Grey writes: "That strife of soul, so long a struggle between the Indian superstitions of his youth and the white teachings forced upon him, ended forever in his realization of the Universal God of Indian and white man."[2] In both versions of the story, Nophaie will die at the end, but in the movie this happens with a glimmer of hope for the future. "It grows dark … dark," Nophaie says. "But through … a veil…. I seem to see our people … coming … home…." At first, the closing pages of the novel seem to strike a similar tone to this. The Indians depart into a glorious, literal sunset, and Marian echoes Nophaie's dying words, "All is well," but then the final sentence, in Grey's own narrative voice, undercuts this perspective: "At last only one Indian was left on the darkening horizon—the solitary Shoie—bent in his saddle, a melancholy figure, unreal and strange against that dying sunset—moving on, diminishing, fading, vanishing—vanishing."[3]

In recent years, the film version of *The Vanishing American* has been criticized for blunting the sharper edges originally present in Grey's novel, although this decision probably helped it go down better with white audiences of the day, who generally loved it. The critics did too, praising its powerful story, its epic scope, the many exciting action sequences, and the stunning landscape photography—including some magnificent Monument Valley settings filmed fourteen years before John Ford discovered the location. Critics then and afterward also recognized the moral significance of the movie. Upon its opening in Charlotte, North Carolina, for example, one local critic wrote, "It will go down in the annals of Motion picture history as one of the masterpieces of all times." After a late-night showing, another reported: "The death-like silence of that after midnight audience was broken … in the final scenes, not by the moving of feet, nor by movements prompted by restlessness,

Richard Dix as Nophaie. *The Vanishing American* (Paramount, 1925).

nor because of lack of interest or attention—it was the weeping of men and women scattered throughout the house, weeping that could not be restrained."[4] A half century later, historian (and rescuer) of silent movies Kevin Brownlow wrote, "The problem of the Indian and his betrayal by the government was more clearly etched in this picture than in any other silent film."[5] *The Vanishing American* may not be the film that we, from our perspective nearly a hundred years later, might wish it to be, but it was the film that the times demanded—and a giant step forward.

Unlike the novel, the movie opens with a lengthy prologue spanning thousands of years, beginning with the first arrival of the "Basket-Makers" far before the dawn of recorded history. The Monument Valley scenery is perfectly suited to this primeval prelude, whose grand historical sweep prefigures the magnificent epic novels of James A. Michener in the era after the next world war. After the great valley is settled initially, wave after wave of new tribes and peoples arrive, each replacing the last, sometimes in breathtaking fashion. The sequence in which the tribesmen of an earlier "Nophaie" lay siege to the less aggressive, more indolent cliff dwellers is a stunning spectacle—watching it, one begins to appreciate why this was one of the most expensive and ambitious productions of its day. As the earlier tribe is vanquished, one of its elders curses his conquerors, saying, "May Paya the Father drive you into darkness, as you drive us! May he send a stronger race to grind you in the dust and scatter you through the Four Worlds of Lamentation!" Then, after the battle has ended, we fade in on the silent stone towers of Monument Valley, ever watching, unmoved and unchanged.

The old man's prophecy comes to fruition centuries later, when Coronado begins his conquest. Still another Nophaie steals a white horse from the Spaniards, only to be shot down from the edge of a cliff by a European rifle. A native shaman proclaims, "It is the end. These men are gods—they work with the lightning." The natives then come and bow down before the Spaniards, whose leader, in a profoundly symbolic visual, places his foot on the neck of one of the prostrate Indians.

After a subsequent episode featuring Kit Carson, we finally arrive at the primary story, beginning about a half hour into the film and taking place in the time just prior to America's entry into the First World War. Dix's Nophaie, the latest in a long line of men carrying that storied name, is a Navajo who will serve the United States gallantly in the war only to be treated abominably upon his return. This theme—an Indian experiencing injustice after fighting bravely in the U.S. military— had already been used

Metaphor made manifest. *The Vanishing American* (Paramount, 1925).

earlier the same year in the movie *The Scarlet West* (now lost) and would reappear a quarter century later in *Devil's Doorway*. It is a powerful image taken from the pages of actual history: people risking their lives in defense of freedom only to have their own freedoms curtailed upon their return.

Although the movie featured hundreds of genuine Native Americans on screen—plus at least one fake one, Charles Stevens, who claimed throughout his career, wrongly, to be the grandson of Geronimo—the lead role of Nophaie and indeed all of the significant Indian parts were acted by whites. Part of this, but not all, connects to the unavailability of experienced Native American actors at the time—which, though a very real challenge, was itself a result of systemic racism. Given the studios of the time, a major Hollywood movie with a Native American actor in the lead could never have gotten the green light. Progress in this regard was going to have to be incremental; for a movie to have important and needed cultural impact, it must first of all be able to be made. (I will address this issue further in the essay on *Broken Arrow*.) Despite this problem, it must be said that Richard Dix is magnetic and powerful as the tragic Nophaie—although, as with his later work in the talkie *Cimarron* (1931), his theatrical mannerisms can strike the modern viewer as rather exaggerated.

Dix is well supported by Lois Wilson as Marian Warner, a white schoolteacher[6] who works with Navajo children and also tutors Nophaie in the ways of Christianity, eventually presenting him with a pocket New Testament that will affect his destiny at least twice. She also articulates an idealistic but still measured and naive ethical position that is presumably that of the filmmakers as well. "Oh, I know—you have been unjustly treated," she says to Nophaie. "But Booker and his men did that—not the Government. This is still your country. You are an American as much as any of us." Regarding Nophaie's entry into the First World War, Marian says to him, "This is a war for freedom, for the right. For oppressed people everywhere. Out of it will grow a new order … a new justice…." And Nophaie responds with equal innocence. "Since we are Americans, we go fight. Maybe if we fight … maybe if we die … our country will deal fairly with our people."

Inevitably Nophaie falls in love with Marian, but—as would be typical even of pro–Indian movies until white audiences became more comfortable with the idea of ethnically mixed romances—the relationship never comes to fruition. Presumably Marian is in love with Nophaie in return; she certainly is in the novel, although this element is soft-pedaled in the film version. Even in the most dramatic demonstration of her love for Nophaie, when she sees him riding off to war and we begin to see the emotional impact this has on her, it is not clear to what degree this represents romantic longing as opposed to the more general love that she has for the Navajo people, as embodied in Nophaie, and her sadness at their fate. I have a feeling that if the sexes were reversed, the movie wouldn't be quite so restrained with regard to the incipient romance between the two leads—a suspicion borne out, perhaps, by comparing the love stories in *Broken Arrow* (white man, Apache woman) and *Devil's Doorway* (white woman, Shoshone man) twenty-five years later.

The main criticism that has been leveled at *The Vanishing American* has to do with its historical and philosophical framing. The prologue is not meant simply to provide a grand historical backdrop to the action; it has a point to make about human history, one which will be one of the central ideas of the film. The opening title card features a quote from Herbert Spencer's *First Principles*: "We have unmistakable proof that throughout all past time there has been a ceaseless devouring of the weak by the strong ... a survival of the fittest." Spencer, of course, was widely popular in the late nineteenth century as a promoter of Darwinism—but a very specific adaptation of Darwin's ideas, applied promiscuously not only to biological evolution but to the realms of sociology and politics. This Social Darwinism— and especially the racist,

Marian (Lois Wilson) sadly watches Nophaie leave for the war. But what does she mourn: a man she loves or the passing of an age? *The Vanishing American* (Paramount, 1925).

fascist, and eugenic ideologies that it later spawned or fueled—would end up taking Darwin's ideas much further than the gentle humanitarian biologist would ever have done or supported.

After this first title card, an ensuing series then describes the setting of the narrative to come:

> In a Western state, far from the present haunts of men, lies a stately valley of great monuments of stone.... A little while—as Nature reckons time—its rocks resounded to the march of feet and clash of battle, or echoed softly the contented babble of a people at peace. Then— stillness again—the hush of the ages. For men come and live their hour and go, but the mighty stage remains.

Later critics found this take on human history problematic, to say the least. Kevin Brownlow may have sung the film's praises in the late seventies, but just a few years later, Jay Hyams wrote: "When [*The Vanishing American*] was made, it was intended to portray the heroic and tragic story of the American Indian, but when viewed today its concern with superior races seems like an adumbration of fascism." Tom Milne echoed this sentiment not long afterwards, criticizing the movie for "steadfastly evading the issues" and calling the prologue "unintentionally fascistic in tone." More recently, Mary Lea Bandy and Kevin Stoehr wrote that the prologue "winds up espousing a principle of Darwinist determinism—and so 'the weak' must accept that they will simply perish in the end, a principle that undercuts the otherwise sympathetic subject matter."

I cannot see the movie, progressive in its day, as fascist in any sense of the word, but the historical/philosophical framing of *The Vanishing American* certainly did let white audiences off the hook to a considerable degree, assuaging whatever guilt they might have felt over the treatment of indigenous Americans by assuring them, fatalistically, that this was simply the way of nature. I find this criticism of the movie to be completely valid; but I also acknowledge that the filmmakers were trying to elicit sympathy for the Native Americans in a way that almost no other movies of the time attempted or were even interested in attempting—a task at which, judging by the contemporary reviews, they succeeded. The movie does not celebrate the falls of civilizations; to the contrary, it finds genuine tragedy in the waning of a noble culture and its heroic representatives. In short, *The Vanishing American* is nothing other than well-intentioned, albeit limited by the social theories and cultural beliefs of its own day. As Dr. King reminded us, progress happens in small steps over great spans of time—a more optimistic take on the "mighty stage" of human history than that of the movie.

Yet in all of this, I would not wish to miss the greater historical insight to which *The Vanishing American* speaks, one that has nothing to do with races being supposedly more or less suited to their environment than others—one instead that applies to *every* culture, whether ancient or modern; weak or strong; new or old; large or small; egalitarian or hierarchical; technologically advanced, developing, or decaying. And it is this more universal insight that gives *The Vanishing American* its deeper metaphorical relevance and emotional power. It isn't about "survival of the fittest"; in fact, it isn't about survival at all, but rather death—the death that awaits us all, as individuals and as societies.

For every civilization that now exists on the face of the earth, how many lie buried beneath the soil and sand, leaving only fragments of artifacts and traces of memory behind? The answer to this is a bitter, sobering, and yet starkly beautiful truth, one that holds even after discarding any pseudo-Darwinian nonsense about "superior" and "inferior" races. Whatever their merits and liabilities, civilizations rise and civilizations fall; this has been the fact of human history since the creation of the very first proto-cities ten thousand years ago. Even the Pharaohs have turned to sand; the Greeks and Romans that gifted the world with classical culture have been gone for centuries; the creators of the Eddas, and the Upanishads, and the *Tao Te Ching*, and the *Bhagavad Gita*, and the Seven Wonders of the World are no more. As countless poets, novelists, and lyricists have observed, all of the efforts of human beings crumble eventually into dust; only the earth and the sky endure.

Zane Grey expressed this idea as well, not only in *The Vanishing American* but continually throughout his later life. In 1929, Grey traveled once more to the Navajo Nation in Arizona and was horrified by how much the situation of the inhabitants had worsened since his last visit. In the guest book of the Kayenta Trading Post, he wrote: "In 1923 I felt the doom of the Navajo. 1929 showed me the truth of the vision I had felt—the ghastly truth of the vanishing American." But the lesson Grey drew from this had nothing to do with individual races and their relative "fitness" or adaptability, but rather with the plight of humanity as a whole. He went on: "The so-called civilization of man and his works shall perish from the earth, while the shifting sands, the red looming walls, the purple sage, and the towering monuments, the vast brooding range show no perceptible change."[7]

Many other twentieth-century authors, before and after Grey, built works around this same theme, from Powys to Michener to Lessing to Aldiss to Le Guin. One of my favorites is the tragically under-read American historical novelist Parke Godwin (1929–2013), who wrote many books set in the British Isles of long ago. Godwin used legendary or semi-legendary tales—of St. Patrick, King Arthur, and Robin Hood, for example—as means of focusing on periods in British history when one cultural group was being superseded by another: *The Last Rainbow* (1985) explores the waning of the fifth-century Picts in Great Britain as the Roman Britons gain the ascendancy; the great Arthurian novels *Firelord* (1980) and *Beloved Exile* (1984) see the Britons giving way to the Anglo-Saxons; and *A Memory of Lions* (1976), *Sherwood* (1991), and *Robin and the King* (1993) are set during the conquest of the Anglo-Saxons by the Normans. All of these are elegiac portraits of the ends of ages. The heroine of *The Last Rainbow* is Dorelei, who leads a small band of Celtic Picts being squeezed out by the encroaching Britons. The analogy between these tragic, noble figures and the Native Americans of the New World is evident throughout the novel, made even more explicit by Godwin in his "Author's Afterword." In this postscript, Godwin compares the image of Dorelei, sitting astride her pony on a hilltop, with that of her Native American counterpart. "Where is the essential difference?" he asks.

> Both had a concept of existence and man's place *in* nature before Christianity placed the human soul apart from it. Both were called devils by the people who pushed them out of the good lands....
>
>   Take them both without tears. Remember them watching from a very real hill, and that both had a truth quite different from our own, but one that worked for them for thousands of years before their time ran out. The same has happened to more than one people who considered themselves chosen of their gods, and perhaps it will again.[8]

Civilizations "come and live their hour and go"; only the mighty stage remains.

Tumbleweeds
(1925)

December 20, 1925 (New York City)
USA—English
William S. Hart Productions
78m—Silent—BW—1.33:1

Direction: King Baggot, William S. Hart (uncredited)
Screenplay: C. Gardner Sullivan, Hal G. Evarts (story)
Principal Cast: William S. Hart (Don Carver), Barbara Bedford (Molly Lassiter), Lucien Littlefield (Kentucky Rose), J. Gordon Russell (Noll Lassiter), Richard R. Neill (Bill Freel), Jack Murphy (Bart Lassiter), James Gordon (Joe Hinman), George F. Marion (Old Couple), Gertrude Claire (Old Couple), Lillian Leighton (Widow Riley)
Production: William S. Hart (uncredited)
Cinematography: Joseph H. August (uncredited)
Music: Artur Guttmann (1939 version)

The day of the William S. Hart Western was drawing to a close. By the mid–1920s, a new kind of Western had emerged, supplanting Hart's grittier, more realistic (in a relative sense) portrayals of the Old West with lighter, flashier, more action-oriented fare.

Tom Mix, Hart's junior by fifteen years, had found stardom even earlier than Hart, and since 1914 the two men embodied what might be thought of as parallel streams in the history of the silent Western. But in the mid-twenties, it was clear that Mix's brand of clean-cut cowboy, jumping into saddles and facing down black-hat-wearing bad guys in simplistic moral situations, had won out. This victory would last until Mix's last screen appearance a decade later, and its influence would persist well after that.

But Hart had one final card to play, and the result was his last and greatest Western, *Tumbleweeds* (1925).

Hart had always wanted to tell true(r)-to-life stories, and the setting of *Tumbleweeds* was taken straight from the pages of history: the Cherokee Strip Land Run of 1893. This was a different event than the 1889 Oklahoma Land Rush later to be depicted in *Cimarron* (1931), although Hart himself mixed up the dates in his 1939 filmed introduction to the film's rerelease. In any case, this epic historical adventure provided the possibility of creating a correspondingly epic Western, and certainly the success of *The Covered Wagon* (1923) and *The Iron Horse* (1924) had shown that there was a market for Western movies of grand scope and ambition. Hart was so passionate about the project that he largely financed it himself, putting at least $100,000 of his own money into the pot.

The result was more than just an epic; it was a bittersweet elegy as well. When we see Hart's little band of wild, ranging cowboys—the "tumbleweeds" of the title—as they watch the cattlemen clear off the land to make way for the settlers, and Hart's character takes off his hat and says, "Boys—it's the last of the West," we soon realize that this film is mourning not only the passing of the Old West but also the end of the Hart-style Western. The frontier has been tamed, the open range has been fenced in, and white-hatted, uncomplicated Tom Mix is in the ascendant. All of this gives the penultimate shot of the film—blowing tumbleweeds caught in barbed wire—an enduring poignancy.

Tumbleweeds grips its audience, and sets its tone, from the first title card: "Man and beast—both blissfully unaware that their reign is over." The "man" in question is represented by Hart's character Don Carver, whom we first meet in communion with the beasts of Nature. We see Carver silhouetted on his horse against the sky; then, as he rides along the trail, his horse shies at a coiled snake. Carver instinctively draws his gun, then reconsiders, saying to the serpent, "Go ahead an' live. You've got a whole lot more right here than them that's comin'." But that's not all: Carver then spots some young wolf pups trying to suckle from their dead mother and rescues them. Later, he hands the pups to his comrades and explains, "We poisoned their ma and pa an' I reckon it's up to us to give them a chanct."

All of this certainly establishes Carver as a man of Nature and gains him the sympathy of the audience, but it also provides an initial point of reference for a character who will prove to be more complex than he appears at first, and one who will grow and evolve over the course of the movie. Like all of us, Carver is multifaceted and often self-contradictory; life in his world (as in ours) is complex, ambiguous, enigmatic. Thus, we have the parallel scene later in the movie, when things aren't going so well for Carver: he has been framed as a "Sooner," and thinks that he has lost both his claim and his girl. Again he sees a snake in his path, but this time he shoots it dead, saying, "You didn't use no sense meetin' up with me today." And here we see that frightening, steely-eyed look so familiar to us since the very opening of *The Bargain* (1914), embodying the shadow that lives in each of us. "This thing of darkness I acknowledge mine," in Prospero's immortal words, and we feel its force through the power of Hart's portrayal.

Tumbleweeds shows us not only Carver's gentle and fearsome sides, but so much more as well. He is a good-natured, hearty companion to his comrades as he horses around with them in the saloon; a defender of virtue, as he rescues a young boy from a beating by his sadistic half-brother; a stiff, laconic veteran who seems out of place in more extroverted company; a friend of Indians, whom he addresses as equals and who are willing to fight for him if he asks; an awkward stumblebum in the presence of a beautiful young lady; a fallible patsy who leaves himself unnecessarily vulnerable to being framed as a "Sooner"; and a wise and world-weary sage who sees, presciently, the coming end of his way of life. He contains multitudes, as we all do—like Carver, we long for both the settled life *and* the wild frontier—and it is a tribute to the wonderful script by C. Gardner Sullivan and Hart's formidable acting skills that these often contradictory parts of Carver's nature come together as a coherent whole in a fully-realized movie character.

But Carver isn't alone; he is surrounded by some delightfully drawn supporting characters as well, particularly his love interest Molly and his sidekick Kentucky Rose (although the villains Noll and Freel, it must be said, are not similarly three-dimensional). It is instructive to consider, just a little more deeply, one method by which *Tumbleweeds* brings some of its characters to life so effectively.

Silent movies, of course, had to prioritize the visual, non-verbal aspects of both storytelling and characterization. Title cards, while often necessary, interrupted the flow of the visual narrative, and so needed to be used sparingly. The best silent filmmakers soon learned how to convey a great deal of information, not only about plot but also about character, simply through the visuals. For many viewers, including myself, this is one of the most delightful and rewarding aspects of silent cinema, in part because—paradoxically, perhaps—it is more realistic. In the real world, we learn a great deal about the people around us—their moods, personalities, and values—through observation of non-verbal cues rather than from hearing them explain their feelings to us aloud. But after the advent of sound in motion pictures, the art of visual storytelling began to recede while the spoken word became more significant. (It's no accident that some of the filmmakers we associate most strongly with masterful visuals—Hitchcock, for example, or John Ford—got their start in silent films.)

One of the pithiest masterclasses in visual characterization was offered by the great detective novelist Raymond Chandler, who gave a cogent example of how to reveal a great deal about the people in a scene through a minimum of action and no dialogue. This brief scenario has been related in many versions; here is William Goldman's, from his essential *Adventures in the Screen Trade* (1983):

> A man and his wife are riding silently upward in an elevator…. The woman carries her purse, the man has his hat on. The elevator stops at an intermediate floor. A pretty girl gets on. The man takes off his hat.

Goldman goes on to say, "This is not a scene about manners. It's about a marriage in trouble. The subtext tells us, with wonderful economy, a helluva lot about that married couple. If, for example, the couple's destination is a divorce lawyer, I wouldn't be a bit surprised."[1]

There are several visually rich but textually economical moments like this in *Tumbleweeds*. For example, when comic relief Kentucky Rose (played beautifully if a bit broadly by Lucien Littlefield) first meets his love interest Widow Riley (Lillian Leighton), we have a wonderful scene that reveals, for the first time, nearly everything we need to know about both of these charming characters. The scraggly Kentucky, who literally sheds clouds of dust at times like a silent-era precursor to Pig-Pen, clearly wants to impress the widow, and he ostentatiously pulls a watch from his pocket. In close shot, however, we see that the watch actually has no hands, and as we linger on that, laughing, we then see a fly crawling its way around the outer edge. Kentucky, in what he thinks is a surreptitious movement, now glances up at the sun to note its location in the sky; this is how he normally checks the time. Meanwhile, Widow Riley smiles ever so gently; we see that she knows exactly what Kentucky is doing but likes him too much to give him away.

All of this takes a grand total of fourteen seconds of screen time, with absolutely no dialogue, but we in the audience have just learned a great deal about these two characters, formed a real affection for both, and now hope to see them get together. Throughout *Tumbleweeds*, the romance between Kentucky and Widow Riley will provide a delightful counterpoint to the growing (and more complex) relationship between the two leads.

In fact, Carver's courtship of Molly (the classically beautiful Barbara Bedford) has its analogous "Chandler moment." As he nervously awaits her entrance into the parlor, he notices a stubborn cowlick on top of his head, and, try as he might, he can't make it lie down properly. Finally, in desperation, he pulls out his knife and cuts off the offending hank of hair. As Molly enters, he hastily places it on top of the piano keys. Molly, who has demonstrated a sort of prim propriety up to now, soon notices the hair as they converse, and, just as with Widow Riley, we feel a wave of affection for her as she discreetly moves to the keyboard and, behind her back, tucks the cowlick safely into her handkerchief, thus saving Carver embarrassment. A few seconds, a simple gesture, effective wordless characterization, and an utterly appealing moment!

A very nervous Don Carver (William S. Hart) courts a very understanding Molly Lassiter (Barbara Bedford). The cowlick is now safely tucked away. *Tumbleweeds* (William S. Hart, 1925).

Hart was sixty when making *Tumbleweeds*, whereas Barbara Bedford, playing his love, was in her early twenties, having been born in the year of *The Great Train Robbery*, 1903. As a young girl, Bedford had actually written fan letters to Hart, and he later helped her land a minor role as Nora in his 1920 movie *The Cradle of Courage*, when she was still a teenager. Bedford would go on to act in over two hundred movies between 1920 and 1945, although her career playing major roles declined after the advent of sound. She would outlive Hart by thirty-five years, dying in 1981.

Bedford is wonderful throughout the film; her indignant response to being accidentally lassoed by Hart in their initial meet-cute is a joy to behold, but she also delivers a powerful sense of her character's nobility, sadness, and capacity for righteous indignation throughout the course of Molly's travails. *Tumbleweeds*, in the end, gives us a hero and heroine who are truly worthy of one another.

For its part, *Tumbleweeds* is a nuanced and intelligent film, well aware of its mythic import and origins. It has its own share of Feirefizian epiphanies, just as *Hell's Hinges* (1916) did. Kentucky Rose, after meeting and being smitten by Widow Riley, says to Carver, "It can't be no disgrace to be a homesteader when a woman like her is one." Carver responds tersely, "We're goin' back to our cows." But then it's his turn: the man who earlier said that "the only land I'll settle down on will be under a tombstone" is now forced to reckon with the impact of Molly on his life. "Kentucky, I'm going to register for a piece of land," he proclaims, newly enlightened. "Ain't nothin' like ownin' land— no sir!"

The movie is very well crafted, although it doesn't rise to the poetic level of John Ford's silent artistry. The land rush sequence, however, is breathtaking, and—for its day—a triumph of film editing. It comes after a long, slow buildup, wherein the clock ticks toward that fateful cannon shot—"the signal for the maddest stampede in American history," whose filmed realization here certainly does not disappoint.

Hart, too, is at the top of his game; over the course of more than seventy movies, he has honed his craft to perfection, and at the age of sixty he is still a force of nature on the screen. He still knows how to sit a horse, rope a steer, face down a villain; and we have no trouble at all believing that young Molly would fall for him. But above all, Hart retains his priceless ability to convey volumes with just a look, a barely perceptible movement of the mouth or eyes, a tensing of the gun hand.

William S. Hart, now in his sixties, shows how well he can still ride a horse in the exciting land rush sequence. *Tumbleweeds* (William S. Hart, 1925).

All of this raises the question: just what exactly is subtlety in film? After all, those with only a passing acquaintance with silent movies often caricature them as being overacted, overemoted, overdone. Part of this is merely a result of style; since the roots of silent cinema are deeply embedded in the stage traditions from which it sprang, there is inevitably a theatricality of expression flavoring silent movies to which we are less accustomed today.

And yet I believe that, when experienced on their own terms, silent movies are amazingly subtle, despite the caricature. Not only do they demand more attention from the viewer than today's typical movies do, largely because of the importance of visuals to the narrative, but they also tend to present what I would consider to be a far more realistic portrayal of human emotions. True, the lingering influences of Romanticism and the nineteenth-century theatrical tradition are still felt in the frequently stylized gestures and facial expressions of the players, but the emotions that the characters feel in a movie like *Tumbleweeds* are themselves authentically human and believable.

Modern viewers may say they find movies like *Tumbleweeds* unsubtle or unrealistic, but is that really what they mean? We have noted the contrasts of style between these two eras; what art form doesn't move through stylistic changes over the course of a century? And yet, in this particular silent film, our hero doesn't kill anybody; there are no earnest professions of love or lengthy passages of exposition; Don's escape from the bull pen is prosaic and realistic, not a James Bond–like overpowering of a dozen hired goons; Hart rides his own horse (proficiently!); the dangerous land rush is filmed with actual people riding actual horses, wagons, and bicycles, rather than CGI creations; characters seem like actual human beings that we could know, rather than idealized Hollywood stereotypes or tights-clad superheroes; and we are enveloped in what feels like an authentic Western atmosphere, down to the cows suckling and the pigs rolling in the muck just next to the town streets.

What then does it mean when modern filmgoers—coming from a movie culture in which tough guys somersault through the air in slow motion shooting guns in all directions, rubber-clad superhero mutants save the world, and erstwhile enemies who initially hate each other end up falling in love—find movies like *Tumbleweeds* to be unrealistic?

The answer, I think, is that what today's viewers perceive as non-realism is instead just a difference in cinematic language. All genres and periods have their own vernacular. Today's audiences understand the conceits of the superhero movie or the romantic comedy or the video game adaptation. Similarly, silent-era audiences were built to respond to the visual symbolism, the Expressionistic lighting, and the theater-born acting styles of their own filmic era.

But in my view, theirs was a more convincing and authentically human style; I wish today's filmmakers had not forgotten so much about visual and narrative craft that the moviemakers of the first few decades already knew. Indeed, I get more from a single great silent-era film like *Tumbleweeds* than I have gotten from all of the comic-book movies I've ever seen put together.

The sage screenwriter William Goldman, in the aforementioned *Adventures in the Screen Trade*, offers yet another example of economical storytelling that is relevant to *Tumbleweeds*, this time concerning the ways in which films can end. When all of the plot elements are either wrapped up or their resolutions are inevitable, then in Goldman's view it's time to "run for curtain." His paradigm of choice is Hitchcock's *North by Northwest* (1959). Goldman describes a tense moment during the famous climax of the film, in which protagonist Roger Thornhill (Cary Grant) and his lover Eve Kendall (Eva Marie Saint) are hanging off the side of Mount Rushmore, dangling over a fatal drop. Roger supports Eve with one hand while clutching the side of the cliff with the other. Meanwhile, the villain Leonard (Martin Landau), holding a small statue with crucial microfilm stashed inside, walks over and begins grinding on Thornhill's free hand with his shoe.

Goldman then notes the number of things that will happen to resolve the plot between this moment and the end of the picture. In his words:

a. Landau is made to cease and desist.
b. Grant saves himself.
c. Grant also saves Eva Marie Saint.
d. The two of them get married.
e. The microfilm is saved for America.
f. James Mason, the chief villain, is captured and handed over to the authorities.
g. Grant and Saint take a train ride back east.

That's a lot of narrative to be successfully tied up. And I would like you to guess how long it takes in terms of screen time for it to be accomplished. Got your guess? Here's the answer— —forty-three *seconds*.[2]

Goldman goes on to explain the masterful way in which *North by Northwest* manages to condense this narrative and end in an eminently satisfying manner. I'll let you read (or better yet, watch) this for yourself, if you don't already know.

But thirty-four years before *North by Northwest*, *Tumbleweeds* does something remarkably similar. There is a moment after the climax of the narrative in which Carver is preparing to enter a hotel. At this point two major threads need to be tied up, but it's clear how things are going to resolve: it's just a matter of characters connecting and conversing. I must confess that, the first time I watched the movie, I felt a preemptive twinge of impatience as I anticipated the inevitable dialogue scenes that would move us to curtain. Brilliantly, however, the film anticipates this response, knows that we know what's coming, and jumps right to the end using only one word of text and a couple of glorious images, including the unforgettable tumbleweeds against the fence. In this case, the elapsed screen time from Carver's entrance into the Caldwell House until "The End" is a mere twenty-five seconds. And it's wonderful. I hope you will see it for yourself.

Apropos of endings: after the film's release and despite its success, the distributor, United Artists, fought with Hart constantly. According to Fenin and Everson, UA first tried to cut the film's length and, when unable to accomplish this, deliberately booked it into minor venues. Hart sued for breach of contract and won, but arguably lost hundreds of thousands of dollars in potential profits.[3]

Discouraged by this, and suffering from the effects of years of physically demanding work, William S. Hart, the greatest of all the silent Western movie stars, retired from films, returned to his ranch home, and wrote Western fiction. Although Hart would have what might be seen as spiritual successors in later eras—Randolph Scott of the 1950s, for example—in truth, his like would never be seen again.

However, *Tumbleweeds* would have a rebirth of sorts, re-released in 1939 by Astor Pictures with a new score and some added sound effects, but most significantly with a newly filmed introduction by Hart himself. This amazing eight-minute footage, featuring Hart at the age of seventy-four on his Newhall, California, ranch, not only provides a touching epitaph for Hart's own film legacy but also, fourteen years after the film's initial release, comes just in time to put a fitting final period on the First Age of the Western—just as *Stagecoach* (1939) was about to usher in the next great era.

William S. Hart delivers his final benediction at the end of an era. One of the most profoundly moving moments in the history of the Western. *Tumbleweeds* (William S. Hart, 1939 version).

Hart's speech—his last film appearance, and his only one with sound—simply must be experienced; no description could do it justice. It is sheer, elegiac poetry, delivered powerfully and movingly by this once Shakespearean actor. As expressive as Hart always was during the silent era of movies, it is staggering to catch this small, tantalizing hint of what his voice must have accomplished on the theatrical stage. The words hit home with a weight that cannot be captured simply in the written text.

These eight minutes of film history are spellbinding; over their span, Hart not only sets up the background to this particular movie itself, but also delivers an eloquent tribute to the mythic Western and the art of filmmaking. Toward the end, he removes his hat, and we receive Hart's own timeless benediction, rendered even more poignant by the fact that his beloved pinto horse Fritz had died the year before:

> My friends, I love the art of making motion pictures. It is as the breath of life to me. But through those hazardous feats of horsemanship that I loved so well to do for you, I received many major injuries that, coupled with the added years of life, preclude my again doing those things that I so gloried in doing.
>
> The rush of the wind that cuts your face, the pounding hoofs of the pursuing posse. Out there in front, a fallen tree trunk that spans a yawning chasm. The noble animal under you that takes it in the same low ground-eating gallop. The harmless shots of the baffled ones that remain behind. And then, the clouds of dust, through which come the faint voice of the director: "OK, Bill, OK! Glad you made it! Great stuff, Bill, great stuff! And, say, Bill! Give old Fritz a pat on the nose for me, will ya?" Oh, the thrill of it all. You do give old Fritz a pat on the nose, and when your arm encircles his neck, the cloud of dust is no longer a cloud of dust but a beautiful golden haze, through which appears a long phantom herd of trailing cattle. At their head, a pinto pony—*(overcome)* a p-, a pinto pony with an empty saddle. And then, a long, loved whinny, the whinny of a horse, so fine that nothing seems to live between it and silence, saying, "Say, boss, what you ridin' back there with the drag for, why don't you come on here and ride point with me? Can't ya see, boss, can't ya see the saddle is empty? The boys up ahead are calling. They're waiting for you and me to help drive this last great roundup into eternity."
>
> *Adios, amigos.* God bless you all, each and every one.
>
> *(He bows, turns, and walks away.)*

William Surrey Hart died seven years later, on this same Newhall ranch, "La Loma de los Vientos"—"The Hill of the Winds"—at the age of eighty-one.

3 Bad Men
(1926)

AKA: *Three Bad Men*
August 28, 1926 (USA)
USA—English
Fox Film Corporation
92m—Silent—BW—1.33:1

Direction: John Ford
Screenplay: John Stone, Herman Whitaker (novel *Over the Border*)
Principal Cast: George O'Brien (Dan O'Malley), Olive Borden (Lee Carleton), Lou Tellegen (Layne Hunter), Tom Santschi (Bull Stanley), J. Farrell MacDonald (Mike Costigan), Frank Campeau (Spade Allen), Priscilla Bonner (Millie), Otis Harlan (Zach Little), Phyllis Haver (Lily), Georgie Harris (Joe Minsk), Alec B. Francis (the Reverend Benson), Jay Hunt (Nat Lucas)
Production: John Ford
Cinematography: George Schneiderman

The most familiar telling of the Holy Grail legend is probably that of the anonymous Vulgate Cycle, made immortal through Thomas Malory's adaptation in *Le Morte d'Arthur* and featuring a familiar cast of characters—Launcelot, Galahad, and so forth. Nevertheless, the greatest of all medieval Grail stories is arguably Wolfram von Eschenbach's thirteenth-century masterpiece *Parzival*. Not only does it exhibit wonderful storytelling in its own right, but *Parzival* also anticipates (and helps set the stage for) many aspects of post-medieval and modern culture through its inclusivism, its amazingly contemporary views on love and marriage, its forward-looking understanding of church and secular society, and its remarkable coda, which contains within it the seeds of modern democracy.

Parzival is also unique among the great medieval Grail legends in elevating *compassion* as the primary virtue that merits the achievement of the Grail, rather than bravery, piety, chastity, or valor at arms. The hero Parzival himself is at first a naïve and foolish child of Nature, unaware of his true heritage, who must unlearn the instruction that society puts upon him (via his mother and an older knight who trains him) and learn instead to act out of his own inner, noble, compassionate character. This foregrounding of personal authenticity, from what we would call a psychological point of view, is surprising indeed in a work which predated Shakespeare by nearly four centuries!

It is not too much of a stretch to assume that Herman Whitaker (1867–1919), who wrote the 1917 novel *Over the Border* on which the great silent Western *3 Bad Men* (1926) was based, would have known *Parzival* and other knightly literature quite well.

Whitaker was born in England, was a fencing master, wrote hundreds of books and short stories, moved in literary circles (Jack London was a close friend), and had a daughter famously referred to as "the Blessed Damozel" by the Bohemian poet George Sterling (also a friend of Whitaker's). When Whitaker first introduces his three outlaws in the novel, he does so in truly *Parzival*-ian terms:

> Yet after granting their "badness," there was about them no taint of the mean, rat-like wickedness of the city criminal. Their composite was of strong impulses, misdirected forces gone to waste, of men cast by birth in a wrong age. In the councils of a nation in the olden time, their strength, ferocity, would have gained them power and place; here, out in the desert, they exactly fitted their environment. As much as the horned toad in the sand at Bull's feet, as much as the lizard that coursed swiftly along the adobe wall above the sleeper's head; as much as the *sahuaro* and the tormented yucca, they belonged to the land. Its gold glowed in their bronze. It were a safe bet that—horses and cattle not being in question—they would, at a given emergency, live in the letter of its best traditions.[1]

All the elements are there, right at the beginning: men born in the wrong place, just like Parzival, unaware of their own nobility; men of Nature whose inner virtue has been "misdirected" and who might, under the right circumstance, reveal their true character.

In Ford's filmed version, the right circumstance—provoking all the major players, good and bad, to show their true characters—is the lovely Lee Carleton (Olive Borden), truly a "Blessed Damozel" in her own right. Lee and her father, Major Carleton,

"Our business is gettin' overcrowded." Bull Stanley (Tom Santschi), Mike Costigan (J. Farrell MacDonald), and Spade Allen (Frank Campeau) face changing times. *3 Bad Men* (Fox, 1926).

are heading to Dakota by covered wagon to find land. The frontier is about to be opened up, largely because of the discovery of gold in the territory, although the film's attitude toward the gold rush is made perfectly clear in an early, nakedly Arthurian title card: "Some sought happiness—some only the horn of plenty—the chalice of gold—the Unholy Grail." This idea is reinforced effectively at several points during the narrative, most especially when the Reverend Benson (Alec B. Francis) sees a group of settlers starting to discard their plow to lighten the load before the land rush, and says to them, "Keep your plow! You'll find the real wealth of this land in the soil!"

In keeping with the Arthurian theme, Lee and her father meet a foolish young Western version of Parzival: Dan O'Malley, acted to perfection by George O'Brien. We first see the smiling O'Malley on horseback playing a harmonica, with his left leg askew, propped over the saddle horn and dangling on the wrong side. This recalls the original Parzival, who, according to Wolfram, initially looks ridiculous when dressed as a knight and mounted on a horse. But there is one major difference between the two characters: in Wolfram, Parzival is the person who, by responding at last to his true noble nature, achieves the Grail and heals the Waste Land, but in 3 Bad Men, it's the title trio instead who need to undergo that transformation. O'Malley, it turns out, is fine just the way he is. He may be simple, but he is noble and heroic throughout.

Not that his naivety goes unremarked by Lee. In fact, she derides him at first, in keeping with Arthurian tales like those of Gawan and Orgeluse (from Parzival), Brewnor and Maledysaunte (from Le Morte d'Arthur), or Gareth the kitchen boy and Lynet (also from Malory), each of which features a noble knight whose eventual lady love first scorns and mocks him. Lee's mockery—which doesn't last long—is precipitated when she and her father lose a wheel from their wagon. O'Malley sees them from afar. He rides over, points, and brilliantly observes, "The wheel came off." Lee rolls her eyes and replies in exasperation, "Oh, did it?" "Something ought to be done about it," he says. "You must have traveled a lot to know all those things," she responds sarcastically. And on it goes. The scene is delightful, and despite Lee's wry irritation, we soon see her charming side, in a memorable moment where she ends up with axle grease on her nose. O'Malley helps the pair and departs, after a failed attempt to steal a kiss from the beautiful and, by that point, not unwilling Lee. He will return later, but now the focus shifts to the title characters, whose future with Lee will become the heart of the story.

The three titular bad men are: Bull Stanley (played by Tom Santschi), the leader of this little gang; Mike Costigan (J. Farrell MacDonald), a sharp-shooting, hard-drinking thief; and Spade Allen (Frank Campeau), an equally hard-drinking card cheat. We learn early on, from wanted posters, that the men are stage robbers, bank robbers, and horse thieves. Their pivotal moment comes when they happen upon a lonely, vulnerable wagon with a handful of horses and decide to ply their trade. Before they can act, however, a larger band of horse thieves appears on the horizon and attacks the wagon first. Mike shakes his head sadly. "Nothin' to it—our business is gettin' overcrowded."

The three then descend upon the other gang and drive them off, with Mike killing two of the bandits. (He laments, however, that it took him three shots to do it.) Now our bad men are ready to seize the horses for themselves. One of the settlers lies dead, and the other one kneels over his body. Bull, the leader, raises his gun and points it at the head of the mourner, who—oblivious to this—removes a hat to reveal her long, flowing hair. It's Lee, weeping over the body of her father. "By golly—he's a woman!" Spade exclaims.

And this is the moment of truth. Lee, sobbing, rushes into Bull's arms for comfort. Behind her head he still holds his pistol, and we see the debate play itself out in Bull's eyes. The other two wait and watch; it's clear that they will follow Bull's lead. Will he be true to the rules of his chosen profession and shoot her down? Or will he listen to that noble voice within and reveal his true character?

It is a magnificent moment, one of many such in this remarkable film, when— behind Lee's head and never noticed by her—Bull tosses his gun backwards, to be caught by Mike. "Put them hosses back!" he cries. From this point on, the three will be Lee's devoted protectors, working for her, without pay at first, each one loving her in his own way. But this love, for all three, is not primarily romantic or sexual (O'Malley will fulfill that role for Lee); it is instead a mix of paternal love and courtly love, fully realized in compassionate self-sacrifice.

What a wondrous thing is Fate! Parzival's horse, unguided, leads him straight to the Grail Castle; and here, our three bad men are transfigured and redeemed through compassion—but only because, at the scene of a robbery, they happened to have gotten there second.

But Lee is given a challenging opportunity to show her true character as well. Arriving in the gold rush town overseen by the oily, corrupt, white-hatted Sheriff Hunter (Lou Tellegen), our unlikely quartet—Lee and her three protectors—make a splash right away. Hunter recognizes the outlaws and, lusting after Lee, reveals their true identities

The moment of truth. Bull (Tom Santschi) ponders what to do with Lee Carleton (Olive Borden) while Mike (J. Farrell MacDonald) and Spade (Frank Campeau) look on. *3 Bad Men* (Fox, 1926).

as thieves to her. Smirking, he "congratulates" Lee on her choice of friends. Lee is at first visibly shaken when she learns the truth about Bull, Mike, and Spade—but then Bull gently passes her a ladleful of water, and we love her all the more as she smiles, accepts it, and says, in front of all the townsfolk and without shame, "Come along, my 3 Bad Men—it's time we were making camp."

All the Arthurian mythology in the world would not, by itself, make *3 Bad Men* the great film that it is. Aside from its mythic resonance, the movie is also visually beautiful; as with so many Ford films, one could pause it at almost any point and see an artistically composed frame. Its characters are wonderfully drawn and superbly acted—Santschi and O'Brien shine as the two halves of the Parzival archetype, and Borden is perfect as both a vehicle of redemption and a fully human object of love. There are so many funny, touching, and human moments brought to life by these excellent actors, from O'Brien's appropriately natural and unaffected approach in the scenes with Borden to Santschi's perfect portrayal of aesthetic arrest, as when Bull sees Lee holding a baby. To top it all off, the dialogue is delightful, as the following examples show:

MAJOR: I'm Major Carleton of Virginia, Suh—this is my daughter Lee.
O'MALLEY: My name and address is Dan O'Malley.
LITTLE: They had a lot of trouble takin' out Spud Taylor's appendix—they had to kill him first.
TOWNSMAN: Parson—this ain't exactly a Sunday School camp—but they's some of us that'll be d—n glad you come along.
BULL (*to Mike and Spade, reproachfully*): Drunk again!
MIKE: So are we!
BULL: I'm thinkin' three ole terrapins like us ain't fit to take care of a gal like her—What our gal needs is a husband!
MIKE: Leave it to us! We'll find a marryin' man—if we have to shoot him.
YOUNG MAN: I've just reached manhood.
MIKE: Then you'd better reach again!
SPADE: If a man's heart is in the right place, it don't matter what sex he belongs to.
MIKE (*as Lee bathes*): You don't reckon she'll be wantin' us to take a bath, do you?
SPADE: I'm a little nervous about it.
SPADE: Mike, your pants may be shabby, but they cover a warm heart.

As fond as we become of O'Malley over the course of *3 Bad Men*, the heart of the film rests first with Lee—our Grail Maiden of sorts, who evokes the best (and worst, in Hunter's case) of the people around her—and, second, with her three protectors, especially Bull. This in itself is a surprise for a Hollywood Western; after all, O'Brien is listed first in the credits, and he is the clean-cut, upright hero who will eventually win the girl. And yet, his scenes occupy only about a quarter of the film's ninety-two minutes; the real focus remains on Lee and her Bad Men.

Olive Borden is radiant and captivating throughout; she makes all four of the men love her, and by the end we, the audience, love her too. Meanwhile, the true Parzival of the picture is Tom Santschi's Bull; it is his transformation that drives both the plot and the emotional arc of the narrative. Santschi shows extraordinary range, conveying everything from tender (paternal?) love to towering rage to awestruck aesthetic arrest to bittersweet resignation to noble self-sacrifice. Bull is also a fearsome force of nature, as evidenced in the moments after his sister's death, when he goes on the most jaw-dropping violent rampage I have ever witnessed in silent cinema, punching his way through walls (and people); everything in his path is obliterated.

3 Bad Men features many of the qualities that John Ford would carry forward into the sound era, and which would make his movies so compelling: wonderful storylines, artistically filmed, with very human, three-dimensional characters and outstanding dialogue. Here we also see many of Ford's visual signatures, especially his penchant for creating "frames" (doorways, windows, arches in the desert) at significant emotional moments, elevating and highlighting the action like an art gallery's frame around a classic painting. And of course, Ford continues to exploit the possibilities of epic landscapes. Monument Valley still lies ahead, but *3 Bad Men* takes full advantage of the locations at which it was shot (primarily the regions around Victorville, California, and Jackson Hole, Wyoming).

The result is certainly a beautiful film to behold, but above all, *3 Bad Men* is profoundly moving, a masterpiece of compassion and redemption. It combines its mythic power with the grandeur of its settings and the humanity of its lovable characters to deliver a tremendous emotional and artistic impact. No other silent Western has moved me so strongly to both laughter and tears or struck me so hard with its beauty. Its images are unforgettable, due to the visuals as well as the mythic narrative, and the final shot— one which deserves to be remembered alongside the closing images of *Ikiru* (1952), *Vertigo* (1958), and *The 400 Blows* (1959)—will stay with me always.

Overshadowed by *Tumbleweeds* (1925) and, sadly, today almost forgotten, *3 Bad Men* stands as one of the monuments of the silent era, its last great Western. The genre may have reached a temporary peak, but an uncertain future lay just over the horizon.

The cast of *3 Bad Men* would meet many different fates. Some, like J. Farrell MacDonald and Frank Campeau, would make the transition to talkies and would have many years of moviemaking ahead of them. Others, like Priscilla Bonner and Phyllis Haver, would leave Hollywood not long after the advent of sound (although Bonner lived later than any of the principal cast, dying in 1996 at the age of ninety-seven).

George O'Brien would soon star in F.W. Murnau's Expressionist masterpiece *Sunrise: A Song of Two Humans* (1927), which would win three prizes at the very first Academy Awards. O'Brien would go on to serve in World War II and act in dozens more movies, including around forty Westerns and six more John Ford films. He died in 1985 at the age of eighty-six, more fortunate by far than many of his *3 Bad Men* costars.

Tom Santschi, who acted in around 250 movies over the course of his career, died of a heart attack five years after *3 Bad Men* was released, at the age of fifty. Bull Stanley may have been his finest achievement.

Lou Tellegen also died tragically just three years after Santschi, at the age of fifty-two. He had led a dramatic life: once Sarah Bernhardt's lover (who was nearly four decades his senior), he married four women, all of whom worked in the arts, and had numerous affairs. In 1929 his face was badly burned in a fire (he had fallen asleep smoking), effectively ending his film career. In 1934, while a guest at a Hollywood mansion, he locked himself in the bathroom, stood in front of the mirror surrounded by newspaper clippings from his career, and stabbed himself to death with sewing scissors. When she learned of his death, Tellegen's second wife, opera singer Geraldine Farrar, reportedly said, "Why should that interest me?"

Olive Borden, so wonderful in *3 Bad Men* and other silent pictures, had a difficult time with the transition to sound. She would make her last film appearance in 1934, and by the late 1930s she was alcoholic and broke. Borden enlisted in the WACS, won a citation for bravery during World War II, and was honorably discharged after a foot injury. But this amazing woman, once one of Holly-wood's leading stars, ended

The first true Western masterpiece? *3 Bad Men* (Fox, 1926).

her life destitute, scrubbing floors in L.A.'s skid row and dying of pneumonia at the age of forty-one. The only item she had in her possession at the time of her death was a signed photo of herself.

Tumbleweeds and *3 Bad Men*, together, represent the culmination of the silent Western, its two finest achievements—one film an ending of its era, the other a harbinger of greatness still to come. That greatness would not arrive immediately, however.

Westerns certainly remained popular throughout the early sound period, providing a source of escapism for millions during the time of the Great Depression, but their glory days already seemed to be behind them. John Ford would make around thirty films in the dozen years after *3 Bad Men*, but not a single Western; instead, he earned a reputation as one of the world's best film directors with such work as *Arrowsmith* (1931), *The Lost Patrol* (1934), and *The Informer* (1935). Tom Mix made several talkies, did some radio and circus work, and when he retired from Westerns in the mid–1930s both Roy Rogers and Gene Autry were ready to fill the clean-cut cowboy gap, but few of these efforts had particularly high artistic aspirations. Marion Morrison, working as a prop boy, was discovered by Raoul Walsh, renamed John Wayne, and cast in his first starring role (*The Big Trail*) in 1930, but his bid for A-list stardom failed, and Wayne moved into making dozens of low-budget and mostly unremarkable Westerns throughout the 1930s.

The Western as a genre was alive and well commercially, but its potential for greatness now lay dormant, waiting for John Ford finally to return to the Western picture after thirteen years; waiting for John Wayne to reclaim his stardom after nine.

Waiting, waiting for *Stagecoach*—and the arrival, at long last, of the Golden Age.

PART TWO

The Talkies

In Old Arizona
(1928)

December 25, 1928 (Los Angeles)
USA—English / Spanish / Italian
Fox Film Corporation
95m—Mono—BW—1.20:1

Direction: Raoul Walsh, Irving Cummings
Screenplay: Tom Barry, Paul Gerard Smith (uncredited), O. Henry (story "The Caballero's Way")
Principal Cast: Warner Baxter (The Cisco Kid), Edmund Lowe (Sergeant Mickey Dunn), Dorothy Burgess (Tonia Maria)
Cinematography: Arthur Edeson
Editing: Louis R. Loeffler
Awards: Oscar—Best Actor in a Leading Role (Baxter)
Nominations: Oscar—Best Picture, Oscar—Best Director (Cummings), Oscar—Best Writing Achievement (Barry), Oscar—Best Cinematography (Edeson)

The outlaw known as the Cisco Kid, portrayed in over two dozen Western movies from 1914 to 1950, made his first appearance in the opening sentences of "The Caballero's Way," a 1907 short story by O. Henry:

> The Cisco Kid had killed six men in more or less fair scrimmages, had murdered twice as many (mostly Mexicans), and had winged a larger number whom he modestly forbore to count. Therefore a woman loved him.

O. Henry envisioned his character as far less noble than Hollywood would eventually make him; in the short story, the Kid is a hot-tempered sociopath who kills "for the love of it," or even just on a whim. "He moodily shot up a saloon in a small cow village on Quintana Creek, killed the town marshal (plugging him neatly in the centre of his tin badge), and then rode away, morose and unsatisfied. No true artist is uplifted by shooting an aged man carrying an old-style .38 bulldog."[1]

How interesting it is, then, that the Cisco Kid is the main character and hero of Hollywood's first major Western talkie, *In Old Arizona* (1928). Although this version of the character, portrayed by Warner Baxter, is far more sanitized and noble than O. Henry's original conception, he is still an unrepentant outlaw thief who is allowed to get away scot-free by the end of the film, something that would never have been allowed had the movie been made a couple years later, when the Motion Picture Production Code (the infamous "Hays Code") was widely adopted.

The first half of the history of the American Western movie is largely the story of the building up of a national mythic orthodoxy—and yet the first hero of a major

94

Western talkie is in fact an antihero, just as the most memorable character in the first true silent Western was the outlaw who emptied his gun directly into the faces of his audience. From the very beginning, the Western mythos has contained the seeds of its own deconstruction.

It is a source of sheer delight to me that Baxter's Cisco Kid serves not only as a precursor to subversive outlaw antiheroes to come (The Man with No Name, Butch and Sundance, the Wild Bunch) but also as a template for the "singing cowboys" of the thirties and forties (Ken Maynard, Gene Autry, Roy Rogers, Tex Ritter). What a varied progeny! O. Henry's literary Kid is a singer too, but an awful one who only knows one tune. "He had a voice like a coyote with bronchitis, but whenever he chose to sing his song he sang it." However, the makers of *In Old Arizona*—billed as "The First All-Talking Picture Filmed Outdoors"—were not about to squander their opportunity to take advantage of the new technology. Eager audiences were treated not only to the thrilling sounds of hoofbeats, gunshots, and ham and eggs sizzling in a pan, but also to the melodious strains of "My Tonia" as sung by Baxter. Thus, in one stroke, two critical things happened: studios became convinced of the commercial potential of the outdoor sound Western, and the singing Western star was born.

Early in the film, we meet both of our male protagonists: the mustachioed, black-hat-wearing, seemingly Mexican outlaw (actually Portuguese, as it turns out) and the clean-cut white sergeant. Silent-era stereotypes have perhaps conditioned us to expect certain things of these characters, especially of the Cisco Kid. We watch as he robs a stagecoach in his first dialogue scene. After he gets the lockbox, he directs all of the passengers back onto the coach—except, he says, for the "pretty lady," who stands frozen, awaiting the inevitable. But then something out of the ordinary occurs, letting us know that the Kid will transcend the noxious stereotypes we've encountered in *Hell's Hinges* (1916) and other early Westerns. The Kid admires the "pretty pin" on the poor, frightened girl's chest and then takes it, saying, "It will look very beautiful on my girl." To the delighted young woman's surprise (and ours), our protagonist then proceeds to give her gold coins in recompense before escorting her

The moment the Cisco Kid (Warner Baxter) wins us over, as he robs a frightened young passenger (Helen Lynch, uncredited)—but chivalrously. *In Old Arizona* (Fox, 1928).

back onto the coach. "I never rob the individual," the Kid says, and we realize that he is in fact both chivalrous and (in his own way) ethical—a Robin Hood of the Old West rather than O. Henry's disillusioned murderer.

As we later learn, he is also a *bon vivant*—"Ah, music, wine, and love; I don't know which one I could give up if I have to"—and a philosopher anticipating French existential nihilism by a couple of decades. "What is my life, after all?" the Kid asks in a transitory moment of melancholy. "The warm breath of a few summers, and the cold chill of a few winters, and then…. By golly, I think I need a drink."

Both versions of the Kid—the original and this Hollywood incarnation—share one common trait in their moral codes: a refusal to bring harm to a woman. As O. Henry writes, the Cisco Kid "could not have spoken a harsh word to a woman. He might ruthlessly slay their husbands and brothers, but he could not have laid the weight of a finger in anger upon a woman." And here lies the critical conflict of the story, embodied (in both cases) in the form of the faithless *femme fatale* Tonia, played here to perfection by an incandescent Dorothy Burgess in her feature film debut. Tonia will challenge the Cisco Kid's chivalric morals, with tragic results, both for him and for her.

The third corner of our eternal triangle here is, to a contemporary sensibility, the most problematic: Edmund Lowe's square-jawed Sergeant Dunn. It's difficult to know how to take this character. Although he is clearly portrayed as the Kid's inferior, my guess is that he is still meant to be comically endearing, in a bumbling sort of way. However, Dunn strikes the modern viewer (or at least this one) as smirking and obnoxious. The Brooklyn wise-guy routine ("Where ya from, goilie?") wears thin pretty fast, and that coupled with the awkward timing of the line deliveries (so common in early talkies still finding their way) makes this character fall flat. The movie certainly provides opportunities for other characters (especially Tonia) to notice his foolishness, but it all comes across as leering and creepy, rather than amusing, to modern eyes. As a result, what could have been a wonderful device for heightening the dramatic tension—our potential affection for both of these noble antagonists as their inevitable conflict looms—ends up as a missed opportunity, because Dunn is so relentlessly grating.

On the other hand, the final twenty-minute segment of the film is gripping and almost agonizingly suspenseful as it builds to its tragic climax. Here is where Baxter is superb. The Kid's anguish as he learns of Tonia's betrayal is palpable, his enigmatic reference to a "long, long journey" is chilling, and as the storyline slowly but inexorably reveals its final surprises, the effect is truly gut-wrenching. This is no lighthearted kiddie fare despite its embroidery-clad singing hero; it is a movie aimed squarely at adults in both its tone and its content.

In fact, the suggestiveness of *In Old Arizona*, pre–Hays, is both surprising and delightful. Double entendre and innuendo are frequent, and the movie is unabashedly sexual. After a long seductive scene between the Kid and Tonia, he plays music from the phonograph (a wax cylinder—the movie is set during the McKinley era) and then calls to her from offscreen. "What you want?" she asks knowingly, leaning against the doorframe and pulling sensually on a cigarette, then grinning because she has always known the answer. She moves to him; the ham and eggs smoke and burn on the stove; the phonograph plays on, the visual symbolism of its horn unmistakable; and we fade to black.

Although it is certainly no masterpiece, *In Old Arizona* is still a worthwhile and affecting film, and Baxter a worthy recipient of the Best Actor Oscar he won for this role. (Dorothy Burgess, however, turns in the most memorable performance!) The virtues the movie upholds are authenticity and honor—in *Parzival* terms, being true to one's inner noble self—and the vices that it deplores are avarice and duplicity. Tonia, the quintessential "material girl," sells her honor for trinkets and baubles, whereas the Cisco Kid is an honorable thief who knows the difference. "The most precious things in the world cannot be bought with gold," he says, holding an infant. "The tender touch of a little baby's fingers, the light in the woman's eyes, and the love in a woman's heart." In that sense, *In Old Arizona* is still true to the morality of its day, even

The person turning in the most stunning performance of the movie—serenaded by the one who won the Oscar. Dorothy Burgess and Warner Baxter, as Tonia Maria and the Cisco Kid. *In Old Arizona* (Fox, 1928).

in its own rather subversive way. Indeed, the fact that our protagonist is an unapologetic thief only gives the movie more moral resonance; future Hollywood Westerns would forget, all too often, that ethical lessons have more impact when imparted via flawed characters. It's difficult to learn anything from Galahad's unapproachable perfection, but Launcelot, whose imperfect humanity we understand (and share), has much to teach.

Tidbits and Trivia

- This was the first talkie filmed largely outdoors, with microphones hidden in trees and behind rocks when necessary. As with most early talkies, there are numerous moments in which the filmmakers linger on what to us seem like relatively banal events, just to give the audience a chance to enjoy the wonder of synchronized sound. One surprising thing, though, to the modern viewer (and listener) is the way in which sound is always experienced as it would be from the immediate environs of the camera. Today we are so used to the fact that visual perspective and sonic perspective need not match that it is almost startling when they do. For example, in a modern Western, we might see a stagecoach off in the middle distance while hearing its galloping sounds with close-up clarity—perhaps even hearing dialogue from within the coach. Here, in contrast, when a stagecoach gallops by our view, we only hear it as we would from that fixed point in space; its sound recedes quickly, even when we still see it clearly. Likewise, when the Kid rides away from the camera singing, we only catch the first phrase, and then both the hoofbeats and the melody fade into silence, despite the fact that he stays in view. Here we are not given that privileged, omniscient aural perspective that would soon become so commonplace in the language of cinema.

- Raoul Walsh, one of the directors of *In Old Arizona*, was originally intended to be its star as well; he had already acted in several dozen films during the silent era. However, prior to shooting, Walsh was involved in a bizarre automobile incident when a rabbit jumped through his windshield and the broken glass damaged his right eye. He would eventually lose the eye, giving him his characteristic eyepatch but ending his acting career. Walsh would continue to direct movies for another thirty-six years, including classic Westerns such as *The Big Trail* (1930), *They Died with Their Boots On* (1941), and *Along the Great Divide* (1951).
- Sharp-eyed viewers can catch all of John Ford's titular *3 Bad Men* (uncredited) in this movie! Tom Santschi is a cowpuncher, Frank Campeau is one of the Kid's pursuers, and—most noticeably—J. Farrell MacDonald appears early on as a wisecracking Irish stagecoach passenger.
- It's hard to miss the homosexual undertones in the first meeting of the Cisco Kid and Sergeant Dunn. They each grope each other's guns at crotch level and comment admiringly. This scene may have inspired the famous (and similarly phallic) exchange between Montgomery Clift and John Ireland in *Red River* (1948).
- True to the Western tradition, the scenery is beautiful. Outdoor sequences were shot in Bryce Canyon, Zion National Park, the Grand Canyon, the Mojave Desert, Joshua Tree, and the Mission San Juan Capistrano, among other locations.

The Virginian
(1929)

November 9, 1929 (USA)
USA—English
Paramount Pictures
91m—Mono—BW—1.20:1

Direction: Victor Fleming
Screenplay: Grover Jones (adaptation), Keene Thompson (adaptation), Howard Estabrook (screenplay), Edward E. Paramore Jr. (dialogue), Owen Wister (novel, play), Kirk La Shelle (play)
Principal Cast: Gary Cooper (The Virginian), Walter Huston (Trampas), Richard Arlen (Steve), Mary Brian (Molly Stark Wood), Helen Ware (Mrs. Taylor), Chester Conklin (Uncle Hughey), Eugene Pallette (Honey Wiggin), Victor Potel (Nebrasky), E.H. Calvert (Judge Henry)
Production: B.P. Schulberg (uncredited), Louis D. Lighton (uncredited)
Cinematography: J. Roy Hunt, Edward Cronjager (uncredited)
Editing: William Shea (uncredited)
Music: Karl Hajos (uncredited)

Very few books have had as much of an impact on the evolution of the American Western genre as Owen Wister's 1902 bestseller *The Virginian*. The work was one of the earliest true Western novels outside of the dime-store tradition, and it is credited with establishing many of the standard elements in Western fiction: chivalric cowboy heroes; frontier justice; climactic showdowns; ranchers vs. settlers; stern codes of manly virtue and honor; a nostalgic, elegiac perspective on the Old West; and a focus on conflicts between the values of the Western frontier and the "civilized" East. True to its era, it also takes positions more distasteful to the modern reader. The novel's sympathies, for example, clearly lie with the elite owners of large ranches rather than the individual settlers. More problematically still, it espouses a sort of social Darwinism with corollary views on race and gender. As Stanley Corkin writes:

> Wister dramatizes the means by which individuals become socially and economically dominant, revealing that such status is the result of biological fitness. The notion of aptitude is infused with notions of American exceptionalism, Anglo-Saxon racial superiority, and the inevitable subordination of women to men. The frontier, as a locale away from the social artifices caused by overcivilization, allows for those who are naturally superior to reign.[1]

For better and worse, almost every canonical Hollywood Western contains influences from the novel, while subversive, revisionist Westerns often directly deconstruct the tropes it established. If, as Alfred North Whitehead observed, the European philosophical tradition is at heart mainly a response to Plato, then similarly, most of the history of the American Western is in some sense responding to *The Virginian*. Western stories and films may work with or against its mythography, but almost all of them feel its effects.

The book was turned into a play in 1904, and there were silent film adaptations in 1914 and 1923. The most significant filmed version, however, was the first sound treatment in 1929, directed by Victor Fleming and starring Gary Cooper in his first important Western role. This movie took all of the elements that had made the novel iconic and brought them home to audiences with the power of sound and spectacle. The Hollywood Western had already been shaped by Wister's work even before the direct movie adaptations, but the 1929 film sealed the deal. The blueprint for the classic Hollywood Western had been drafted; the majority of the pictures to follow, for quite some time, were variations on a theme.

Wister's novel is rich in detail, and its hero undergoes many adventures; for this ninety-minute adaptation, however, the plot had to be boiled down to essentials. The movie focuses on four primary characters from the book: the Virginian (Gary Cooper), unnamed in both book and movie, a mischievous and untutored but ethical cowboy; his best friend Steve (Richard Arlen), an amiable arrested adolescent and trickster archetype who becomes involved in a cattle rustling scheme; Molly Stark Wood (Mary Brian), the cultured Eastern schoolteacher they both desire; and Trampas (Walter Huston), the leader of the rustling gang and the Virginian's nemesis.

The movie is very deliberately paced, as were many of the early sound pictures as filmmakers adapted to the new technology; but whatever the reason for the pacing of the film, it works well. *The Virginian* is a slow burn and an intense one. The film stays with scenes longer than we expect, not to advance the plot but to provide a sense of realism and local color. The sound recording is natural, featuring the noises of the frontier—cattle lowing, people mumbling and muttering, realistic speech complete with interruptions and false starts, and many atmospheric ambient sounds. Minor characters provide an authentic background (Eugene Pallette's Honey Wiggin is particularly delightful), and in moments of high drama, the people of the story don't rush the action—they proceed warily, lingering and hesitating in a very human way, giving the viewers a chance to fully experience the emotional pregnancy of the situation.

Two scenes in particular are gut-wrenching in a way we don't expect: the terrible lynching, which is played with great nuance, emotional authenticity, and pain; and the final showdown between the Virginian and Trampas. As

The two best friends, *puer aeternus* Steve (Richard Arlen) and the laconic Virginian (Gary Cooper), in happier times. The latter will end up lynching the former in the film's most heartbreaking scene. *The Virginian* (Paramount, 1929).

familiar as we are with climactic gunfights, this one still can tie one's stomach in knots. It brings us directly inside the feelings of the main character as he steels himself for the awful conflict to come. What must it feel like to wait all alone for the hour when you know you must either leave town or walk out into the streets to kill or be killed? Just as in the novel, this showdown is neither cathartic nor romanticized; instead, the emotional weight is carried by the long, slow buildup to the gunfight rather than the actual moment itself, which is actually over in a flash—blink and you'll miss it. This is very true to the same moment in the book: the Virginian is pondering things as the duel approaches, watching the sunset, waiting for what must come. The approach to the showdown has gone on for several pages at this point, and our hero has not even spotted his opponent yet. Suddenly the text reads:

> A wind seemed to blow his sleeve off his arm, and he replied to it, and saw Trampas pitch forward. He saw Trampas raise his arm from the ground and fall again, and lie there this time, still. A little smoke was rising from the pistol on the ground, and he looked at his own, and saw the smoke flowing upward out of it. "I expect that's all," he said aloud.[2]

That is the extent of the gunfight; it has happened automatically, unconsciously, with the Virginian not even aware of it until it is over.

The film version of *The Virginian* also set the pattern for the relationship between the male and female leads in many conventional Westerns to come. It is worth examining the dialogue from the primary courtship scene in some detail, because the text itself says more than any analysis of mine could. Here, the hero and heroine are enjoying a moment of rest out in the woods after riding out together; and everything we need to know about the film's attitudes regarding relations between the sexes (not to mention between West and East) is contained in their conversation.

> MOLLY: You haven't told me about that book I lent you last week. Did you finish it?
> VIRGINIAN: That Romeo and Juliet? Yes, ma'am, I finished it.
> MOLLY: Don't tell me you didn't like it!
> VIRGINIAN: Well, I ain't read any poetry before, but soon as I get the hang of it, it'll be as easy as readin' the patent medicine catalog.
> MOLLY (*laughing*): Well, didn't you like the story?
> VIRGINIAN: Well, they raised a mighty strange breed o' men in them days, but in some respects this Romeo was a pretty good hombre.
> MOLLY: Oh, indeed, just a pretty good hombre!
> VIRGINIAN: Yes'm, he had his enemies, and he killed 'em. Shows he wasn't no coward and I s'pose he was quick on the draw.
> MOLLY: You approve of killing your enemies? An eye for an eye?
> VIRGINIAN: Not if there's an honorable way out, no ma'am. But them enemies was particular ornery. They had it comin' to 'em.

The Virginian goes on, however, to criticize Romeo's behavior in the famous balcony scene; he doesn't understand why the hero would "traipse" around sneakily, rather than confronting Juliet's father man-to-man. Molly, amused rather than irritated, posits that "perhaps men in those days realized just how much women love the gallantry of courtship." The Virginian replies that, in Romeo's shoes, he would not waste time "fritter[ing] around on rope ladders, makin' up poetry."

> MOLLY: No, you're hardly a Romeo. But what would you do?
> VIRGINIAN: Molly—I'll show you what I'd do. (*He lifts her up and kisses her. She acts offended.*)

MOLLY: You're just as sure of yourself as ever, aren't you?

VIRGINIAN: Molly, don't play-act with me. We don't fool each other. We ain't on no balcony. Don't you think the spring is the prettiest time of year to be married?

MOLLY: But I don't want to get married yet! I've got my school, and I'm just getting started, and those children could get—

VIRGINIAN: Teachin' school—that ain't no real woman's job in life. Listen, Molly, I don't aim to stay here. Now that you'll be my wife and partner, what I aim to do, I'm pushin' out further west, to Utah or Nevada, to do out there what Judge Henry done right here in Wyoming: make more United States out o' raw prairieland.

MOLLY: I like you, and I admire you more than any man I've ever known. But I'm not sure of myself yet. This country is so new and strange. I feel like an alien, an outsider. Oh, I don't know how to explain it, but I just feel that I'm different.

VIRGINIAN: Women are funny, Molly. I don't understand 'em.

MOLLY: Oh, yes you do—but I'm glad you think you don't.

This dialogue may seem egregiously sexist by today's standards, but of course it reflected perfectly well the ideals of its own day, bolstered by a romantic conception of the values of the mythical Old West. The scene is very effective in bringing us, as modern viewers, close to the ideals of another time, another generation. We may be glad that we have moved beyond the assumptions about gender roles implicit here, but we also like these characters; the film allows us to see how far we have come but also to find at least a modicum of empathy for the people of a different era, struggling—like we do—to make sense of the eternal puzzle of the sexes, even if, nearly a century removed from us, they reach different conclusions.

In addition, setting its problematic content aside, this excerpt gives a sense of the engaging nature of the dialogue throughout the movie, especially when delivered so well. Not only does the title character, in an early scene, get to speak one of Western cinema's most famous lines ("If you wanna call me that, smile," taken directly from the book), but the other characters get some wonderful speeches too. When Steve attempts to calm a nervous rustler around a nighttime campfire, he ruminates on life and death in a way that recalls the Cisco Kid's similar wistful philosophizing in the near-contemporaneous *In Old Arizona* (1928), not to mention the musings of Gus McCrae and the other cowboys in the masterpiece *Lonesome Dove* (1989) six decades later. "What's life, anyway?" Steve asks. "A few winters waitin' for spring, a few summers wishin' they'd last, a few bottles of whiskey and a half a dozen girls you can remember. And then your little six by three feet under the ground, and that's all. Hmm. Might as well be now as later."

The title character (Gary Cooper) and Molly (Mary Brian) discuss Shakespeare and other matters. *The Virginian* (Paramount, 1929).

This tendency toward elegiac philosophy is not the only similarity between *The Virginian* and *Lonesome Dove*, to the point where it seems likely to me that the latter contains deliberate homages to the former. Both start with a long sequence—a first act—in which the plot is moving barely at all, but which spends a great deal of time just witnessing the quirky conversations of the local cowboys, providing a powerful sense of local color and helping us feel like we know the characters. Most strikingly, both films feature a gut-wrenching scene in which the heroes feel compelled to dispense frontier justice, through lynching, on a wayward, happy-go-lucky friend who has drifted fecklessly into criminal activity. Even sixty years after the fact, *The Virginian* was still making its influence felt in the creation of great Westerns, and it would continue to do so.

Cowboys reflecting on life, death, and morality; men and women going through the baffling dance of courtship under rules neither of them fully understand; the contrast between Eastern civilization (represented by both lovely women and weaselly villains) and the Western frontier (embodied in the cowboy heroes); love triangles involving both friends and enemies; chivalrous but uncultured knights of the plains riding to the rescue of maidens fair; hot-headed bullies and cool, laconic heroes facing each other down in saloons; and, ultimately, men strapping on their guns and walking slowly down a dusty street to meet their fates: these things have become a part of America's cultural DNA, familiar and usually taken for granted. But it all started here.

Hell's Heroes
(1929)

December 27, 1929 (New York City)
USA—English / Spanish
Universal Pictures
68m—Mono—BW—1.20:1

Direction: William Wyler
Screenplay: Tom Reed, C. Gardner Sullivan, Peter B. Kyne (novel *The Three Godfathers*)
Principal Cast: Charles Bickford (Bob Sangster), Raymond Hatton (Barbwire Tom Gibbons), Fred Kohler (Wild Bill Kearney), Fritzi Ridgeway (Mother), Jo De La Cruz (José), Walter James (Sheriff), Maria Alba (Carmelita), Buck Connors (Parson Jones)
Production: Carl Laemmle, Jr. (uncredited)
Cinematography: George Robinson
Editing: Del Andrews, Harry Marker
Music: Sam Perry (uncredited)

The author Peter B. Kyne's first significant work, a Western short novel called *The Three Godfathers*, was published in 1913 and became so popular that Hollywood made no fewer than five filmed versions between 1914 and 1948. Two from the silent era are now considered lost, but in 1929 there appeared the first, and best, of three sound versions.

The plot of Kyne's story is a relatively straightforward Christian allegory. Four bandits rob a bank in Wickenburg; one is killed in the escape (by a preacher, no less!), but the remaining three ride out into the Colorado Desert. They are forced to kill their horses along the way and proceed through the wasteland on foot.

The three outlaws call each other by their names, but the narrator refers to them simply as the Wounded Bad Man, the Youngest Bad Man, and the Worst Bad Man. After a time, they come upon a covered wagon containing a young woman about to give birth. Her husband is missing, presumed dead, after having foolishly dynamited the only source of water in the area.

The young woman's plight evokes sympathy in these hardened criminals; they comfort her and assist with the birth. It's a boy—but the mother's life is doomed. Before dying, she asks the three men to save her baby's life, and names them as his godfathers. This is the turning point for our three bad-men-turned-heroes, who, in true *Parzival* fashion, are now guided by their authentic inner nobility and dedicate themselves to saving the child's life, even knowing that this will almost certainly mean their own capture. Two die along the way; the third delivers the child safely to the town of New Jerusalem on Christmas Eve.

William Wyler's *Hell's Heroes* (1929), as mentioned above, is the earliest film adaptation of this story that still survives. What a pity it is that it is marred by uneven production values—especially in terms of its photography and editing—because in many ways it is the rawest, most powerful, and least sentimental of the three versions we have. It is mainly the missteps in its production, in my view, which keep it from being an all-out masterpiece, perhaps even on a par with John Ford's similarly themed *3 Bad Men* (1926). (Ford's great silent film, despite its different source material, has inevitably been compared with the various adaptations of Kyne's story, given that both stories feature three hardened criminals redeemed through their compassion for someone in need of their protection—either a woman or a baby—alone on the frontier. This must have been a theme that appealed to Ford, given that he himself was responsible for two of the filmed versions of Kyne's story: the lost 1919 silent *Marked Men* and 1948's *3 Godfathers*.)

Despite its flaws, there is so much to recommend Wyler's *Hell's Heroes*, not least the outstanding script. The dialogue—much of it taken directly from Kyne's short story—is wonderful, but what truly sets the movie apart from the other adaptations is the fearlessness of its characterization. A quick note about the screenwriters: Tom Reed, credited with "Adaptation and Dialogue," was a prolific writer whose best-known script today is also the last one he created for Hollywood before moving to television—*Night People* (1954). C. Gardner Sullivan, the "Supervising Story Chief," was at one point perhaps the most famous writer in Hollywood, helping to create such anti-war landmarks as *Civilization* (1915) and *All Quiet on the Western Front* (1930) as well as canonical Westerns like *Tumbleweeds* (1925) and *Union Pacific* (1939), both discussed in this volume. When these two experts combined their talents for *Hell's Heroes*, they must have realized that the most effective way to heighten the emotional impact of the outlaws' redemption was to magnify their initial wickedness. I imagine them asking themselves: just how far can this script go in making the three men reprehensible at the beginning, while still evoking the audience's love for them by the end?

Our first meeting with these bad men is in the opening scene, as Wild Bill Kearney (Fred Kohler) and Barbwire Tom Gibbons (Raymond Hatton) ride across the desert, accompanied by their compatriot José (Jo De La Cruz). They approach a sign reading:

> 3 Mi to New Jerusalem
> A Bad Town
> For Bad Men

"I wonder how they knowed we was coming!" laughs Bill. Barbwire looks grimly at the noose hanging from the sign, which frames his face in a medium close-up as he says, "Looks just about your size, Bill." (This terrific shot, through the hangman's noose, would later be echoed in Sergio Leone's *The Good, the Bad and the Ugly*, 1966.) When José looks forward to the opportunity to kill the town sheriff, however, Barbwire pats his arm and says, "The Lord frowns on bloodshed, my boy." This establishes Barbwire—who already seems like the most seasoned, and jaded, of the bunch—as the closest thing the gang has to a conscience.

The men then proceed to New Jerusalem, where their ringleader, Bob (Charles Bickford), has been casing the town bank. Introduced in a cantina scene, Bob strikes us as the vilest of them all—an obnoxious, leering braggart with no visible redeeming qualities. He kisses, then slaps, a dance-hall girl who is obviously smitten with him, then pulls another girl to his side while she sings; he laughs in delight as the two girls fight each other for his affections. We also see him bully his way around a craps table and mock the elderly town sheriff to his face. At this point we have no love for him whatsoever, and it is difficult to see how he will ever evoke our sympathy.

Then comes the bank robbery. José waits outside with the horses while Bob, Bill, and Barbwire are inside. The thieves pull their pistols, and Barbwire growls menacingly at one of the two cashiers: "Start reaching for heaven, stranger, or you're headed straight for hell." (We will remember this exchange later.) The frightened cashier lunges

Barbwire Gibbons (Raymond Hatton) contemplates his likely fate. *Hell's Heroes* (Universal, 1929).

for a hidden gun and both Bill and Barbwire fire, cutting him down. "Got him straight through the pump," Bill proclaims proudly. "You're a liar," says Barbwire. "You missed him a full inch!" Barbwire may have been cautioning about the sin of killing a few minutes earlier, but now both he and Bill want to claim credit for this murder.

As the men make their escape, they ride past a church. The old, bearded preacher (Buck Connors) steps out the front door, hears about the robbery, pulls a big pistol from his coat and fires three shots at the backs of the thieves, wounding Barbwire and killing José, who falls to the ground with his stolen loot. Bob wheels his horse around and rides back toward the body of his comrade, and for a fleeting moment we think, "Ah, honor amongst thieves." But Bob merely leans down to scoop up a fallen money bag from the ground, then gallops away.

At this point today's Western buff cannot help but recall *The Wild Bunch* (1969), which starts with a similar robbery committed by a murderous band of outlaws. In both films, we see that the "good Christian" townsfolk are just as violent and bloodthirsty as their foes. They may not have initiated the violence, but still, at this point it's hard to see anyone having a particularly strong claim to any moral high ground.

Three criminals, cold-blooded killers all, flee into the desert, pursued by a posse. Their horses run off during a sandstorm, and they are left to make their way on foot, searching for water as well as an escape. Their situation will become increasingly grim. At one point, the wounded Barbwire begins to muse.

> BARBWIRE: Once there was three wise hombres rode outta Jerusalem.
> BOB: We ain't ridin', we're walkin'.
> BARBWIRE: Yeah? I said wise. Wasn't speakin' of us 'uns. You two birds don't know your Scriptures. Now once upon a time, the King of the Jews—
> BILL: Heh? I never knowed them Jews had a king.

Soon after, we see the three figures on a ridge, silhouetted against the evening sky, and we are reminded of the similar visual trope of the Magi following their star. Only here we have the anti–Magi—or at least, so we think. True to its source material, *Hell's Heroes* is rife with biblical allusions such as this, not only setting up the Christmas allegory still to come but also prefiguring the severe biblical imagery we will find decades later in the era of Clint Eastwood and the spaghetti Western.

The next day in the narrative holds the turning point: the trio's encounter with the pregnant woman (Fritzi Ridgeway) near Terrapin Tanks, which has, up to now, always been a reliable watering hole. In Kyne's story, this immedi-

Menace personified: the worst of the bad men, Bob Sangster (Charles Bickford), asserts his claim to the woman inside the wagon. His intention, at this point, is unmistakable. *Hell's Heroes* (Universal, 1929).

ately catalyzes the redemptive process for our three outlaws; but here, the screenwriters first push things even further to show the depravity of these men before they begin their transformation. Bob is the first to look into the covered wagon which shelters the desperate young woman. Lying stretched out under a blanket, she moans and is clearly in distress, but her condition is not immediately apparent to Bob (or to us); all he can tell is that she is beautiful, helpless, and many miles from succor. He pulls the curtains closed to hide her from the others. "Whatcha got, Bob?" asks Bill. "Nothin'!" Bob answers; but the two others then hear a feminine moan issuing from the wagon. Bill grins knowingly and spits, then goes around to the front of the wagon and looks in. "Nothin', huh?" "I seen her first," says Bob, defensively. At this point Barbwire indicates that he isn't interested because of his wounds: "Lucky for you I'm crippled," he says. At this point, the movie leaves no doubt that Bob and Bill intend to rape the poor woman. Bill, however, is happy to wait his turn, walking away with Barbwire toward Terrapin Tanks. "Come on up to the hole, Bob, when you're thirsty," he says cheerfully; and we understand this to mean, "Let me know when you are finished so I can take my turn."

This, then, is the nadir for our characters, the answer to the question of just how far the screenwriters are willing to plumb the depths of the men's wickedness before the shifting of their ethical arcs. Accustomed as we now are to gritty reboots and antiheroes, it may be hard at first to appreciate just how daring this movie was for its time; even to our modern sensibilities, though, *Hell's Heroes* comes across as strikingly raw, pulling no punches. The depth of the brutality and loathsomeness in our three main characters is what will ultimately make their transformation so powerful.

That transformation, of course, is set in motion by the birth of the child and the appointing of the three men as the boy's godfathers by the mother before she dies. "Will you … three … *good men* … save my baby?" she asks, and Bill responds first. "Us three good men'll do what we kin, ma'am," he promises. From here on in we will see each one wrestle, in his own way, with his own demons and angels before rising to the occasion—but rise to the occasion the men do, and then some. The wonder of this film is that within only a few minutes of screen time it will have us, the audience, completely on the side of these three "good men." By the end, we will love them for their courage, nobility, and self-sacrifice.

Not only did the filmmakers paint the three leads as, initially, even more villainous than they were in the original story, but they also made other changes heightening the impact of the narrative. First, in this version the three men must choose to go back to the town they just came from in order to save the child; that is, they have to return to the scene of the crime, where the vengeance of the Law will be inevitable. In addition, our three outlaws in this version soon learn that the baby's father was actually the cashier that they gunned down in the bank robbery. ("Start reaching for heaven, stranger, or you're headed straight for hell.") This adds an extra layer of culpability and atonement that was not present in the original short story; it is a brilliant masterstroke of narrative with a potent payoff.

Another change: in the original book, the baby is finally delivered to a woman singing Hosannas on a melodeon on Christmas Eve, and the narrative closes on a pious note: "Who knows? Perhaps in that moment the woman, too, like The Three Bad Men, beheld The King!"[1] But in the film, the baby is delivered to clean-cut, hymn-singing churchgoers on Christmas morning—churchgoers who have just been listening to their preacher (José's killer) praise one of their own for his "sacrifice" in obtaining a beautiful Christmas tree for the worship service. Meanwhile, the three men who have offered up the true sacrifice would, we feel certain, be held in contempt by this preacher and congregation. Thus, the movie makes a noticeable left turn from the straightforward devoutness of the original short story, contrasting the showy piety of the churchgoers with the true moral virtue of the outlaws.

Wild Bill Kearney (Fred Kohler) offers comfort to Barbwire (Raymond Hatton), holding the child who will redeem both of their lives. The thorny tree, we will soon see, is in the shape of a cross. *Hell's Heroes* (Universal, 1929).

But the most stunning alteration from (and improvement on) the original text is in the handling of the film's decisive and climactic moment: the final decision that Bob will make in order to save the life of the infant. I will say no more about it here, because it is a scene whose power must be experienced firsthand; but for me it ranks as one of the most memorable moments in the history of the Western.

If the preceding sounds as if I have been describing a masterpiece—well, I have: a masterpiece of screenwriting and acting. And to be clear, there are amazing and artistic visual moments as well: Barbwire's face framed within the hanging noose; dust streaming from the outlaw's hats as they ride into town; José contemptuously flicking away a cigarette, its smoke leaving a meteor's trail in the air, while he waits on his horse outside the bank; the "Magi" silhouetted against the sunset; the cross-shaped desert tree that figures prominently both in the opening shots of the movie and at a critical, full-circle moment later in the story.

All of this makes it difficult to understand the almost amateurish visual missteps, especially given William Wyler's directorial skill and extensive experience making Westerns. There is an overabundance, especially early on, of self-conscious and gratuitous panning shots and dolly shots. (One long, wobbly dolly shot spends seventeen seconds of screen time only to show Bob crossing a New Jerusalem street to tie up his horse.) There are editing and continuity problems as well. But perhaps the most egregious error in judgment is the way in which the last scene of the movie is handled— again, not in terms of its acting or script, but the editing and, above all, the treatment of sound. Had this scene simply been allowed to play out without any music (source or otherwise), using only the natural ambient sounds of the location, the result would have been soul-shattering; instead, we are left with an intrusive, self-consciously arty and pretentious effect whose final sonic expression in the closing seconds of the film actively works against the entire aesthetic tenor of the movie up to that point, and distracts us from contemplating what we should at this moment, namely the fate of this child who— in this version—is now alone without a history, without a name.

One cannot help but imagine what Wyler himself could do with this film were he alive today and able to make a "director's cut"—especially given what he would later prove he could accomplish in classics like *Wuthering Heights* (1939), *Mrs. Miniver* (1942), *The Best Years of Our Lives* (1946), *Roman Holiday* (1953), and *Ben-Hur* (1959). Indeed, Wyler would go on to become one of the greatest directors in Hollywood history, known (among other things) for his sense of nuance and his ability to take great advantage of strong scripts. So what happened with *Hell's Heroes*? Was Wyler simply less secure in this, his first sound outing? Was he still finding his voice within a rapidly changing medium? The widespread adoption of the Hays Code was just around the corner; was there outside pressure for him to bow to more pious sensibilities in the movie's final scene? (Wyler once joked about the very Christian *Ben-Hur*: "It takes a Jew to do this stuff well.")[2]

Hell's Heroes is an interesting enigma; nevertheless, despite its inconsistencies, it remains, in its finest moments—and there are many—a wonderfully moving drama, magnificently written and acted, that stays with the viewer long afterward. It should be remembered as the best of the three surviving versions of Kyne's short story, even while serving as a reminder of the incredibly short aesthetic distance—a mere hair's-breadth—that separates "memorable" from "masterpiece."

I noted earlier that the Western movie mythos, since its very inception, has contained the seeds of its own subversion. *Hell's Heroes*, with its initially evil lead characters and hypocritical townsfolk, certainly shows the countercultural potentialities that would eventually come to the fore in the sixties and seventies. But the Hays Code was about to become standard practice, and so for the next three decades subversive Westerns, while still present, would have to be more discreet and subtle. The next two versions of *The Three Godfathers* would be considerably more sanitized, and movies which attempted to deconstruct Western orthodoxy were rare—indeed, practically non-existent—from this point until the 1940s. Nevertheless, films like *The Ox-Bow Incident* (1943), *Yellow Sky* (1948), *The Gunfighter* (1950), *Johnny Guitar* (1954), and *Vera Cruz* (1954) would eventually appear, bubbling beneath the mainstream surface, anticipating and laying the groundwork for the heretical eruption of the Silver Age.

Tidbits and Trivia

- In keeping with the gritty realism of the characters and the rawness of the script, Wyler shot some of the exterior scenes (in the Mojave Desert and Panamint Valley) in 110-degree heat. There is a reason why we can palpably feel the thirst and exhaustion that these characters are suffering—the actors were suffering it too!
- A silent version of *Hell's Heroes* was also prepared to accommodate those theaters which were not yet equipped for talkies.
- Wyler holds the record for most Best Director Oscar nominations (twelve). His nearest competitors, Martin Scorsese and Billy Wilder, have eight apiece. However, John Ford has the most Best Director wins (four); Wyler and Frank Capra are tied for second with three each. (Wyler's three wins: *Mrs. Miniver*; *The Best Years of Our Lives*; *Ben-Hur*.)
- There is a bizarre symmetry to William Wyler's directorial career. He was the credited director for sixty-seven films between 1925 and 1970. The middle film in that list is *The Storm* (1930), the next Wyler film released after *Hell's Heroes*. In the thirty-three Wyler movies preceding *The Storm* (including *Hell's Heroes*), all but three are Westerns. In the thirty-three films that follow, however, *only* three are Westerns—a negative image, in one sense, of the first half of Wyler's career.

The Big Trail
(1930)

October 2, 1930 (Los Angeles)
USA—English
Fox Film Corporation
125m / 108m—Mono—BW—2.10:1 / 1.20:1

Direction: Raoul Walsh, Louis R. Loeffler (uncredited)
Screenplay: Hal G. Evarts, Marie Boyle (uncredited), Jack Peabody (uncredited), Florence Postal (uncredited), Raoul Walsh (uncredited)
Principal Cast: John Wayne (Breck Coleman), Marguerite Churchill (Ruth Cameron), El Brendel (Gus), Tully Marshall (Zeke), Tyrone Power, Sr. (Red Flack), David Rollins (Dave Cameron), Frederick Burton (Pa Bascom), Ian Keith (Bill Thorpe), Charles Stevens (Lopez), Louise Carver (Gus's Mother-in-Law)
Production: Winfield R. Sheehan (uncredited)
Cinematography: Arthur Edeson (70 mm version), Lucien N. Andriot (35 mm version)
Editing: Jack Dennis
Music: R.H. Bassett (uncredited), Peter Brunelli (uncredited), Alfred Darby (uncredited), Arthur Kay (uncredited), Jack Virgil (uncredited)
Awards: National Film Registry

The path has been a potent mythic symbol for as long as human beings have been travelers. The *Tao Te Ching*, for example, is centered around the metaphor of the Way, and famously refers to the long journey that begins with a single step. Similarly, in Greek, Celtic, and Brazilian mythologies (not to mention the Blues), crossroads were supernaturally magical locations, suggesting those potent moments of critical decisions in human lives when multiple directions present themselves. The path to the Grail, standing in for the individual's quest for fulfillment, features prominently in several Arthurian romances, including the Vulgate Cycle, in which the knights seeking the Grail intentionally *avoid* paths that have already been laid, finding their own ways instead; and *Parzival*, in which the hero's path actually leads him to the Grail Castle early on (when he lets go of his horse's reins), but then takes a surprising turn when he initially fails in his quest and now must spend years wandering in the Waste Land before finding his way back to his destiny.

The symbol of the road or path (evoking the course of a life) pervades modern literature and art as well, from Robert Frost to Tolkien to the Beat poets to road movies to popular music. Nowhere in American art has this metaphor been more prevalent than in the Western picture, most especially so in its earlier years. By the 1950s there were plenty of Westerns that had a fixed and concentrated unity of place—*The Gunfighter* (1950), *High Noon* (1952), and *3:10 to Yuma* (1957), for example—but the vast majority of the earlier Westerns were about *movement*: wagon trains, cattle drives, scouts and

111

trappers, settlers and railroads pushing relentlessly westward. The trail was life, and the trail led west, from sunrise to sunset.

In hindsight, the life-trail of the greatest and most iconic of all Western stars might seem as if it were laid before his feet, but in fact it was far from inevitable. The phenomenon of John Wayne nearly didn't happen; like Parzival, Wayne had to find his Grail Castle twice.

By 1930, young Marion Morrison had appeared in a string of uncredited bit parts in twenty pictures, only two of them Westerns. For nine of these, he also served as a prop man or costumer. By this point, he had only one actual screen credit to his name (as Duke Morrison), playing the fraternity brother who doesn't get the girl in the 1929 collegiate comedy/musical *Words and Music*, for which he also served as property assistant.

John Ford made a connection with young Morrison early on, employing him in small roles in seven of his silent films and early talkies starting with *Mother Machree* in 1927; but it was Raoul Walsh who first took advantage of Morrison's star potential. The story goes that Walsh spotted Morrison, then in his early twenties, moving furniture on a set and knew he had found his leading man for *The Big Trail* (1930). The director renamed his discovery John Wayne (after Revolutionary War general "Mad" Anthony Wayne), and the rest was history.

Well, history delayed, because *The Big Trail* was a commercial flop despite its large budget and epic scope. After its failure, Wayne would return to bit parts in A-movies, supplemented by a long string of lead roles in mostly forgettable Poverty Row B-Westerns. Like Walsh, John Ford had spotted something of interest in Wayne, but he felt that the time wasn't yet right. "Duke wasn't ready. He had to develop his skills as an actor," Ford later recalled. "I wanted some pain written on his face to offset the innocence."[1] John Wayne, like Parzival, had to return to the Waste Land and await his moment. The Golden Age of the Western movie, ushered in and led by the partnership of Ford and Wayne, was still nine years distant.

On the surface, *The Big Trail* seemed to have all of the ingredients of a Western success: an accomplished director, a historic setting (the Oregon Trail), eye-popping photography, and epic scenes filmed in over a dozen locations across seven states using Grandeur, a new 70 mm widescreen process developed by Fox. Although certainly not a great Western, it's enjoyable on its own terms and has much to recommend it. So why did *The Big Trail* fail?

One answer might be that it was the right idea at the wrong time. The film was costly to make, not only because of the enormous production expenses involved in staging a massive wagon caravan on screen, but also because the filmmakers shot six different versions: one in widescreen, one in standard aspect ratio, and four in foreign languages (French, German, Italian, Spanish). Of the two English-language incarnations (both of which are available today), the widescreen one is definitely the better, but unfortunately, many theaters were not equipped to project in that format, nor—in the early days of the Great Depression—were they typically willing to eat the cost of upgrading their equipment. Had *The Big Trail* been of higher quality overall, on the level of *The Iron Horse* (1924) or even *The Covered Wagon* (1923), it might have recouped more of its expenses by drawing more viewers through positive word-of-mouth; but as simply a

The eternal Western triangle: slick con artist Bill Thorpe (Ian Keith), plucky heroine Ruth Cameron (Marguerite Churchill), and true Western man Breck Coleman (John Wayne). *The Big Trail* (Fox, 1930).

perfectly serviceable Western dressed up with amazing (and costly) visuals, it was sunk, financially, under the weight of its own grand designs.

Despite its imperfections, there is still much to praise about *The Big Trail*. Most obviously, the widescreen photography is breathtaking, with epic vistas, gargantuan cities of covered wagons stretching back to the horizon, a compelling ride on an enormous riverboat, a kinetic buffalo hunt, a heart-pounding Indian attack sequence, and a wonderfully thrilling scene as the massive wagons and cattle are lowered by ropes down a perilous cliffside. The film also takes great care with historically accurate details, giving it a potent authenticity. The wagon train itself seems realistic to an almost documentary degree, down to the oxen pulling the prairie schooners, the grimy clothing of the settlers, and the constant sounds of dogs, cattle, and other background noises that must have been ever-present on the actual Oregon Trail. As a viewer, it is easy to believe that this is how a genuine wagon train would have looked and sounded.

The Big Trail also feels like the beginning of something; it resonates with freshness, optimism, and youth. This is the opening of the West, when all the great adventure still lies ahead, and the frontier waits, beckoning. If *Tumbleweeds* is our autumnal senescence, an elegy for the passing of an era, then *The Big Trail* is our glorious youth, when the future is still an undiscovered country and possibilities are endless.

Speaking of beginnings, the most obvious high point of *The Big Trail* is the arrival at long last of John Wayne, even as a rather awkward and amateurish newcomer, in his first starring role. Yes, there is much still to be ironed out. Wayne's line delivery is stilted and wooden, despite the fact that he was coached by, among others, the Shakespearean actor Lumsden Hare. As John Ford noted, the young actor needed experience, development of his skills, seasoning. Nevertheless, Wayne as Breck Coleman exhibits a natural, rugged, self-confident physicality (not far removed from that of George O'Brien) that hints of things to come. The raw material is evident, at least in hindsight; the seeds of the Ringo Kid and Thomas Dunson and Ethan Edwards and Tom Doniphon and Rooster Cogburn are all here, waiting to germinate.

The weaknesses of *The Big Trail* are simply those that were quite common among the early talkie Westerns. The dialogue is stagy and often obscured by poor choices in sound recording. The three villains are caricatures, especially Red Flack, played by Tyrone Power, Sr., in his only sound role. In symmetry with this trio's unambiguous badness, Wayne's character is just a little *too* perfect; witness, for example, the following exchange of dialogue between Red and Lopez (Charles Stevens) as they discuss our fearless hero.

> RED: Lopez? Who's that young buck over yar with no hair on his face?
> LOPEZ: That's Breck Coleman. He very quick with his knife.
> RED: Where's he come from?
> LOPEZ: He come from the plains, the mountains, he live with the Indians. He can throw a knife through the heart in twenty feet. He's the best shot in all this country. He knows everything.

Really? That all seems like a bit much, especially for this amiable young galoot. It's almost as if the movie is trying to sell us on two very different characters for Wayne: a pure-hearted, straightforward, "aw-shucks" kid and a tough, seasoned man of Nature on a vendetta quest. Wayne in his later years was certainly capable of playing complex and contradictory characters (in *The Searchers*, most notably), but he doesn't yet have the acting chops to pull it off here. And, in fairness, he doesn't get much help from the script.

The storytelling is also a bit awkward at times. For example, at the very moment in which we learn about Coleman's vendetta from his own lips, the man he has been looking for just happens to be right there listening. That is, we learn the backstory and meet the villain at the same time and in the same place; this is serendipitous, to say the least, given that the whole of the West is the stage on which Coleman's manhunt plays out. The narrative would be more compelling if it were to reveal its plot points more gradually as we move along the trail.

True to its time, *The Big Trail* is predictable in its attitude toward Native Americans. There are signs of hope at first: Coleman is talking with some kids before the wagon train sets out, and one asks him if he has ever killed an Indian. "No, you see, the Injuns are my friends," Coleman says. He later demonstrates this friendship along the trail, to the benefit of the settlers. This is our hero wearing his "man of Nature" hat, symbolized by his familiarity with the ways of the Indian. But as the plot rolls on, the potential for a more positive view of Native Americans vanishes. "Injuns have never yet prevented our breed of men from travelin' into the settin' sun," proclaims Pa Boscom (Frederick Burton), the leader of the wagon train. From this point in the movie forward, the Indians will become the usual dehumanized obstacles to the destined expansion of white civilization. As William Indick writes, *The Big Trail* "depicted Indians as faceless forces of

Four characters, but only two dimensions: hero Breck Coleman (John Wayne) confronts villains Lopez (Charles Stevens), Red Flack (Tyrone Power, Sr.), and Bill Thorpe (Ian Keith). *The Big Trail* **(Fox, 1930).**

nature amidst the other natural dangers of the Great Plains. The film's treatment of the Indian was emblematic of the way they would be treated throughout Depression-era Hollywood, when Westerns were relegated to B-movie status and the Indian limited to the role of anonymous natural threat."[2]

Most of the Westerns in the early sound era exemplify this dangerous side to a mythology. As Joseph Campbell reminds us, one of the primary functions of myth is to reinforce the rules, customs, and beliefs of a culture. As a positive, this can bring people in a society together and foster social cohesion, but of course, as we have seen all too often, the power of mythic symbolism can also be used to dehumanize and demonize the people of other regions, races, and cultures—and, as a corollary, to whitewash history and ease the guilty consciences of the beneficiaries of injustice. It would be two more decades before the American Western movie began to address this problem in earnest.

Beyond any doubt, the makers of the early Westerns knew that they were helping to craft a grand American mythology. Magical realms became the American frontier; knights became cowboys; swords became pistols; kings became ranchers. And just as the image of the Way had pervaded mythologies of the past, East and West, so the writers of the American Western turned to the metaphor of the trail.

The Big Trail, as its title signals, is centered around this image, and in many ways the organizing symbol is an effective one. Breck Coleman, like his mythic forebears, is the man who has been out there in the unknown lands, making trails for others to follow; and the film itself follows not only a literal trail but also a seasonal one, progressing from spring to winter like the course of a human life. (It's understandable, and yet unfortunate, that the movie ends with the rebirth of spring; in many ways I think it would have been more effective had it ended six minutes earlier, still in the winter's cold, and the future still open.)

However, the viewer can feel a bit bludgeoned by the unsubtle and constant underscoring of the trail image by the dialogue. "Our trails fork here." "Old Windy's gone on another trail." "Well, we all get off on the wrong trail once in a while." "We're blazing a trail that started in England!" "No great trail was ever blazed without hardship." "You're the breed of man that would follow a trail to the end." And Coleman, bidding farewell to his love interest Ruth Cameron (Marguerite Churchill), says, "Someday, somewhere, our trails will cross again." (Again, leaving the relationship there, on an uncertain but still promising note, would have made for a more memorable ending. Later Westerns—1946's *My Darling Clementine* springs to mind, for example—would learn the power of leaving some threads dangling, unresolved.) All of this goes to show, I think, the perils of mythic symbolism. When presented simply and allowed to work with subtlety, nuance, and artistic sensibility, symbols can be immensely powerful; but when overemployed, overexplained, or used ham-fistedly, the effect is lessened, and they become wearying or even grating. The balance is difficult to achieve. Mythmaking is hard.

In most legends, the adventure that the hero receives is exactly the one that he is suited for, that fits him well, whether he seeks the adventure or has it thrust upon him. This is certainly true in the American Western. But there is one striking way in particular, perhaps peculiar to the Western, in which the hero seems always to match his adventure perfectly: his age. One can predict with surprising accuracy where a Western will fall on the scale from "pioneering and optimistic" to "nostalgic and elegiac" simply by noting the (apparent) age of the hero. Pictures evoking the "morning of the West" tend to feature young heroes like Breck Coleman; elegiac Westerns feature old, weathered veterans who have ridden too many trails to recall. Perhaps these veterans were once Breck Colemans. Perhaps all orthodox Westerns feature the same eternal, archetypal hero at various points in his life, moving slowly but inexorably from sunrise to sunset.

Billy the Kid
(1930)

October 18, 1930 (USA)
USA—English
Metro-Goldwyn-Mayer
98m—Mono—BW—1.20:1

Direction: King Vidor
Screenplay: Laurence Stallings, Charles MacArthur, Harry Behn (uncredited), Willard Mack (uncredited), John T. Neville (uncredited), W.L. River (uncredited), Walter Noble Burns (novel *The Saga of Billy the Kid*)
Principal Cast: Johnny Mack Brown (Billy), Wallace Beery (Garrett), Kay Johnson (Claire), Karl Dane (Swenson), Wyndham Standing (Tunston), Russell Simpson (McSween), Blanche Friderici (Mrs. McSween), Roscoe Ates (Old Stuff), Warner Richmond (Ballinger), James A. Marcus (Donovan), Nelson McDowell (Hatfield), Jack Carlyle (Brewer), John Beck (Butterworth), Chris-Pin Martin (Santiago), Marguerita Padula (Nicky Whoosiz), Aggie Herring (Mrs. Hatfield)
Production: King Vidor, Irving Thalberg (uncredited)
Cinematography: Gordon Avil
Editing: Hugh Wynn
Art Direction: Cedric Gibbons
Music: Fritz Stahlberg (uncredited)

The story of Billy the Kid has been filmed many times, but King Vidor's 1930 version is the first important one. It is an uneven but tremendously engaging Western, very powerful in its best moments, decidedly odd in others. As with *The Big Trail* (1930), the movie was filmed in both standard aspect ratio and in 70 mm widescreen, but unfortunately the widescreen version is considered lost today.

One of the most far-reaching impacts of *Billy the Kid* is that it established certain storytelling conventions that would persist in later filmed versions of Billy's legend: the complex relationship of friendly antagonism between Billy and his eventual killer Pat Garrett; Billy's simple-mindedness; his attachment to the English rancher John Henry Tunstall (called "Tunston" here) as a much-needed father figure whose murder will inspire the outlaw's spree of vengeance; and an interpretation of Billy as a sort of Robin Hood of the West, fighting for justice and freedom against the corrupt representatives of the law.

Billy the Kid as a folklore hero had begun to fade into obscurity by the 1920s, but then Walter Noble Burns published *The Saga of Billy the Kid* in 1926, and the book quickly became a bestseller, revitalizing Billy's legend and inspiring King Vidor to create a movie adaptation—in this case, with much of it actually filmed in Lincoln County,

New Mexico, the setting for the climax of Billy's career in the Lincoln County War (1878–81), and featuring a pistol supposedly used by the real Billy himself and lent to the filmmakers by William S. Hart, who served as a consultant on the film. Unfortunately, this centerpiece of Hart's gun collection was later revealed to be a fake, but this still shows the lengths to which the filmmakers were willing to go in order to give *Billy the Kid* a sense of gritty authenticity. And they succeeded; in fact, Fenin and Everson call this one of the few sound Westerns to "recapture successfully the primitive quality and stark realism of the early Hart films, not only in plot, but also in characterization, photography, and direction."[1]

Despite this commitment to a more realistic aesthetic, Vidor's adaptation wastes no time in whitewashing the life and actions of its killer protagonist. Directly after the opening credits we see the great seal of the State of New Mexico (incorporated only eighteen years before), and beneath it a scrolling written statement from Governor Richard C. Dillon:

> It seems to me that this picture of Billy the Kid, though it has taken liberties with the details of his life, presents a true drama of his career, and proves that this gunfighter of early New Mexico played his part in the story of the West. Billy had a keen sense of justice which had been deeply outraged, and he set about with his gun and invincible courage to even up the scores, and in that way to restore to life on the range its personal liberty.

Throughout the film, Billy (Johnny Mack Brown) kills without any apparent compunction or regret—usually, in fact, with a smile—and so, without this opening frame, I'm not sure that we would read Billy's actions as primarily about "restoring personal liberty" to the range. Governor Dillon's statement therefore does a significant amount of work in shaping the audience's appraisal of Billy from the beginning; it is also balanced by the words of Billy's love interest Claire (Kay Johnson) toward the end of the movie, when she—a respectable English lady—absolves Billy of his sins, saying, "Every killing you've done has been needed. You made this town a decent place to live in." This is quite a blessing indeed, given the body count that Billy has generated up to this point.

Just as Billy's ultimate impact on the West is essentially just explained to us in words, so his personality as cold-blooded killer (already there at the beginning of the movie) is explained only through one bit of dialogue in Billy's introduction scene, when he guns down a thug threatening Tunston, saying, "Killin' rats comes natural to me. You see, when I was twelve years old, I saw one of 'em shoot down my mother, in cold blood—and another got my father in the back." That's all we get by way of explanation for how Billy became the way he is, and his character doesn't change. He ends the film the same man he was at the beginning.

However, Johnny Mack Brown's performance throughout the film is powerful and compelling—idiosyncratic enough at first to take some getting used to, but ultimately one that stays with the viewer. In fact, it is surprising to see the nuances of character that former football star Brown is able to convey. He gives us a Billy who, while essentially unchanged by the events in the movie, nevertheless contains layers of complexity beneath his deceptively simple façade. Given Brown's fine performance in his breakout role, it is interesting—and a little sad—to compare his career trajectory with that of John Wayne. Both men had their first significant role in a 1930 widescreen Western (released within weeks of each other, in fact); both were former football players who played athletes in their early silent film work before gravitating toward Westerns; and both, not long after their breakthrough role, found themselves in the relative backwater of the Poverty Row B-Western. Brown would go on to be a very successful and popular B-movie cowboy up until the early 1950s, but he would never be a major motion picture star again. Wayne, in contrast, would become a legend, dominating and personifying his genre like no actor before or since. Comparing the contemporaneous performances of Brown in *Billy the Kid* and Wayne in *The Big Trail* may make one question the justice of the world, because—at this point in their careers, at least—Brown was by far the superior actor.

Billy (Johnny Mack Brown) is absolved of his sins by Claire (Kay Johnson). *Billy the Kid* (MGM, 1930).

The emotional crux of most Billy the Kid movies, including this one, is the relationship between Billy and Sheriff Pat Garrett, who—in real life and in *most* filmed versions—eventually will kill Billy. From the beginning we appreciate the friendship between Billy and Garrett (Wallace Beery, excellent here as well). They have a respectful, friendly rivalry as crack shots, which we learn about through a charming exchange about shooting dollar coins, then half-dollars, then quarters. The two men clearly have genuine affection for one another, which is what makes their eventual conflict more powerful. Their fates are intertwined, but much must still unfold before their ultimate confrontation.

The archetypal Western "frenemies"—Pat Garrett (Wallace Beery) and Billy the Kid (Johnny Mack Brown). *Billy the Kid* (MGM, 1930).

One of the most exciting sequences in the movie is its centerpiece, when Billy and his allies are holed up in McSween's ranch house, under siege by crooked lawmen (and the ethical, reluctant Garrett). The standoff lasts several days and takes up nearly a half hour of screen time; the suspense slowly builds and violence accumulates until finally, one night, the besiegers roll flaming barrels down the hillside to set the house on fire. At this point Billy's remaining allies, trapped in the burning house with him, begin to contemplate escape, and yet everyone still stays cool—there is a great deal of humorous repartee even in this moment of crisis. The noble outlaws begin to flee the house, but several are gunned down in the darkness by the well-sheltered besiegers. Eventually, just Billy is left inside; he must run across the yard and scramble over a wall in order to reach his

The epitome of cool under fire: Johnny Mack Brown in his most riveting scene. *Billy the Kid* (MGM, 1930).

horse. It's a tense situation, leading to one of Brown's finest acting moments. The house has begun to collapse, burning rafters dropping onto the floor at random. Billy leans in, lights his cigarette on one, then calmly proceeds to the mirror, where he turns on a music box, adjusts his attire, watches unperturbed as another piece of the ceiling falls in, and takes a few more drags on the cigarette. It's a fantastic, epic moment. Finally, the time has come; Billy coils himself like a spring, rushes outside with guns blazing, and cuts down several of the attackers. In seconds he has transformed from ice-cold calm into a furious blaze of deadly energy. Leaping over the wall, he vaults into the saddle *backwards* so that, as his horse rides away, he can continue to rain gunfire upon his enemies.

But a one-on-one confrontation between Billy and Garrett is still inevitable. The stage is set by the best scene between the two men, which occurs on the outdoor steps of the Lincoln County Courthouse after Billy has "come in from the cold" to discuss an offer of amnesty from the governor, General Lew Wallace (Frank Reicher, uncredited). Billy meets Garrett on the steps, and the two men are clearly glad to see one another, even after being on opposite sides of the siege.

> BILLY: Hello, old kid!
> PAT: Hello, Kid. The governor's waitin' for you upstairs.
> BILLY: All right—I'll walk on up there.
> PAT: It'd be pretty polite if you left that hardware with me.
> *Billy considers for a long moment, then hands Pat his rifle and gun belt.*
> BILLY: Sure, Pat. Here you are.
> PAT (*joking*): I'll stay here and see that nobody hurts ya.
> BILLY LAUGHS: Yeah! Stick around, Pat, and I'll have ya tuckin' me in my little bed and
> puttin' on my little night pants for me! (*Both men laugh good-naturedly.*)

Then, after rejecting Wallace's offer and preparing to ride back to his life of outlawry, Billy returns to the courthouse steps to reclaim his hardware from his friend.

> BILLY (*gesturing to his guns*): Give 'em back to me like you promised, I'm gonna need 'em
> some more.

PAT: I don't want to give them back to you, Billy. Why don't you stand up like a man and take the offer General Wallace made you?

BILLY (*smiling*): I don't want your advice, Pat; I want my guns.

PAT: All right. I'll give 'em back to you, Billy. (*He gives back the pistol belt.*) But if you walk out of here still an outlaw, I ain't gonna waste any more time on you—I'm comin' after you myself, and I ain't comin' back without you. (*He hands Billy the rifle.*)

BILLY: Then come shootin', Pat.

Pat nods, and Billy rides off.

WALLACE (*joining Pat on the staircase*): Well, Garrett, looks like a manhunt for you. I hate to see it. Funny—I like that boy.

PAT: Yeah, me too.

We like Billy as well, partly because of the range that Brown shows in his portrayal, from the force of nature with ice water in his veins that we see in the ranch house siege to the desperate, weakened, starving wretch who eventually surrenders—temporarily, at least—to Garrett for a few miserable pieces of bacon (which Garrett provides, with sympathy and compassion).

Billy the Kid is an idiosyncratic film, with an odd way of juxtaposing gritty violence and genteel humor, but that is also its charm. It's true to its own strange vision—at least, up until the last moments. The surprising end of the movie anticipates the final scene of *Stagecoach* (1939) by nine years, but what will work tremendously well as a conclusion for the Ringo Kid's story arc is quite a disappointment here. All of the threads, narrative and historical, have been leading to one critical outcome, the avoidance of which robs us of what could have been an astoundingly strong catharsis, given the emotional investment that the movie has evoked from us so far. All of this narrative tension, violence, suspense, and pathos has been driving us inexorably to a crisis point, one which then—bafflingly—never comes. Apparently, there was a European cut of the movie that did indeed bring things to a satisfying, if tragic, conclusion, but the poor Americans were "treated" to a happy ending instead. From *Billy the Kid* to *Frankenstein* (1931) to *Breakfast at Tiffany's* (1961) to the original version of *Blade Runner* (1982) to *The Scarlet Letter* (1995) to *The Hunchback of Notre Dame* (1996), Hollywood has spent a century under the misapprehension that tacking on happy endings to storylines that should be tragedies is a good idea. It isn't—as Aristotle could have told us a couple thousand years ago. This mistake doesn't ruin *Billy the Kid*—nowhere near it; there is too much that's good here— but it does make the film fall short of what it could have been.

Despite its ending, however, the movie is unsparing in its violence and unambiguous in its sympathy for its killer-outlaw antihero. It was not a film that could have been made even just a handful of years later, when the Hays Code went into full effect. This raises the question: if the Code had never been adopted and enforced, would the rise and eventual dominance of the subversive Western have come sooner than the sixties and seventies? And if it had come earlier, would that have been a good thing? Or did Hollywood need the long period of orthodoxy and legend-building from the thirties to the fifties in order to create a more fully constructed mythic edifice, something that would inspire more creative and iconoclastic energies—and therefore, better art forms—devoted to its eventual destruction?

Cimarron
(1931)

January 26, 1931 (New York City)
USA—English / French
RKO Radio Pictures
123m—Mono—BW—1.20:1

Direction: Wesley Ruggles (uncredited)
Screenplay: Howard Estabrook, Louis Sarecky (uncredited), Edna Ferber (novel)
Principal Cast: Richard Dix (Yancey Cravat), Irene Dunne (Sabra Cravat), Estelle Taylor (Dixie Lee), Nance O'Neil (Felice Venable), William Collier, Jr. (The Kid), Roscoe Ates (Jesse Rickey), George E. Stone (Sol Levy), Stanley Fields (Lon Yountis), Robert McWade (Louis Hefner), Edna May Oliver (Mrs. Tracy Wyatt), Judith Barrett (Donna Cravat), Eugene Jackson (Isaiah)
Production: William LeBaron, Wesley Ruggles (uncredited)
Cinematography: Edward Cronjager
Editing: William Hamilton
Art Direction: Max Rée
Music: Max Steiner (uncredited)
Awards: Oscar—Best Picture, Oscar—Best Writing, Adaptation (Estabrook), Oscar—Best Art Direction (Rée), National Board of Review—Top Ten Films, Photoplay Medal of Honor (Sarecky)
Nominations: Oscar—Best Actor in a Leading Role (Dix), Oscar—Best Actress in a Leading Role (Dunne), Oscar—Best Director (Ruggles), Oscar—Best Cinematography (Cronjager)

Of all the entries in the American Western film canon, few have suffered the ravages of age to the extent that *Cimarron* (1931) has. When it was released, critics raved, and the film famously went on to win the Academy Award for Best Picture (called "Outstanding Production" in those days)—the only example of a Western being so honored during the first six decades of Oscar history. (*Dances with Wolves*, 1990, and *Unforgiven*, 1993, are the only other pure Westerns to win Best Picture to date, along with the "neo–Western" *No Country for Old Men*, 2007.) Today, however, *Cimarron* is far from beloved—for example, it currently holds just a 50 percent rating ("Certified Rotten") among critics on the review-aggregation website Rotten Tomatoes, and an audience score of only 25 percent.[1]

The film is an epic, sweeping, big-budget Western adapted from an acclaimed novel by Edna Ferber (published just the year before), with strong direction, acting, and production values. It starts with a marvelous, eye-popping spectacle, the most famous of the various Western land rush scenes, and the scope of the film is historic and grand, spanning a forty-year slice of history from the opening of the Oklahoma Territory to the end of the Roaring Twenties (essentially contemporary with the movie itself). It was the

The most famous land rush sequence ever filmed. *Cimarron* (RKO, 1931).

biggest Western epic of the early sound era and single-handedly rekindled RKO's interest in making Westerns. So how do we account for *Cimarron*'s striking fall from grace in critical and public estimation over the last ninety years? Why does it no longer hold up well with viewers today? And is this justified?

In the Introduction, I indicated (accurately) that this book is not primarily focused on politics or questions of identity—but in the case of *Cimarron*, there is no good way to understand its history or read it in artistic terms without considering its political content, in both specific and general senses, because the movie itself prioritizes politics. *Cimarron* was certainly a progressive film in its own day: both small-p "progressive" and big-P "Progressive." (Witness the reverential showing of Teddy Roosevelt's picture and signature, as well as Yancey's candidacy for Oklahoma governor and Sabra's eventual election to Congress as a Progressive.) *Cimarron* stays generally true to the left-wing perspectives that animated Ferber's original novel, but the viewpoints that made the movie liberal in 1931 are generally accepted by both liberals and mainstream conservatives today. By modern standards, though, there are jarring contradictions in the film's treatment of these themes, especially with regard to race. This makes *Cimarron* simply a product of its time, but because its liberalism is so front-and-center in the narrative, and because this is a 1930s version of American liberalism—forward-looking on race and gender but still weighted down by racist tropes—the movie's bizarre (by our standards) juxtaposition of progressive idealism with howling racial stereotypes is likely to be grating for today's viewers, no matter where they might fall on the political spectrum.

Having recognized this, one must still credit *Cimarron* for being so far ahead of its time in its treatment of women, Native Americans, and minorities—*as abstract groups.* Our hero Yancey Cravat (Richard Dix) stands up for Native Americans ("The time has come for full citizenship for the Indians!"), is kind to the young Black child Isaiah (Eugene Jackson), and treats the Jewish Sol Levy (George E. Stone) with dignity and respect. After being asked to lead his town's first church service, Yancey shows his ecumenical bent by

Sabra Cravat (Irene Dunne) and Yancey Cravat (Richard Dix) amid the chaos that is Osage, Oklahoma. The West of *Cimarron* is always a bustling, crowded, noisy place. *Cimarron* (RKO, 1931).

allowing Sol to participate, saying: "Fellow citizens, I have been called upon to conduct this opening meeting of the Osage First Methodist Episcopalian Lutheran Presbyterian Congregational Baptist Catholic Unitarian *Hebrew* Church." Sol himself delivers one of the movie's most devastating deflations of bigotry when the stuffy old dowager Mrs. Wyatt (Edna May Oliver) says pompously, "Sorry, Mr. Levy, about you not being on the committee. But you see, we invited representatives of our principal families. One of my ancestors was a signer of the Declaration of Independence." Sol's reply: "That's all right. Relative of mine, fella named Moses, wrote the Ten Commandments."

In harmony with these progressive stances from the men, Yancey's wife Sabra (Irene Dunne) shows amazing grit and determination over the years, eventually becoming an important politician and, ultimately, the true protagonist of the picture. Although Ferber by her own account intended to satirize American womanhood in the novel, the film version shows Sabra emerging as a proto-feminist hero. "The women of Oklahoma have helped build a prairie wilderness into the state of today," she proclaims in a speech near the end of the film. "The holding of public office by a woman is a natural step." Unlike Yancey, her character genuinely evolves with the times; for example, she starts out by calling the natives "dirty" and "filthy," but ends by accepting, and indeed being proud of, her Indian daughter-in-law. Sabra's heroic trajectory is truly powerful, and we love her by the end.

In dissonant contrast to these features, however, *Cimarron* frequently resorts to tired stereotypes and racist tropes. The young servant boy Isaiah is in truth a heroic figure in the story; he is incredibly loyal to the Cravat family, even abandoning his own family and stowing away so he can accompany the Cravats on their trek to Oklahoma. (Our progressive Yancey sees nothing unusual about this, and apparently feels no conflict of conscience when he notes that the young servant possesses "loyalty ... that money can't buy.") In perhaps the movie's most moving scene, Isaiah lays down his life in an ultimately unnecessary attempt to save the life of young Sim, the Cravats' son. The filmmakers recognize the power of this, and the Cravats' eventual silent tribute to Isaiah is wonderful. Unfortunately, the character of Isaiah up until this point has been a virtual compendium of minstrel-show clichés; he is mainly played for laughs, a caricature providing comic relief. Perhaps Isaiah's most cringeworthy moment is when the family first arrives in Osage, and the young boy, spotting a wagonload

The servant boy Isaiah (Eugene Jackson) will commit the film's most heroic act; unfortunately, the rest of the time his character is reduced to minstrel-show stereotypes. *Cimarron* (RKO, 1931).

of watermelons, grins beatifically and exclaims, "I sho glad I came to Oklahomey!" In *Cimarron* we also have Indians who are little but cardboard cutouts, an over-the-top stutterer (Roscoe Ates, also played also for broad comic relief), and of course Sol Levy, who, while certainly sympathetic, is nevertheless a timid, furtive street vendor who relies on Yancey's beneficent graces to compensate for his lack of gumption. (At one point he says to Sabra, "It's men like [Yancey] that build the world; the rest of them, like me—well, we just come along and live in it.") Minorities in general are not shown to be strong in themselves but instead dependent upon the benevolent assistance of the progressive white man as epitomized by Yancey Cravat. While the film holds an enlightened position on minority groups in the abstract, it tends to depict actual individual representatives from these groups in mere caricature.

Characterization is not only a problem in *Cimarron* among its minority representatives, however. Yancey's theatrical manner and habit of deserting his wife and child (and disappearing from the narrative) simply as a result of a vaguely defined wanderlust serves to keep us at arm's length from him as a character. We never fully understand what drives him, aside from a certain faith in the romantic notions of historical inevitability and Manifest Destiny. He is an instrument of history, but not a real human being.

Other characters' motivations can also be baffling to a modern viewer. For example, during the church service Yancey is fired upon by the villain Lon Yountis (Stanley Fields), who was responsible for the death of the previous newspaperman in town (again, with motivation never explained—nor do we learn how Yancey knows he was the culprit). Yancey guns down Lon and brings the service to a close. Afterwards, he speaks briefly with Dixie Lee (Estelle Taylor), a young woman whose path he has crossed before, and who is now one of the town courtesans. When the Cravats arrive home, Sabra is shaken—not, it turns out, because her husband was just fired upon and forced to kill a man in the middle of the church service and in front of their young son. Instead, Sabra is upset that Yancey was kind to the prostitute. "That woman—smirking and smiling, and you stood there actually talking to her, holding her hand!" she exclaims indignantly.

Perhaps this would have made some sense to the film's contemporary audience, but I think most of today's viewers will scratch their heads.

Another bizarre moment is when Yancey returns to his family after wandering on adventures for five years. We might expect this homecoming to be emotional—Yancey tearfully embracing his family, holding on to his children to make up for all the lost time. Instead, he quotes from the *Odyssey* about the faithful Penelope. ("You and your miserable Milton," Sabra says, in a line directly from the novel. Ferber then writes, "He looked only slightly surprised and did not correct her.")[2] And then Sabra says, "Run along to school now, children—you're going to be late," as if it's an ordinary morning, before running along herself, in order to make sure that the hussy Dixie Lee gets appropriately sentenced.

Earlier Western epics like *The Covered Wagon* (1923), *The Iron Horse* (1924), and *Tumbleweeds* (1925) understood the importance of putting real, believable human beings in front of these grand historical backdrops, but in *Cimarron*, every character is either a caricature or impenetrable, with the exception, eventually, of Sabra.

At first blush, compassion seems to be the primary virtue extolled by the film—Yancey can be tremendously compassionate toward the Indians, and the Kid, and Sol, and Dixie, who is eventually abandoned by her bigamist husband and loses her child; and yet Yancey too abandons his wife and children, seemingly on a whim and with no particular concern shown for them. There is of course something about this that rings true, that touches on a more profound phenomenon: often people with the loftiest ideals for humanity don't put those ideals into practice closer to home. But Yancey's theatricality and frequent absence from the drama on screen keep this observation from having the impact that it could have.

Indeed, many of the most dramatic events in the narrative occur offscreen or in highly compressed fashion. When Yancey leaves his family for the second time, we never see the moment when he breaks his decision to Sabra; instead, we are given only a title card that tells us about how he has "ridden away to newer fields" because of his wanderlust. The episode with true dramatic and emotional potential has been conveniently avoided. It is as if the film deliberately wants to keep us absorbed (which it does), but always at a certain remove.

These moments of evaded drama, baffling character choices, and reactions that seem either too little or too much for the situation all serve to create a distancing effect at odds with the engrossing spectacle built into the story, and ultimately the whole enterprise comes across as too mannered, too contrived—an outcome not helped by dialogue that tends to be either overwrought or pedestrian, but never sings.

Yet, despite all this, there are moments when *Cimarron* is truly wonderful. When it works, it works spectacularly. The land rush is breathtaking; Isaiah's sacrifice is heartbreaking; the church service is first delightfully funny and then grippingly tense; and it is hard not to be moved when Yancey quietly replaces the Kid's gun in its holster after reluctantly shooting down his former friend (played by William Collier, Jr.). Irene Dunne also draws us in beautifully: we feel Sabra's aching loneliness after Yancey deserts her (not least because we never witness his adventures without her), and we watch her transform, over the four decades of the movie's timeline, from shrinking violet to woman of steel. Above all, Sabra's final scene—"Sleep, my boy"—is moving and unforgettable, as is the last juxtaposition of the movie, the unstained, mythically heroic statue of the Oklahoma pioneer contrasted against the grime and anonymity in which Yancey, the true pioneer, has been living.

In sum, *Cimarron* is an important, impressive, and compelling film with a powerful narrative and genuinely artistic execution, but its characters' motivations and priorities are sometimes baffling, and its politics, when viewed today, are guaranteed to please no one. Yes, the movie upholds values that were progressive for its time and would have existed primarily on the left; it celebrates the ideals of racial equality, women's suffrage, and women as political leaders. But few ordinary viewers today—left, right, or libertarian—would argue any of these points. (True, rabid right-wing white supremacists have been in the news a great deal recently, but to a degree that, I dearly hope, belies their relatively small numbers. I omit them from this discussion; I don't consider these vile racists to be genuine Americans in spirit, in that they are not committed to democratic values, nor do I care one bit whether they would like *Cimarron* or not.) Extremist fanatics aside, rational mainstream American culture takes for granted that, for example, an African American or Native American or Jew or woman should have the same rights as anyone else. The fact that this is now a generally accepted aspect of American society robs *Cimarron* of whatever progressive power it may have carried in its day; for most of us, it's preaching to the choir. Instead, modern political sensibilities are more likely to be startled by the racist stereotyping, and in addition to the ethical issues raised by such treatment, this gives the film an unevenness of tone that weakens not only its politics but also its aesthetics. I will be the first to argue that political content should always be subordinate to aesthetic considerations when evaluating a work of art; however, when the work of art is so overtly political to begin with, when it puts so many of its eggs in that basket, then inconsistency or jarring contradictions in political positioning cannot help but weaken the artistic impact as a whole.

Having said this, I do not wish for the perfect to become the enemy of the good in this case. True, *Cimarron* will never make my top twenty list; I would never argue that it is a great film. However, I do believe that if one can temporarily switch off one's modern political sensibilities—difficult to do, perhaps, in these hyper-politicized times—and take the movie on its own terms, it can be an effectively moving experience. Furthermore, from an artistic point of view and stripped of all politics, there is a grandeur to the story and an artistry to its cinematic realization, despite the flaws I've noted, that rightly garnered acclaim in its day. It remains a good movie. I do not believe the Academy or the contemporaneous critics erred; I simply believe that, in the intervening nine decades, time and society marched on, absorbing *Cimarron*'s noble ideals while moving beyond its less enlightened perspectives.

Cimarron was the last big-budget epic Western for a while; the impact of the Great Depression would soon make the scope of the typical American Western much more modest, while adult film audiences began gravitating toward other entertainments—particularly gangster movies—throughout the remainder of the 1930s. The genre as a whole began to stagnate in its ambitions, relying mostly on recycled plots and stale clichés, finding its vitality mainly in cheaply made Poverty Row B-pictures.

The Western had entered the doldrums.

Viva Villa!
(1934)
(Including an Interlude in Poverty Row)

April 10, 1934 (New York City)
USA / Mexico—English
Metro-Goldwyn-Mayer
115m—Mono—BW—1.37:1

Direction: Jack Conway, Howard Hawks (uncredited), William A. Wellman (uncredited)
Screenplay: Ben Hecht, Howard Hawks (uncredited), James Kevin McGuinness (uncredited), Howard Emmett Rogers (uncredited), Edgecumb Pinchon (book), O.B. Stade (book)
Principal Cast: Wallace Beery (Pancho Villa), Leo Carrillo (Sierra), Fay Wray (Teresa), Donald Cook (Don Felipe de Castillo), Stuart Erwin (Jonny Sykes), Henry B. Walthall (Francisco Madero), Joseph Schildkraut (Gen. Pascal), Katherine DeMille (Rosita Morales), George E. Stone (Emilio Chavito), Phillip Cooper (Pancho Villa as a Boy), David Durand (Bugle Boy), Frank Puglia (Pancho Villa's Father), Francis X. Bushman Jr. (Wallace Calloway), Adrian Rosley (Alphonso Mendoza), Henry Armetta (Alfredo Mendoza), Pedro Regas (Tomás), George Regas (Don Rodrigo)
Production: David O. Selznick
Cinematography: James Wong Howe, Charles G. Clarke
Editing: Robert Kern
Art Direction: Harry Oliver
Music: Herbert Stothart
Awards: Oscar—Best Assistant Director (John Waters), National Board of Review—Top Ten Films, Venice Film Festival—Best Actor (Wallace Beery), Venice Film Festival—Special Recommendation (Conway)
Nominations: Oscar—Best Picture, Oscar—Best Writing, Adaptation (Hecht), Oscar—Best Sound Recording (Douglas Shearer), Venice Film Festival—Best Foreign Film

As I write this, there has been a recent brouhaha in online circles: the great filmmaker Martin Scorsese has made some oral and written comments critical of the currently dominant Hollywood genre of superhero movies. Scorsese has likened comic-book movies to theme-park rides and criticized the Hollywood machinery for simply following tried-and-true formulas to make money rather than taking any artistic risks. It occurs to me that we have seen an analog to the superhero movie hegemony before, in the Poverty Row Western of all places! In each case, we have a subset of Hollywood dedicated to churning out a formulaic product on an assembly line—a popular product aiming to provide entertainment and escapism on an adolescent-fantasy level, following established formulas and avoiding risks, with no lofty artistic aspirations, and guaranteed to make money. True, the scale is completely different: Poverty Row Westerns were made on shoestring budgets, but reliably appearing as second features to draw in young audiences and making money due to their low overheads; whereas franchise comic-book features today are Big Business. It's a bit surprising, perhaps, to draw a connection between the lowest of low-budget B-movies during the Depression and the mega-budgeted, mega-marketed blockbusters of today, but in many ways they show two sides of the same phenomenon, one that has always been present whenever the interests of Art and Business are in tension, and Business wins out.

The eight-year stretch between *Cimarron* (1931) and *Stagecoach* (1939) was a bleak time for the serious Western. Just like far too many of today's Hollywood "creative" types, the makers of Westerns in the 1930s tended to rely on one of two things: simple, formulaic, crowd-pleasing plots aimed at providing audiences with escapist entertainment while making a quick buck; or remakes of earlier successes.

One of the best examples of the latter is from 1931, not long after *Cimarron*: Cecil B. DeMille's third filmed version, and first sound version, of his own 1914 landmark *The Squaw Man* (discussed earlier in this volume). The 1931 version features Warner Baxter in the lead role and a captivating Lupe Velez as the Indian savior Naturich. The film is not as strong as DeMille's original—the Hollywood slickness of production makes the scenes in England much more engaging but weakens the portrayal of life on the raw frontier, where the heart of the drama takes place. Nevertheless, the film has much to recommend it, especially Velez's heartbreaking performance. She seems just too glamorous (and impeccably made-up) for the part of this woman of Nature—minimizing the contrast between her and the "classically beautiful" Diana (Eleanor Boardman)—but her powerful portrayal of maternal anguish in the film's closing scenes is soul-crushing. The pitiful symbol of the crude toy horse that she carves for her child (who, significantly, spurns it for a fancy new train set) is used to devastating effect, and Naturich's eventual demise is all the more chilling as a premonition of Velez's own tragic suicide thirteen years later.

But by far the most common Westerns of the thirties were those which were much less ambitious: the B-Westerns. According to *The BFI Companion to the Western*, there were 1,073 Western features released during the 1930s, and of these, the book identifies only 44 as A-list films[1]—meaning that during the thirties, 96 percent of all Westerns were B-Westerns! There is no question that the so-called Poverty Row studios (Republic, Monogram, Lone Star, Grand National, et al.) knew how to turn out a product quickly, cheaply, and to crowd-pleasing effect. The best of these movies are simply fun—but ephemeral as well, virtually interchangeable diversions that, while providing audiences of the day brief escape from the worries of the Great Depression (and children of the day countless hours of entertainment), do not linger in the memory. As mentioned before, Johnny Mack Brown had a long string of these, as did others such as Tom Keene, Ken Maynard, Gene Autry, Roy Rogers, Buck Jones, Tex Ritter, and of course John Wayne. Some of Wayne's better B-movie efforts—filled with the Western equivalents of courtly damsels, knightly chivalry, ladies' tokens, loyal squires, and the like—come from the first half of the thirties; they include *The Man from Monterey* (1933), which, in keeping with its Arthurian forebears, even features a climactic swordfight; *Riders of Destiny* (1933); *The Lucky Texan* (1934); *Randy Rides Alone* (1934); and *The Trail Beyond* (1934).

Riders of Destiny features Wayne in his first "singing cowboy" role, mouthing along to a recording of a dubbed baritone, which, in Wayne's words, made him feel like "a god-damn pansy."[2] Wayne's threatened masculinity aside, this is actually quite an enjoyable film, one which also features Wayne's first pairing with Gabby Hayes. Most startlingly, it anticipates two iconic moments in later films: a bad guy delivers the line "I've made Denton an offer he can't refuse" nearly forty years before *The Godfather* (1972); and Wayne's character (actually stunt double Yakima Canutt) works his way underneath a runaway stagecoach, front to back, in a manner virtually identical to the famous stunt featuring Indiana Jones and a speeding Mercedes truck in *Raiders of the Lost Ark* (1981)! *Randy Rides Alone* features not only one of the most delightfully cheesy titles in the history of the genre, but also a surreal opening worthy of any acid Western, as Wayne's character rides toward a saloon from which emanates the sound of a pianist poorly playing Juventino Rosas's *Over the Waves* waltz. Upon entering, Wayne discovers an unmanned player piano droning on amidst a roomful of corpses!

Most 1930s B-Westerns deliberately emphasize the virtues of the two-fisted man of action. Poverty Row heroes are doers, not talkers. An early exchange between the weaselly Don Luis Gonzales (Donald Reed) and the heroine Dolores Castanares (Ruth Hall) in *The Man from Monterey* is illustrative:

> Luis: Dolores, there must be some way that I can make you believe that I love you, that life without you is not worth living.
> Dolores: Your speeches are delightful, Luis. If only your deeds were half as stirring and romantic, I might be tempted—but you never do anything!
> Luis (*angrily*): Oh, I see! You want a storybook hero, one you can dream about at night! One who will—
> Dolores: Well, what if I do? At least he will be a man of energy and ambition and will not waste all of his time talking!

Soon Dolores will meet the storybook Captain John Holmes (played by John Wayne), who will embody these ambitious, energetic traits. He and his counterparts set the tone for the heroic American male in the thirties Western. The Poverty Row films may not have been great, but they were seen by many, many children who adored them, and whose ideals of American masculinity were almost certainly shaped as a consequence, even as these Westerns themselves were being shaped by the ethos of the older generation making them. Westerns, like all modern art forms, are—among other things—vehicles for the transmission and amplification of evolving cultural values.

A great number of the B-Westerns were set in exactly or relatively contemporary times to those in which they were made, as if to reassure Americans that these heroic figures and noble quests still existed in the here and now. This accounts in part, I think, for their widespread appeal. To their credit, their portrayal of ideal masculinity was far less problematic than we might at first assume. Yes, their heroes were more physical than mental in their orientation, but they were also honest, courteous, modest, generous, and merciful to their enemies—in other words, they embodied the traditional knightly virtues. The B-Western hero was very likely to resort to fisticuffs, but—contrary to modern assumptions—he was not trigger-happy. In fact, it was the villains in these pictures who were far more likely to pull a gun; the heroes rarely killed anyone, relying far more frequently on the rule of law for the meting out of justice, and if they had to fire a weapon, it was most often (unrealistically, of course) to disarm their opponent. As corny and idealized as these white-hatted heroes may seem to our sensibilities today, the values they represented were largely positive ones; a society that lived up to their virtues (adjusting for our generally more enlightened views on, for example, race, gender, and civil rights) would not be a bad one in which to live.

In fact, the Poverty Row Westerns even contained socially and racially progressive elements on occasion, including a much greater respect paid toward Mexicans (and Hispanics in general), who were now more often viewed with affection and even idealized. There are echoes of *Don Quixote* in *The Man from Monterey*, for example—guitar music, serenades, beautiful girls tossing flowers, and a sidekick inevitably recalling Sancho Panza—and Captain Holmes becomes the beloved of the beautiful Mexican girl Dolores with no one's eyebrows raised. (Ruth Hall, who appeared with Wayne in several B-Westerns, was genuinely Hispanic herself—born Ruth Gloria Blasco Ibáñez.) Blacks and Native Americans still had a way to go in the Western, but at least the odious "oily Mexican" stereotype had been partially laid to rest.

Riding this wave of liberality toward Hispanics was MGM's 1934 A-movie *Viva Villa!* In this superbly crafted picture, Wallace Beery turns in one of the most extraordinary performances of his career as the Mexican bandit-turned-revolutionary Pancho Villa (1878–1923). One should not approach the film with any hope that it portrays history as it really happened; the creators themselves knew this, as evidenced by the accurate "Foreword" disclaimer at the beginning of the picture: "This saga of the Mexican hero, Pancho Villa, does not come out of the archives of history. It is fiction woven out of truth, and inspired by a love of the half-legendary Pancho and the glamorous country he served." Knowing from the very beginning that this narrative will be more legend than historical fact, we can relax and enjoy the movie on its own terms, and the most affecting part of it, without question, is its unflinching portrayal of its amoral protagonist—part heroic revolutionary, part uneducated and violent brute, just as Villa was in true life. By the film's end, authentic history may not have been served, but we have been presented with a powerful portrait, authentic in spirit if not in literal fact, of a human being both great and terrible—and we recognize parts of ourselves in him, at least dimly. As Terence wrote, "I am a human being; nothing human is alien to me." Villa stands in for all of us, complicated beings that we are, with our light and dark sides constantly in play, and our biological and cultural heritage of both civilization and savagery.

The movie begins when Pancho Villa is just a child. The Mexican aristocracy has stolen his father's land, along with the land of all the *peones* in the area. Villa's father protests, respectfully, and is subsequently whipped to death. Young Villa, without shedding a tear (on screen), soon stabs his father's killer and embarks upon a life of banditry. Our first introduction to Villa as an adult follows, and it is unforgettable. A group of aristocrats is subjecting six peon servants to a travesty of a trial. The effete judge, when asked if the names of the accused should at least be read into the record, says, "There is no need to clutter up proceedings of justice with trivial detail…. It has been proven to my satisfaction that these six servants are guilty of misdemeanors against the noble house of my friend Don Miguel. I pronounce you guilty. I sentence you to be hanged. I command that your miserable bodies be left hanging as a lesson to the *peones* of this district." This terrible sentence is carried out; but then Villa shows up with his band of outlaws, brings the bodies of the dead peasants into the courtroom and props them up to make a "jury," then proceeds to hold a mock trial of his own, the outcome of which is the gunning down of the aristocrats in cold blood, in Villa's stated ratio of two-to-one. We soon become acquainted with our own dark sides viewing this scene; as with other

The light and dark sides of revolution (and of us all): Francisco Madero (Henry B. Walthall) and Pancho Villa (Wallace Beery). *Viva Villa!* **(MGM, 1934).**

moments of explosive, vengeful violence in Westerns—the climaxes of *The Wild Bunch* (1969) and *Unforgiven* (1992), to name just two examples—it is disturbing to realize just how satisfying this rough justice is to behold. Our reptilian brains, we are reminded, do not lie all that deeply buried beneath the thin veneer of civilization.

Throughout the film, Beery as Villa continues to earn our sympathy and admiration, as well as our contempt and horror. He is fearless and passionate in his fight for the downtrodden peasants, and as loyal to his friends as he is ruthless to his enemies. He is also a brutal killer who is not above torturing a captured opponent to death or horsewhipping a woman (shown, as so many dark things in the picture, through shadows on the wall). In one particularly haunting scene, Villa orders that his most wicked adversary, the fictionalized Pascal (Joseph Schildkraut), be covered in honey and slowly devoured by ants—and we suddenly feel pity for this evil man whom we previously loathed. One of the great strengths of the film is that it never lets us rest comfortably in our sympathies; we never have the luxury of black-and-white ethical thinking, because this story has another, deeper purpose, forcing us to acknowledge and confront the hidden shadows buried in the murky depths of the human psyche. Villa is the beast that lies within each one of us, which is only kept under control—to the extent that it is—by culture and civilization.

In *Viva Villa!* the title character has many wives whom he has serially married along his travels, as was true of the authentic Villa, who had dozens of wives (claims run as high as seventy-five) with whom he fathered dozens of children. In the film, we watch Villa meet the beautiful Rosita (Katherine DeMille) early on and immediately offer to marry her; she accepts, and the wedding is on, to the surprise of the young journalist Jonny Sykes (Stuart Erwin), who will become Villa's (fictional) follower and biographer. "Holy suffering catfish," Sykes exclaims. "He's going to get married!" Villa's right-hand man Sierra (Leo Carrillo) responds, "That's what he like. He like to get married. He get married all the time." "That's the way I was brought up—religious!" Pancho explains. Sykes goes on to perform the wedding ceremony himself, saying: "And if there's anybody present who objects to these doings, let him speak up now and he will be buried with full military honors." But Villa moves beyond mere womanizing to a genuinely violent misogyny, as when he physically assaults Teresa (Fay Wray), the sister of a former ally, and prepares to sexually assault her as well, although this is interrupted. This scene, difficult as it is to watch, is also true to the real Villa's nature; for example, because of a personal vendetta the Villa of history attacked the small town of Namiquipa, then ordered his troops to throw the captured women in an animal pen and rape them before burning the town to the ground.

Although its title character is not painted quite this darkly, *Viva Villa!* is still a movie that could not have been released in the following year, after the Hays Code had been adopted. Villa's polygamy and womanizing are overt, as are his final intentions toward Teresa. The movie oozes a primitive, lusty sexuality throughout; for example, a young saloon girl in Juarez (Anita Gordiano) does a brazenly provocative dance—lifting up her skirt and caressing her own breasts—the likes of which would not appear again in Hollywood movies for decades to come.

Moreover, the film is surprisingly violent for its day, and brutality and iniquity often go unpunished, which the Hays Code would never allow. Yes, Villa himself will yield up his life before the end, but many others—such as his right hand, Sierra—will commit atrocities and escape without retribution. (Sierra's real-life inspiration, Rodolfo Fierro, was a vicious murderer known as "El Carnicero"—"The Butcher"—who died by falling into quicksand several years before Villa's death.) Even Villa's death in *Viva Villa!* is more of an apotheosis than a punishment; he dies completely unrepentant. The journalist Sykes comforts the mortally wounded revolutionary, shot to pieces:

VILLA: What a funny place to die, a butcher shop. Maybe you fix it up more better, huh?
SYKES: I'll fix it, kid.
VILLA: I hear about big men, what they say when they die. You write something pretty big about me.
SYKES: I'll write, uh, I'll write about how Pancho Villa died with a medal that had once been given him for the rescue of Mexico still around his neck!
VILLA: And the ring Mr. Madero give me, you write that too?
SYKES: I'll, I'll throw that in for good measure.
VILLA: What else, Jonny? I like to hear.
SYKES: Well, I'll, I'll ... the peons! "From near and far, from north and south, the peons who had loved him came to see him as he lay. They gathered in silence, a tattered multitude kneeling wretchedly in the streets, and then, once again, the thrilling strains of 'La Cucaracha' rang out on the night air."
VILLA: That's fine, Jonny. You tell me more.
SYKES: "Until Villa spoke for the last time. He said, he said ...."
VILLA: Hurry, Jonny! Jonny, what, what were my last words?
SYKES: "'Goodbye, my Mexico!' said Pancho Villa. 'Forgive me for my crimes. Remember, if I sinned against you, it was because I loved you too much.'"
VILLA: "Forgive me"? Jonny, what I done wrong?

This scene is likely a nod to a legend surrounding the real Villa's demise at the hands of assassins. One report said that his last words were, "Don't let it end like this. Tell them I said something"—although in truth, Villa almost certainly died instantly from a hail of bullets, no dying words spoken.

As cinematic art, *Viva Villa!* is one of the true high points in the long, dry stretch between the birth of the talkies and *Stagecoach.* Its production values,

Journalist Jonny Sykes (Stuart Erwin) composes his eulogy for the dying Villa (Wallace Beery). *Viva Villa!* (MGM, 1934).

including the magnificent photography, stand out in an era of low-budget quickie Westerns. Wallace Beery, at that time the highest-paid actor in the world, gives an astoundingly rich and complex portrayal of a historical figure who, although dead for just over a decade, had already entered the halls of legend. (The real Villa added to his own lore by appearing in several early Hollywood documentary features, including *Life of Villa,* which he himself produced in 1912; *The Life of General Villa,* 1914; *The Great Mexican War,* 1914; and *Following the Flag in Mexico,* 1916. The first two of these movies employed both genuine battle footage and recreations.)

Herbert Stothart's score for *Viva Villa!* is another superb element of the film and features one of the most winningly nuanced musical moments in the early talkies. When Pascal and his cronies are plotting against the angelic President Madero (Henry B. Walthall) at a fancy ball, the waltz being played in the background—from the middle of Johann Strauss's famous *On the Beautiful Blue Danube*—subtly shifts into minor mode, contrary to the score of the original piece.

Viva Villa! is a cold hard punch to the gut during an era of ethically simple, sanitized Western flicks. It shows the extent to which the mythologically subversive, iconoclastic character of the anti–Western was already waiting to burst into being, had the Hays Code not driven it underground for three more decades. In its day, *Viva Villa!* was a tantalizing hint of things to come, even if there would be some delay before its artistic progeny would finally be born.

I wonder whether today's audiences, though, are capable of taking *Viva Villa!* on its own terms, appreciating it for what it is—a gritty, psychological exploration of the darkness and light that live, for better or worse, within us all. In our current hyper-politicized environment, it seems like the movie would be disliked by the right for its pro-socialist idealism (embodied in the character of the real-life "Christ-fool" Francisco Madero) and called out by the "woke" left for its misogynist protagonist and its failure to include even one genuine Hispanic actor in its primary cast (a transgression that almost certainly, and rightly, would not happen today).

What a pity. What a squandered opportunity, if a film as accomplished and powerful as this were to be dismissed, and missed, simply on the basis of its lack of acceptable content to ideological purists on both the left and the right. Art has the capability of taking us beyond our self-assured pieties and speaking to us on a far deeper level than mere politics. The best art, in fact, is fully aware of the primacy of its aesthetic, human-centered, metaphorical power over any surface-level pedantic content. As Joyce articulated beautifully in *A Portrait of the Artist as a Young Man*, didactic art is just the mirror image of pornography, and both are vastly inferior to "proper art." May the apprehenders of the arts (including film) in our current, confused time rediscover the transcendent value of moving past politics, sanctimony, and didacticism in order to touch something far deeper and more fully human.

Ruggles of Red Gap
(1935)

February 19, 1935 (USA)
USA—English / French
Paramount Pictures
90m—Mono—BW—1.37:1

Direction: Leo McCarey
Screenplay: Walter DeLeon, Harlan Thompson, Humphrey Pearson, Harry Leon Wilson (novel)
Principal Cast: Charles Laughton (Ruggles), Mary Boland (Effie Floud), Charles Ruggles (Egbert Floud), Zasu Pitts (Mrs. Judson), Roland Young (Earl of Burnstead), Leila Hyams (Nell Kenner)
Production: Arthur Hornblow, Jr.
Cinematography: Alfred Gilks
Editing: Edward Dmytryk (uncredited)
Art Direction: Hans Dreier (uncredited), Robert Odell (uncredited)
Music: John Leipold (uncredited), Heinz Roemheld (uncredited)
Awards: National Board of Review—Top Ten Films, National Film Registry, New York Film Critics Circle—Best Actor (Laughton, shared with *Mutiny on the Bounty*)
Nominations: Oscar—Best Picture

The Western frontier is a wonderful place to put larger-than-life characters involved in mythic, heroic exploits. As it turns out, it is also a wonderful place to plunk down misfits for comic effect. During the silent era, many famous comedians took advantage of the possibilities of Western comedy, often playing fish out of water in outrageous circumstances. Buster Keaton's own favorite from his catalog was *Go West*, a 1925 silent about a hapless Midwesterner who tries to make his fortune in the West; and Will Rogers starred in around a dozen silent Western comedies from 1918 to 1927, one of the most charming being *Hustlin' Hank* (1923), in which Rogers plays a bumbling ranch hand who gets into a host of extraordinary situations during the film's mere twenty-four minutes.

It took the advent of sound, however, for the Western comedy to come fully into its own; visual humor, facial expressions, and body language were now enhanced by nuances of dialogue, vocal timbre, and timing to great comedic effect. The first outstanding example of the comic Western, far outstripping any of the silents and rarely equaled since, is the delightful *Ruggles of Red Gap* (1935). Like many of its silent predecessors, it is built around a central character who (at first) seems woefully out of place in the Wild West—in this case, the proper English manservant Marmaduke Ruggles, played wonderfully by the great Charles Laughton. The primary cast as a whole is top-notch, and the picture is helmed by Leo McCarey, one of the superb comedy

136

directors of his era—see, for example, *Duck Soup* (1933), *The Awful Truth* (1937), and *Going My Way* (1944).

Harry Leon Wilson's *Ruggles of Red Gap* was a bestselling novel in 1915 and had already been adapted twice during the silent era, first starring Taylor Holmes (1918) and then Edward Everett Horton (1923). But the role was tailor-made for Charles Laughton, who in the 1930s was at the peak of his career. (The National Board of Review's Top Ten List for the year 1935 included three Laughton films: *Ruggles of Red Gap, Mutiny on the Bounty*, and *Les Misérables*.) Among all of Laughton's movies, this was the one that he liked the best,[1] and for good reason.

The setup is simple: Ruggles is valet to the Earl of Burnstead (Roland Young), who loses him in a Parisian poker game to a Western *nouveau-riche* couple, the uncultured but genial Egbert Floud (Charles Ruggles) and his social-climbing wife Effie (Mary Boland). The Earl must then explain to Ruggles about his upcoming situation half a world away in the remote boomtown of Red Gap, Washington. The scene is a masterpiece of comic timing and understatement, as both characters discuss this shocking development with stereotypically British stiff upper lips, each almost but not quite managing to conceal his emotions—awkward embarrassment for the Earl, shocked horror for Ruggles. The Earl eases into the subject, recalling a Spanish dancer he once knew:

> EARL: Oh yes, I nearly chucked everything and went to ... went to America with her.
> RUGGLES: America would never do for you, milord.
> EARL: Well, I don't know, a lot of opportunities over there, you know, the right kind of fellow. I, um—(*plunging in*) You'll do very well for yourself there, I think, Ruggles.
> RUGGLES: Me, milord?
> EARL: Oh, yes, yes, I forgot to tell you. You're ... you're going out to America.
> RUGGLES (*containing his shock*): America, milord? (*with distaste*) A country of slavery.
> EARL: No, that's all finished, I believe. Some fellow called Pocahontas or something did something about it, or the other.
> RUGGLES: Indeed, milord. (*He gathers himself.*) Would it be North or South America, milord?
> EARL: Oh, oh, North, I think, yes. Somewhere on the West Coast, you know, Idaho or Omaha, one of those Indian places. Chap's a sort of a millionaire.
> RUGGLES: "Chap," milord?
> EARL: Yes, plenty of money, you know. Mines, lumber, domestic animals, and that sort of thing. Yes, the wife took quite a fancy to you, and, er, so they ... won you.
> RUGGLES (*fumbles a jar lid on the breakfast tray*): Ahem—"won me," milord?
> EARL: Oh yes. Yes, yes, we were playing this game of "drawing poker," you see, and it seems there's a thing called bluffing. Though I say it myself, I'm particularly good at it.
> RUGGLES: Do I understand—ahem—(*quavering slightly*) that I was the stake, milord?
> EARL: Oh yes, yes, rather, yes. Yes, you see, I didn't realize that they were bluffing too. I, er, I had three of the eights against a ... a flush of clubs. So, you really only lost by one eight.
> RUGGLES: Indeed, milord.
> EARL: Oh yes. I do hope you don't think that I didn't lose you gamely, as a gentleman should, Ruggles.
> RUGGLES (*nods politely*): North America, milord. Quite an untamed country, I understand.
> EARL: Yes, I expect so, yes.

And so Ruggles is off to his new home, where he will be surrounded by people with whom he has, on the surface, absolutely nothing in common.

One of the delightful things about *Ruggles of Red Gap* is that it manages to poke fun of everyone—stoic British aristocrats, *nouveaux riches*, untutored American yokels—and yet it does so with unfailing gentleness and affection for all of its characters. In one of the most memorable scenes of the film, Egbert, speaking with Ruggles in a saloon, refers to the Gettysburg Address, then realizes he can't recall it. He asks around, but neither the saloonkeeper nor any of the patrons know it. Then, to everyone's surprise, Ruggles himself begins to recite it, and the patrons slowly begin to gather around him, reverent and awestruck at Lincoln's stir-

The valet Ruggles (Charles Laughton) struggles to keep his stiff upper lip when learning that his employer, the Earl of Burnstead (Roland Young), has lost him in a poker game. *Ruggles of Red Gap* (Paramount, 1935).

ring words. Our hearts are moved by the looks on the faces of the grizzled old cowboys as they hear, as if for the first time, these words of freedom and higher purpose. The movie has teased these folks, along with Ruggles and Egbert, but lovingly; and thus, we respond empathetically to the barkeep when he buys everyone a drink, because we now want to sit down and have a beer with all of them.

As it turns out, this scene had great significance to Laughton, who yearned for American citizenship, eventually obtaining it in 1950. According to many reports, the actor kept becoming so emotional during the filming of the Address that it took over a day to record. Preview audiences actually chuckled at close-ups of Laughton's emotional rendering of the speech—not the effect the filmmakers were striving for—and so the scene was re-edited, focusing more on the reactions of Ruggles's scruffy but rapt listeners. The result is one of the most highly praised scenes in a highly praised picture. Laughton later called reading the Gettysburg Address for this scene "one of the most moving things that ever happened to me."[2]

Moving it is indeed, but lest anyone get the wrong idea, the vast majority of *Ruggles of Red Gap* is simply laugh-out-loud funny, one delirious scene after another. The comic timing is nearly perfect throughout, not surprising under the direction of McCarey, who just two years before had given us the Marx Brothers' most consistently funny escapade, *Duck Soup*. Hilarity abounds in *Ruggles*, but its lovable, stoically suffering protagonist keeps the movie centered; the touching moments only serve to increase our fondness for him and are never over-sentimental.

Another enjoyable aspect to the picture is the growing affection between Ruggles and Egbert. The gregarious, unpretentious Egbert takes to Ruggles right away, but unsurprisingly it takes a little while for Ruggles to reciprocate; when he does, however, the result is both charming and funny. There must be something archetypal about friendship between opposite types: whether Don Quixote and Sancho Panza, Robinson

Crusoe and Friday, Elizabeth Bennet and Charlotte Lucas, Huck and Tom, Holmes and Watson, Aubrey and Maturin, Kirk and Spock, or Harry and Hermione, some of the most enduring friendships in literature and film seem deliberately constructed to highlight the differences between complementary traits. There may be some real-world truth to this: while romance may best be served by a balance between similarities and differences, great friendships often seem to tolerate and even embrace widely contrasting

The old cowboys in the Silver Dollar Saloon are spellbound by the Gettysburg Address in a scene that Charles Laughton described as "one of the most moving things that ever happened to me." *Ruggles of Red Gap* (Paramount, 1935).

personality types. But perhaps, as readers and viewers, we also respond strongly to the friendship of opposites because, with apologies to Whitman, we *all* contain multitudes. The pairs listed above, as well as Ruggles and Egbert, can be seen to embody counterbalanced forces that we each have within us, even if one side of the coin is more evident to ourselves and to others. For example, personality models typically consider complementary characteristics like introversion and extroversion to be present in everyone, even if one or the other predominates. In this light, perhaps the union of opposite types in fictional friendships symbolizes the integration and harmonization of the varying and often contradictory parts of our own psyches.

The error of overthinking comedy has been committed countless times; alas, I have clearly added to that tally here. As E.B. White wrote, "Humor can be dissected, as a frog can, but the thing dies in the process and the innards are discouraging to any but the pure scientific mind."[3] Enough, then! Suffice it to say that, whatever its other virtues may be, *Ruggles of Red Gap* is above all a genuinely funny movie, brimming over with joy and great silliness. It set the stage for many films to come, showing the comic possibilities of the Western format while still, arguably, remaining the best of them all.

Following are just a few examples of comedic Western misfits over the years; the characters (and their films) vary widely, but they all owe a debt to *Ruggles*:

- Laurel and Hardy's delightful bumblers in *Way Out West* (1937);
- Jimmy Stewart's loquacious pacifist lawman in *Destry Rides Again* (1939);
- Jimmy Durante's highly-strung Easterner in *Melody Ranch* (1940);
- Gary Cooper's mild-mannered wanderer (mistaken for a bandit) in *Along Came Jones* (1945);
- Bob Hope's traveling dentist in *The Paleface* (1948), reprised by Don Knotts in *The Shakiest Gun in the West* (1968);

Great friends and charming people: Prunella Judson (Zasu Pitts), Marmaduke Ruggles (Charles Laughton), Egbert Floud (Charles Ruggles), and Ma Pettingill (Maude Eburne) brainstorm names for the valet's new business venture. *Ruggles of Red Gap* (Paramount, 1935).

- Jane Fonda's aspiring schoolteacher and Lee Marvin's inept gunslinger in *Cat Ballou* (1965);
- Dustin Hoffman's Zadig-like jack-of-all-trades in *Little Big Man* (1970);
- Jack Elam's down-and-out slob turned incompetent gunslinger in *Support Your Local Gunfighter* (1971);
- Cleavon Little's cool Black sheriff in *Blazing Saddles* (1974);
- Jack Nicholson's hapless outlaw in *Goin' South* (1978);
- Gene Wilder's naive rabbi in *The Frisco Kid* (1979);
- The title trio in *City Slickers* (1991);
- Evan Adams's nerdy Native American in *Smoke Signals* (1998).

The Plainsman
(1936)

November 16, 1936 (USA)
USA—English
Paramount Pictures
113m—Mono—BW—1.37:1

Direction: Cecil B. DeMille
Screenplay: Waldemar Young, Harold Lamb, Lynn Riggs, Grover Jones (uncredited), Jeanie MacPherson (material), Courtney Ryley Cooper (stories), Frank J. Wilstach (stories)
Principal Cast: Gary Cooper (Wild Bill Hickok), Jean Arthur (Calamity Jane), Charles Bickford (John Lattimer), James Ellison (Buffalo Bill Cody), Porter Hall (Jack McCall), Helen Burgess (Louisa Cody), Victor Varconi (Painted Horse), Fred Kohler (Jake), John Miljan (General George A. Custer), Paul Harvey (Yellow Hand)
Production: Cecil B. DeMille, William H. Pine (uncredited)
Cinematography: Victor Milner, George Robinson (uncredited)
Editing: Anne Bauchens
Art Direction: Hans Dreier, Roland Anderson
Music: George Antheil

Cecil B. DeMille's *The Plainsman* (1936) was an attempt to resurrect the epic Western using iconic figures from the Old West as focal points—Wild Bill Hickok, Calamity Jane, Buffalo Bill, and General Custer. Although uneven and overlong, the movie contains many gripping scenes and some compelling performances, especially from Gary Cooper in the lead role as Hickok and Helen Burgess as Louisa Cody, Buffalo Bill's new wife. *The Plainsman* combines and recombines various bits of fact, legend, and original story to present an intimate, interpersonal drama set within the sweeping context of grander historical events, as Western epics were wont to do. Inevitably, this meant that literal-minded critics would find fault with the movie for playing fast and loose with history.

Of course, there is nothing wrong *per se* with a film eschewing historical verisimilitude in the service of the drama. After all, most movies are stories; the goal of a Western is the creation of a powerful or artistic or entertaining fictional experience, not a documentary record of historical events. *The Plainsman* is honest about this from the start. Immediately after the credits, there is an image of tumbleweeds blowing in a sandstorm, followed by a printed disclaimer: "Among the men who thrust forward America's frontier were *Wild Bill Hickok* and *Buffalo Bill Cody*. The story that follows compresses many years, many lives, and widely separated events into one narrative—in an attempt to do justice to the courage of the plainsman of our West." The lie that tells the (larger) truth: the filmmakers were up-front and unapologetic about this, which is exactly right. *The*

Plainsman has certainly endured its share of criticism for its creative approach toward historical fact, but this is not fair either to the movie or to the reason why narrative films (and indeed, all fictional works) exist.

Despite its internal historical inaccuracy, *The Plainsman* is a piece of history in its own right, because it almost perfectly encapsulates the dilemmas, conflicting loyalties, and tensions of the mid–1930s Western—and, by extension, of mid–1930s America itself. Society was in a state of transition: opinions about race, gender, art, history, culture, religion, and violence were greatly in flux. It was difficult for the makers of Westerns to know just how to position their movies with regard to these things: most (like the filmmakers of Poverty Row) ran backwards to the comforts of established forms and formulas, while a few others took serious artistic risks, some of which, like those in *Viva Villa!* (1934), yielded rich results. But in general, when one watches a decent number of Westerns from the thirties, one feels like the filmmakers were not certain what to do with this genre that, up until recently, had been so successful. It clearly needed to evolve—but how?

So many of the ambiguities inherent in this situation are present within *The Plainsman*, resulting in a motion picture that is definitely uneven—trying to be too many things to too many people—and yet also engaging, for essentially the same reason. The contradictory tensions within *The Plainsman* generate contradictory outcomes: they contribute to the film's inconsistency while also providing it with a great deal of its energy and interest. Following are a few areas in which opposing tensions and ambiguities are particularly striking.

American expansion and the "Indian." The movie makes its overall stance toward Manifest Destiny clear from the very beginning. In the first scene, no less than Abraham Lincoln himself (played by Frank McGlynn Sr.) grants his blessing on the westward expansion in a conversation with members of his cabinet, recalling a similar Lincoln moment at the beginning of *The Iron Horse* (1924). As if that weren't valediction enough, Lincoln then excuses himself, explaining that he has promised to take Mary to a play at Ford's Theatre that evening. In other words, in *The Plainsman*'s universe, the primary importance of the settling of the West is literally Lincoln's last statement of policy before his assassination—his final words to his country, so to speak. As viewers, we now have Lincoln's comforting assurances on our side so that we may root wholeheartedly for the expansionists, George Antheil's stirringly patriotic score sealing the deal.

In general, the movie follows suit with its treatment of the natives, who are portrayed as stupid, savage brutes with little to redeem them. One scene strongly implies that a group of marauding Indians gang-rapes Calamity Jane (Jean Arthur); others show them fascinated by simple trinkets, baffled by mirrors, and gleefully torturing prisoners. Although, as was frequently the case in Westerns of this era, the ultimate villain is a traitorous white man (Lattimer, played by Charles Bickford) who sells guns to the Indians, the whites in the picture are generally blameless and even sanctified. General Custer (John Miljan) shines forth as an unsullied hero; he dies covered in glory, eyes ecstatically raised toward the heavens as he embraces the American flag—an image which would put even the tackiest of black velvet paintings to shame.

And yet America's views about its own past were becoming more complicated at the time of *The Plainsman*'s release, a fact perhaps tacitly acknowledged by the film itself in the degree to which it works so hard to justify its own propaganda (the Lincoln prelude, for example). But the film does make some concessions. For example, one of

Lincoln's cabinet members takes care to specify that the problem is "*hostile* Indians" rather than Indians as a totality (although we are never treated to an example of a non-adversarial Indian during the film). Our hero, Wild Bill Hickok (Cooper), is described as a friend of the Indian chief Yellow Hand (Paul Harvey); he speaks Yellow Hand's language and has respect for him, although he will kill him before the movie's end.

Extraordinary kitsch: General George Armstrong Custer (John Miljan) dies, beatified. *The Plainsman* (Paramount, 1936).

Perhaps the closest *The Plainsman* gets to a more fair-minded portrayal of Native Americans is in the scene where Hickok and Calamity Jane are prisoners in Yellow Hand's tepee; here the Chief is given a chance to explain his own point of view.

> HICKOK: What started you on the warpath, Yellow Hand?
> YELLOW HAND: Where sun rise, white man's land. Where sun set, Indian land. White man come, take our land, kill buffalo—our food. White man promise us food. White man lie. Now Cheyenne buy white man thunder-stick. Soon war drums sound in all Indian land. All tribes ride with Yellow Hand. We drive white man like buffalo, away, back to rising sun. Yellow Hand has spoken.
> HICKOK: Yellow Hand has spoken, and you may be right, but you can't drive the white man away.

The Plainsman is generally one-sided in its understanding of the battles between whites and Native Americans, but for this one brief moment we catch a glimpse of another perspective—acknowledging both the unfairness of the white man's coming triumph as well as its inevitability—that would express itself more fully in movies like *Broken Arrow* (1950), *Little Big Man* (1970), and *Dances with Wolves* (1990).

Women. There are only two significant female characters in *The Plainsman*, and they are polar opposites: the wild, reckless, sexually liberated tomboy Calamity Jane and the young wife of Buffalo Bill, Louisa Cody (played magnificently by Helen Burgess in her film debut), who is cultured, proper, and gentle. As it turns out, DeMille had to fight with the Production Code Administration to keep Jane's character as it was. They didn't like some of the lines in the script that accentuated her easy virtue, but DeMille argued the lines back in, saying: "Calamity Jane's virtues were her own. Her faults were those of her time. And since she was a real emancipated woman, she was truly natural."[1]

From the beginning it is clear that our hero Hickok scorns both of these women. Although Calamity Jane adores him, and he carries her picture in his pocket watch, he is nevertheless repulsed by her, constantly wiping off the kisses that she bestows upon him with some frequency throughout the movie. To Hickok, Jane is a woman of easy virtue, and his disapproval is palpable. It's a funny thing to see a character who is renowned for his ability to kill being prudish about sex; this bizarre acceptance of violence alongside a puritanical attitude toward sexuality is a long-standing tradition in Hollywood. (The most famous—or infamous—succinct summary of this strange cultural double standard was given by Jack Nicholson in a 1992 *Vanity Fair* interview. Commenting on the hypocrisy of the MPAA rating system, Nicholson said, "Kiss a tit, it's an X. Hack it off with a sword, PG.")[2]

Hickok also clearly disdains Jane's opposite, Buffalo Bill's wife Louisa; throughout the movie he mocks Buffalo Bill (James Ellison) for letting himself be civilized, to the point where it becomes genuinely grating. Yes, we get it—poor Bill has been emasculated by actually settling down with a fine, brave woman in a little windblown cabin in the Indian wilderness. It's never clear just what Hickok objects to about Louisa, other than that he feels his formerly wild friend is now becoming domesticated. (He actually isn't; Louisa is supportive of Buffalo Bill throughout his continuing adventures.)

All of this is a prime example of the longstanding, pervasive, ambivalent attitudes that the Hollywood Western would continue to exhibit toward women: with very few (refreshing) exceptions, Westerns during the first half of the genre's history didn't know what to do with female characters. These tended to fall into two types, paralleling the two represented here, and each one evoked contradictory reactions from the male stars and, presumably, many male audience members. On the one hand, there was the woman of easy virtue, the harlot, the dance-hall girl, always portrayed in a sexually provocative and enticing way. To her audience, both real and on screen, she was both exciting and frightening. Men were drawn to her independence, her grit, her brazen sexuality—and threatened by all of that as well. Running in counterpoint to that type, there was the civilized and civilizing woman, representing hearth and home. She was morally upright, decent, often the film's conscience—and usually forced to play the role of the nagging wet blanket who wants to keep our hero housebound and safe. She is the force that must be overcome for the adventure to move forward.

The dynamics of this are pretty easy to understand from a distance, since many heterosexual men of that era (and subsequent ones) were drawn to those elements in the female which also frightened them. They wanted a strong, independent spirit in a partner—but then were jealous of those qualities, wanting to reserve them for the adventurous male. They wanted their own sexual freedom and licentiousness, but also were judgmental toward the women who provided it. They craved the comforts and security of home, and simultaneously resented the women whom they felt restricted their freedom to roam. There may be no other American genre in the twentieth century that so clearly shows the conflicted views that most straight men held (and often still hold) toward women than that of the Western—and *The Plainsman* is a fine representative of this, though by no means the first or last that we will encounter in these pages.

What the film gets right is that, to a degree, it understands this dichotomy and its lead character's own awkwardness around it. This approach leads to one of the two most satisfying sequences of the movie, when Calamity Jane and Louisa Cody are left alone in Louisa's little house and begin to bond. At this moment *The Plainsman* begins to transcend the stale Western stereotypes of women by bringing both characters together, and a larger and more mythic understanding of the feminine begins to emerge, contained within the boundaries that each woman represents.

Religion. Another area in which Westerns were frequently ambivalent was religion. On the one hand, these were films made mainly by people raised in Judeo-Christian

A study in feminine contrasts: adventuress Calamity Jane (Jean Arthur) and homemaker Louisa Cody (Helen Burgess, in the stunning debut performance of her tragically short career). *The Plainsman* (Paramount, 1936).

traditions for Judeo-Christian audiences, and although Westerns were not afraid to call out false piety—witness the religious hypocrites in *Hell's Hinges* (1916), *Hell's Heroes* (1929), and *Cimarron* (1931), for example—the traditional religious virtues were still primarily upheld and celebrated, especially among the supporting characters. Yet the pacifist precepts and moral codes of Judeo-Christian ethics were pretty confining for the larger-than-life rugged individualists who served as Western heroes. They wandered freely, unbound by buttoned-up societal conventions, laws unto themselves, relying on no one else's help—even God's—and so there was automatically a tension between their adventurous natures and the dominant cultural norms of Christianity. This echoes an analogous tension in medieval Grail legends: why should the Grail knights seek their salvation by questing out in the world when the Church regularly offered (it was claimed) the literal body and blood of Christ through the Eucharist? The doctrine of *extra Ecclesiam nulla salus* ("no salvation outside the Church") was diametrically opposed to the worldly philosophy of the Grail legends, despite their quasi-ecclesiastical trappings. Both the chivalric romances and American Westerns, then, had an unspoken theme in common: most people needed to find their salvation within the respectable confines of organized religion, but the truly great heroes found their own way.

In *The Plainsman*, Louisa Cody (representing civilization and Christian practice) is surprised to learn that people in the West travel by stage on the Sabbath. "But tomorrow's Sunday! Do we ride on Sunday?" she asks Hickok. He laughs and replies, "Well, there's no Sunday west of Junction City, no law west of Hays City, and no God west of Carson City." The way Hickok says this, it is abundantly clear that he does not disapprove of this arrangement. Similarly, after Hickok is wounded in a shootout, Louisa tends his wounds, reluctantly at first—she refers to him as a murderer before relenting—and so we have yet another opportunity to see these conflicting viewpoints come into contact.

> HICKOK: I never was a murderer. I never did fight unless put upon.
> LOUISA: "Thou shalt not kill."
> HICKOK: No ghosts ever come bothering me. It was always the other man or me, in a fair fight.
> LOUISA: Well, what right have you to judge who is to live or to die? Put away your guns, Mr. Hickok.
> HICKOK: I can't do that, ma'am—not till I find John Lattimer.

To the film's great credit, it embraces the ambiguity here. We truly care about both of these characters; they are treated respectfully by the movie, and both actors wring a great deal of meaning out of these simple lines. We sympathize with (or at least understand) both viewpoints, and *The Plainsman* rightly lives there with us, amid the contradiction.

All mythologies, even secular ones, replace one "religion" with another, or at least place the new and the old side by side. In this case, the new religion is patriotism, even jingoism—Manifest Destiny is its central creed, and General George Armstrong Custer its preeminent saint and martyr. (In support of this, Antheil's score features patriotic tunes played in the style of, and with the solemnity of, church hymns.) Bookending the expansionist beginning of the movie is its equally "religious" ending. Hickok has died, and a shot of his body slowly dissolves into an image of "amber waves of grain" in the wind; martyred like Custer, Hickok has become the very land itself. Then we see a dreamlike image of Hickok and Custer riding side by side, carrying the American flag forward into history. The closing title card, slightly misquoting a passage from Algernon Charles Swinburne's poem "A Word for the Country," reads: "It shall be as it was in the past … / Not with dreams, but with strength and with courage, / Shall a nation be molded to last." (The British original had blood and iron in place of strength and courage.)

Guns. In traditional Westerns, including this one, the deadliest sin is providing the Indians with guns. While the right of whites to own and use guns, even for purposes of "frontier justice," is never questioned, only the most despicable characters would ever deal in arms with the natives. Guns are a part of civilization, and civilization is for whites only. (Tellingly, those who deal guns to the Indians are often described as "half-breeds," though that is not the case in *The Plainsman*.)

But there is one scene, early on, which again seems to swim in murky waters. After Lincoln's departure, a few gun manufacturers gather in a smoky room to discuss what happens next. The beginning of their conversation sets forth a pro-gun argument that would please even the staunchest member of the National Rifle Association; it actually prefigures some of the rhetoric that the NRA would use in later decades. But then the dialogue takes a sudden turn, and we realize that these men are the villains of the piece, willing to sell their guns to anyone as long as they can make a profit, no matter to what use the weaponry will be put.

> FIRST EXECUTIVE: But the war is over, and we have on our hands order after order cancelled by the government—hundreds of thousands of rifles unsold!

SECOND EXECUTIVE: Once we were the saviors of our country! Now we're outcasts, our money invested in an unsaleable product.

THIRD EXECUTIVE: But a good product, gentlemen. The new repeating rifle would have made short work of the war had it been introduced earlier. But now the subject of guns is an unpopular topic—for those who needed them so badly a short while ago. I'm afraid we'll have to look to Providence for a market.

FIRST EXECUTIVE: Providence, hah! Where?

THIRD EXECUTIVE: I've been told that the Indians hunt with bow and arrow. Still, they obtain furs, valuable buffalo hides, otter, fox, and beaver. With our new repeating rifle....

At this point the wicked Lattimer enters, ready to run guns to the Indians, and our plot is underway.

Here yet again we see the ambiguity of this conflicted picture. What is, on the one hand, a red-blooded, nakedly patriotic movie also shows American gun manufacturers as conniving crooks who manipulate history to their own pecuniary ends. Hickok, our protagonist, is known far and wide for his proficiency in killing with a gun, and yet we have no reason to believe that these corrupt moguls who are selling out their countrymen are not the same ones providing Hickok, Cody, and Custer with their instruments of salvation. After all, four major executives are shown in that scene; how many large gun companies were there in nineteenth-century America? Furthermore, the movie shows just how much undeserved power a gun puts in the hands of a coward, in this case Hickok's murderer Jack McCall (Porter Hall), who—as in true history—shoots Hickok from behind while the latter is engaged in a game of poker. Hickok became a legend, dying over his "dead man's hand" of aces and eights, but cowards continued (and continue) to slay better people than themselves with the twitch of a finger.

Although *The Plainsman* aims for epic, its best moments are intimate ones: the aforementioned conversation between Calamity Jane and Louisa Cody, and a wonderful scene between the two Bills when Cody has been assigned to track down Hickok after the latter has gunned down three traitorous Union officers. The two old friends sit down in the woods and have coffee together—and yet the tension between them is palpable. Both actors play the nuances of this complex moment perfectly, and the result is gripping. The events of the narrative keep the potential of this exchange from being fully realized, but it brings the characters of both men sharply into focus and lends genuine weight to the drama.

Moments like this make *The Plainsman* a fulfilling experience, despite its flaws. It is indeed overlong; it is indeed uneven; it is indeed uncomfortably jingoistic, and unenlightened in its views of Native Americans. The dialogue is stilted, as is often the case in DeMille pictures. (Howard Hawks once reportedly asked Cooper, "How in the hell can you read those goddamned DeMille lines?" Cooper replied, "Well, when DeMille finishes talking to you, they don't seem so bad. But when you see the picture, you kind of hang your head.")[3] The use of rear projection, so obvious and artificial-looking to us today, detracts from the excitement of the action sequences, as it would do in countless Hollywood adventures to come, even great ones as late as *North by Northwest* (1959) or *Goldfinger* (1964)—yet another contradiction, calling to our attention the abundant use of the studio in these epics purportedly unfolding in the great outdoors.

Yet the movie is redeemed by its unapologetic embrace of its own ambiguities; by the spectacularly good acting of Gary Cooper and Helen Burgess; by a number of scenes

that are viscerally grip-
ping and exciting; and by
its personification of the
contradictions that were
so abundant at that time,
both in Westerns and in the
country as a whole.

Tidbits and Trivia

- The opening credits
of *The Plainsman*
appear as a crawl
moving from the
bottom of the screen
upward, receding
toward a vanishing
point—a technique
familiar to viewers

Two old friends, Buffalo Bill (James Ellison) and Wild Bill
Hickok (Gary Cooper), regard each other warily in the film's
best scene. *The Plainsman* (Paramount, 1936).

of the *Star Wars* franchise. George Lucas has famously explained his title crawl
as an homage to the *Buck Rogers* and *Flash Gordon* serials, but *The Plainsman*
predates the first appearance of the "receding scroll" in either of these (1939)
by three years, as it does the next DeMille Western *Union Pacific* (1939), whose
similar crawl was cited by Lucas's title designer Dan Perri as an inspiration. Is it
possible that *The Plainsman* actually features the earliest filmed version of this
effect?
- George Antheil (1900–1959), who wrote the score for *The Plainsman*, was an
American *avant-garde* composer perhaps best remembered for his *Ballet
Mécanique*, featuring a battery of mechanical pianos as well as a siren and
airplane propellers in the orchestra. In the mid–1930s, Antheil began composing
music for Hollywood movies, beginning with 1935's *Once in a Blue Moon*. (He
had also written a score for *The Scoundrel* that same year, but it was rejected.)
Little survives of Antheil's Futurist and Dadaist roots in his film music.
- The story of Helen Burgess is a tragic one. After making such a strong debut in
The Plainsman, she acted in two other movies (to be released in 1937) and was
at work on another. Then, in early 1937, Burgess eloped with a piano teacher,
had the marriage annulled seven weeks later, and soon after that developed
lobar pneumonia. She died in April of 1937, just months after the release of
The Plainsman and just weeks before her twenty-first birthday. Watching her
outstanding performance in *The Plainsman*, one can only wonder at what might
have been.

Jesse James
(1939)

AKA: *Darryl F. Zanuck's Production of Jesse James*
January 14, 1939 (New York City)
USA—English
Twentieth Century–Fox
106m—Mono—Technicolor—1.37:1

Direction: Henry King, Irving Cummings (uncredited)
Screenplay: Nunnally Johnson, Gene Fowler (uncredited), Curtis Kenyon (uncredited), Hal Long (uncredited)
Principal Cast: Tyrone Power (Jesse James), Henry Fonda (Frank James), Nancy Kelly (Zerelda, aka Zee), Randolph Scott (Will Wright), Henry Hull (Major Rufus Cobb), Slim Summerville (Jailer), J. Edward Bromberg (Mr. Runyan), John Carradine (Bob Ford), Brian Donlevy (Barshee), Donald Meek (McCoy), Johnny Russell (Jesse James, Jr.), Jane Darwell (Mrs. Samuels)
Production: Darryl F. Zanuck
Cinematography: George Barnes, W. Howard Greene
Editing: Barbara McLean
Art Direction: William S. Darling, George Dudley
Music: Cyril J. Mockridge (uncredited), Alfred Newman (uncredited), Louis Silvers (uncredited)

The last important pre–*Stagecoach* Western was Henry King's *Jesse James*, released in January of 1939; it would become one of the most popular movies of that incredible year, with greater domestic box-office receipts than any 1939 movie except for *Gone with the Wind*, *The Wizard of Oz*, and *Mr. Smith Goes to Washington*.[1] The 1930s had been hard on the quality of the Western movie genre, despite a few bright spots—the films discussed earlier, as well as crossover gems such as the musical quasi-Western *Rose-Marie* (1936) and the Laurel and Hardy comedy *Way Out West* (1937). There were a handful of good but not extraordinary remakes—*The Squaw Man* (1931) and *Three Godfathers* (1936), for example—and of course the modestly resourced but prolific machinery of Poverty Row continued to hum along. Overall, though, it seemed like the sunset of the artistically ambitious A-list Western picture had arrived.

But then, in the *annus mirabilis* of 1939, something extraordinary happened. (In fact, *everything* extraordinary happened in American film, but that's an entirely different book.) For reasons not entirely clear, the big studios began releasing major Westerns. The best explanation I have found for this comes from William Indick:

> It is often claimed that *Stagecoach* reinvigorated the genre single-handedly, though this is clearly not the case. Multiple A-list Westerns came out that year that as a group, reestablished the Western film as a marquee headliner, rather than as a perennial second bill tacked on for

the kids. A better explanation for the revival is that one studio decided to make a big-budget Western, and the other studios, always interested in blocking the other studios' moves, decided to offer competing big-budget Westerns in their theater chains, resulting in a bandwagon effect in which every Hollywood studio entered an A-list Western into the competing market.[2]

This certainly rings true, given the major Westerns released by most of the big studios that year. MGM and Columbia didn't have any big-budget Westerns in the offing, but of course they were about to release, between them, the three biggest moneymakers of the year: *Gone with the Wind* and *The Wizard of Oz* for MGM, and *Mr. Smith Goes to Washington* for Columbia. But six other big studios were going all-in on the Western in 1939: Fox (*Jesse James*), Paramount (*Union Pacific*), RKO (*Allegheny Uprising*), Walter Wanger and United Artists (*Stagecoach*), Universal (*Destry Rides Again*), and Warner Brothers (*Dodge City*). Of these, *Jesse James* deserves a large portion of the credit for resuscitating the Western movie: after all, it was the most popular representative of the genre during the year which brought about its rebirth.

There are certainly many reasons to like *Jesse James,* but it's not hard to imagine that what really connected with audiences was the film's particular perspective on its outlaw heroes and, in this telling, the predatory fat cats that drove them to a life of crime. After all, Depression-era audiences were not overfond of bankers and business tycoons. Gone was the lionizing of the great railroads pushing ever westward, as we saw in *The Iron Horse* (1924) and other early Westerns. Instead, the railroads here are greedy land-grabbers, bilking the honest struggling farmers out of their livelihoods, and audiences of the day must have felt a certain vicarious, cathartic thrill in seeing the James Gang fight back against these ruthless tycoons and racketeers.

The film sets this new subversive tone with its opening titles: "After the tragic war between the states, America turned to the winning of the West. The symbol of this era was the building of the trans-continental railroads. The advance of the railroads was, in some cases, predatory and unscrupulous. Whole communities found themselves victimized by an ever-growing ogre—the Iron Horse." How things have changed since John Ford's rendering of the Golden Spike! This theme pervades the movie consistently. When Jesse (Tyrone Power) and his beloved Zee (Nancy Kelly) interrupt a church service and ask the preacher (Spencer Charters) to marry them, the startled officiant is even more astonished when he learns Jesse's identity. "We don't want no trouble," Jesse says.

> MINISTER: Trouble? Why, son, you're as welcome as rain to the flowers. Do you realize, boy, that I had a farm giving nine hundred bushels of corn, until that railroad had taken it from me? Why, I'd given up preaching and was making an honest living off the land, until that dag-swinged railroad swindled me out of my own home!
> PARISHIONER (*offscreen*): Well, that's true, Mr. James!
> MINISTER: By golly, son, do you know, I had a big house, two barns, three outhouses, until that gol-danged railroad hornswoggled me!
> PARISHIONERS: Amen. Amen.

Note the sly dig at organized religion here, delivered by the preacher himself. This is consistent with the movie's irreverence; for example, during the train robbery scene the outlaws move up and down the aisle bowing and saying *Thank you, brother* and the like as the frightened passengers put their items in the bag—mimicking the passing of the plate at a church service.

Our killer outlaw has now been blessed by the church's representative (however tainted), and at the end of the film he receives a post-humous benediction from the press as well, as the journalist Rufus Cobb (Henry Hull) delivers a eulogy over Jesse's grave.

An atypical wedding: Zee (Nancy Kelly), Jesse (Tyrone Power), and Frank (Henry Fonda) listen as the preacher (Spencer Charters) blesses them for standing up to the railroads. *Jesse James* (Twentieth Century–Fox, 1939).

> There ain't no question about it: Jesse was an out-law, a bandit, a criminal. Even those that loved him ain't got no answer to that. But we ain't ashamed of him! I don't know why, but I don't think even America is ashamed of Jesse James. Maybe it's because he was bold and lawless, like we all of us like to be some-times. Maybe it's because we understand a little that he wasn't altogether to blame for what his times made him. Maybe it's because for ten years he licked the tar out of five states! Or maybe it's because he was so good at what he was doin'. I don't know. All I do know is, he was one of the dog-gonedest gol-dingedest dad-blamedest buckaroos that ever rode across these United States of America!

From the beginning to the end of the movie, Jesse James and his gang are portrayed as heroic outlaws, stealing only from predatory capitalists. During the train robbery, Jesse is careful to remind the passengers that they need to sue the railroad to get compensated for their losses, thus absolving him from any guilt about robbing ordinary folks. Here we have a Robin Hood and his Merry Men set down in the Old West. This Romanticism is only enhanced by the lyrical, and often gorgeous, Technicolor photography.

In keeping with this approach, the true history of the James Gang was ignored or whitewashed within the film, which earned it a decent amount of criticism even at the time. The real Jesse James didn't learn to be a killer when the evil railroads descended upon his family; as a one-time member of the Confederate guerrilla band Quantrill's Raiders, he is thought to have already participated in the infamous massacre that took place in the abolitionist town of Lawrence, Kansas, well before his outlaw days began. Likewise, there is no reason to believe that economic justice had anything directly to do with the workings of the James Gang after the Civil War. But that's as may be. We look, or should look, to narrative films for meaningful stories and aesthetic experiences, not for historical insights, and here the movie acquits itself well. It's no masterpiece, but it's still a cracking good tale, and would be so even if it were completely fictionalized, with all the names changed.

One important area that *Jesse James* explores is the question of whether a person can be an outlaw or a killer—even if "justified"—and not lose his humanity. (Here, as in more recent films on the same theme such as *Casino Royale*, 2006, the fact that the lead character is already an iconic cultural figure does add to the impact.) As it digs deeper, *Jesse James* adds more nuance to its initial idealization of its Merry Men outlaws. Jesse is frequently compared to an animal—often a wolf—and the movie reinforces this in one of its most compelling images: the extraordinary tracking shot featuring a silhouette of Jesse, crouched and animalistic against the violet night sky, scampering across the top of a moving train while the civilized passengers sit unaware, bathed in orange light, beneath him. This image is directly echoed in its composition later on, when Jesse is escaping from his hunters; wounded, he hides in the water at the edge of a river, underneath a thick tangle of limbs, while one of his pursuers creeps and slouches overhead.

The heartbreaking culmination of the animal imagery is when Zee has just given birth to Jesse's son in his absence and confides her horror about Jesse's devolution to the sympathetic lawman Will (Randolph Scott). "We live like animals, scared animals," she says, then continues: "Jesse'll be an outlaw as long as he lives. I know it now. He's wild, Will. He's like a horse you can't break. He's crazy with wildness and there's nothing either you, or me, or him, or anybody else can do about it!" Zee has lost all hope, and in her anguish confesses to Will that she even prayed for her own death as well as that of her baby's. It's a bitter, hopeless scene whose imagery is echoed later, after the Northfield raid, when Will says to Zee, "He ain't a knight anymore fightin' a bad railroad; he's a wild animal." But contrary to Zee's, and Will's, expectations, Jesse does manage to rise above his animal nature; he returns, after five years, to his family, beholds his young son and namesake, is embraced by his loving wife, and gives up his outlaw ways.

However, all Jesse James stories are tragedies, as was the true history: Jesse cannot escape his past and is destined to be gunned down for the reward money by the Judas within his gang, the most infamous traitor in Western lore. Like Wild Bill before him, Jesse James will die shot from behind, done in by a coward. There is a mythic truth here, as old as Achilles being slain by Paris's arrow: even the strongest among us are still vulnerable to the deceits of the schemers, who often deliver devastating blows without ever confronting their adversaries face-to-face. The movie underscores this point by upping the ante on Bob Ford's cowardice, making his treachery responsible not only for Jesse's death (which it was in real life) but also for the Northfield disaster (which it wasn't).

The most gripping parts of *Jesse James* are the breathtakingly filmed action scenes: the train robbery twenty minutes into the movie and the Northfield raid twenty minutes before its end. Movies about the James Gang often make a great deal of dramatic hay out of the Northfield debacle—*The Great Northfield Minnesota Raid* (1972) and *The Long Riders* (1980) provide two particularly gut-wrenching examples—but the pattern for them all was set here. From the first gunshot to the last, the footage of James's band being cut to pieces lasts for only about a minute of screen time, but it seems excruciatingly long;

Jesse prowls, lupine, along the top of the train. *Jesse James* (Twentieth Century–Fox, 1939).

we flinch from the cannonade of shots, agonize when every way out of the town seems to be blocked, and finally start breathing again when the two James brothers crash their way through to the open gallop and eventual freedom. It is a masterful scene, as is the train heist, and it is startling to realize that these two bookends to Jesse's outlawry (as told in the film) are actually the only two robberies shown on screen in the entire movie apart from a couple brief images in a montage sequence.

The great Henry Fonda as Frank James. *Jesse James* (Twentieth Century–Fox, 1939).

The other great asset to the film is the phenomenal performance of rising star Henry Fonda as Frank James. He is a force of nature from the moment he first appears, and in fact this is paradoxically one of the movie's greatest weaknesses as well: in any scene with Fonda, he blows the other actors off the screen. Just watch the sequence where Frank confronts Jesse in the cabin and notice the difference between the two actors. For me at least, it's impossible to watch *Jesse James* without wishing that the brothers' players had been reversed, with the meatier role going to Fonda, who is frankly far more compelling than Tyrone Power in this picture. (Contemporary audiences were drawn to Fonda's performance as well, no doubt a primary reason why Fox immediately began work on a sequel, *The Return of Frank James*, released the following year and featuring Fonda in the lead.) If only the other actors in the movie were able to match Fonda's dark intensity. Nancy Kelly is fine and even touching, and Randolph Scott does a solid job playing the compassionate lawman, but Henry Hull's jaw-droppingly overacted Rufus Cobb is virtually unwatchable and comes close to wrecking every scene in which the character appears. Hull's over-the-top portrayal of the grating geezer makes one long for the sophisticated nuance of a Gabby Hayes!

Tidbits and Trivia

- This is the movie that would jumpstart the American Humane Association's monitoring of movie sets for animal welfare, because of the sequence where two horses fall off a cliff and into the water. Accounts vary about the outcome of this; some say that one horse was killed in filming the scene, others claim that both were, and still others neither one. But whatever the fate of these two animals, Hollywood from this point forward would have to take more care to avoid animal cruelty. (Horses in early Westerns had it particularly bad. One of the most notorious practices, invented by stuntman Yakima Canutt, was the use of the so-called Running W, a wire contraption that would trip a horse in order to simulate the horse being felled in a battle by gunfire. Often this resulted in the crippling or outright death of the animal.)

- John Carradine plays Bob Ford in the picture; his sons David, Keith, and Robert would play the Younger brothers (allies of Jesse and Frank in the Northfield raid) in *The Long Riders* four decades later.
- Jesse's headstone at the end of the film is pretty accurate. In fact, James's mother (still alive at his death, contrary to the movie) wrote his actual epitaph: "In Loving Memory of my Beloved Son, Murdered by a Traitor and Coward Whose Name is not Worthy to Appear Here."

Boundary lines are always artificial. I have chosen to consider the Golden Age of Westerns to have begun with *Stagecoach*, released just three weeks after *Jesse James*— after all, *Stagecoach* is the one that truly paved the way, setting the tone for what was to come in the American Western and featuring the historic first pairing of John Ford as director and John Wayne as leading man. It makes a convenient milestone. But the same culture at the same time created both *Stagecoach* and *Jesse James*. In truth they are both part of a surge of renewed vitality in the Western genre, and in many ways, it is a shame that *Jesse James* has been so overshadowed by its near contemporary. The movie is a Janus figure, standing at the threshold of a new era and looking both forward and backward. It was the last American Western to be both made and received by an audience without the experience of *Stagecoach*; and yet its approach also anticipated things yet to come, including many stories about outlaws that would owe it a debt. I present it here as a worthy conclusion to an era, but—save for the historical accident of three weeks—it would be equally at home in the Golden Age. Human beings place dividing lines in history to try and make sense of it all; but the river of art flows, unbounded.

PART THREE

The Golden Age

Stagecoach
(1939)

February 10, 1939 (Miami)
USA—English / Spanish / French
Walter Wanger Productions
96m—Mono—BW—1.37:1

Direction: John Ford
Screenplay: Dudley Nichols, Ernest Haycox (story "Stage to Lordsburg"), Ben Hecht (uncredited)
Principal Cast: Claire Trevor (Dallas), John Wayne (Ringo Kid), Andy Devine (Buck), John Carradine (Hatfield), Thomas Mitchell (Doc Boone), Louise Platt (Lucy Mallory), George Bancroft (Curley), Donald Meek (Peacock), Berton Churchill (Gatewood), Tim Holt (Lieutenant)
Production: John Ford (uncredited)
Cinematography: Bert Glennon
Editing: Otho Lovering, Dorothy Spencer, Walter Reynolds (uncredited)
Art Direction: Alexander Toluboff
Music: Gerard Carbonara (uncredited), Richard Hageman, W. Franke Harling, Louis Gruenberg, John Leipold, Leo Shuken
Awards: Oscar—Best Actor in a Supporting Role (Mitchell), Oscar—Best Music, Scoring (Hageman, Harling, Leipold, Shuken), National Board of Review—Top Ten Films, National Board of Review—Best Acting (Mitchell), National Film Registry, New York Film Critics Circle—Best Director (Ford)
Nominations: Oscar—Best Picture, Oscar—Best Director (Ford), Oscar—Best Black-and-White Cinematography (Glennon), Oscar—Best Art Direction (Toluboff), Oscar—Best Film Editing (Lovering, Spencer)

In the dusty Western town of Tonto, eight individuals from different walks of life prepare to board a stagecoach bound for Lordsburg; they will soon be joined along the way by a crucial ninth person. Each character seems at first like a simple stereotype lifted from a Poverty Row Western, but no one is as straightforward as that. Most will reveal unexpected depths and complexities before the journey is done. Rote B-movie stock characters have been transformed into genuinely powerful—and genuinely American—archetypes. Even the terrain looks new, like nothing we've seen before—vast, wide open, mythic. The result is *the* pivotal moment in the history of the Western, the moment at which the genre showed that it could move beyond the mere re-clothing of European knights-errant in the garb of the Old West and instead emerge as a fully adult, fully *American* mythology.

As is true of most American art forms, the Western movie's early history clearly shows the influence of its Old World forebears. Just as American concert music needed its Charles Ives to begin shaking off the weighty burden of its European inheritance;

**The first of many times John Ford would use the epic grandeur of Monument Valley to prop-
erly frame his artistic vision. *Stagecoach* (Walter Wanger, 1939).**

just as American poetry needed its Whitman and Dickinson; just as American visual
art needed its Hudson River School—so too did the American Western need *Stagecoach*
(1939). This essential, transformational movie underscores the cry for artistic independence issued by Ralph Waldo Emerson a century earlier in "Self-Reliance":

> Our houses are built with foreign taste; our shelves are garnished with foreign ornaments;
> our opinions, our tastes, our faculties, lean, and follow the Past and the Distant.... And why
> need we copy the Doric or the Gothic model? Beauty, convenience, grandeur of thought and
> quaint expression are as near to us as to any, and if the American artist will study with hope
> and love the precise thing to be done by him, considering the climate, the soil, the length of
> the day, the wants of the people, the habit and form of the government, he will create a house
> in which all these will find themselves fitted, and taste and sentiment will be satisfied also.[1]

Seen in this light, *Stagecoach* feels like the start of something fresh, a genre beginning
to distinguish itself from its worthy predecessors, to fit itself to a new world and a new
time, to make its own way.

Our nine stagecoach passengers will have to make their own way as well, through a
vast, unfamiliar, impersonal, unknowable frontier represented perfectly by the magnificent Monument Valley landscapes that Ford chooses for the backdrop to his drama. The
travelers, in order of appearance, are:

- Buck (Andy Devine), the good-natured, comical simpleton who will drive the
  stagecoach;

- Lucy Mallory (Louise Platt), the upper-class pregnant wife of a cavalry officer, whom she hopes to rejoin at the end of her journey;
- Peacock (Donald Meek), a soft-spoken whiskey salesman;
- Hatfield (John Carradine), a sly, aristocratic Southern gambler;
- Curley (George Bancroft), a gruff but honorable marshal riding shotgun on the trip;
- Gatewood (Berton Churchill), a pompous banker escaping town with a valise full of embezzled funds;
- Dallas (Claire Trevor), a good-hearted prostitute whom the holier-than-thou ladies of the "Law and Order League" are running out of town;
- Doc Boone (Thomas Mitchell), an alcoholic physician who is similarly being run out of his practice; and finally,
- The Ringo Kid (John Wayne), an escaped prisoner who meets up with the stagecoach en route, pursuing a vendetta against the men who framed him and murdered his father and brother.

The movie takes twenty of its ninety-six minutes to introduce these characters, one by one, and none of it is time wasted. We need to get to know each one, at least a little bit, at the beginning; we will then learn more as the person's journey, through both geographical space and individual story arc, proceeds. These characters work as archetypes, representing elements within the psychology of all of us, but at the same time they are also three-dimensional and believable human beings.

It is fascinating how the characters counterbalance and play off against each other, both in dyads and triads. In one sense the movie is very much about class, and here the group divides very neatly into thirds: the "aristocrats" (Hatfield, Gatewood, and Lucy Mallory); the "decent working men" (Peacock, Curley, and Buck); and the disgraced "outcasts" (Ringo, Dallas, and Doc Boone). But there are also very interesting dynamics that develop between some of the pairs of characters: the alcoholic doctor and the whiskey peddler; the respectable officer's wife and the "whore with a heart of gold"; Lucy and Hatfield; Doc Boone and Dallas; and, of course, the relationship between Dallas and Ringo.

The film centers around a journey, which is naturally one both geographical and metaphorical. For six of the nine travelers—the "aristocrats" and the "outcasts"—this short trip will transform their lives; each has an interior journey to undergo as well as the exterior one. The proud will be humbled, and the humbled will be exalted. And although our three straightforward working men—Curley, Buck, and Peacock—may emerge less obviously transformed by the adventure, they nevertheless serve as catalysts for the dramatic arcs of the other characters. Whatever the final outcome, everyone's story evolves in stages, from one stop to the next along the route.

Point of Departure: Tonto

The setting in Tonto serves, of course, to place all of the main characters on the board, with the exception of Ringo. It also sets the humanist tone of the movie from the very beginning. Ford's movies tend to delight in providing refreshing slaps in the face to false piety, hypocrisy, and priggishness, and *Stagecoach* is no exception—in fact, it might be the prime example. We immediately loathe the smugly sanctimonious old biddies who run Dallas out of town—"There are worse things than Apaches," Dallas says aptly, eying them through the stagecoach window—and the moment we first fall in love with Doc Brown is when we watch the reactions of the "Law and Order League" crones to the doctor's "Farewell, ladies!" and his (offscreen) obscene gesture. (We experience the gesture through their reactions, which are priceless.)

These opening moments also provide us with a chance to meet the haughty Lucy Mallory, and to observe class-conscious gambler Hatfield's aesthetic arrest as he first beholds her. We encounter the duplicitous banker Gatewood, hastening out of town with his stolen loot, but without losing one shred of his self-righteous pomposity. ("And remember this: what's good for the banks is good for the country!") These five people, plus the Ringo Kid still to come, serve as the crux of the story, and they are handled expertly by Ford from the start. In the opening minutes of the film, it is already clear that we are in the hands of a master cinematic storyteller.

Ringo himself arrives eighteen minutes into the picture—and so does John Wayne, forever. The director treats this moment with an absolutely mythic flourish, as if already aware of its historic significance. But how could Ford have possibly known that this was the turning point, the true grand entrance of the most enduring icon in the history of the Western movie? And what an entrance it is! The stagecoach is proceeding along the trail when, without warning, we hear a gunshot, and a voice cries, "Hold it!" The stage pulls to a halt; even the soundtrack music stops. There he stands, John Wayne, holding a saddle in one hand and twirling a rifle in the other, the craggy landscape of Monument Valley framing him in the background. The camera closes in and sharpens on Wayne's face—piercing eyes, sweat trickling from his brow—and something has just permanently changed.

Whether knowingly prescient or not, this moment serves as an allegory for the impact of the film itself. The titular vehicle, like the 1930s Western up to that point, rolls along its well-worn path, until suddenly, with a literal bang, everything jolts to a halt. Wayne's cry of "Hold it!" is directed at both the stagecoach of the narrative and the genre as a whole. John Ford has returned home to the Western after thirteen years, and John Wayne

The transformative moment: John Wayne arrives as the Ringo Kid, and as the greatest icon of the American Western. *Stagecoach* (Walter Wanger, 1939).

is back in an A-list starring role after nine—this time to stay. The genre's greatest director and its greatest leading man have come together at last. From this moment onward, everything will be different.

First Stop: Dry Fork

My favorite scene in the movie occurs when our pilgrims stop off at an establishment in Dry Fork and take a little refreshment while they debate whether they should risk Indian attack by pressing on with their journey or simply head back for Tonto. Dallas, who has been self-consciously aware of her own low status in the eyes of her fellow travelers, sits off against the wall rather than joining the others at the table. Meanwhile, Curley insists that the group's difficult decision be made democratically. Chivalrously, he turns first to Lucy for her vote, saying, "I ain't gonna put a lady in danger without she votes for it." After Lucy insists on going on, Curley then turns to Peacock to ask him for his vote. "Where's your manners, Curley?" Ringo interrupts. "Ain't you gonna ask the other lady first?" Dallas is surprised at this humane treatment from Ringo; she looks at him wonderingly, and it is clear that people have rarely shown such solicitude for her feelings before.

Soon after, the matron brings food for the table and invites everyone to sit down. Lucy settles at one end. Dallas makes as if to leave the area of the table altogether when Ringo intervenes. "Sit down here, ma'am," he says, gesturing to the seat next to Lucy. The others turn, startled. After a long moment Dallas sits, and then Ringo joins her. Lucy looks uncomfortable until Hatfield "rescues" her, suggesting she move to the other end of the table: "May I find you another place, Mrs. Mallory? It's cooler by the window." As they move away, joined by the remaining "aristocrat" Gatewood, Dallas looks embarrassed. But then Ringo—in a moment of true nobility—is apologetic, taking the responsibility for the snub upon himself: "Looks like I got the plague, don't it?" "No, no, it's not you," Dallas responds sadly, but he continues: "Well, I guess you can't break out of prison and into society in the same week." He starts to leave, but Dallas pulls at his arm and entreats him to stay. This entire scene is handled perfectly and touchingly. Our hearts go out to both of these characters; indeed, this is the moment when Wayne as Ringo wins us over entirely. This will be the first of many instances in which these outcasts are ennobled while their supposed societal betters are diminished.

Among the many masterful aspects of this scene, and others like it between Ringo and Dallas, is that we are never quite sure whether Ringo knows or suspects the nature of Dallas's past. He plays it innocent throughout, and it's just possible that the character is that naive; but it's also possible that he is fully aware, and that his own noble nature—truly genteel, contrary to the false chivalry of Hatfield—compels him to avoid embarrassing or demeaning Dallas. Is he unaware that she is a prostitute? Or does he know, but not care? Curley seems to be pondering the same question; at one point, after observing Ringo and Dallas, Curley pointedly asks Ringo just how old he was when he first went to prison. "Pushing seventeen," Ringo answers, which probably leaves the question still open. Brilliantly, the movie never resolves this ambiguity, and we as viewers are allowed to read Ringo according to our own lights.

We've gotten a closer look at Lucy and Hatfield at the lunch; but Gatewood, our third "aristocrat," will get his moment after the stagecoach departs Dry Fork for Apache

Inversion underscored by photography: the "aristocrats" Lucy Mallory (Louise Platt) and Hatfield (John Carradine) have been made small, while "outcasts" Ringo (John Wayne) and Dallas (Claire Trevor) occupy the foreground. *Stagecoach* (Walter Wanger, 1939).

Wells, the travelers having voted to continue. Gatewood has already shown himself to be a two-faced windbag by his faux-patriotic praise for the cavalrymen that soon turns to bullying once they fail to fulfill his wishes, but perhaps his most memorably revealing speech comes in the coach, when he bombastically preaches the gospel of *laissez-faire* while holding his bag full of embezzled funds. Gatewood's hypocritical pontification seems remarkably prescient today:

> I don't know what the government is coming to. Instead of protecting businessmen, it pokes its nose into business! Why, they're even talking now about having bank examiners—as if we bankers don't know how to run our own banks! Why, Boone, I actually had a letter from a popinjay official saying they were going to inspect my books! I have a slogan that should be blazoned on every newspaper in the country: America for Americans! The government must not interfere with business! Reduce taxes! Our national debt is something shocking, over one billion dollars a year! What this country needs is a businessman for president!

Nearly seventy years after this extraordinary speech, America—and the world—would experience the full-powered consequences of under-regulated banks. We have also certainly seen a resurgence of the idea of "America for Americans" over the last few years. And as I write this, the United States has a business tycoon for president.

In *Stagecoach*, Gatewood fails and is discredited; in the real world, he won.

Second Stop: Apache Wells

At the next outpost, Apache Wells, Lucy goes into labor, and it is time for Doc Boone's apotheosis—he must sober himself up and rise to the occasion. (Has there ever been a more heroic ordering of black coffee?) We are also treated to a rare moment of respite, a gentle outdoor Mexican song accompanied by guitar, although this is cover for the desertion of Apache sympathizers. Nevertheless, this scene prefigures similar campfire nocturnes in countless Westerns to come, especially including *The Wild Bunch* (1969).

Back inside, as Dallas presents Lucy's just-arrived little girl to the travelers, all of the men—except for Gatewood, the one character of the bunch with no visible redeeming qualities, and Doc Boone, who is still in the back room with Lucy after her difficult delivery—come together in aesthetic arrest as they behold the little miracle. This is wonderful: often we love characters for what they themselves love. We are moved by what moves them. As Goethe wrote in *Faust*, "The shudder of awe is humanity's highest faculty."[2] This birth has brought out the best in nearly everyone, and most notably in Dallas, who has been unfailingly compassionate to Lucy, helping her and sitting up with her all night through her labor, despite Lucy's coldness. Now Dallas, holding the baby, beams as we haven't seen her yet, and this seems like the perfect moment for the nascent love between her and Ringo to ripen. The other men are fixated on the baby in Dallas's arms, but in a masterful low-angle shot we can tell that Ringo's eyes are on Dallas herself. Wayne—consistently underrated as an actor—is perfect here; we can see exactly what his character is thinking—and so can Dallas. Each is seeing a vision of a future together, and children of their own.

The remarkable acting of both Wayne and Trevor in this scene, coupled with Ford's expert direction, provides a masterclass for today's filmmakers, who seem to have forgotten how to convey anything of the inner life of their characters without either (a) having them simply voice their thoughts aloud; or (b) presenting posed shots of pensive characters accompanied on the soundtrack by pop songs with vaguely relevant lyrics. Today's completely commercialized machinery of no-risk profit-making movie ventures may be expert in ensuring the financial security of Hollywood corporations, but sadly this system does not lend itself well to nuance, or artistic power, or emotional veracity, or human insight.

Among many other things, *Stagecoach* is a school, and a lesson.

Third Stop: Lee's Ferry

The travelers reach Lee's Ferry only to find it devastated by Geronimo's Apaches on the warpath, and the subsequent run from the ferry to Lordsburg contains the bulk of the film's action sequences as the nine pilgrims attempt to outrun their Indian pursuers. Typical of the time, the Indians here are rendered simply as nameless, savage forces of nature, obstacles to be overcome rather than human characters. This should be familiar to us across years and genres: our action blockbusters today still rely on impersonal enemies whom our heroes can kill without remorse—and, whether stormtroopers in *Star Wars* or monstrous creatures in *The Lord of the Rings*, they are easier on our consciences as well. We can cheer their demise without guilt, given the lack of any tragic, genocidal history between Americans and, say, orcs. But Native Americans were true human beings who lived, loved, suffered, and were killed or robbed of their lands by the people whose representatives serve as heroes in the classical American Western. This, always, will be the hardest part of these movies to live with. We watch *Stagecoach* and love it for its humanity, its psychological insight, its drama, its subtlety, its grandeur, and its beauty; but we simply endure its treatment of the Indians, perhaps seeing it as a product of its time, reading it metaphorically, and taking the natives depicted here as symbols of the challenges that nature will throw our way, whatever our race or identity. We can do this—indeed, I have argued that we *should* do this in my Law of Metaphor. ("In general, Westerns are best read metaphorically, not literally.") Nevertheless, what a relief it will be when the films of the sixties, seventies, and beyond (as well as a handful prior to that!) begin to question and eventually deconstruct this narratively facile and harmful portrayal of a great diversity of peoples whom the United States treated abominably. But this evolution itself is distinctly American: we genuinely do get better, we progress. We become older, wiser, and sadder too.

Our movies grow along with us. If only it didn't take so long.

Arrival: Lordsburg

By the time the stage reaches Lordsburg, the stories of all but three of the characters have essentially concluded. Gatewood will face a brief and inevitable reckoning, but beyond that, only Dallas and Ringo still have uncertain futures. The first thing that Dallas does upon entering Lordsburg is make her peace with Lucy—the two feminine archetypes from the journey in their final scene together. But even here, *Stagecoach* shows its brilliance. Consistently throughout the narrative, the movie has deliberately avoided easy, pat outcomes. Trite Hollywood convention would have Doc's redemption followed by him giving up the booze; he doesn't. Hatfield would either be redeemed or condemned; he isn't either one, and his character exits the action as enigmatically as he entered it. And after Dallas's care for Lucy, a typical movie today would have the two bonding together over their shared sisterhood. But *Stagecoach* is far too wise for that. These are characters from different worlds, and there is no way that the entire weight of the culture in which they live—epitomized by the "Law and Order League" from the opening (whose reproachful looks toward Dallas are echoed by the Lordsburg townswomen)—could possibly allow them to be friends. Both characters know this. As Lucy, still weak from her childbirth, is carried away from the stagecoach and toward her waiting husband, she attempts to reach out: "Dallas, if there's ever anything I can do for...." She trails off; there isn't, can never be, and both are aware of it. "I know," says Dallas, smiling sadly; she drapes a blanket over Lucy and the two women part. Their paths will likely not cross again. (It is interesting to note, however, that the whiskey peddler Peacock invites Dallas to visit him in Kansas City. Although *Stagecoach* is pessimistic about the American upper class, this moment seems to suggest some hope for reconciliation, charity, and compassion among the middle and lower classes.)

Now it is time for Ringo to fulfill his vengeance quest, and for Ringo and Dallas together to determine their fate as a couple. Dallas is caught between two worlds; as she walks down the streets in the shadier section of Lordsburg, she sees—and we see—her future in the world-weary face of an aging prostitute on the front porch of a bordello.

Soon Dallas will stand, literally, on a bridge between two futures, and everything will hinge on what happens next to Ringo as he finally comes face-to-face with his enemies.

The showdown looms and suspense builds, but here, brilliantly, *Stagecoach* turns the pattern established in *The Virginian* completely on its head. The earlier film allowed us to witness the tension, the anxiety, the gut-wrenching moments that our hero Gary Cooper experienced as he headed toward the inevitable confrontation.

Dallas (Claire Trevor) knows there are social divides that cannot be bridged, like the one between her and Lucy Mallory. *Stagecoach* (Walter Wanger, 1939).

This time, in *Stagecoach*, the focus is on Luke Plummer (Tom Tyler), the villain. The agonizingly slow buildup to the climactic battle is experienced mainly through Luke's eyes, and those of his two brothers. They are clearly terrified, and all of the portents—including the infamous "dead man's hand" of aces and eights—are against them. I always thought it was an amazing feat Hitchcock accomplished in *Dial M for Murder* (1954) when he actually made us, his audience, nervous on behalf of the villain of the picture when it looked like the devious plan to kill his own wife was going to go awry. But *Stagecoach* got there fifteen years earlier. In the long, dreadful silence in the saloon during which Luke Plummer prepares to face his adversary, we actually feel for him. We share his anxiety. Inexorably Plummer is swept toward his fate, and the suspense becomes almost unbearable. It's a masterstroke by both screenwriter and director; but even after this, the movie still has surprises to deliver. I will say no more about the climactic events in Lordsburg that happen next; let the first-time viewer experience them fresh!

Looking back over the events of the narrative, Doc Boone has the honor of placing the final period on the story arcs of Ringo and Dallas, saying, "Well, they're saved from the blessings of civilization." Civilization, it turns out, is one of the things that *Stagecoach* is about: its characters represent American culture in a microcosm, people of different backgrounds and personalities and classes who nevertheless must come together and work together to survive, despite their differences and even, sometimes, their open dislike for one another. There will never be any love lost between ex-rebel Hatfield and ex–Yankee Doc Boone, for example, and yet they have a shared interest in Lucy's welfare, and each contributes something essential to the journey. In today's fractured political climate, one in which powerful forces try to inspire good Americans to hate other good Americans and deem them enemies, *Stagecoach* offers a powerful and much-needed lesson about democracy, about people setting aside their differences in order to work for the common good. The only irredeemable characters in *Stagecoach* are the inflexible dogmatists (Gatewood; the "Law and Order League") or those who harm others by being motivated exclusively by self-interest (the Plummers; Gatewood again).

The heroes of *Stagecoach*, on the other hand, are those who, while flawed, nevertheless act nobly and without hypocrisy when the situation requires it. The three representatives of the upper class pretend to be genteel, brave, solicitous; but it is the outcasts—the outlaw, the whore, and the drunk—who, in the end, display true courtesy, true courage, true compassion. Despite their very human shortcomings, these three are no poseurs, but rather authentic exemplars of the virtues to which all of us might aspire.

Stagecoach marks the beginning of the American myth as it would be presented by the classic Westerns of the Golden Age. Its characters are no longer just European knights-errant in Western costumes; they are avatars of American personalities and classes as they mix together in a varied and messy democracy. The power of this shift is amplified by the use of American folk tunes ("Bury Me Not on the Lone Prairie," "Jeanie with the Light Brown Hair," "Shall We Gather at the River?," and many others) as the basis for the musical score, and by the use of other elements of American lore as accents in the narrative. For example, American card-playing folklore carries symbolic weight, as when a cut ace of spades prefigures death after the decision has been made to proceed to Lordsburg, or when Luke Plummer is dealt Wild Bill's "dead man's hand." And all this happens within a work of art that is consistently moving, insightful, and beautiful.

A myth, of course, is many things. It serves the functions delineated by Joseph Campbell that I cited in the Introduction—in the case of *Stagecoach*, most especially the sociological and psychological functions. The film presents a vision of American society that is contemporary, not trapped in the nineteenth century. Its combination of archetypal characters poses a question about twentieth-century American democracy voiced wonderfully by the philosopher Robert B. Pippin: "*Can* such a collection of people, without much common tradition or history, without much of what had been seen as the social conditions of nationhood, become in some way or other a unity capable of something greater than the sum of its parts?"[3] The movie's answer is ambiguous; it suggests a democratic ideal, but we also see the limitations of this ideal, as in the conclusion of the relationship between Dallas and Lucy, and of course the movie ends with Doc's voiced acknowledgment that for some people, the only solution lies beyond the blessings of civilization altogether. In *Stagecoach*, no person or philosophy or ideology is simple. Those seeking easy answers or trite homilies can go to the B-Westerns; this movie offers something different and more real.

On the individual, psychological front, *Stagecoach* delivers genuine insights about the drives, hopes, and fears that move us. A mythology, after all, is the collective dream of a culture, and we recognize that the characters who populate our own individual dreams are really parts of ourselves. The nine main characters in *Stagecoach* represent not just their sociological counterparts in the actual political world—they also, with all of their nobility and venality, honor and shame, live within each of us. Thus, the movie becomes an allegory not just for American democratic society but also for the integration of the various and often contradictory elements of the human psyche.

These mythographic contributions would already be enough to ensure *Stagecoach*'s immortality, but—like the grand megaliths that dominate the landscape in which it is set—the movie is also a towering artistic monument. Orson Welles called the movie a textbook and claimed to have watched it over forty times in preparation for *Citizen*

Kane. (In a 1967 *Playboy* interview of Welles, British drama critic Kenneth Tynan asked him how he felt about contemporary American directors. Welles responded, "Stanley Kubrick and Richard Lester are the only ones that appeal to me—except for the old masters. By which I mean John Ford, John Ford and John Ford.")[4]

And of course, how incredible to think that, in addition to its other genre-transforming qualities, this is also the film that truly and finally gave John Wayne to the Western! The star of *The Big Trail* (1930) has now evolved, keeping all of the elements of promise his earlier character showed, but adding in the layers of darkness and depth that Ford knew were needed. Here is a John Wayne that we can find likeable, compassionate, heroic—just as we did in *The Big Trail*—but we can also believe in him as a man on a vengeance quest. Nor is Wayne's development finished yet. Breck Coleman has grown into the Ringo Kid, yes, but darker complexities still lie ahead, waiting to be uncovered, as Ringo's simpler desire for frontier justice morphs into the single-minded obsession of *Red River*'s Tom Dunson (1948) and eventually becomes, at the zenith of Wayne's career, the destructive, vengeance-fueled fury of Ethan Edwards in *The Searchers* (1956). These characters, and others like them inhabiting many Westerns to come, will truly roam the outer darkness of the wild frontier, far beyond the "blessings of civilization."

Dodge City
(1939)

April 1, 1939 (Dodge City, Kansas)
USA—English
Warner Bros.
104m—Mono—Technicolor—1.37:1

Direction: Michael Curtiz
Screenplay: Robert Buckner
Principal Cast: Errol Flynn (Wade Hatton), Olivia de Havilland (Abbie Irving), Ann Sheridan (Ruby Gilman), Bruce Cabot (Jeff Surrett), Frank McHugh (Joe Clemens), Alan Hale (Rusty Hart), John Litel (Matt Cole), Henry Travers (Dr. Irving), Henry O'Neill (Colonel Dodge), Victor Jory (Yancey), William Lundigan (Lee Irving), Guinn "Big Boy" Williams (Tex Baird)
Production: Robert Lord (uncredited)
Cinematography: Sol Polito
Editing: George Amy
Art Direction: Ted Smith
Music: Max Steiner, Adolph Deutsch (uncredited)

Richard Slotkin, in his magisterial 1992 study of frontier mythology, *Gunfighter Nation*, provides a thorough discussion of the "town-tamer" Western narrative paradigm, contrasting it with three other classic types of Western structure ("outlaw," "psychological," and "gunfighter" Westerns). However, Slotkin did not originate the term, nor did he introduce it into pop culture. For example, there was a 1965 Western called *Town Tamer* made from a 1957 novel of the same name by Frank Gruber; and a short story called "Johnny, the Town Tamer" appeared in the August 1949 issue of *Famous Western*, written by none other than L. Ron Hubbard!

Dodge City (1939) preceded all of these, however, and serves as an excellent early Golden Era example of this narrative paradigm, executed with skill and great production values. Swashbuckler star Errol Flynn plays Wade Hatton, a reluctant cattleman-turned-lawman patterned after the legends of Wyatt Earp but provided with an Irish background, presumably to accommodate Flynn's speech. Hatton's challenge, like that of all town-taming heroes, is to cleanse the area of criminal elements so that civilization and progress can come to the frontier.

The Technicolor West of *Dodge City* is resplendently beautiful, a symphony of pastels, blue skies, and endless vistas. Even the paintings of the West that accompany the opening credits are gorgeous, suggesting the American equivalent of an aboriginal Dreamtime, a lost golden era of boundless horizons slowly receding from the modern memory. But the credit paintings also tell a linear story of progress, as they move from images of wagons to cattle drives to stagecoaches to towns to homesteads, and then, finally, open land and open sky. This seeming contradiction is at the heart of the film's worldview: progress can bring back Paradise.

In keeping with this, the railroad magnates, representing the advance of civilization and the taming of the frontier, are the good guys; when the train they ride on outraces a horse-drawn stagecoach at the beginning of the movie,

Errol Flynn as town-tamer Wade Hatton. *Dodge City* (Warner Bros., 1939).

it's a triumph made clear by the eponymous Colonel Dodge (Henry O'Neill), who proclaims, "Gentlemen, that's a symbol of America's future—progress! Iron men and iron horses—you can't beat 'em!" Later, he articulates this vision even more completely in an outdoor speech to a receptive crowd:

> Ladies and gentlemen, today a great chapter of history has been written, and we take justifiable pride in bringing this railroad to the terminal furthest west in this country. Someday, and I believe it will be in the near future, a great city will spring from this very spot upon which we now stand, a city which will represent all that the West stands for—honesty, courage, morality, and culture—for all the noble virtues of civilization. I can see a great metropolis of homes, churches, schools: a fine, decent city which will become the flower of the prairie!

The magnates' agent is Wade Hatton, whose job (eventually) it will be to clean up the towns they create, to remove from them the stain of evil men who stand in the way of progress. In town-tamer Westerns, this is done decisively and surgically, with no ethical qualms; the protagonist selectively targets evil men and eradicates them with his gun, an exterminator ridding Eden of its serpents one by one. When his work is done, there is joy and elation, not to mention a final prize awaiting the hero, the love of a good woman. Tragedies have occurred, innocents have been sacrificed, and much blood has been spilled, but at the end, we rejoice: the bad guys are dead, God's in his Heaven, all's right with the world—thanks to one good man with a gun. Violence has been the solution, and—*contra* Gandhi, King, and the Gospel of Matthew, not to mention the lessons of history—it begets no further violence. Paradise has been restored, and civilized life may now continue.

Dodge City was the first of several Westerns in which Errol Flynn would star; after the film's success, *Virginia City* (1940), *Santa Fe Trail* (1940), and *They Died with Their Boots On* (1941) would soon follow, the latter two also featuring Flynn's frequent co-star Olivia de Havilland—the longest surviving major star from the Golden Age of Hollywood, who died at the age of 104 not long before this book went to press! De Havilland reportedly disliked her role in *Dodge City*, but her character Abbie Irving is strong and

The West has never looked so idyllic on screen. *Dodge City* **(Warner Bros., 1939).**

independent, and her repartee with Flynn is one of the high points of the movie. Their best scene together prefigures the battle-of-the-sexes sparring between strong-willed career women and their hard-headed lovers that Hepburn and Tracy would later perfect, as lawman Wade confronts Abbie at the newspaper office, pronounces that journalism is no career for a lady, and then, in his grand exit, trips over a box and falls unceremoniously to the ground. Abbie laughs, which irritates Wade further:

> WADE: Is this showing proper respect for the law?
> ABBIE: I never saw the law fall on its face before!
> WADE: I didn't fall on my face. You know, there's an old saying in the British Army: "The law must always save its face in front of the natives."
> ABBIE: And what if the natives object to its face?
> WADE: We just put them across our knee and spank them soundly! (*He moves as if to do so.*)
> ABBIE: You're not suggesting that I'm a native?
> WADE: No. The only real native of Kansas is the buffalo. He's got a very hard head, a very uncertain temper, and a very lonely future. But apart from that, there's hardly any comparison between you.

By today's standards, Wade's attitudes about both women and colonialism are problematic, of course, but they were typical of the time in 1939, and would have been positively enlightened in 1870s Dodge City.

The movie as a whole is in fact unabashedly progressive, relative to its era. Our hero, in the furtherance of progress, raises taxes, initiates gun control, and stands up for the rule of law in the face of a lynch mob. Wade is no lone wolf on a personal quest; he represents the communitarian values of society and civilization rather than the Romantic ideal of the primacy of the individual. As Slotkin writes about Flynn's character, "The new age will demand a hero different from the individualistic old-time plainsman, a conservationist rather than a free hunter, a redistributor of misappropriated wealth rather than an exploitative entrepreneur—a New Dealer on horseback."[1] The aptness of the community's ethos is not questioned as it is in *Stagecoach*; here, the biddies of the Law and Order League have been replaced by the far more lovable women of the Pure Prairie League, and there is no Doc Boone in sight to comment ironically on the "blessings of civilization." *Stagecoach*, of course, was progressive as well, but in a very different way—the society it envisioned was a melting pot of very different people, not necessarily agreeing but working together through the messy business of democracy, whereas the ideal of *Dodge City* has very much to do with shared community values, the "honesty, courage, morality, and culture" that Colonel Dodge expected to be held in common. Watching both of these movies reminds us just how much our current political fault-lines are a product of recent decades, how the divisions and distinctions between what we call "left" and "right" change over time. We would not divide so neatly if we were all transported back to 1939, nor would our counterparts if they lived today. Americans in the twenty-first century are so used to being harshly polarized; it is easy to forget that, prior to the traumas of Vietnam and Watergate, American political culture was far more nuanced, ambiguous, and subtle. There was more common ground, a greater potential for communication, cooperation, and coalition.

There is a great deal to like about *Dodge City* apart from its breathtaking visuals. Wade Hatton is an appealing hero, well-played by Flynn, and de Havilland's Abbie, as mentioned earlier, is a woman of fiercely independent spirit who is every bit Wade's match. In contrast to the typical role played by Western movie women when a gunfight seems imminent—preaching a pacific moral code that the male hero must reject—Abbie has the situation sized up from the start (at least, according to the film's worldview). "What Dodge City needs is a man with a sense of public pride and the courage to back it up by shooting it out with men of equal skill," she proclaims, and although at the time she doesn't think that Wade is that man, her solution to the problem is one which he will ultimately accept and fulfill.

The pivotal event that changes Wade's perspective and overcomes his reluctance to take the sheriff's position is the tragic death of the young boy Harry Cole (Bobs Watson), caused inadvertently by the actions of the reprehensible Jeff Surrett (Bruce Cabot) and his gang. The boy, with whom Wade has bonded, lies dead, a homemade paper sheriff's star still pinned to his vest. A close-up on the star then dissolves into another badge, a real one now worn next to the bullets on Wade's belt. As corny as this moment sounds (and is), I defy anyone to watch it and not get goosebumps.

Perhaps the most famous scene in *Dodge City* is the barroom brawl, supposedly the largest such ever filmed—and a genuine riot it is. Strikingly, music sparks the explosion here. Prior to 1939, other films had already acknowledged the stirring potential of patriotic anthems—most notably Jean Renoir's masterpiece *La Grande Illusion* (1937), which features a powerful "cabaret" scene in which French prisoners-of-war spontaneously burst into a singing of "La Marseillaise" while in the presence of their German captors. In *Dodge City*, the colossal brawl is precipitated by dueling Civil War

Abbie Irving (Olivia de Havilland) holds her own with Wade Hatton (Errol Flynn). *Dodge City* **(Warner Bros., 1939).**

anthems: the former Confederate cowboys allied with Wade Hatton try to drown out "Marching Through Georgia" with their own rendition of "Dixie," with predictably disastrous consequences. It is interesting to note that Michael Curtiz, who directed *Dodge City*, would go on to film cinema's most famous "dueling anthems" sequence just three years later—"Die Wacht am Rhein" battling "La Marseillaise" in *Casablanca* (1942).

All in all, *Dodge City* is quite a satisfying movie, taken on its own terms. Although the final showdown is somewhat anticlimactic, the story is gripping throughout, and even the film's excesses—and there are some—are forgivable in the service of such an enjoyable cinematic experience. There is little that will be unfamiliar to the modern viewer; only Wade's inability to save the young boy's life and Abbie's stubborn refusal to fit into the conventional Western stereotypes will come as something of a surprise. Nevertheless, *Dodge City* stands as perhaps the best early exemplar of the classic town-tamer story, influencing the style of countless other Westerns, including such Golden Age monuments as *My Darling Clementine* (1946) and *High Noon* (1952).

Who could have predicted the staying power of the town-tamer paradigm, or the far-reaching impact it has had on our culture? Despite bearing little resemblance to the way that anything ever works in real life, this template has persisted (and fruitfully multiplied) through at least nine decades and across a dozen film genres. Whether in cop movies, swashbuckling adventures, gangster flicks, sci-fi spectacles, spy movies, comic-book blockbusters, or Westerns, the hero selectively killing the right people and then walking off with the beautiful girl has resolved the vast majority of action-adventure plots for generations, to the point where it has become a part of our national consciousness.

Sadly, this fantasy continues to be confused with reality by a great many people. Taken literally, Hollywood movies tell us continually that cops aren't apprehenders on behalf of the legal system; they're exterminators. Spies aren't gatherers of intelligence; they're assassins. You don't beat crippling societal problems like crime, drug addiction, rape, and violence through social work, treatment, or rehabilitation; you beat them by one-upping the violence, being better at killing than the bad guys are. There are few big problems that can't be solved by a good eye and a steady trigger finger. This is one reason why it is so incredibly important for us as a culture to *relearn* how to read films metaphorically rather than literally. We can cheer a hero who conquers the evils that confront him while staying true to his inner virtue *without* having to buy into the notion that actually appointing proficient killers to root out and destroy evildoers in our society, rather than trusting to the workings of the American legal system and due process, is a better way to go. When we are able to make this transition from superficial literality to a deeper metaphorical understanding, then movies like *Dodge City* come alive; they are relevant once again, meaningful and no longer socially destructive.

The funny thing is that the people who created these original templates in the early years of Hollywood knew that they were myths, symbolic rather than historic. Within the context of their metaphorically literate society, the filmmakers understood exactly what they were doing, and would no doubt have been baffled by the ways in which, over time, American culture would seize on these metaphors, literalize and fetishize them, and fashion out of them a lens through which many Americans now view reality. Part of the problem is that these particular symbolic treatments are rooted in very concrete, commonplace things—guns, crime, corruption, and the American town. It doesn't take too many leaps of the imagination to put ourselves into these situations vicariously, as it would within more obviously symbolic, fantastical, or otherworldly settings. In real life we don't walk through wardrobes into magical lands, or move objects with our minds, or attend wizarding schools, or wield lightsabers—it's not hard to read these things as fantasy, and thus very few of us actually believe in Narnia or cite our religious affiliation as Jedi or try to find Hogwarts on Google Earth. But many of us own guns, and many of us have, in one way or another, had our lives or the lives of people we know impacted by gun violence. There is something less elusive and more temptingly tangible about the mythic figure of the gunman; we may not be able to believe in hobbits or Klingons or zombies or mutants with superpowers, but can't there at least be town tamers in real life? (And if so, can I be one? I may not be particularly strong or agile or smart—but I *can* pull a trigger!)

Nothing can illuminate the human experience quite like metaphor. The response that symbols can evoke in us, the energies that they can unleash in our psyches, the impact that moving in myth can have on our lives—these are profound. Symbolic thinking is a gift to our species. But the fundamentalist literalization of metaphor—reading fiction as fact, symbol as history, the finger that points to the Moon as the Moon itself—leads to fanaticism, dogmatism, and destructive ignorance. A cultivated understanding of art is critical in helping us to manage, negotiate, and utilize this innate, quintessentially human faculty while minimizing the risks of literalization. Among the many fine arguments for arts education in this country, the opportunity to help reestablish, in generations to come, a healthy relationship to the world of myth, symbol, and metaphor is one that I find particularly powerful, perhaps even necessary for our survival.

Union Pacific
(1939)

April 27, 1939 (Omaha)
USA—English
Paramount Pictures
135m—Mono—BW—1.37:1

Direction: Cecil B. DeMille
Screenplay: Walter DeLeon, C. Gardner Sullivan, Jesse Lasky, Jr., Stanley Rauh (uncredited), Jack Cunningham (adaptation), Ernest Haycox (novel *Trouble Shooter*)
Principal Cast: Barbara Stanwyck (Mollie Monahan), Joel McCrea (Jeff Butler), Akim Tamiroff (Fiesta), Robert Preston (Dick Allen), Lynne Overman (Leach Overmile), Brian Donlevy (Sid Campeau), Robert Barrat (Duke Ring), Anthony Quinn (Cordray), Stanley Ridges (General Casement), Evelyn Keyes (Mrs. Calvin), Henry Kolker (Asa M. Barrows), Francis McDonald (General Dodge)
Production: Cecil B. DeMille
Cinematography: Victor Milner
Editing: Anne Bauchens
Art Direction: Hans Dreier, Roland Anderson
Music: Sigmund Krumgold, John Leipold, Gerard Carbonara (uncredited), Leo Shuken (uncredited), Victor Young (uncredited)
Awards: *Boxoffice*—Best Picture of the Month for the Whole Family, Cannes Film Festival—Palme d'Or, Western Heritage Award
Nominations: Oscar—Best Special Effects (Farciot Edouart, Gordon Jennings, Loren L. Ryder)

As a story about the creation of the first transcontinental railroad and the driving of the Golden Spike, Cecil B. DeMille's *Union Pacific* is fairly mediocre. That story has been told far more compellingly before—most notably, in John Ford's silent epic *The Iron Horse* (1924), upon which *Union Pacific* draws in liberal measure. (Although, if anything, its treatment of Native Americans is even more appalling than that of the earlier film—a depressing development coming from the three-time director of *The Squaw Man*.) This doesn't mean that DeMille didn't pull out all the stops for his own epic attempt at the story. Not only did *Union Pacific* make use of the true historical Golden Spike (on loan from Stanford University), but it is also crammed full of the usual DeMille excesses—epic battle sequences, stirring music and visuals, hyper-patriotism, and hundreds of actors and extras filling the crowded screen. The world premiere of *Union Pacific* in Omaha, part of a multi-day festival celebrating the seventieth anniversary of the Golden Spike, was equally epic in scope: a quarter of a million attendees traveled to the city where the real Union Pacific Railroad laid its first rails (temporarily doubling Omaha's population); the National Guard was called in to keep order; and

174

President Roosevelt himself, from the White House, pushed a telegraph key to kick off the festivities.

Despite all this grandiosity in both the film's content and debut, the most memorable element of *Union Pacific* is still the intimate love triangle between upright railroad trouble-shooter Jeff Butler (Joel McCrea); the young Irish "daughter of the railroad" Mollie Monahan (Barbara Stanwyck); and Butler's old friend Dick Allen (Robert Preston), an amoral gambler selling his services to the highest bidder and currently working for the corrupt bosses of Union Pacific's rival railroad company. Trickster archetypes who follow their own rules and live outside the normal societal demarcations of good and evil often make the most fascinating characters, and that is certainly true in this case. While McCrea's square-jawed, ramrod-straight Jeff Butler is the bore that such characters typically are, Dick Allen, brought to life in a beautifully nuanced performance from Robert Preston, seizes our attention from his first scene to his last. In many ways, Preston's character is the spiritual ancestor to the subversive antiheroes of the Silver Era: the Wild Bunch, the Professionals, and most especially the greatest morally ambiguous Western character of them all, Eli Wallach's Tuco from *The Good, the Bad and the Ugly* (1966).

Mollie Monahan is also a complex character, and it is fascinating to observe how she is actually led into immoral behavior by her own inner morality, piety, and kindness

Mollie Monahan (Barbara Stanwyck), Jeff Butler (Joel McCrea), and Dick Allen (Robert Preston), the only survivors in a wrecked train surrounded by hostile natives, contemplate a grim use for their three final bullets. Together they embody one true romantic love and two great friendships. *Union Pacific* (Paramount, 1939).

Scoundrel Dick Allen (Robert Preston) and straight-arrow Jeff Butler (Joel McCrea) embrace their contradictory relationship as adversaries and best friends in one of the film's most effective scenes. *Union Pacific* **(Paramount, 1939).**

toward others. Truly the road to iniquity is paved with good intentions, if Mollie's own journey is any example. Stanwyck, already established as one of the greatest actresses of the time and fresh from her triumph in *Stella Dallas* (1937), presents Mollie as a woman full of contradictory impulses being torn apart by the conflicting demands of her loyalty, her religiosity, her compassion, and her romantic feelings. Stanwyck takes us into the heart of her character with both subtlety and power.

But it is fourth-billed Preston who steals the show. Reportedly, the actor disliked working with DeMille, and though he would go on to participate in the director's next two pictures (*North West Mounted Police*, 1940, and *Reap the Wild Wind*, 1942), once Preston had established himself more securely in Hollywood he declined further opportunities to work with DeMille. Even given this difficult working relationship, however, Preston turns in one of the best performances of his career in *Union Pacific*. Like Stanwyck, Preston is able to convey so much by so little—a gesture, a half-smile, the subtle inflection of a line of dialogue that evokes even more from the script than was originally there.

Perhaps Preston's best scene, and McCrea's as well—to which my mere transcription of the dialogue cannot do justice—is the moment when the two men bid farewell to each other after they and Mollie have escaped from a horrific train wreck and a bloody battle with Sioux Indians. Mollie, off being treated for wounds she sustained in the attack, is now Dick's wife despite being desperately in love with Jeff, and both men know that they are about to return to their respective positions on opposite sides of the rail-road struggle—Dick as a wanted man who stole a massive payroll (even though he later returned it at Mollie's bidding), and Jeff as the trouble-shooter who is tasked with making sure that justice is done. The two old friends, taking shelter beneath a craggy rock overhang, banter in a way that recalls similar scenes between friendly enemies in other films, especially two cited earlier: Gary Cooper and James Ellison in *The Plainsman* (1936), and Johnny Mack Brown and Wallace Beery in *Billy the Kid* (1930).

> JEFF: Dick, you and I have fought side by side many times. We've been through hell and high water—robbed the same chicken coop and chewed on the same bone. But you're on the other side in this fight. (He pulls out a pipe.) The next time I see you on Union Pacific property, I'll have to…. You got a match?
> DICK (*reaching for a match*): Won't your conscience bother you for letting me go?
> JEFF: There's grub and blankets in the pack on that horse.
> DICK (*smiling*): I won't be hung for horse-stealing, will I?
> JEFF (*shakes his head, chuckling*): Belonged to an Indian. He won't need it anymore.
> DICK (*laughs*): All right. All right, I'll get going.
> JEFF: Where to?
> DICK: Oh—Central Pacific.
> JEFF: You're gonna help the road that's trying to beat us?
> DICK (*ironically*): Yeah. I'm gonna help them the same way I helped the Union Pacific.
> JEFF (*smiles and hands him a gun*): Here. You might need that. Don't deal any cards off the bottom with it.
> DICK: Thanks.
> JEFF: Extra cartridges in the pack.
> DICK: Thanks. You're all aces, bucko. But you're in love with Mollie—and don't you ever forget she's my wife.
> JEFF (*smiling*): I might; she wouldn't.
> *They mount their horses.*
> DICK: Now when the Central meets the Union's tracks, I'll be there, Jeff. And you and the Union Pacific and the devil himself won't keep me from my wife. I'd hate to kill you with your own gun.
> JEFF (*smiles*): I'll be there, Dick.
> *They shake hands.*

What a shame it is that the Hays Code constrained the possibilities for stories and characters like this. We know ahead of time just how all of this must turn out, the ultimate fates of all three players in this interesting triangle. Dick must die for his sins. Even if redemption comes for his character (which it does, nobly), it still must cost him his life, and this will then clear the way for the two true lovers to be together. The filmmakers clearly must have known that Preston's character is far more compelling than McCrea's, and indeed they exploit this to the greatest extent possible—Dick actually gets to marry Mollie, and performs the film's most heroic act—and yet it is Jeff and Mollie who are predestined to get their happy ending.

Having said all this, we should be careful about too one-sided an interpretation of the effect of the Hays Code on film quality. As *Parzival* reminds us, every phenomenon has both positive and negative results, and this was true in Golden Age cinema as well. Consider, for example, the dialogue in a classic Hollywood romantic scene (whether *noir*, melodrama, or screwball comedy) and how it tends to be far wittier, sharper, better crafted, and more sparkling than what is produced in today's freer environment, largely because of the need to be indirect, oblique, and clever that the Hays restrictions necessitated. Film characters under the Code couldn't talk bluntly about sex, and yet classic Hollywood romances are awash in sexuality due to the tantalizing suggestiveness and nuance of the dialogue (and visuals) brought about, ironically, by prudish censorship.

Igor Stravinsky once addressed the problem of creating art within constraints, and how, paradoxically, it can result in better outcomes. "In art as in everything else," he wrote, "one can build only upon a resisting foundation." The great composer went on:

> My freedom will be so much the greater and more meaningful the more narrowly I limit my field of action and the more I surround myself with obstacles. Whatever diminishes constraint diminishes strength. The more constraints one imposes, the more one frees one's self of the chains that shackle the spirit.[1]

Stravinsky's constraints were mainly self-imposed, but the principle still applies. Classic Hollywood filmmakers working within the limits of the Code actually found that its strict framework provided a structure that encouraged and fostered subtlety, metaphor, and creative development. This was a benefit that we should not ignore. However, the cost was not being able to take full advantage of subversive ideas and subversive characters. Later, when the Hays Code began to dissolve, the floodgates opened, and Westerns were free to explore in greater depth complex characters like Preston's Dick Allen. At that point, the true Western antihero was born.

Frontier Marshal
(1939)

July 28, 1939 (USA)
USA—English / Spanish
Twentieth Century-Fox
71m—Mono—BW—1.37:1

Direction: Allan Dwan
Screenplay: Sam Hellman, Stuart N. Lake (book *Wyatt Earp: Frontier Marshal*)
Principal Cast: Randolph Scott (Wyatt Earp), Nancy Kelly (Sarah Allen), Cesar Romero (Doc Halliday), Binnie Barnes (Jerry), John Carradine (Ben Carter)
Production: Sol M. Wurtzel
Cinematography: Charles G. Clarke
Editing: Fred Allen, Robert Bischoff (uncredited)
Art Direction: Richard Day, Lewis H. Creber
Music: Samuel Kaylin (uncredited), Charles Maxwell (uncredited), David Raksin (uncredited), Walter Scharf (uncredited)

History is written by the victors, they say, and nowhere in the lore of the Old West is the truth of this adage shown more clearly than in the story of Wyatt Earp. The real Earp had a checkered history—a tough lawman who was a tireless opponent of wild Western outlaws, but also a gambler, brothel manager, saloon owner, miner, teamster, occasional (and controversial) boxing referee, and not so occasional lawbreaker. But the actual event that conferred immortality upon him happened in the boomtown of Tombstone, Arizona, on October 26, 1881: a gunfight on Fremont Street between Earp, his two brothers Virgil and Morgan, and Doc Holliday on one side, and five members of the outlaw gang called the Cowboys on the other. Three of the Cowboys—Billy Clanton and the brothers Tom and Frank McLaury—were killed, while the other two—Ike Clanton and Billy Claiborne—fled the scene. Earp's party survived with only minor injuries, and Wyatt himself was untouched. The battle lasted just thirty seconds, but its legend has endured for well over a century: the erroneously dubbed "Gunfight at the O.K. Corral," the most famous shootout in the history of the Wild West.

Wyatt Earp himself would eventually become an unpaid consultant for early Western movies. He became a frequent visitor to John Ford's movie sets, and when he died in 1929 at the age of eighty, pallbearers at his funeral included William S. Hart and Tom Mix. During the latter part of his life, Earp and his wife Josephine (who survived him by fifteen years) worked hard to establish and control his image (which was not originally so heroic), and their efforts have a great deal to do with how Earp has been remembered by posterity. But the most important event in the cementing of the Wyatt Earp legend was the publication, two years after his death—and fifty years to the month after

179

the fabled gunfight—of Stuart N. Lake's largely fictionalized and completely romanticized biography *Wyatt Earp: Frontier Marshal*. Lake interviewed Earp several times, along with other figures such as Bat Masterson, but his resulting opus was far closer to myth than to history. Writing for Depression-era audiences desperately in need of heroes, Lake portrayed Earp and his brothers as gallant knights cleansing the West of villainous outlaws. He made no mention of Josephine or Earp's previous common-law wife, former prostitute Mattie Blaylock, nor did Lake dwell on any of the more unsavory aspects of Earp's true history. His book did draw upon actual fact in one important regard, establishing perhaps the most important relationship in all of Western lore: the unlikely friendship between "upright" Wyatt and the enigmatic, terminally ill gunfighter and gambler Doc Holliday.

The first film adaptation of Lake's book came just three years after its publication—*Frontier Marshal* (1934), directed by Lewis Seiler and starring George O'Brien. However, Earp's widow Josephine, always anxious to control her late husband's image, sued Twentieth Century–Fox to try and keep the movie from being made, and while she failed to do so, the studio did rename the lead character as "Michael Wyatt." Also, there is no climactic gunfight at the O.K. Corral or anywhere else outside; instead, the inevitable showdown takes place in a saloon.

Other early sound Westerns inspired by Earp's legend—such as *Law and Order* (1932), *The Arizonian* (1935), and *Dodge City* (1939)—likewise renamed the lead character and strayed far enough from Earp's own history to avoid similar lawsuits. However, in 1939 there appeared the second official adaptation of Lake's book, also titled *Frontier Marshal*, and here, for the first time, Wyatt Earp appears as protagonist while bearing his true name. (The 1923 silent Western *Wild Bill Hickok*, starring William S. Hart in the title role, did feature Wyatt Earp as a minor character, appearing briefly in one scene. As a result, Bert Lindley holds the honor of being the only movie actor to portray Wyatt Earp under his proper name prior to the real Earp's death.) Although *Frontier Marshal* did use Earp's name for the lead character, the filmmakers made two concessions: in response to pressure from Josephine, they dropped her husband's name from the title of the picture; and, fearing a lawsuit from Doc Holliday's family, they changed the character's last name to "Halliday."

The picture is a perfectly serviceable town-tamer Western, but one which is primarily important to history for moving the legend of Wyatt Earp, Doc Holliday, and the O.K. Corral into the mainstream of Western movies and establishing many of the tropes that would become permanently attached to the Tombstone story. The film would serve as a template for its more important remake, John Ford's *My Darling Clementine* (1946), which in turn forever altered the history of the Earp legend as it then played itself out in dozens of movies, television shows, and novels over the next seven decades.

The 1939 version of *Frontier Marshal* opens with a two-minute montage featuring the founding of Tombstone and its transformation into a rough, murderous boomtown in need of taming. "We are growing rapidly, but it is getting to be a question whether the city or the cemetery will be the larger," writes the editor of the local paper—named, as it was and is in real life, the *Tombstone Epitaph*. Into this chaos, just passing through, arrives Wyatt Earp (Randolph Scott), who quickly rises to the occasion by subduing the drunk and murderous "Indian Charlie" (Charles Stevens, who would play the same role in *Tombstone, the Town Too Tough to Die* in 1942 and again in *My Darling Clementine* four years after that) when the local lawman is unwilling to do so. Earp then becomes the new town marshal and soon comes across the tuberculous gambler Doc (Cesar Romero), as well as corrupt dance-hall girl Jerry (Binnie Barnes) and the virtuous Sarah Allen (Nancy Kelly). Real-life comedian Eddie Foy—who was a friend of Wyatt and Doc and may have been present in Tombstone when the famous gunfight happened—also figures prominently in the plot; the character is played here by Foy's son, Eddie Foy, Jr., who would go on to repeat the role of his father in three more feature films over the next five years: *Lillian Russell* (1940), *Yankee Doodle Dandy* (1942), and *Wilson* (1944). (Interestingly, the vaudeville world that would eventually become Foy Senior's milieu was birthed almost simultaneously with the shootout that would eventually immortalize his friend Wyatt Earp. The first true American vaudeville show premiered in New York on October 24, 1881—just two days prior to the Gunfight at the O.K. Corral.)

The saloon scene in *Frontier Marshal* in which Wyatt and Doc first become friends is a genuine classic. Wyatt has just caught Jerry helping the gambler Blackmore (Edward Norris) cheat at poker, and Earp pulls her outside and dumps her unceremoniously into a watering trough. Soon after, Jerry's sometime lover Doc strides menacingly into the bar, looking every inch the standard Western villain with his clipped mustache, black hat, and dead eyes. There is no love lost between him and Blackmore, but his beef for the present is clearly with Wyatt. Slowly he moves toward the table where Wyatt and Blackmore are playing cards; Blackmore eyes Doc with malice.

> BLACKMORE: He'd better not try anything with me.
> *Doc reaches the table; Wyatt stands to face him.*
> DOC (*to Wyatt*): I don't like the way you're running this town. And I especially don't like the way you treated a certain young lady. (*He holds up a handkerchief to initiate a pistol duel.*) Take hold of—
> *Doc is suddenly seized with a fit of tuberculous coughing and doubles over. Blackmore, seeing his chance, draws a pistol from a concealed shoulder holster to shoot the incapacitated Doc. Quick as a flash, Wyatt knocks the gun away and seizes Blackmore's wrist.*
> WYATT: You always want an edge, don't you, Blackmore? Suppose you wait till he quits coughing.
> DOC (*recovering*): Thanks, Mister Earp. Now if you'll please step aside—
> WYATT (*smiling kindly*): No, Doc. I'm the marshal here, y'know; I gotta keep the peace.
> DOC: Yes, of course, of course. Will you join me in a drink?
> WYATT: Glad to. (*He turns to Blackmore.*) Better try another camp; this one's unhealthy.

In the blink of an eye, Wyatt has established himself as a man of honor and lived up to Doc's chivalrous standards. Within the space of a few seconds, the Western movie's most enduring and unlikely friendship has been forged for the first time.

What makes the Tombstone legend so immortal? Well, for one thing, like all great legends it has at least some basis in historical fact. Wyatt and Doc and their adversaries were real people, and the shootout in Tombstone was an actual thing that happened. The story itself—together with the events that precede and follow the fateful gunfight—is a compelling one, filled with drama, violence, betrayal, courage, cowardice, and loyalty. It's also difficult to resist a tale that so clearly depicts the victory of good over evil, simply by means of the intrepidity of a handful of brave men standing up against a gang of ruffians.

But one of the primary appeals of the legend must be the surprising friendship of opposites that we find in Wyatt and Doc. Depending on the version of the myth, the two characters can represent law vs. lawlessness; ethics vs. amorality; reason vs. emotion; common sense vs. erudition; physicality vs. intellectualism; reformed lawman vs. fallen angel; Apollo vs. Dionysus; stoicism vs. epicureanism; life affirmation vs. death wish. When the story is done right, though, we are eventually led to see the two men as complementary halves of the same whole. Together they represent parts of the self that are

Crooked gambler Blackmore (Edward Norris) looks on as the West's most iconic friends meet for the first time on film: Wyatt Earp (Randolph Scott) and Doc "Halliday" (Cesar Romero). *Frontier Marshal* (Twentieth Century–Fox, 1939).

frequently in tension with one another, and yet which come together and work together within an integrated personality. And of course, just as significantly, Wyatt and Doc embody the true value and power of human friendship.

Oddly, history would be more accurately represented in many ways as the American Western continued producing versions of Wyatt Earp's story, contrary to the manner in which legends typically accrete over time. In both *Frontier Marshal* and *My Darling Clementine*, for example, Doc is dead before the Gunfight at the O.K. Corral has occurred or concluded; likewise, in both films the participants and casualties do not correspond to those of the actual shootout. In contrast, more recent films such as *Tombstone* (1993) and *Wyatt Earp* (1994) take pains to get at least these broad historical details correct, even while (rightly) feeling free to take artistic license in the service of the story.

Randolph Scott was already an established screen presence before *Frontier Marshal*. He had appeared in over three dozen movies to this point, typically playing tough, no-nonsense characters with square jaws and stringent codes of honor. During the thirties, Scott had gained notice for his starring work in such pictures as *Heritage of the Desert* (1932), *The Last of the Mohicans* (1936), *High, Wide, and Handsome* (1937), *Rebecca of Sunnybrook Farm* (1938), and *The Texans* (1938), as well as his strong supporting turn as the sympathetic lawman in *Jesse James* (1939). By the time of *Frontier Marshal*, Scott was forty-one and had been acting in films for over a decade, and yet more than sixty movies (about three-quarters of them Westerns) still lay ahead. Scott's Western persona seems cut from the same cloth that gave us William S. Hart; and strikingly, both men also did their greatest work past middle age in the final films of their careers. No one could have guessed that Scott's own apex as an actor would come during his late fifties and early sixties—a series of seven low-budget but masterful Westerns made under the direction of Budd Boetticher (starting with *7 Men from Now*, 1956), as well as his final (and magnificent) performance in Sam Peckinpah's *Ride the High Country* (1962).

As solidly enjoyable as Scott is in *Frontier Marshal*, however, the character of Wyatt Earp in Westerns is usually overshadowed by the more compelling figure of Doc Holliday. In this version, Doc's primary internal conflict is that between his prior role as a compassionate giver of life and his current status as a despairing, terminally ill killer in the service of death. Toward the end of the film, he will redeem himself heroically, pulling a young boy back from the brink of death with his surgical skill. "Isn't

The Angel of Death (and Life): Cesar Romero as Doc. *Frontier Marshal* (Twentieth Century–Fox, 1939).

it more thrilling to give life than to take it away?" his true love Sarah says to him; seconds later, in a shocking turn, Doc lies dead, gunned down by villains firing from the shadows, and leaving Wyatt to face the shootout at the O.K. Corral all alone, contradicting both history and Stuart Lake's now well-known version of it.

Throughout the lore of the American Western, there is something about Doc—as a character first crystallized by Cesar Romero in this film and perfected gradually over time in movies like *My Darling Clementine* (1946, played by Victor Mature); *Gunfight at the O.K. Corral* (1957, Kirk Douglas); *Hour of the Gun* (1967, Jason Robards); and most especially *Tombstone* (1993, Val Kilmer)—that resonates with us on a purely archetypal level. Doc is the enigmatical shadow self; a philosophical, erudite, cold-blooded killer; the Angel of Death who is himself mortally wounded; a despairing former saint now become the deadliest of sinners; and the dark, ironic, cynical trickster who nevertheless befriends the virtuous Earp, fights for law and order not for ethical reasons but out of love for his friend, and dies redeemed by that very same friendship. In these Hollywood retellings, Wyatt Earp is undoubtedly the hero—but, in most cases, it is the elusive, doomed character of Doc who stays with us.

Destry Rides Again
(1939)

November 30, 1939 (New York City)
USA—English / Russian
Universal Pictures
95m—Mono—BW—1.37:1

Direction: George Marshall
Screenplay: Felix Jackson, Gertrude Purcell, Henry Myers, Max Brand (novel)
Principal Cast: Marlene Dietrich (Frenchy), James Stewart (Tom Destry, Jr.), Mischa Auer (Boris), Charles Winninger (Washington Dimsdale), Brian Donlevy (Kent), Allen Jenkins (Gyp Watson), Warren Hymer (Bugs Watson), Irene Hervey (Janice Tyndall), Una Merkel (Lily Belle), Billy Gilbert (Loupgerou), Samuel S. Hinds (Judge Slade), Jack Carson (Jack Tyndall), Tom Fadden (Lem Claggett), Virginia Brissac (Sophie Claggett)
Production: Joe Pasternak
Cinematography: Hal Mohr
Editing: Milton Carruth
Art Direction: Jack Otterson
Music: Frank Skinner
Awards: National Film Registry

To this point, we have looked at some of the ways that Hollywood Western versions of the Hero's Adventure have been shaped by, responded to, or reacted against the inherited traditions of Judeo-Christianity and the myths and legends of Greece and Western Europe. In the Judeo-Christian traditions, the hero is generally the person who submits himself fully to the will of God, whereas in the European traditions, the hero is more often a rugged individual who forges his own way, whether the gods are for him or against him. Classic Hollywood Western pictures, which construct a uniquely American mythology while still showing the influences of their Old World antecedents, often embody the tension between these Levantine and European ideals. The Western hero is ostensibly a god-fearing Christian and allies himself with those who uphold Christian values, but he must also walk his own individual path, which may involve ranging on his own beyond normal societal boundaries, wreaking violence and retribution himself rather than leaving vengeance to God.

These traditions, however, are not the only sources of human myth. Just as Europe and the Middle East provided fertile soil for most of the Occidental mythologies and religions still working in the world today (including the three major Abrahamic religions, as well as the Western cultural inheritance from classical mythology and the Celtic and chivalric legends), so India and the Far East were nurseries for their own systems of belief and philosophy, including Hinduism, Buddhism, Taoism, Shinto,

184

Confucianism, and Jainism. Each of these mythologies, East and West, offers differing takes on aspects of metaphysics, human culture, and human life: the place of the individual versus that of the community; whether the divine is separate from nature or a part of it; the relative importance of action and contemplation; whether deity is personal, impersonal, immanent, transcendent, or nonexistent; whether history is linear or cyclical; and the fate, if any, of individual consciousness after death. Importantly, the Eastern religions and philosophies also offer differing perspectives on the role and nature of the hero—who, in the case of Far Eastern systems such as Taoism, may appear in the form of the "Master" or sage.

(In my experience there is no better delineation of the differing characteristics of these belief systems, as well as those from both earlier and more recent times in human history, than Joseph Campbell's *magnum opus*, the four-volume masterpiece titled *The Masks of God*, published between 1959 and 1968. Although some of Campbell's archaeological and anthropological claims, especially regarding the dating of ancient pre-historical cultures, have been superseded by more recent discoveries, this still remains the best and most penetrating overview of the religions and mythologies of the world written in the last hundred years. All four volumes are listed in the Bibliography.)

The foundational text for both religious and philosophical Taoism is the classic Chinese *Tao Te Ching*, a collection of eighty-one short "chapters" (each only a few verses long) ascribed to the sage Laozi (Lao Tzu, Lao-Tze), who may have lived sometime between the sixth century and fourth century BCE, or, like his ancient Greek counterpart Homer, may never have existed at all. The *Tao Te Ching* explores the concept of the Tao—literally, the "Way" or path, but seen here as the fundamental natural principle underlying the Universe. The text suggests rather than elucidates, because one of its primary assumptions is that the Tao is ultimately unknowable, unnamable, beyond all categories of thought. Indeed, the *Tao Te Ching*'s first sentence is: "The tao that can be told is not the eternal Tao."[1]

At first blush, the pattern for the cowboy or gunfighter hero of an American Western movie would seem to be at odds with the ideals of a philosophy such as Taoism. The traditional Western hero is a man of action and intention who takes matters into his own hands; but the *Tao* advocates for *wu wei*, acting without acting, saying (in Chapter 2), "The Master acts without doing anything and teaches without saying anything." The traditional Western hero is quick with a gun; but the *Tao* (Chapter 31) says, "Weapons are the tools of fear; a decent man will avoid them except in the direst necessity and, if compelled, will use them only with the utmost restraint…. He enters a battle gravely, with sorrow and great compassion, as if he were attending a funeral." Western gunslingers and town-tamers are hard men who win through by being even tougher than their opponents; but we read in the *Tao Te Ching* (Chapter 78) that "the soft overcomes the hard; the gentle overcomes the rigid." Finally, the classic Western protagonist is visibly heroic, an ideal of adeptness, skill, and bravery whom we cannot help but admire; and yet the *Tao* (Chapter 45) says: "True wisdom seems foolish. True art seems artless."

The Bible, the Greek myths, and the Arthurian legends have shown just how much they can contribute to the Hollywood Western mythos, but given the classic Western's standard formulas, it might seem that the perspectives reflected in Taoism and other philosophies of the East have little relevance to the genre.

Enter Thomas Jefferson Destry, Jr., played marvelously by Jimmy Stewart in his first Western role. Many words have been written about the offbeat *Destry Rides Again* (1939):

its place in the comic Western tradition, its subversion of established tropes, its relation to a Jeffersonian concept of law, and—most especially—its questioning of the dominant culture's assumptions regarding gender roles.[2] When our town-taming hero, the son of a famous lawman, first steps off the stage onto the wild streets of Bottleneck, he is holding a parasol and a canary in a cage. He orders milk instead of whiskey at the saloon and doesn't carry a gun. When first confronted by the corrupt boss of the town, the land-grabbing Kent (Brian Donlevy), Destry responds mildly and passively, albeit with a certain unflappable strength. Stewart's Destry is indeed a subversive hero, contradicting just about everything that we have come to expect from the genre's typical protagonists.

Again, many analyses have focused on Destry's character as a satirical critique of American masculinity, and they are not wrong to do so. But, viewed mythologically, Destry can also represent simply an *alternative* way to be an American male, as Taoism is an alternative to Christianity. In fact, I would argue that Destry is the American Western's first true Taoist hero. Please note that I am not claiming this is intentional; there is nothing in the biographies and output of the film's writers that suggests any particular acquaintance with or interest in Taoism. (Felix Jackson, the German-born composer, playwright, and drama critic who created the story—which bears almost no resemblance to the Max Brand novel that supposedly inspired it—wrote mainly romantic comedies for Hollywood, none of which have a noticeable Eastern flavor.) Whether consciously or not, however, the creators of *Destry Rides Again* tapped into a deeper human truth, the same one that inspired many Eastern philosophies—namely, that gentleness and a certain passive acquiescence to the natural flow of events can often yield more productive results than aggression or forcing the action. It was almost certainly unintentional, yet the creators of *Destry* ended up drawing water from the same wells of the psyche that had previously nourished the philosophies of Laozi, Zhuangzi, Mencius, and Confucius.

(I would be remiss if I failed to note that the virtue of gentleness is also an important thread running through Occidental religion: the Hebrew Scriptures aver that "a soft answer turneth away wrath," Jesus tells us to turn the other cheek and love our enemies, and the Quran extols the virtues of peacemaking. "Acting without acting," however, is a concept that is much more at home in the Far East—and in *Parzival*—than it is in the Levantine traditions.)

Destry Rides Again may be as philosophically oriented as its offbeat hero, but that doesn't change the fact that it is also a whole lot of fun. Stewart is a delight in his first Western role—his comic timing is superb, his character is eminently likeable from the very beginning, and he even has the opportunity to show occasional glimpses of the dark, quiet intensity that would later inhabit his characters in the masterful 1950s Westerns directed by Anthony Mann. Meanwhile, top-billed Marlene Dietrich is incandescent in the role that was meant to rekindle her film career. (It did.) Dietrich plays Frenchy, Kent's corrupt dance-hall girlfriend and a genuine fireball. As the saloon's featured performer, she gets to deliver three very memorable tunes by Frank Loesser and Friedrich Hollaender: "See What the Boys in the Back Room Will Have"; "You've Got That Look"; and "Little Joe, the Wrangler." (As is typical of Western dance-hall songs, these are in contemporary musical style rather than the popular idioms of the actual Old West.)

The primary plot is set in motion when, after killing the prior sheriff, Kent—through his accomplice Judge Slade (Samuel S. Hinds)—has the town drunk Washington

"Wash" Dimsdale (Charles Winninger) installed as the new sheriff, to the uproarious laughter of the townsfolk. However, Dimsdale—a former deputy to Destry's father—takes his new role seriously, and soon sends for Destry Jr. to assist him with the mess that is Bottleneck. "He ain't got as big a name as his Pa," Dimsdale proclaims, "but he cleaned up Tombstone, and I'm sendin' for him to be my deputy! And when he gets here, Destry will ride again!"

Destry himself arrives on screen twenty minutes into the picture, and, like Frenchy, captivates our

After helping corrupt boss Kent (Brian Donlevy) cheat a man out of his ranch, Frenchy (Marlene Dietrich) pockets her share. "There's gold in them thar hills," her character said originally, but the censors nixed the line. *Destry Rides Again* (Universal, 1939).

attention from that moment forward. He is in a stage riding toward Bottleneck, accompanied by Janice Tyndall (Irene Hervey) and her hot-headed brother Jack (Jack Carson). The stage bounces along violently, irritating Jack, but Destry occupies himself carving a simple piece of wood into a napkin ring. (Again, it's hard not to be reminded of an Eastern sage working on a rock garden or a bonsai plant.) When the angry Jack fantasizes aloud about blowing the driver's head off, Destry—in what will soon become his trademark—smilingly relates a parable while he carves.

> DESTRY: I had a friend once, his name was Stubbs, he was always goin' around threatenin' to blow people's heads off. One day a fella came along and took him up on it.
> JACK: Well?
> DESTRY: Well, folks say that now Stubbs's forehead is holdin' up the prettiest tombstone in Greenlawn Cemetery.
> JACK: Very funny. You know, I've been handlin' cattle around these parts for quite a spell. I've met some of the toughest hombres they got. I'm still here. (*He pulls out a pistol.*) This ain't no ornament. Pretty good with it.
> DESTRY (*blowing shavings off his carving*): So was Stubbs.
> JACK (*irritated*): Meanin' just exactly what?
> DESTRY: Well, I just mean, you gotta be careful who you meet up with.
> JACK: You know, you got some pretty peculiar ideas for a deputy sheriff.
> JANICE (*chuckling*): But they make sense.
> JACK: Oh, so I'm supposed to ride in this confounded contraption gettin' bumped around like this and grin like a baboon!
> DESTRY: Well, maybe you should take up a hobby like me. You'd be surprised the genuine rage you can work off just by carvin' a little piece of wood.
> JACK: Are you sure your name is Destry?

Jack is heat to Destry's cool. Compared to Destry, he seems "manlier" in the traditional sense. He brandishes his weapon proudly, while Destry tells stories. But *stillness overcomes heat,* says Laozi. *True wisdom seems foolish. Weapons are the tools of fear.* Right here, in the protagonist's first appearance, the film immediately establishes a direct contrast between the standard Western hero, epitomized by Jack's macho posturing, and Destry's alternative paradigm—a beautiful rendition, even if unintentionally, of an Eastern sage. Watching Destry's unusual approach gradually unfold itself is one of the many joys of this movie.

Tom Destry (James Stewart) explains his philosophy on guns. Even his posture is sagelike. *Destry Rides Again* (Universal, 1939).

Destry may recall the *wu wei* ideal of a Taoist sage, but he can also be seen as Confucian in his respect for social duty and the right ordering of society—in this case, his reverence for the rule of law. He first has the opportunity to articulate his positions on both weapons and the law in a charming scene opposite Sheriff Wash Dimsdale in a hotel room. Wash is convinced that Destry is hopeless as a lawman and harangues him about his *laissez-faire* approach (while simultaneously helping him off with his boots).

> DESTRY: What'd you expect me to do?
>
> WASH (*pulls out his two pistols and waves them dramatically*): I expected you to be like your Pa, comin' out blastin' behind shootin' irons! And what happened? You didn't have any! Why?
>
> DESTRY: I don't believe in 'em.
>
> WASH: Huh? You did the last time I heard about ya! What in thunder's come over ya since then?
>
> DESTRY (*pulls a gun belt out of his suitcase*): Well, Wash, my Pa had these on that day down in Tombstone—but he got shot in the back. Didn't seem to do him much good, did they? (*He throws the guns back in the suitcase with distaste.*) That's one reason I don't believe in 'em.
>
> WASH: What in tarnation do ya believe in?
>
> DESTRY: Law and order!
>
> WASH: Without guns?
>
> DESTRY: Without 'em!
>
> WASH: Well, if that don't beat all let go. (*He pulls his shirttails out in frustration, then softens.*) Oh, Tom. The reason they made me sheriff here is because I was the town drunk. They wanted someone they could kick around, someone who wouldn't ask questions. But I was aimin' to fool 'em, do things right, sendin' for you. And now, you fooled me.
>
> DESTRY (*smiling*): Well, you will fool 'em, Wash. We'll fool 'em together.
>
> WASH: The only way to do that is fill 'em full o' lead!
>
> DESTRY: No, no, no. What for? You shoot it out with 'em, and for some reason or other, I

don't know why, they get to look like heroes. But you put 'em behind bars and they'll look little and cheap, the way they oughta look! And it serves as a warnin' to the rest of 'em to keep away!

WASH: Oh, that won't work here in Bottleneck. Oh, you go on home, and I'll go back to bein' the town drunk. That's all I'm good for.

DESTRY: Now, you're not goin' back to bein' the town drunk, and I'm gonna stay here and do this job I come for. My Pa did it the old way, and I'm gonna do it a new way.

WASH: Mmm.

DESTRY: (*tucking in Wash's shirt for him*). And if I don't prove to you that I'm right, I'll get out of town quick enough, don't worry. But first you got to give me a chance, Wash!

Wash reluctantly agrees, and Destry begins his work as an official lawman, in the truest sense of the word. He upholds the law even when it favors crooks like Kent, trusting in the slow grinding of the wheels of justice to eventually sort things out. Although Destry shows a grim intensity many times, the closest we see to an angry outburst is when the primacy of the law is challenged, as when the hothead Jack Tyndall declares, "Well, I'll get something done about [Kent], if I have to take the law in my own hands!" Destry responds with heat: "Nobody's gonna set themselves up above the law around here, you understand?" Later, Destry loses control and socks Tyndall in the jaw when the latter accuses him of being corrupt. This, to Destry, is blasphemy—working outside the law is clearly the ultimate sin in his eyes.

Running in parallel with Destry's journey is the storyline of the hapless, comical immigrant Boris (Mischa Auer), whose character presents another view of masculinity to add to those of Destry, Jack Tyndall, and the villain Kent. Boris starts out as a terribly henpecked husband—to the extent that his wife forces him to assume the last name of her dead first husband. In his first major scene, Boris plays five-card stud with Frenchy, and loses not only all of his money but, in the final hand, his pants as well. When she insists that he give her his pants right there at the table, humiliating and symbolically emasculating him, he protests in disbelief: "Oh, but Frenchy, I can't, it's undignified! Think of my position! I've met every king in Europe!" "Now you met two aces in Bottleneck," Frenchy replies. "Off with those pants!" But by the end of the movie, Boris will have learned to stand up for himself, to others and to his wife, in a way more in accord with the traditional American masculine virtues. However, Boris still remains a slightly ridiculous character at the end; the film shows us his transformation into a "man" just as it shows the *machismo* of Tyndall and Kent, but these models are set up in opposition to that of Destry, beyond a doubt the true hero of the picture. Most of the world must content itself with the poor options provided by Kent, Tyndall, or Boris (in ascending order of desirability); whereas the true sage, the fully centered man who acts in accord with both the flow of nature and his own inner truth, regardless of what society thinks of him, is a rare thing indeed. Destry is the genuine ideal, not cut from anyone's mold but his own—one of a kind, "certainly different from the rest of the men you meet out in this country," as Janice Tyndall describes him. The *Tao Te Ching* itself recognizes how uncommon people like Destry are. After the assertion that softness overcomes hardness, the text goes on to say, "Everyone knows this is true, but few can put it into practice."

One challenge presented by sages in movies—whether Destry, Merlin, or Yoda—is that they tend not to evolve; their character arcs are often slight. For dramatic interest, then, they usually require being surrounded by others who change more over the course of the story. In *Destry Rides Again*, the bulk of this work is achieved by the character

Lily Belle (Una Merkel), phallic symbol in hand, confronts her emasculated husband Boris (Mischa Auer), still missing his proper pants. *Destry Rides Again* **(Universal, 1939).**

of Frenchy, who begins the movie quite corrupt—a crook, a cheat, and an accessory to murder—but ends it ennobled. Her journey as a character, brought to life magnificently by Dietrich, is a critical part of the backbone of the narrative. Frenchy captivates our attention in many unforgettable scenes—the poker game just mentioned, all of her interactions with Destry, and especially the infamous knock-down-drag-out brawl with Boris's wife Lily Belle (Una Merkel), who clearly wants to be the only one with the right to emasculate her husband. (According to many accounts, the fight scene was not choreographed; Dietrich and Merkel improvised, and they were serious—to the extent that Merkel was bruised for quite some time afterwards.)

Over the course of the movie Frenchy's relationship to Destry becomes a focal point, driving the storyline just as strongly as the town-taming structure. Ultimately, driven both by narrative necessity and the compulsions of the Hays Code, Frenchy must sacrifice herself in order to atone for her sins, and when this happens it is a powerful moment indeed, one made even more touching in a subsequent scene, in which we (along with Destry) get to see, tangibly, just how Frenchy's spirit will endure into the next generation. Meanwhile, Destry's story resolves in a satisfying manner as well, ending on a delightful "fade-out" as he starts another parable and the credits begin to roll. In the end, Destry has tamed the town and brought peace—while firing only a single shot at another man. *Weapons are the tools of fear; a decent man will avoid them except in the direst necessity and, if compelled, will use them only with the utmost restraint.* The hero reluctantly picking up his guns has become a common trope in Westerns, and it is often read, somewhat condescendingly, as the peaceful idealist learning the error of his ways and becoming the warrior that all true men are meant to be. But I don't think that is how *Destry* is meant to be viewed. Here, our hero, like the Taoist sage, truly does take up his gun with great reluctance and only as a last resort, even though it is a stirring moment when he does so. Like the *Tao Te Ching*, Destry is not purely pacifistic; like Laozi, he recognizes that there are times of last resort when violence is unavoidable. When that moment comes, Destry does indeed enter the battle in true Taoist fashion, "gravely, with sorrow and great compassion, as if he were attending a funeral." Then, after things have been resolved, Destry once more walks the now-peaceful streets of Bottleneck without a weapon at his side. As a character, he didn't need to "see the light" about violence; he held the truth all along.

There is so much to love about *Destry Rides Again*. Dismissed as a simple comedy Western by some critics, and misunderstood or undervalued by many more,[3] the movie actually stands as one of the great triumphs of the genre. Just like its hero, it is unapologetically different from all of its peers, faithfully consistent to its own inner logic, wise, heroic, wonderfully funny, and frequently misread. However, like its heroine, it is also brash, uninhibited, over-the-top, delighted at its own chaos, and brazenly unconventional. The acting from the two leads is superb, leading to a string of saloon-girl characters in subsequent films played by Dietrich, although Stewart would not make another Western until Mann's *Winchester '73* (1950). The screenplay, direction, and production values are similarly first-rate. And of course, *Destry* is one of the very few classic Westerns that actually challenges the assumption that the best way to respond to violence is with more violence. In that sense, this rambunctiously offbeat Western might also be one of the most realistic representatives of the genre. After all, in real life, how often has the assertion of one man's will through sheer physical force and violence proven to be the best answer to a problem?

Destry Rides Again is unquestionably a comedy, and yet it has no shortage of powerful (and tragic) moments as well. I will always remember the way Stewart's voice sounds when he says, "That's how they shot my father. They didn't dare face him either." Or the way he delivers the first remark that really hits home with Frenchy, while smearing the lipstick off her mouth: "You know, I bet you've got kind of a lovely face under all that paint. Why don't you wipe it off someday and have a good look?" And Frenchy's sacrifice, with its long-delayed kiss and its poignant aftermath, stirs the soul. What is amazing about *Destry* is the way in which it blends

Destry (James Stewart) first gets through to Frenchy (Marlene Dietrich). *Destry Rides Again* (Universal, 1939).

outrageous hilarity and touching human drama seamlessly, maintaining a sense of an artistically coherent and integrated whole throughout, with no unevenness or artificiality. The masterful script bears a great deal of responsibility for this success, as does the multilayered acting of the two stars. Dietrich runs the gamut of humanity over the course of the movie, and Stewart manages to convey both lightness and gravity in every scene. As a wise and yet vastly entertaining Western that expertly blends comedy and tragedy, satisfying the viewer while staying true to its own eccentric character, *Destry Rides Again* is as rare and unique as its own offbeat hero.

The Westerner
(1940)

September 5, 1940 (London)
USA—English
The Samuel Goldwyn Company
100m—Mono—BW—1.37:1

Direction: William Wyler
Screenplay: Jo Swerling, Niven Busch, W.R. Burnett (uncredited), Lillian Hellman (uncredited), Oliver La Farge (uncredited), Dudley Nichols (uncredited), Stuart N. Lake (story)
Principal Cast: Gary Cooper (Cole Harden), Walter Brennan (Judge Roy Bean), Doris Davenport (Jane Ellen Mathews), Fred Stone (Caliphet Mathews)
Production: Samuel Goldwyn
Cinematography: Gregg Toland
Editing: Daniel Mandell
Art Direction: James Basevi
Music: Dimitri Tiomkin, Alfred Newman (uncredited)
Awards: Oscar—Best Supporting Actor (Brennan)
Nominations: Oscar—Best Original Story (Lake), Oscar—Best Black-and-White Art Direction (Basevi)

It's truly a shame that Walter Brennan, today, is most commonly remembered in caricature. We recall his strikingly idiosyncratic voice, his odd mannerisms, and the old, grizzled sidekicks that he memorably played. We think of him in the same category as Gabby Hayes and imagine that he must have portrayed such characters a hundred times, but in fact, the lasting image we have of Brennan as Western sidekick is primarily due to only three movies—*Red River* (1948), *The Far Country* (1954), and *Rio Bravo* (1959). We forget that Brennan was actually a profoundly good performer, one of the greatest character actors of all time, comfortable across a multitude of genres, playing villains, patriarchs, society men, preachers, and war heroes. We also forget that he won three Best Supporting Actor Oscars—still more than any other performer—and was nominated for a fourth. Of these four nominations, only one was for work he had done in a Western picture—the Oscar he won bringing Judge Roy Bean to life in *The Westerner* (1940). It was arguably the finest performance of his extraordinary career.

Judge Roy Bean was an actual historical figure, of course, although his story was very different than that portrayed here. The real Bean was not particularly a "hanging judge"; in fact, we only know of two men he sentenced to be hung, one of whom escaped first. And of course, the genuine Bean died peacefully in his sleep, having lived a few years into the twentieth century. But classical Westerns are about legend, not history—and rightly so. Nevertheless, *The Westerner* does build some of its characterization around truths of Bean's biography. Bean was indeed an eccentric self-proclaimed judge with no official credentials but who nevertheless styled himself as the "Law West of the Pecos," and he was truly infatuated with the British-American actress Lillie Langtry, naming his saloon The Jersey Lilly in her honor. (Contrary to the movie's assertion, however, the town of Langtry, Texas, was not named after the actress, but rather an unrelated railroad foreman who coincidentally had the same last name.)

Walter Brennan as hanging judge Roy Bean—one of the greatest performances of his career. *The Westerner* (Samuel Goldwyn, 1940).

The Westerner, like many other Westerns, structures its plot around the historical conflicts between cattlemen and farmers. In the film's opening moments, Bean sentences a young farmer, Shad Wilkins (Trevor Bardette), to be hung for "the most serious crime west of the Pecos, to wit, shootin' a steer." In truth, the farmers were being shot at by cattlemen; Wilkins returned fire but killed the animal by accident. About to be hung, the poor man, bizarrely, defends himself by pointing out that he was shooting at a man and didn't mean to hit the steer. "Yeah, it's your bad luck you missed him," says Bean, evoking general laughter from the onlookers when he adds, "That's the trouble with you sodbusters: you can't shoot straight!" Soon the man is dangling dead from a tree. This is justice west of the Pecos.

The next person we see judged by Bean's kangaroo court is the movie's hero, Cole Harden (Gary Cooper), who has made the mistake of legally purchasing a horse that was stolen. "You can rest assured that in this court a horse thief always gets a fair trial before he's hung," the Judge says. But the quick-thinking Harden learns of Bean's obsession with Lillie Langtry and soon persuades him that he possesses a lock of her hair, sealed safely away back in El Paso. Bean is starstruck, and thus Harden is able to talk himself out of a hanging by implying he will deliver to the Judge this non-existent trophy from his imaginary encounter with the famous actress. The two men then begin a complicated relationship, the evolution of which is the primary delight of the movie.

In my opinion, many excellent critics and scholars have gotten Brennan's Judge Bean wrong when writing about *The Westerner*, seeing his character mainly as an object lesson about the importance of not being fooled by the apparently likeable characteristics of tyrants. Michael Coyne notes the time period of the film's release and sees Bean as a symbol of the fascism that was drawing the world into war[1]; and Mary Lea Bandy and Kevin Stoehr write, "Despite his moments of displaying humor, affection, and folksy charisma, making it difficult for the viewer to despise him outright, Bean is rotten to the core, and anyone who forgets that basic fact is liable to suffer his wrath at some point."[2]

One danger inherent in our postmodern, hyper-politicized, ultra-polarized times is that we are becoming blinder to the nuances and complexities of human beings. Instead, we have been conditioned to make simplistic, black-and-white snap judgments, placing people as quickly as possible into Worthy Ally and Loathsome Enemy buckets. This is true of movie characters as well, especially after we, from our twenty-first-century position, have now endured several recent decades of Hollywood movies pounding away at facile tropes, sorting characters into clearly defined categories of "Hero" and "Villain" utilizing a widely understood but uncreative shorthand. As much as we deride the (inaccurate) stereotype of the White/Black Hat oater, most of our movies today are far guiltier of the sins of oversimplification and laziness of characterization than are the more morally complex and ambiguous Westerns of the Golden Age and afterwards.

As presented in *The Westerner*, Judge Roy Bean is a brutal, autocratic town boss, but he is also a desperately lonely man, self-imprisoned in his own fiefdom, distanced from all those around him by his lone-wolf authoritarianism. He longs for the human warmth and intimacy promised by the plentiful sensuous portraits of Lillie Langtry with which he adorns his tavern walls. When Harden comes along, Bean senses—perhaps for the first time—a man who is his equal, capable perhaps of understanding him. His need for Harden's friendship is palpable, as is his genuine affection for this basically upright but occasionally cunning adversary. At one point the two men even wake up together in a bed, limbs entwined, after a night of overindulgence. One doesn't have to work hard to see homosexual subtext here, but I think that this scene is more interested in the ways in which both the personalities and the destinies of these two men are interwoven. Harden and Bean are two halves of the same coin, both strong men making their own way through a wilderness of toadies and the weak-willed.

The key to Bean, and to the amazing relationship between these two opposed characters, comes in one of the film's most memorable scenes, when Bean pursues the escaping Harden on horseback and eventually knocks him off his horse. Both men wind up sprawled on the sand after this dramatic pursuit, but then proceed to have a leisurely conversation.

BEAN: That lock of hair—Lilly's hair. You promised to ride to El Paso fer it! Don't you remember? We drank on it! When you gonna do it? Huh? You ain't gonna crawfish?
HARDEN: No! The first post office I come to.
BEAN (*indicating his own back*): Straighten her out, will ya, son?
Harden knocks Bean's arm, causing him to fall on his stomach. This does the trick.
BEAN: Thank ya.
Bean gets back up on his

Cole Harden (Gary Cooper) and Judge Roy Bean (Walter Brennan): two enemies, also friends, enjoying a conversation in the dirt. *The Westerner* (Samuel Goldwyn, 1940).

hands and knees, and his pistol falls out of its holster. He replaces it, and flops back down
on the sand next to Harden.
HARDEN: You mangy old scorpion, you mighta got us both killed!

Bean laughs at this. Harden, watching him, smiles slowly, then starts to laugh as well. At this point, the Judge asks Harden why he intends to go to California; after all, he notes, there is a lot of fun to be had—together!—in Vinegarroon. Bean's longing for a real friendship is palpable here, but right now Harden has other concerns, primarily his own safe escape from this perilous territory. As the two men continue to talk at close quarters, Harden slowly sneaks Bean's pistol out of its holster.

BEAN (*chuckles*): Ya know, I cottoned to ya the first time I seen ya. Why don't you put in
   with me?
HARDEN (*concealing Bean's pistol in his own boot*): Well, I tell you, Judge, it's nice of you to
   ask me, but I, uh, I'm headin' for California and nothin' short of hangin' can stop me.
He rises, followed by Bean.
BEAN (*worried*): Wait a minute! You can't go; you're under suspended sentence.
HARDEN: Why, you hung Mr. Evans for that!
BEAN (*desperately*): Huh? Er, you're under suspendence anyhow! Who are ya, what do
   I know about ya, how do I know they ain't lookin' for ya? You're under arrest fer …
   disorderly conduct, fer … disturbin' the peace, uh, vagrancy, and you're on the way back
   to town with me and that's my rulin'!
Harden's smile has been growing. He pats Bean's arm and moves to get on his horse.
HARDEN: So long, Judge!
Bean watches him go, thinking. He slowly reaches for his pistol, misses it, begins looking
   around in the sand. Then he straightens up and turns toward Harden, now riding away in
   the distance.
BEAN: By gobs, he stole my gun!
But then, gradually, Bean begins to smile in appreciation. Fade out.

Despite themselves, the two men have a genuine affection for each other. From this moment on, Bean will think of Harden as a friend, even to the moment of their inevitable showdown. For his part, Harden will continue to respect Bean, in the end making the most compassionate gesture he can to his defeated opponent. We, the audience, are not meant to see Bean as simply a "fascist villain" or "rotten to the core." Instead, we are invited to see him as Harden sees him: a corrupt authoritarian, yes, but with a redeeming humanity buried inside. It is only the lack of the love and friendship that Bean so clearly craves that keeps him from being on the side of right; he stands a hair's breadth away from virtue, villainous only because of the void—symbolized by the two-dimensional portraits of the idealized Langtry—where genuine human connection should be. From *The Westerner*'s perspective, friendship can save a soul. Perhaps it can even redeem the world.

The greatest ancient discourse on friendship may be found in Chapters VIII and IX of Aristotle's *Nicomachean Ethics*. The philosopher opens by stating that "without friends no one would choose to live, though he had all other goods; even rich men and those in possession of office and of dominating power are thought to need friends most of all; for what is the use of such prosperity without the opportunity of beneficence, which is exercised chiefly and in its most laudable form towards friends?"[3] Judge Roy Bean, as portrayed in *The Westerner*, is a living negative example of this principle; he lacks the "opportunity of beneficence" because of his own tyrannical ways, and learns only too late, through his encounter with Cole Harden, about the critical element his life has been missing. Harden, however, does have the capability and opportunity to express the Aristotelian ideals in a positive way, and will do so before the end.

In the *Ethics*, Aristotle delineates three types of friendship, extrapolating from the differing ways in which we might love an object. The simplest of these, and the most common, is a relationship based upon *utility*. This is Harden's initial response to Bean—he reaches out and tries to find some common ground with the Judge (or, more accurately, invents it) for the obvious purpose of saving his own life from a hanging. Midway through the movie, however, in the conversation mentioned above, we see Harden beginning to enjoy his interaction with the Judge. In spite of himself, he can't help but like the eccentric old bastard. Harden has progressed to Aristotle's second level of friendship, that of *pleasure*. (It should be noted that Bean's own evolution mirrors this pattern: he is initially interested in Harden for utilitarian reasons, seeing him as a means for obtaining the treasured lock of hair, but in the later scene, Bean is clearly enjoying their conversation as much as Harden is.)

The third and highest form of Aristotelian friendship is the relationship based upon *virtue*, upon the good. Here we care for the other person as an end in themselves; we want what is best for them simply because it is best for them. Their usefulness to us and their ability to bring us enjoyment are secondary issues. This is the stage that the two men have reached by the end of the picture, when Harden's primary motivation turns from meting out frontier justice to the granting of a final vision of Paradise, and the blessings of an angel, to his fallen adversary/friend. There is no selfish gain for Harden here; his actions are entirely altruistic, a way of reaching out, one last time, to that which is the purest and noblest in Bean's soul. And the vision granted to Bean is granted to us, the audience, as well. We see what Bean's dying eyes see; by implication, we become him and partake in his absolution. We are Bean, all of us—living for ourselves and the things that we think we need, but inside, longing for beauty, love, and connection to others.

Ambiguity pervades *The Westerner*, not only in the paradoxical relationship between its two primary characters, but also in its approaches to history, conflict, freedom, security, home, nature, and civilization. If Harden and Bean encapsulate, between them, the dualities present within the human spirit, then Harden and the farmer's daughter Jane Ellen Mathews (Doris Davenport) show us the tensions between entirely different, external dichotomies: man and woman, of course, but also the individual and the community; freedom and responsibility; nature and culture; adventure and security; tradition and progress; the wilderness and civilization. Harden is a man of the open range; Jane Ellen is a woman of hearth and home. The interplay of these two opposing forces, reflected also in the conflict between the free-ranging cattlemen and the fence-building farmers, pervades the classical Western.

Westerns have always been ambivalent about civilization. On the one hand, civilization means the spread of Christian values, the conquering of the West, the realization of Manifest Destiny, and the delivery of the Promised Land to America. On the other hand, it also means prioritizing culture over nature, law over frontier justice, feminine society over masculine independence, a sense of place over a sense of freedom, community needs over rugged individualism. Perhaps most difficult for the fantasizing males who make up the bulk of the Western audience, civilization means settling down. One cannot reconcile all of these opposing forces without something being sacrificed.

The classic Western duality embodied: free-ranging Cole Harden (Gary Cooper) and Jane Ellen Mathews (Doris Davenport), woman of hearth and home. *The Westerner* (Samuel Goldwyn, 1940).

In their wonderful kitchen conversation, Harden and Jane Ellen make all of this explicit. "My house is all out there, all one room, with a sky for a roof," he says. She responds, "I'd want my house so that nothing could ever move it, so down deep that an earthquake couldn't shake it." This essential conundrum threads through the history of the Western, from *The Squaw Man* (1914) through *Tumbleweeds* (1925), *Cimarron* (1931), *Stagecoach* (1939), *Red River* (1948), *Shane* (1953), *The Searchers* (1956), *The Tall T* (1957), *The Outlaw Josey Wales* (1976), *Lonesome Dove* (1989), and beyond. Each of these Westerns addresses the ambiguity and answers it in its own way. Here, Harden will give up his tumbleweed existence to build a home with Jane Ellen; others—Ethan Edwards in *The Searchers*, for example—will find a different solution.

It's clear that the classical Western evokes something archetypal in continuing to explore these themes. Images this pervasive must be about more than just the literalities of cattlemen and settlers, open ranges and fences, trails and homes, individual men and women. As human beings, we stand right in the middle of so many contradictions and must somehow negotiate them, every single day. We are animals, but we have a culture. We are brutes who created civilization. We are self-centered individuals who built communities. We must learn how to live together while remaining true to ourselves. This is yet another reason why Westerns are so powerful, so necessary—in many ways, the best of them are all about this essential problem. How can we reconcile so many seemingly opposed forces in our lives and societies? How can we bring these conflicting tensions into harmony? And what must we sacrifice in order to do so?

The Westerner provides one answer to this, both in its internal narrative and its external history. By all accounts, Walter Brennan—like the corrupt judge he portrays here—had the capacity to be a pretty loathsome human being. He is reported to have been terribly racist and anti–Semitic; for example, workers on the set of his last television series, *The Guns of Will Sonnett*, recall him reacting with joyous laughter upon hearing of the assassination of Dr. King in 1968.[4] And yet, over the course of his illustrious career, Brennan gave us characters both demonstrating and evoking great compassion, sympathy, courage, and wisdom.

So what do we make of him, and those like him?

This movie shows a way forward: not just how we can make our peace with Brennan the individual actor, or Bean the character, but how we can do so with all of those around us, whether they live up to our ideals or not. Judge Roy Bean, in *The Westerner*'s telling, hangs people for little or no reason and imposes his ill-informed will on an entire community, regardless of the destructive consequences. His actions are deplorable, and the movie makes no bones about this from the first scene to the last. And yet we, along with the film's protagonist, also see Bean as a human being, capable of longing for beauty (Langtry) and friendship (Harden). We end up bestowing upon him our sympathy and affection, in spite of the horrors of his character and behavior, because of his human side. We recognize in ourselves what we see in him, both the light and the dark, and as a result, we have compassion for the murderous judge, even while (like Harden) still opposing his actions and the principles in which he believes. Perhaps we need to do the same for Walter Brennan, the actor—and for many, many other real-life human beings, despite their flaws.

This is what the arts can do for us, among many other things: help us get in touch with our shared humanity. When movies are at their best, as this one is, they can serve to take us out of judgmental mode and encourage us to see all of the parts that make up a human being, the ugliness and the beauty that we all carry around within us. They can encourage the favoring of sympathy over dogmatism, of compassion over condemnation, of forgiveness over self-righteousness. The profound value of this for human society has been recognized by artists through the ages. As Nathaniel Hawthorne wrote in *Twice-Told Tales*: "Man must not disclaim his brotherhood, even with the guiltiest."[5]

Tidbits and Trivia

- As a winner of three Oscars for acting, Brennan is in select company indeed: only Ingrid Bergman, Daniel Day-Lewis, Jack Nicholson, and Meryl Streep have matched this figure. Brennan remains the only one to win all three in a Supporting category. Katharine Hepburn is the only person to have won four acting Oscars.
- This was the third of seven movies with Cooper as the star in which Brennan would play a supporting role. They were: *The Wedding Night* (1935); *The Cowboy*

and the Lady (1938); *The Westerner* (1940); *Meet John Doe* (1941); *Sergeant York* (1941); *The Pride of the Yankees* (1942); and *Task Force* (1949). The two men had also appeared in the lost silent feature *Watch Your Wife* (1926), both uncredited and in bit parts.

Melody Ranch
(1940)

November 15, 1940 (USA)
USA—English
Republic Pictures
84m—Mono—BW—1.37:1

Direction: Joseph Santley
Screenplay: Jack Moffitt, F. Hugh Herbert, Bradford Ropes, Betty Burbridge
Principal Cast: Gene Autry (Gene Autry), Jimmy Durante (Cornelius Jupiter Courtney), Ann Miller (Julie Shelton), Barton MacLane (Mark Wildhack), Barbara Jo Allen (Veronica Whipple), George "Gabby" Hayes (Pop Laramie), Jerome Cowan (Tommy Summerville), Mary Lee (Penny Curtis), Joe Sawyer (Jasper Wildhack), Horace McMahon (Bud Wildhack), Clarence Wilson (Judge "Skinny" Henderson), William "Billy" Benedict (Slim)
Production: Sol C. Siegel
Cinematography: Joseph H. August
Editing: Lester Orlebeck
Art Direction: John Victor Mackay
Music: William Lava (uncredited), Paul Sawtell (uncredited)
Awards: National Film Registry

This book deals very little with the phenomenon of the "singing cowboy" Western, for reasons explained earlier, and yet I would be remiss if I did not at least write a handful of words about a subgenre that was unquestionably a significant part of American culture, especially for those who were young during the 1930s and 1940s. Ken Maynard, Roy Rogers, Tex Ritter, Gene Autry, and their fellow "sons of the saddle" portrayed a Western cross between two medieval ideals, the knight errant and the troubadour. Their cowboy characters were chivalrous itinerant minstrels who sang their way into ladies' hearts while righting injustices.

Ken Maynard is often credited with being the screen's first true singing cowboy, due to his performance of a song called "Drunken Hiccoughs" in a 1929 short, but the film that truly set the pattern for the subgenre was a Maynard vehicle from 1934, *In Old Santa Fe*. Not only was this movie the debut of Smiley Burnette and also the first appearance of Gabby Hayes's persona as cranky but loveable sidekick; it also featured the arrival of Gene Autry, soon to become "America's Favorite Singing Cowboy," in an uncredited musical performance. Aspects of *In Old Santa Fe*'s plot would soon become commonplace in Westerns of this type: the modern setting, the uncomplicated morality, and the use of Eastern racketeers as the villains.

Autry makes an interesting contrast with his eventual box-office rival, Roy Rogers ("The King of the Cowboys"). Roy is more genteel, smoother, and unfailingly graceful—no one sits a horse like Roy does; whereas Gene is a little rougher, a little meaner, a little more muscular, a little more hard-edged. For me, Gene Autry is to Roy Rogers as Gene Kelly is to Fred Astaire.

Movie studios wanted to take advantage of the pop-idol appeal (on- and off-screen) of their singing cowboy heroes, and it was clear that these stars were just playing versions of themselves anyway. For this reason, in over eighty films from 1938 to 1952, the name of Roy's character was simply "Roy Rogers." Likewise,

The budding romance between two genuine oddballs, Cornelius J. Courtney (Jimmy Durante) and Veronica Whipple (Barbara Jo Allen), is the most charming part of a charming movie. *Melody Ranch* (Republic, 1940).

in over ninety pictures from 1934 to 1953, Gene Autry bore his own name. Sidekicks and female leads, however, were varied and fictional.

Rogers first starred in the enjoyable 1938 Republic picture *Under Western Stars*; Autry was originally intended for the role but became embroiled in a salary dispute with the studio. The plot centers around water rights in an unnamed Western state. Roy, the son of a former congressman, runs for Congress himself to stand up for ordinary Western folks against the Eastern corporate interests, while simultaneously romancing the daughter of the biggest bigwig. The movie is great fun; mythic it isn't, but certainly entertaining, and Rogers is an appealing star. Even the famously hard-to-please *New York Times* film critic Bosley Crowther wrote about the film's release: "Republic Pictures, which is always prospecting around, has discovered a new Playboy of the Western World in the sombrero'd person of Roy Rogers, who has a drawl like Gary Cooper, a smile like Shirley Temple and a voice like Tito Guizar." (Although Crowther, in his brief review, is clearly impressed by Rogers, his thoughts on the film itself are more lukewarm. He closes: "In modest and sometimes unintentional ways, the incidents are amusing, the score has a certain folksy exuberance, and the dust-bowl film shown to Washington society by Roy after his election to Congress on a free-water platform is a darn good documentary. Too bad we couldn't just review that.")[1]

Though in general I prefer Rogers to Autry, the latter's *Melody Ranch* (1940) is one of my favorite singing cowboy pictures. In many ways this vehicle for Autry is a weaker picture than Rogers's *Under Western Stars*. The tone is uneven, the "message" (extolling Western virtues over "city" ones) is ham-handed, Autry's acting is stilted, a love triangle is set up and then quickly dismissed before it can generate any real conflict, and one moment—a character's death—seems unnecessarily dark in a picture otherwise clearly made to be a lark. But it's a B-picture after all, and whatever flaws *Melody Ranch* has are redeemed for me, and then some, by the comic moments, the colorful supporting cast, and especially by the delightful secondary romance between the two eccentrics Cornelius J. Courtney (Jimmy Durante) and Veronica Whipple (Barbara Jo Allen, a comedienne already famous at the time for her spinster character Vera Vague). To watch the interplay of these two great comics as their characters' relationship begins to blossom is to enjoy (in microcosm) a sense of the possibilities of Hollywood romantic comedy as it existed in the early 1940s.

Movies like *Under Western Stars* and *Melody Ranch* are meant to be nothing but fun. And they succeed, admirably. Relax and enjoy them on their own terms and set aside mythic significance for a while. The path through the history of the Western is a long and complex one; it's always nice to stop along the way for a little laughter and refreshment.

They Died with Their Boots On
(1941)

November 20, 1941 (New York City)
USA—English
Warner Bros.
140m—Mono—BW—1.37:1

Direction: Raoul Walsh
Screenplay: Wally Kline, Æneas MacKenzie
Principal Cast: Errol Flynn (George Armstrong Custer), Olivia de Havilland (Elizabeth Bacon), Arthur Kennedy (Ned Sharp), Charley Grapewin (California Joe), Gene Lockhart (Samuel Bacon, Esq.), Anthony Quinn (Crazy Horse), Stanley Ridges (Major Romulus Taipe), John Litel (General Phil Sheridan), Walter Hampden (William Sharp), Sydney Greenstreet (Lt. General Winfield Scott), Regis Toomey (Fitzhugh Lee), Hattie McDaniel (Callie)
Production: Robert Fellows
Cinematography: Bert Glennon
Editing: William Holmes
Art Direction: John Hughes
Music: Max Steiner

They Died with Their Boots On (1941) follows—or rather, purports to follow—the life of George Armstrong Custer from his earliest days as a discipline problem at West Point through his military career in the Civil War and the American Indian Wars, concluding with his death at Little Bighorn. There are many odd or unexpected aspects to this movie: its wildly inaccurate, revisionist history; the large number of indoor dialogue scenes relative to action sequences; and the casting of Aussie Errol Flynn, accent and all, as the Ohio native Custer. However, by far the most surprising aspect of this patriotic Custer biopic is its relatively sympathetic take on the Indians. Later Westerns featuring Custer (notably *Little Big Man*, 1970) would portray the general's campaigns, more accurately, as part of a larger genocidal war on America's native peoples. Naturally, in these more recent narratives Custer is shown as a villain, a lunatic, or both. What is striking about *They Died with Their Boots On* is the way in which it tries to have its cake and eat it too: the Indians are treated unfairly by the whites, and yet Custer is still a noble American hero.

In this version of the tale, Custer wants to do right by the natives. He negotiates a peace with the Sioux in which, on behalf of the government, he grants them the Black Hills as their own land. However, unscrupulous Eastern businessmen—colluding with, coincidentally, two of Custer's former enemies from West Point—deal arms to the Indians, and then spread a rumor that there is gold to be found in the Black Hills, thus insuring that whites will flock to the area and drive the Indians from the land. In real life, the

Errol Flynn as the spirit of George Armstrong Custer in the film's last shot. *They Died with Their Boots On* **(Warner Bros., 1941).**

Black Hills Gold Rush was actually sparked in part by Custer's own reports of gold, but in the movie's reality, Custer's role is to right the wrong perpetrated by these war profiteers. Testifying in Washington, he learns (from one of the conspirators) of plans for two American generals to concentrate their forces in the Yellowstone Valley, and exclaims:

> Why, you fool! Those troops are infantry! Useless against Indians! And they won't find any three thousand Sioux. The sanctuary of the entire red race has been violated. They'll find every tribe in the West massed there, ready to overwhelm them! Not only the Sioux, but the Cheyenne, the Blackfeet, the Sans Arcs, all the rest of them! And who's to blame them? Not I, gentlemen. If I were an Indian, I'd fight beside Crazy Horse to the last drop of my blood!

An unconventional Custer indeed; Flynn's version has all of the heroism of earlier flag-waving portrayals, and yet carries none of the genocidal guilt that would be assigned to the general's figure by later movies (and history). Other sympathetic whites echo Custer's sentiments, such as his British adjutant Butler (G.P. Huntley), who, on the eve of the Last Stand, proclaims to Custer, "The only real Americans in this merry old parish are on the other side of the hill, with feathers in their hair."

I'm torn in my response to this. On the one hand, I appreciate the more enlightened sensibility of *They Died with Their Boots On* toward the Native Americans, relative to other films of its day. On the other, this all seems like taking the easy way out, hedging one's bets. We get to keep our noble vision of Custer, guilt-free, while still sympathizing with the plight of the Indians. Inconvenient ethical problems are cast aside; we can all agree that the greedy profiteers who incite the battle in order to profit from it are villains, enemies to both the United States and the natives. Why delve any further into the messiness of history? The movie lets us off too easy, absolves us of any guilt or the need to question our own reactions—thus, in that sense, lacking the moral courage of its own hero.

In the climax of the film, Custer goes into Little Bighorn not as a general who has made a tactical error but rather as a willing sacrifice. He knows that he and his men will be massacred but chooses this course to buy time for other forces to assemble. Custer dies so that others can live—including the Indians, whose right to the Black Hills he secures with a posthumously prophetic letter. General Sheridan (John Litel) adds the final touch to the movie's glorification of Custer when he says to Libbie, Custer's widow (Olivia de Havilland, in her last film pairing with Flynn): "Come, my dear. Your soldier won his last fight after all." The movie shows Custer's Last Stand as a brilliant tactical move, and the general himself as both the savior of his country and friend to the natives, wanting to do right by everyone, finally sacrificing himself for both the Indians and the whites. Frankly, it's a lot to swallow.

None of this is what made me choose to write about *They Died with Their Boots On*, however. I include the movie here because of a conundrum that it presents, a question for which I do not feel that I have a definitive answer.

It must be said that, in general, the film is middling in quality. It does show some fine production values, especially the cinematography by Bert Glennon, which—in the interior scenes, featuring brightly lit surfaces dappled with organic shadows—recalls the visually captivating style of George Barnes in Hitchcock's Best Picture-winner *Rebecca* from the previous year, one of the most beautifully photographed movies of all time. Despite its visual splendor, however, *They Died with Their Boots On* is overlong, its sentiments often bloated and overstated, and the interest sags in many places. Although the score by Max Steiner can be excellent and stirring (making great use of the real Seventh Cavalry's signature "Garryowen" tune), the music is oddly incongruous in many places, especially in its awkward use of whole-tone harmonies during dramatic moments, sounding to modern ears more whimsically eccentric than foreboding. (Listen to the scene where the Sharps make their business offer to Custer for a particularly striking example.) And though the movie clearly attempts to glorify the American soldiers, the cavalry never really gets its due. Other than Custer and his adjutant, the men of the Seventh are just background extras; we don't know them as people, not even as stock characters. It would require the skills of John Ford, a few years down the road, to compose the quintessential filmed paeans to the U.S. Cavalry.

Given all these reservations, the question I am driven to ponder is this: can a mediocre film be redeemed by one incredible moment? In fact, can it even be made great?

The scene in question is Custer's final farewell to his devoted wife before departing to meet his destiny at Little Bighorn. By accident, he discovers a diary in which Libbie has written down her fears that she will never see her husband again. "Tomorrow my husband leaves, and I cannot help but feel that my last happy days are ended. A premonition of disaster such as I have never known is weighing me down." Custer already knows that he is riding to his doom, having chosen this outcome himself, but both he and Libbie try, at first, to put a brave face on things. Libbie ad-libs about how she has probably written similar things on the eve of all of her husband's departures for battle, and Custer

Libbie Custer (Olivia de Havilland) and her husband (Errol Flynn) share what they both know to be their final moment together. *They Died with Their Boots On* (Warner Bros., 1941).

responds in kind. "The more sadness in parting, the more joy in the reunion," he asserts, smiling unconvincingly. But then the bugle call sounds outside, and we see the two look at each other in a split second of transcendent honesty. Each is fully aware of what is about to happen, and they see it in each other's eyes. This moment is acted brilliantly by Flynn and de Havilland as lovers knowingly together for the last time on earth. It is profoundly thrilling, moving, heartbreaking. Custer then declares, with great feeling, "Walking through life with you, ma'am, has been a very gracious thing." He kisses his wife one final time, then leaves without looking back. Libbie leans against the wall, tears running down her face, and the camera pulls back, showing her isolated and small among the home's rich furnishings. After a moment, she drops to the ground in a dead faint. I cannot help but be reminded of Wolfram's *Parzival* once more—specifically, the moment when Parzival bids farewell to his mother and rides off to meet his own destiny (one with a happier outcome than Custer's). His grief-stricken mother watches the hero ride away, and then falls to the ground, dead.

The farewell scene between Custer and Libbie is spectacularly powerful. Might it be one which fully justifies, and then some, the two hours of less effective screen time it has taken to get to this point? In a film that often manages to avoid opportunities for deeply satisfying payoffs, can this one staggeringly good instance make up for all the rest? I can't answer with certainty; but I will say that, for me, at the least, it comes very, very close.

Tidbits and Trivia

- The real Elizabeth Custer lived until 1933, just eight years before this film's release. Like Josephine Earp, Libbie would go on to spend a good portion of her widowed years cultivating her husband's image for posterity.
- The character of Butler, a heroic Englishman who gives his life for America, was presumably present in *They Died with Their Boots On* to elicit sympathy for contemporary England, under attack by the Nazis at the time. (The actual Custer did not have a British adjutant.) Many movies of this era sought, in ways subtle and unsubtle, to stir Americans from their isolationism. In this case, the point would be moot: seventeen days after the film's release, the Japanese attacked Pearl Harbor.

The Ox-Bow Incident
(1943)

AKA: *Strange Incident*
December 4, 1942 (St. Louis)
USA—English / Spanish
Twentieth Century-Fox
75m—Mono—BW—1.37:1

Direction: William A. Wellman
Screenplay: Lamar Trotti, Walter Van Tilburg Clark (novel)
Principal Cast: Henry Fonda (Gil Carter), Dana Andrews (Donald Martin), Mary Beth Hughes (Rose Mapen), Anthony Quinn (Juan Martínez), William Eythe (Gerald Tetley), Harry Morgan (Art Croft), Jane Darwell (Ma Grier), Matt Briggs (Judge Daniel Tyler), Harry Davenport (Arthur Davies), Frank Conroy (Major Tetley), Marc Lawrence (Jeff Farnley), Paul Hurst (Monty Smith), Victor Kilian (Darby), Chris-Pin Martin (Poncho), Willard Robertson (Sheriff Risley), Ted North (Joyce)
Production: Lamar Trotti
Cinematography: Arthur C. Miller
Editing: Allen McNeil
Art Direction: Richard Day, James Basevi
Music: Cyril J. Mockridge
Awards: National Board of Review—Best Film, National Board of Review—Best Actor (Morgan, shared with *Happy Land*), National Board of Review—Best Director (Wellman), National Film Registry
Nominations: Oscar—Best Picture, New York Film Critics Circle—Best Director (Wellman)

In 1919, when he was fourteen years old, Henry Fonda witnessed a lynching in Omaha. Will Brown, a Black man awaiting trial for the alleged rape of a white woman, was dragged from his jail cell by a white mob, stripped, castrated, and hung. The rabid crowd then fired bullets into the corpse, dragged it through the town, and set it ablaze. Fonda's father had let him see this atrocity on purpose; according to Fonda, he offered no commentary, but simply wanted his son to witness the event and, presumably, process it in his own way. It was a horrific experience that Henry Fonda would never forget.[1] Later in his life, the actor would seek out and win roles in numerous movies decrying the tyranny of the angry mob, including *Young Mr. Lincoln* (1939), *12 Angry Men* (1957), *The Tin Star* (1957), and *Warlock* (1959). But perhaps the greatest such film—and one of Fonda's personal favorites—was the grim, groundbreaking Western *The Ox-Bow Incident* (1942).

The movie—adapted relatively faithfully from Walter Van Tilburg Clark's 1940 anti-fascist novel—tells the story of Gil Carter (Fonda) and Art Croft (Harry Morgan, billed as Henry Morgan in those days), two Western drifters who get swept along with a posse hunting after unknown cattle rustlers who, according to rumor, have also killed a local rancher. Out in the wild, the posse captures three men in possession of the cattle in question; the men say they purchased the cattle legally, but most of the mob believe them to be the culprits and argue fiercely for their execution. Gil, Art, and a handful of others stand against the lynching—there is time to investigate and clear up any doubts before justice is administered—but the vengeful contingent prevails after a gut-wrenching debate, and the three men are hung. Afterward, the posse members learn that the rancher was only wounded, not killed, and that the true rustlers have already been apprehended. The sheriff who breaks this news, then says to the lynch mob, "God better have mercy on you—you won't get any from me."

This primary storyline is powerful stuff in itself, but the movie is filled with many additional narrative touches that give it a gritty realism and clear-eyed humanity unparalleled in any prior Western. These include Gil and Art's colorful arrival in the dusty tavern at the beginning of the movie; the Oedipal conflict between a bloodthirsty, tyrannical ex–Confederate and his cowed but compassionate son; the chance encounter with a former flame of Gil's, now a newlywed, along the trail; and dialogue scenes which flesh out the personalities of some of the secondary characters. Moments like these bring us, as viewers, with full force into the world of the movie, and connect us to the characters in a way that is startlingly strong, especially given the relatively short running time of the picture.

The Ox-Bow Incident is not just the best Western made during the Second World War; in fact, it is one of the greatest Westerns ever, and the earliest example of a movie not just partially but fully committed to the dismantling of the standard Western mythos. It questions everything, all of the assumptions of its predecessors about violence, vengeance, frontier justice, true heroism, and moral certitude.[2] Every deconstructionist, revisionist Western made during the 1960s and after looks back, in some way, to this moment in time when—incredibly—the mythmaking machinery of Hollywood began demolishing the received wisdom of its own deeply entrenched culture by way of one extraordinary film. Some earlier Hollywood Westerns contained subversive elements, of course—outlaw heroes, sympathetic treatment of Native Americans, differing takes on masculinity and violence, etc.—but none until *Ox-Bow* was completely subversive, start to finish.

As played by Henry Fonda, Gil is the protagonist of the film, and he and his friend Art are the closest things we have to stand-ins for the audience. Nevertheless, Gil is far from perfect, no idealized Western hero. When we first meet him, he is a broody drifter who seeks out bar fights and overindulges in alcohol. (After vomiting outside the saloon after a binge, he looks at the result on the ground and says, "Holy cow, now I'm going to have to start all over again!") And although he will eventually stand with those opposed to the lynching, he is not the first to reach that conclusion, and he never moralizes about it. In fact, the movie allows us to see a certain amount of self-interest in Gil's position—for example, when he says to Art, "I got nothin' particular against hangin' a murderin' rustler, it's just I don't like doin' it in the dark. There's always some crazy fool who'd lose his head and start hangin' everybody in sight." "Us?" Art asks. "Funnier things have happened," Gil replies, aware of the suspicion held by many of the posse members toward Art and himself. And yet Gil has his noble side too: he is unhesitatingly kind to the old Black preacher Sparks (played magnificently by Leigh Whipper), whom most of the posse deride or talk down to, and by the end of the movie, Gil and Art will take it upon themselves to care for the bereaved family of Martin (Dana Andrews), the leader of the trio who ended dangling from a tree in the ox-bow. Overall, Gil is no Western hero in the traditional sense. He's just a life-sized man, imperfect and self-contradictory, but one whose better nature can and will be evoked by the end. (In many ways, Fonda's character here prefigures the great, ethically complex roles that his dear friend James Stewart would play a decade later in five classic Anthony Mann Westerns, from 1950's *Winchester '73* to 1955's *The Man from Laramie*.)

A revealing conversation between the saintly preacher Sparks (Leigh Whipper) and the drifter Gil (Henry Fonda). *The Ox-Bow Incident* (Twentieth Century–Fox, 1942).

However, *The Ox-Bow Incident* does have a genuine hero, in the sense of a role model to be emulated: the vastly compassionate Sparks. This character is the film's true moral center, saintly and yet real, believable. Fonda's performance may be a masterpiece of smoldering intensity, but Leigh Whipper's portrayal of the old preacher, in his few brief scenes, is just as stunning. The extraordinary Whipper, virtually unknown today, brings to vivid life the character of this gentle, humble man while at the same time endowing him with great gravity, wisdom, and quiet power; how bizarre it is that neither the actor nor the unforgettable character he plays are even listed in the film's opening or closing credits.

Leigh Whipper himself had a fascinating life and career. He was born in South Carolina in 1876 at the end of Reconstruction—that is, prior to the time in which the movie is supposed to have taken place. The son of an educator and the nephew of a prominent abolitionist, Whipper attended Howard University Law School for a time, left to begin a significant career on the stage (starting with *Uncle Tom's Cabin* in 1899), became an accomplished pianist, co-founded the Negro Actors Guild of America, and was the first Black member of the Actors' Equity Association. His earliest movie appearance was in the 1920 silent *Within Our Gates*, an anti-lynching drama which is the oldest surviving film directed by an African American (Oscar Micheaux). Whipper originated the role of Crooks in *Of Mice and Men* on Broadway and played the character in the 1939 film version as well. Between 1920 and 1957, Whipper acted in twenty-five movies, seven of them (including this one) without being credited. After retiring from films in his early eighties, he lived for nearly two decades more, dying shortly before his ninety-ninth birthday in 1975.

One of the best moments in *The Ox-Bow Incident* is a dialogue between its two most compelling characters, Gil and Sparks. During the cold night vigil as the posse pauses in its hunt, the preacher rides over to Gil and asks, "Mind my comin' in a little closer, Mr. Carter?" Gil immediately responds, "No, come on. I'm findin' it kinda lonesome myself."

Despite the racist culture of the time, Gil speaks naturally with Sparks as an equal, and Sparks trusts Gil enough to open up to him. The ensuing conversation, in just a few lines of dialogue, takes full advantage of Sparks's vulnerable nobility and Gil's flawed humanity.

> Sparks: Powerful cold tonight, ain't it?
> Gil (*kindly*): I got a blanket if you want it.
> Sparks: No, thank you just the same, Mr. Carter, but it takes all my hands to stay on this old horse.
> Gil (*offering a whiskey bottle*): Better have a couple of shots.
> Sparks: I never use it. I sure wish we was well out of this here business.
> Gil: Ah, it's a way of spendin' time.
> Sparks: It's man taking on himself the vengeance of the Lord.
> Gil (*snorts*): Think the Lord cares much about what's happenin' up here tonight?
> Sparks: He marks the sparrow's fall. (*Sparks hesitates a moment.*) I seed my own brother lynched, Mr. Carter. I weren't nothin' but a little fella, but sometimes, now, wakes up dreamin' about it.
> Gil (*moved*): Had he done what they picked him up fer?
> Sparks (*sadly*): I don't know. Nobody never did know for sure.
> Gil (*sighs*): Well, a couple shots more whiskey can't do my soul any harm. (*He drinks.*)

Even citing this excellent dialogue doesn't do the scene justice. To watch and hear Whipper and Fonda deliver these lines is to witness a one-minute masterclass on the actor's craft.

When Sparks talks about being present at his brother's lynching as a child, we see the reaction in Gil's eyes—one that undoubtedly echoed Fonda's own feelings as well. And yet it is to the movie's great credit that it avoids extremes of didacticism (with one notable exception, discussed later). Sparks could have told us that his brother was innocent—but he doesn't know; the brother may have done what he was hung for. Gil could be so moved by the saintly Sparks that he becomes a pure-hearted character—but he doesn't; he just leans a little more toward the good. The innocent men facing lynching could be caricatures of wronged innocence—but they aren't; they are flawed and human just like their executioners. Our protagonists, Art and Gil, could be the first to raise their voices against the lynching—but they aren't; as the handful of men move across to stand with the shopkeeper Davies (Harry Davenport) and Sparks, indicating their opposition to the hanging, Art and Gil are among the last to decide, after nearly a full minute of hesitation.

This is the great thing about *The Ox-Bow Incident*: it never takes the easy way out, never oversimplifies its characters or its storyline. The pat, simplistic, black-and-white morality that typifies mainstream pop culture is almost completely absent in this movie. Obvious and lazy narrative shortcuts are avoided, as is cheaply bought emotional manipulation. For example, there is a potentially cathartic explosion of Gil's pent-up rage when he sees Deputy Mapes (Dick Rich) brutally slug the prisoner Martin just before the hanging. Without a second's hesitation, Gil leaps upon Mapes and attacks him with his fists. And yet we never really see the fight; it's lost in a crowd of onlookers, just indiscriminate bodies rolling around, without any of the typical Hollywood ringing punch sounds, just dull thuds. The movie avoids the easy manipulation of a romanticized, choreographed fight scene, and our catharsis is denied. The full weight of the slow-burning and tragic plot still lies on us. Similarly, when the three prisoners are

Yin and yang, the union of opposites: Sparks (Leigh Whipper) comforts Dad Hardwicke (Francis Ford) before the lynching. *The Ox-Bow Incident* (Twentieth Century–Fox, 1942).

finally hung, there is nothing sentimental about the scene. The camera lingers for just a second on their shadows, and then moves on. This honest, unpretentious approach yields a Western so completely human, realistic, and powerful that it stands apart from any of its predecessors (and most of its successors).

One of the most unforgettable mythic moments in the entire movie occurs when Sparks comforts the addle-minded old Dad Hardwicke (played by John Ford's brother Francis) before he is hung. As Sparks immediately and instinctively kneels down to embrace the poor man cowering on the ground, we are given a vision of pairs of opposites—saint and sinner, Black man and white man, wise man and fool—dissolved in unity, bound together through compassion. (Perhaps the German *Mitleid*—"with-suffering"—captures the nature of this highest human virtue even more aptly.) For me, this is the most powerful image in a movie filled with powerful images—and an archetypal one as well. Many of the world's great mythologies have evoked this same notion, that while on the surface we as human beings seem as if we were separate individuals, in reality we are all one. The unitary nature of apparent dualities that we see visualized in circular images such as the Taoist *taijitu* (the *yin-yang* symbol), the ancient Egyptian "Secret of the Two Partners" (who are actually one), the Nataraja dance of Shiva within the wheel of flames (*prabha mandala*), or Nicholas of Cusa's circle with center everywhere and circumference nowhere—all of these find a distant echo in the round embrace of these two poor souls, each an outcast in his own way, one embodying pure Love, the other just moments away from Death.

I have already remarked on the way in which *The Ox-Bow Incident* avoids both narrative laziness and cheap manipulation—and that's true. There is one false note at the end, however, an uncharacteristic moment when things tip too far into the obvious, the sentimental, the didactic. Before his lynching, Martin is allowed to write a letter to his wife. He gives it to the kindly storekeeper Davies to deliver; Davies secretly reads it, and shows it to some of the others, convinced that the nobility of the letter shows that Martin could not be the kind of man to kill a rancher and steal his cattle. Martin is actually upset by this; he meant for the letter to be a private communication for his wife and children. After the hanging, when the horrified posse members learn that they have killed three innocent men, they return to town and sit silently, devastated, in the saloon, awaiting their fate at the hands of the sheriff. At this moment, Gil reads Martin's letter aloud to the bunch—a passionate argument for the rule of law as opposed to the rough justice of the mob. Unfortunately, the moment falls completely flat. It's heavy-handed and stagy, preachy and didactic, spelling out points that the movie has already made far more powerfully through the events of the narrative. It's also inauthentic—we strain to believe that this philosophical dissertation is what a man about to die would write to his beloved family, rather than something more intimate and personal.

The letter was a plot point in Clark's original novel, but the author wisely did not reveal its contents. Lamar Trotti's original script followed suit, understanding that some things are better suggested than literally enunciated. We have already seen the storekeeper's reaction to the letter and understand all we need to know about its content. Any text that the film reveals is bound to be a disappointment; better to keep it a mystery, let each viewer's imagination fill in the gaps, and with emotion rather than discourse. A screenwriter as accomplished as Trotti—who gave us, among others, the classic scripts to *Young Mr. Lincoln* (1939), *Wilson* (1944), and *Yellow Sky* (1948)—certainly knew all this. However, during the journey from concept to execution, director William Wellman became convinced that the contents of the letter must be made explicit, and so

The reading of the letter: Gil (Henry Fonda) and Art (Harry Morgan). *The Ox-Bow Incident* (Twentieth Century–Fox, 1942).

he overrode Trotti's (and Clark's) original intent.[3] The result is the one glaring weakness within a masterpiece of cinema.

In many ways this scene is analogous to another penultimate monologue, the one just before the end of *Psycho* (Alfred Hitchcock, 1960) in which the psychologist takes several minutes to explain to us what has just happened. Both of these are unnecessary digressions, over-pedantic and redundant; each represents the only obvious flaw in an otherwise near-flawless movie. Fortunately, these scenes do not ruin their respective movies; they are surrounded by too much that is glorious.

Overall, *The Ox-Bow Incident* pulls no punches. Although brimming with humanity, it is also gritty and gut-wrenching from the first scene to the last. It never lets the audience off easily, nor, for that matter, any of its characters except for Sparks and Davies. After the hanging, when the sheriff confronts the posse, he turns to the gentle storekeeper: "Mr. Davies, I know you well enough to know that you didn't have a thing to do with this. I'm depending on you to tell me who did." The face of the once-kindly Davies is now stone hard. He looks around for a very long moment, and then replies coldly, "All but seven." With that flat statement Davies indicts not just the instigators and active participants in the lynching, but everyone else who stood passively by while this injustice was carried out, rather than standing up against it. In the narrative of *The Ox-Bow Incident*, this means a full three-quarters of the posse—but what proportion in the larger world? How many of us would pass Davies's test of character? What wrongs have been and are being wrought by our culture, our nation, or our species for which we share culpability, even if only through our silence?

The movie features another more immediate piece of iconoclasm as well. Running in parallel to the main narrative is the storyline involving the tyrannical ex–Confederate Major Tetley (Frank Conroy) and his sensitive son Gerald (William Eythe). The father is a bloated blowhard, clearly covering weakness with braggadocio, and other townsfolk are clearly aware that the Major's manly posturing covers a tarnished past. When the lynching party is first formed, Tetley forces his meek son to come along, saying, "Perhaps this will do what I've already failed to do: make a man out of you!" Throughout the movie the Major abuses his son, beats him down mercilessly, and eventually tries to compel him to initiate the hanging of one of the prisoners even after his son has stood with the handful of others against the lynching. But after the return home, Gerald confronts his father at last, shouting at him. "I saw your face—it was the face of a depraved, murderous beast! There are only two things that have ever meant anything to you: power and cruelty. You can't feel pity, you can't even feel guilt!" After the end of his son's diatribe, Major Tetley retreats to his study alone, and we hear a gunshot from behind the closed door.

The mythic content of this is clear: the son must metaphorically kill the negative father figure—that is, reject the claims of a now obsolete inherited tradition—in order to step into mature humanity and begin walking his own path. I can't help but wonder, however, if this is not only a symbolic commentary on the human condition but also a meta-commentary on the genre of the Western itself. The filmmakers must have been aware of the degree to which they were tearing down all of the old Western edifices when they made *The Ox-Bow Incident*, and so the Oedipal conflict between the Tetleys may also have something to say, at least in retrospect, about the evolution of the Western movie. In this reading, the father is the Old Hollywood Western, the paradigm of the classic American myth—full of *machismo*, overdressed, overstuffed, glorifying summary frontier justice over the rule of law, presenting a grand surface while covering over a problematic, embarrassing past. The son is the Birth of the New Western, starting out in his father's shadow but eventually finding his own way. Gerald stands for the ethos of the individual conscience, skeptical of inherited wisdom, willing to rethink the old masculine stereotypes, neither bound by the past nor fooled by its superficially gaudy trappings. At this point, he is taking his first faltering steps, still unsure of himself and on completely new ground, just as the antithetical elements within the Western genre had at first been presenting themselves tentatively, cautiously, a little bit at a time. The end of the film is the moment at which Gerald comes into his own, just as, with *The Ox-Bow Incident*, the subversive strain running beneath the Western genre had finally burst forth, brazenly and unequivocally rejecting the old tradition's articles of faith.

Every great mythology contains the heretical seeds of its own destruction, dismantling, reconstruction, and eventual rebirth in a new form. The Western is no exception; antithetical elements had been bubbling beneath the surface from the very beginning. *The Ox-Bow Incident* was the first movie to show the true potential of the deconstruction to come—two decades ahead of its time.

My Darling Clementine
(1946)

AKA: *John Ford's My Darling Clementine*
October 16, 1946 (San Francisco)
USA—English / Spanish
Twentieth Century–Fox
97m / 103m (pre-release version)—Mono—BW—1.37:1

Direction: John Ford
Screenplay: Samuel G. Engel, Winston Miller, Sam Hellman (story), Stuart N. Lake (book *Frontier Marshal*)
Principal Cast: Henry Fonda (Wyatt Earp), Linda Darnell (Chihuahua), Victor Mature (Doc Holliday), Cathy Downs (Clementine Carter), Walter Brennan (Old Man Clanton), Tim Holt (Virgil Earp), Ward Bond (Morgan Earp), Alan Mowbray (Granville Thorndyke), John Ireland (Billy Clanton), Roy Roberts (Mayor), Jane Darwell (Kate Nelson), Grant Withers (Ike Clanton), J. Farrell MacDonald (Mac), Russell Simpson (John Simpson)
Production: Samuel G. Engel
Cinematography: Joseph MacDonald
Editing: Dorothy Spencer
Art Direction: James Basevi, Lyle R. Wheeler
Music: Cyril J. Mockridge
Awards: Italian National Syndicate of Film Journalists—Best Foreign Film, National Board of Review—Top Ten Films, National Film Registry

In 1942, Henry Fonda starred in the most subversive Western of its time, *The Ox-Bow Incident*. Soon after filming wrapped, Fonda enlisted in the Navy to serve in World War II. He completed his service in 1946, returned to Hollywood, and immediately began work on his next film, one that (in polar opposition to *Ox-Bow*) might be considered a quintessential realization of the classical American Western mythology: John Ford's *My Darling Clementine* (1946). We journey from the most fearless deconstruction of the Western myth to one of its most reverent reconstructions in just two consecutive Fonda Westerns—both masterpieces.

My Darling Clementine is a remake of *Frontier Marshal* (1939), the pre-war rendition discussed earlier of the legendary shootout at the O.K. Corral. *Frontier Marshal* was a free adaptation of historical events in the service of an absorbing town-tamer Western, culminating in an exciting shoot-'em-up. Although very different in tone, *My Darling Clementine* still follows the lead of its predecessor, playing just as fast and loose with history. For example, in real life the Earps were never cattlemen, as they are in Ford's version; the character Clementine did not exist; Doc Holliday, a dentist rather than a surgeon, survived the O.K. Corral, which he doesn't in *Clementine*; Old Man Clanton was not at the gunfight, having died some time before; James Earp lived well into the twentieth century; and it was Morgan, not Virgil, who was shot in the back, and this happened months after the famous gun battle. None of this mattered to Ford, however, since his aim was to create a mythic story rather than a historically accurate account. A film historian once asked Ford why the movie altered the factual details. Irritated, Ford asked, "Did you like the film?" When the historian replied enthusiastically in the affirmative, Ford snapped, "What more do you want?"[1] Rather than presenting history as it happened, Ford's primary interest in *Clementine* was to turn the exploits of the Earps and Doc Holliday into mythology, to contribute something enduring to the folklore of the American West—and he succeeded spectacularly. If *Frontier Marshal* is prose, *My Darling Clementine* is poetry.

It is important not to downplay the role of *Frontier Marshal* in getting many of the standard elements of the Earp legend in place, and *Clementine* borrows noticeably from its predecessor, especially in the events that are completely fictionalized. Both movies have Wyatt overcoming a character named Indian Charlie (Charles Stevens each time) in a saloon and dragging him out feet first, thus inspiring the town leaders to ask Earp to be marshal. Both involve Doc in a love triangle between an immoral saloon girl and an upright woman from the East. (In contrast to later films—and history—*Frontier Marshal* and *Clementine* present Doc's true love as the straitlaced girl, not the woman of easy virtue.) In both versions, Doc performs a heroic operation on an innocent victim just before the climactic gunfight. (In the moodier *Clementine*, however, his patient dies.) Both movies have Doc failing to survive the O.K. Corral, contrary to history, though in *Clementine* he at least gets to participate in the gunfight, however briefly. Although John Ford would later claim not to have seen *Frontier Marshal* before making *Clementine*, there is evidence that he screened the movie in late 1945 while working on his own version.[2] Whatever the truth of that may be, *Frontier Marshal* was clearly an important template for the basic narrative skeleton of *My Darling Clementine*. Nevertheless, it is the differences and not the similarities between the two films that are fascinating, the ways in which both sets of filmmakers build from the same basic structure and yet manage to create such radically varying cinematic experiences.

John Ford and producer Darryl Zanuck were at odds a great deal throughout the making of *Clementine*. As the script was being developed, Ford was unhappy enough about the way things were proceeding to try and convince Zanuck to change all the character names to fictional ones; Zanuck refused.[3] For his part, after viewing a cut of the film, the producer wrote to Ford: "You have a certain Western magnificence and a number of character touches that rival your best work, but to me the picture as a whole in its present state is a disappointment. It does not come up to our expectations."[4] It was Zanuck who insisted that Fonda, as Wyatt Earp, kiss Clementine (Cathy Downs) before riding away into the desert in the movie's final scene, rather than awkwardly shaking hands with her as Ford had originally filmed. Zanuck would eventually edit together his own version of *Clementine* from Ford's footage, trimming about a half an hour of running time. John Ford's original version of the movie has not survived; however, we do have a restored "pre-release" cut of the film that is about six minutes longer than Zanuck's theatrical release and preserves more of Ford's original vision—it contains additional subtleties of characterization, features a different musical score (and more silences), avoids some of the sentimentality of Zanuck's version, and reinstates the wonderful handshake at the end, a far better choice.

Usually in film versions of the Tombstone story, the enigmatic Doc Holliday is a more interesting and compelling character than the straight-shooting Wyatt Earp. *My Darling Clementine* is an exception to this: Doc (played by Victor Mature) is fine, but more or less a one-note presence, whereas Fonda as Wyatt displays a range that has never been equaled for this character. Here, Wyatt can be menacing in one scene, courteous and gentle in another, self-deprecating and awkwardly shy in still another. He shows himself to be open and friendly at times, but in others incredibly dark—grimmer and more chilling than Doc, in fact—hinting at the actor's ability to play much more sinister roles, as he would most notably in Sergio Leone's *Once Upon a Time in the West* (1968).

Wyatt's character also evolves over the handful of days in which the action takes place. In early scenes, he seems cold and casually racist, as when he speaks derisively about Indian Charlie and the dance-hall girl of mixed ethnic heritage, Chihuahua (Linda Darnell). Later, however, when Chihuahua is severely wounded, Wyatt shows intense concern for her, and when an older white townswoman asks him if it would be all right for her to take Chihuahua home and nurse her back to health, Wyatt beams and says, with great relief, "Sure!" Witnessing and then becoming a part of the growing sense of community in Tombstone has changed him, as has the negative experience of the Clantons' inhumane cruelty. In a matter of days, Wyatt has learned to feel compassion for people other than his immediate family. The complexity and development of this character, brilliantly played by Henry Fonda, yields the most fully realized, multifaceted Earp we have ever seen on screen.

Wyatt Earp as written is the bringer of civilization who cleanses the town of the wicked men who keep the West from becoming a paradise. As Tom Milne wrote about the film's conclusion, "With the serpent of evil at last driven out of Tombstone, the wilderness could become a garden."[5] Earp starts, however, as a disinterested party seeking only to pass through the territory with his brothers; the adventure he gains is a serendipitous one. Nevertheless, as Joseph Campbell points out, whether serendipitous or deliberately chosen, the adventure that the hero gets is always the one for which he is ready.[6] Wyatt's destiny is to tame the town of Tombstone. As he says over his brother's grave—in a scene actually directed by Lloyd Bacon, but imitating Ford's style[7]—"Maybe when we leave this country, young kids like you will be able to grow up and live safe."

In this way, *My Darling Clementine* becomes a hybrid of two Western paradigms: the town-tamer Western and the vengeance quest. The movie's hero is a blend as well. As William Indick brilliantly points out, over the course of the narrative Wyatt Earp moves progressively through all four of the classical Western hero archetypes (as delineated by Indick): the cowboy knight, the honorable marshal, the lone crusader, and the rebel outlaw.[8] It is a credit to the script, the direction, and Fonda's acting that these remarkable transformations occur within a character who nevertheless remains coherent and believable throughout the film.

Fonda's Earp is matched in intensity by Walter Brennan's portrayal of the primary adversary, Old Man Clanton. Brennan reportedly hated working with Ford, but one would never know it by the outstanding performance he delivers. (Perhaps some of that hostility made its way into Brennan's portrayal of the villainous patriarch.) The way in which Brennan plays the scene where Old Man Clanton learns of Earp's identity is priceless; likewise, it is impossible to forget Clanton's voice after he punishes one of his sons with a horsewhip beating, saying, "When you pull a gun, kill a man!"

Although Doc is less compelling than Wyatt in this rendering, his story still adds a necessary counterpoint to the action. His friendship with Earp, while less central here than in *Frontier Marshal*, carries an important part of the interest and emotional weight, and his death is both appropriately tragic and required by the film's worldview. Despite Doc's charm and ultimate inner nobility, he belongs more to the pre-civilized, law-of-the-jungle ethos that characterized Tombstone before Wyatt's arrival. In some sense, Doc must die in order that Tombstone might live—a Christ figure of sorts, who perishes crucified on a wooden railing, taking the sins of the town with him.

However, it must also be said that Doc might have been a stronger character, on a par with Wyatt, had he been cast differently. Victor Mature was famously self-deprecating about his abilities as an actor, occasionally referring to himself by his Coast Guard appellation "The Beautiful Hunk of Junk" in recognition that his career was probably due more to his good looks than anything else. (In a 1966 interview, Mature recalled the time he applied for membership in the Los Angeles Country Club and was told by the chairman that the club could not accept any actors. Mature replied, "Let me know when your board of directors meets next, and I'll bring over a projector, all my films and all my reviews—I'll prove to you I'm no actor!")[9] It is said that Zanuck originally wanted Jimmy Stewart for the role of Doc Holliday, and one can only imagine what the pairing of Stewart and Fonda, two spectacular actors who were also great friends in real life, might have done for the Doc/Wyatt relationship—a tantalizing history that might have been.

None of this takes away from the splendor of the actual *My Darling Clementine*, however. It is filled with wonderful moments, large and small. Some of the best instances of characterization occur in simple grace notes. For example, when the departing stage actor Thorndyke (Alan Mowbray) shares a tender moment with the old soldier Dad (Francis Ford), we realize that a genuine friendship has formed between these two minor characters behind the foreground action of the narrative. Tombstone, it turns out, is a real town filled with real people living real lives. Similarly, the love triangle between Doc, Clementine, and Chihuahua—soon broadened to a quadrangle to encompass Wyatt—is handled with nuance; it is understated, real, and effective. Elements like these—in a "print the legend" Western, no less!—make one cry a question to the heavens: when, and why, did Hollywood decide to stop making movies about real people? I cannot help but be reminded of the ridiculous contracts that today's action-hero "stars" have, stipulating (for example) that they can never be shown to lose a fight. The fallible humanity and vulnerability of fully realized protagonists such as Wyatt and Doc has seemingly gone the way of the dinosaur, and audiences today are much the poorer for that.

My Darling Clementine is a beautiful film, a genuine work of art. It is lyrical, poetic, visually stunning, and masterfully written. In this movie brimming over with unforgettable scenes, four in particular stand out.

Wyatt's recumbent dance. On a quiet Sunday morning, Wyatt sits on a porch and leans back in his chair, supporting himself with a foot against the railing. Spontaneously he begins a playful little "dance" against the rail, tipping back and forth between his two feet like a child might do. What is it about this scene that is so perfect? The entire event lasts only a few seconds, and yet it is one of the most vivid and frequently recalled images from the movie. Somehow our understanding of the character is dramatically enhanced by this little diversion. The dance was completely improvised on the spot by

Chihuahua (Linda Darnell) watches in dismay as Wyatt Earp (Henry Fonda) amuses himself. Fonda said that he was asked more about this spontaneous moment than any other from his career. *My Darling Clementine* **(Twentieth Century–Fox, 1946).**

Fonda, who later reported that he was asked more about this moment than any other in his career.[10]

The church social. Tombstone is in the process of building a church; at this point, only the frame is present, but the metaphor is evident: the church will be the center-piece not only of the town's spiritual life but of its social life as well. In other words, it is the symbol for Tombstone's growing sense of community and culture. As the townsfolk begin to move toward the gathering place on Sunday morning, it is clear that Wyatt has no intention of going, but then Clementine comes along, clearly intending to attend the dedication service, and asks Wyatt, "Marshal, may I go with you?" Earp looks startled, and she continues, "You are going to the services, aren't you?" Wyatt readily accepts, becoming religious in an instant to be with a beautiful woman, in true Feirifiz fashion.

In the absence of a minister, the church dedication quickly transforms into a town dance. Clementine clearly wants to be invited to dance by Wyatt, and the scene where he battles his shyness while she, fully aware of his inner conflict, smiles gently to herself is a truly delightful masterpiece. (This inevitably recalls the equally charm-ing moment involving William S. Hart's lock of hair in *Tumbleweeds*.) Once Wyatt and Clementine commence their dance, the result—indescribable in mere words—is what Robert B. Pippin called "perhaps the single most beautiful image in Hollywood Westerns,"[11] and what William Indick labeled "the emotional heart of the picture. It is the grand purpose behind the violence, the thing worth fighting for, and the positive, promising side of romance and love, as opposed to the dark, doomed relationship between Doc and Chihuahua."[12] The dance, we come to understand, is not only a moment spilling over with joy and humanity; it is also the beginning of the new era, the moment at which the daylight of civilization overtakes the darkness of lawlessness. Only one more act of violence will be required in order to complete the process.

Wyatt (Henry Fonda) wrestles with his shyness while Clementine (Cathy Downs) looks on in understanding. Compare with the image of William S. Hart and Barbara Bedford in *Tumbleweeds* (1925). *My Darling Clementine* (Twentieth Century–Fox, 1946).

The gunfight at the O.K. Corral. This is the moment when the famous shootout achieves its mythic status. In both cuts of the film, the entire climactic sequence, nearly ten minutes in length, is accompanied by no music on the soundtrack. For long stretches, we hear only the wind, the distant early morning sounds of horses and dogs, and the slow footsteps of the Earp party as they march deliberately and inexorably toward their destiny. The space of the action is vast, situated amid a boundless desert and under an infinite sky. The Earps start out as distant specks on the other side of town, and a full four minutes elapses between the moment of their departure for the corral and the first gunshot. Once the action is fully underway, it is intense and surprising, spanning well over three minutes from first bullet to last. (The historical gunfight lasted about thirty seconds.)

The only difference between the pre-release and theatrical versions of the shootout sequence is at the very end, where the latter version cuts about fifteen seconds from the stretch when Wyatt and Morgan stand mournfully over Doc's body. The theatrical version is missing one line of dialogue—Wyatt saying "I'll get his boots"—and the appearance of the two supporting townsfolk after Wyatt walks off screen. Other than this, Zanuck seems to have kept Ford's deliberately paced climax intact.

If any gun battle from the Golden Age of Westerns could be described as mythopoetic, it is this one; we won't see its equal again until the (very different) climaxes of *High Noon* (1952), *The Good, the Bad and the Ugly* (1966), and *The Wild Bunch* (1969). The open spaces and hypnotic, deliberate pacing take us as viewers to a place beyond geography and time. The shootout has been carved into the edifice of myth; the combatants have walked out of time and space and into immortality.

The ending. Only about three minutes remain in the movie after the conclusion of the gunfight—less, in the theatrical version. Ford does not let us return to the familiar motions of everyday town life after the battle; instead, we remain in stillness and the wide-open spaces. At the edge of town, Wyatt bids an awkward but sincere farewell to Clementine, who—as the embodiment of the civilization to come—will remain

In the film's final scene, Clementine (Cathy Downs), the bringer of civilization, watches as Wyatt (Henry Fonda), his work accomplished, rides off into the vast unknown. *My Darling Clementine* (Twentieth Century–Fox, 1946).

in Tombstone as the new schoolteacher. The taming of the wilderness, Wyatt's work, is done; the age of Clementine is beginning. After kissing her (or shaking her hand, in Ford's original version), Wyatt rides off into the vast landscape. He may or may not return—the movie brilliantly leaves the resolution of this nascent relationship ambiguous.

Artistically, everything about *My Darling Clementine* revolves around the unifying motifs of open space and open time. The cinematic frame often features large expanses of empty space, even in interior scenes. Tombstone itself, in this rendition, is set right amid the vastness of Monument Valley, surrounded by miles of expansive landscape and crystal-clear sky, engulfed in a gorgeous emptiness. Stanley Corkin notes that the extremely long shots "emphasize the openness of the land, a geographical condition that creates the terms of freedom as it invites the exercise of individual will."[13] The landscapes seem to dwarf the characters, and yet at the same time endow them paradoxically with a certain grandeur and stature. As with space, so with time: even though the action of the narrative only takes a handful of days, the unhurried pacing of the film provides a powerful sense of timelessness.

All of this emphasizes the possibilities inherent in negative space, and as a result, *My Darling Clementine* becomes an artistic exploration of the beauty of the undetermined. No matter how constrained it might seem, life in actuality is endlessly open, teeming with infinite potential. This is why the unresolved situation of Wyatt and

The poetics of (empty) space, exterior and interior. From upper left: the Earps march toward destiny at the O.K. Corral; Wyatt (Henry Fonda) and Mac (J. Farrell MacDonald) in the saloon; Clementine (Cathy Downs) awaiting the stage; Clementine watching Wyatt's departure. *My Darling Clementine* (Twentieth Century–Fox, 1946).

Clementine is the perfect ending to the movie. Hamlet's "undiscovered country, from whose bourn no traveller returns"—presented by Thorndyke in his performance of the famous soliloquy—may originally have referred to death, but in *My Darling Clementine* it takes on a different meaning. Here the undiscovered country is the future, containing as it does all of the unknown possibilities and experiences that may become real within its encircling horizons—horizons that, just like those in the wide open spaces of Monument Valley, continue to recede from us as we make our way across the immeasurable landscape.

Duel in the Sun
(1946)

AKA: *King Vidor's Duel in the Sun*
December 29, 1946 (Los Angeles)
USA—English
Selznick International Pictures
144m—Mono—Technicolor—1.37:1

Direction: King Vidor, Otto Brower (uncredited), William Dieterle (uncredited), Sidney Franklin (uncredited), William Cameron Menzies (uncredited), David O. Selznick (uncredited), Josef von Sternberg (uncredited)

Screenplay: David O. Selznick, Oliver H.P. Garrett (adaptation), Ben Hecht (uncredited), Niven Busch (novel)

Principal Cast: Jennifer Jones (Pearl Chavez), Joseph Cotten (Jesse McCanles), Gregory Peck (Lewton "Lewt" McCanles), Lionel Barrymore (Sen. Jackson McCanles), Herbert Marshall (Scott Chavez), Lillian Gish (Laura Belle McCanles), Walter Huston (The Sinkiller), Charles Bickford (Sam Pierce), Harry Carey (Lem Smoot), Joan Tetzel (Helen Langford), Tilly Losch (Mrs. Chavez), Butterfly McQueen (Vashti), Scott McKay (Sid), Otto Kruger (Mr. Langford), Sidney Blackmer (The Lover), Charles Dingle (Sheriff Hardy)

Production: David O. Selznick

Cinematography: Lee Garmes, Harold Rosson, Ray Rennahan

Editing: Hal C. Kern

Art Direction: James Basevi

Music: Dimitri Tiomkin

Awards: Venice Film Festival—Cinecittà Cup (Selznick)

Nominations: Oscar—Best Actress in a Leading Role (Jones), Oscar—Best Actress in a Supporting Role (Gish), Venice Film Festival—Grand International Award (Vidor)

Once, when I was a teenager, my paternal grandmother came for a visit. She was a wonderful woman, loving and kind, devoted to her family, and we all adored her. She was also devoutly fundamentalist, belonging to a very strict Pentecostal church that disapproved of many of the activities that were of no small interest to my adolescent self—among them movies, drinking, playing cards, and chasing girls. Nevertheless, Grandma was more tolerant than her church: she herself did not go to the movies, but she never judged or criticized when my brother, my sister, or I did. She was also an avid card player who would beat the pants off her grandchildren at penny poker—although later she would tiptoe into our rooms and return the money she had won to our coin jars, plus a little extra.

Like many women of her generation, Grandma was also seriously addicted to her "stories"—the ever-present soap operas filled with deceit, betrayal, lust, venality, and titillation that permeated the daytime schedules of the three network channels. By the time I was a teenager, the soaps had even invaded primetime television. It was the era

225

of *Dallas*, *Dynasty*, *Knots Landing*, and *Falcon Crest*. One evening during Grandma's visit, she was staying up to watch the end of one of her nighttime dramas while the rest of us trailed off to bed. I retired to my room, turned out the light, and prepared to go to sleep. My door was open, however, and my bedroom was just at the top of a flight of stairs directly off the living room, so I could still hear my grandmother's soap as it drew to its lurid, cliffhanging close. The end credit music began to play, and Grandma switched off the television, leaving the house now silent and still. As she rose and began turning out the lights before making her way toward the guest room, I heard her sigh and say quietly to herself: "Sin, sin, sin." The actions of the characters in these soaps represented everything that my grandmother abhorred; nevertheless, she would return to this genre—dare I say, religiously—day after day, year after year, until the end of her life.

American culture has always had a split personality when it comes to the sexy and the seamy. Has there ever been a people more puritanical on the one hand, and so voyeuristic on the other? Over the years, there have been many cultural products ready to help repressed Americans find outlets for their carnal curiosities, and what nearly all of these have held in common is a surface-level disapproval of "immoral behavior," giving Americans a certain amount of safe cover while still letting them indulge their guilty fantasies. Reality television is today's obvious (and most tragic) example, but in earlier years we patted ourselves on the back for our moral superiority as we tut-tutted over the antics of soap opera characters. Further back, before the primacy of the soaps, there were pulp magazines and paperbacks with heaving bosoms on the covers, featuring characters who indulged in all of the forbidden pleasures that upright Americans wouldn't allow for themselves—promiscuity, marijuana, kinky sex, adultery, graft. During the heyday of pulp fiction, characters who acted immorally by society's standards usually got their comeuppance, but not before first providing the reader with a heavy dose of cheap thrills.

No movie of the pulp era better exemplifies this approach—wearing the trappings of a morality play and cautionary fable, while simultaneously reveling in its own debauchery—than the massively controversial (and massively profitable) *Duel in the Sun* (1946). *Duel*'s formula: first, surround the lurid story with a moralizing disclaimer at the beginning (spoken in voice-over by Orson Welles) and an ending where the misbehaving characters pay for their sins; next, cloak the entire endeavor in the garb of the serious Hollywood epic; then, wait for the inevitable controversy to arise, fanning its flames when necessary; and finally, ride the movie's forbidden-fruit status all the way to the bank. The film's excesses led it to be nicknamed "Lust in the Dust" by critics and the public, in this case a moniker fully deserved. (According to some accounts, the nickname originated in a quip made by Gregory Peck to Jennifer Jones during shooting and was soon picked up by others. The appellation was later honored in the title of the 1985 camp Western *Lust in the Dust*, featuring Tab Hunter and drag queen Divine in the lead roles.)

Predictably, the naughtiness of *Duel in the Sun* was the key to its financial success. Many groups were outraged, of course; the Catholic church called the film "morally offensive and spiritually depressing."[1] Meanwhile, Selznick cashed in. *Duel* was not the first Western to profit handily from the public's prurient interest, however; that honor goes to Howard Hughes's *The Outlaw* (1943), an appallingly bad and brazenly titillating Western ostensibly centered on the imaginary trio of Pat Garrett, Billy the Kid, and

Doc Holliday but remembered primarily for Jane Russell in her breakthrough role as Rio, a character whose primary service to the movie is having large breasts and displaying them as prominently as possible. (Hughes supposedly had engineers design a special cantilevered bra to accentuate Russell's natural gifts, and the movie's bosomy promotional posters would later ask, "What are the two reasons for Jane Russell's rise to stardom?" Wink wink, nudge nudge.) Even though production on *The Outlaw* had finished in 1941, controversy over its overt eroticism kept it from release until 1943, and the picture would not see a wide release until 1946. By that point, however, so much public interest had been generated that it became a huge hit.

Duel in the Sun's writer and producer, David O. Selznick, certainly hoped to top the success of *The Outlaw*, but he had other ambitions as well, among them the glamorization of his lover (and future wife), the film's star Jennifer Jones. Selznick used the great Austrian-American filmmaker Josef von Sternberg for some scenes, but only as a lighting expert to help the camera flatter Jones maximally. Even more obviously than his desire to showcase his inamorata, Selznick hoped to position his Western as a natural successor to his all-time triumph, *Gone with the Wind* (1939),[2] and he spent the unprecedented sum of two million dollars to promote the film in that way. *Duel* has all the trappings of Selznick's earlier epic: eye-popping Technicolor cinematography, substantial running time, first-rate production values, a lushly Romantic score (featuring orchestral Prelude/Overture, Intermission, and Exit music), sprawling historical context, overwrought family drama on an immense estate, and a tempestuous green-eyed heroine torn between a bland but decent fellow and the scoundrel (and occasional rapist) who is her heart's true desire. However, the provocative sexuality already present in *Gone with the Wind* was ratcheted up several notches for *Duel*, as was the level of melodrama and violence. The end result would be both a monument of trashy excess and, adjusted for inflation, the most commercially successful Western ever made.

Perhaps the weakest thing about *Duel in the Sun* (aside from one cringingly stereotyped minor character, Butterfly McQueen's Vashti) is the way in which the movie approaches its controversial material by first hedging its bets—although this may not be entirely the fault of the filmmakers. Yes, they nakedly capitalized on the movie's titillations in order to stimulate public interest, but they also had to be able to show the film in American theaters under the Hays Code and needed a way to signal (even disingenuously) that they were by no means condoning the "sin, sin, sin" depicted in the narrative. From this need came the device of the initial voice-over disclaimer delivered by Orson Welles, which may have helped to placate the Puritans but also, unfortunately, sucks some of the energy out of the film's brash sensationalism before the plot even gets going.

On top of the Overture, which follows a ten-minute orchestral Prelude but precedes the film's opening credits, Welles provides the socially acceptable context for the movie's outrageousness, condemning (for the record) the licentiousness of its characters while assuring us that they will ultimately pay for their sins—after we've reveled in them for two hours. In 1880s Texas, we are told, "the forces of evil were in constant conflict with the deeper morality of the hardy pioneers; and here, as in the story we tell, a grim fate lay waiting for the transgressor upon the laws of God and man." Welles's narration also undermines the movie's religious critique by clarifying that the movie's only non-secular character, fiery evangelist Crabbe (Walter Huston), does not represent true Christianity. "The character of the Sinkiller is based upon those bogus, unordained evangelists who preyed upon the hungry need for spiritual guidance, and who were recognized as charlatans by the intelligent and God-fearing."

Are all the bases covered? Good—now let the games begin.

Jennifer Jones plays the heroine, Pearl Chavez, a mixed-race firecracker orphaned when her father kills his adulterous wife and her lover, then hangs for it. Pearl makes her way to the estate of her father's one-time benefactress, Laura

Jennifer Jones as Pearl Chavez. *Duel in the Sun* (Selznick International, 1946).

Belle (Lillian Gish), who is now married to the rancher and senator Jackson McCanles (Lionel Barrymore). The old couple have two sons, the kindly and upright Jesse (Joseph Cotten) and hypermasculine bad seed Lewt (Gregory Peck, cast against type). The family takes Pearl in, and the inevitable love triangle between her and the McCanles boys soon develops. Lewt is a charismatic but terrible man; he exploits Pearl, and sexually assaults her on multiple occasions, and yet all of her passion winds up directed at him rather than Jesse. She recognizes the horror of this—in one famous scene, she calls herself "Trash, trash, trash, trash, trash!" In this sense, we can see Pearl as a symbol for the movie itself: both are wildly over-the-top and melodramatic, yet still compelling and memorable; both reject reasonableness in favor of unrestrained, irrational passion; and both have pretentious aspirations that fail to fully overcome their earthier origins.

Nevertheless, the most obviously mythic moment in this overstuffed Western may very well be a tribute to a genre often accused of being similarly grandiose: the Wagnerian music drama, and specifically *Tristan und Isolde*. Wagner's *Tristan* is a monumental work based upon Gottfried's medieval romance but updated with a Schopenhauerian sensibility. The opera, with its constantly yearning instability of key, is credited with hastening the eventual breakdown of traditional tonality that led, ultimately, to the birth of modern music. Its famous ending, the "Liebestod" ("Love-Death"), sees the lovers perishing together, entwined. However, this is played as blissful transfiguration rather than tragedy, the pair finally united in death while the restless music settles at last into its ultimate (major) tonality. The dying Isolde sings over Tristan's body:

How softly and gently he smiles, how sweetly his eyes open—can you see, my friends, do you not see it? How he glows ever brighter, raising himself high amidst the stars? Do you not see it? How his heart swells with courage, gushing full and majestic in his breast? How in tender bliss sweet breath gently wafts from his lips—Friends! Look! Do you not feel and see it? Do I alone hear this melody so wondrously and gently sounding from within him, in bliss lamenting, all-expressing, gently reconciling, piercing me, soaring aloft, its sweet echoes resounding about me? Are they gentle aerial waves ringing out clearly, surging around me? Are they billows of blissful fragrance? As they seethe and roar about me, shall I breathe, shall I give ear? Shall I drink of them, plunge beneath them? Breathe my life away in sweet scents? In the heaving swell, in the resounding echoes, in the universal stream of the world-breath—to drown, to founder—unconscious—utmost rapture![3]

This is death as an erotic consummation, and the music that accompanies this extraordinary text is transcendently beautiful, one of the most famous passages in the history of opera. (If you don't yet know the "Liebestod," please consider finding a performance on YouTube—sung by Flagstad, Nilsson, Norman, or Meier, for example. Your life will be the richer for it, I promise.)

In contrast to Wagner's (and Gottfried's) doomed pair, who move in a straight line from being enemies to being lovers, Pearl and Lewt walk a more complicated path. She starts by despising him—appropriately enough, given that he tries to assault her the first time they are alone together—but then, against her own better judgment, begins to long for him. Numerous betrayals and atrocities ensue, until finally, at long last, Pearl has had enough. In the titular confrontation at the climax of the film, the lovers—spoiler alert!— shoot each other to pieces under the broiling desert sun, only to die rapturously in each other's arms, locked in a final erotic kiss. The camera then pulls back to reveal the landscape, which previously looked realistic but now appears—not accidentally—like operatic stage decoration. This eight-minute scene is the Western version of the "Liebestod," complete with Dimitri Tiomkin's Wagnerian chromaticism on the soundtrack as the two undergo their apotheosis. Yes, the road to the lovers' demise is different from Wagner's version, and the quality of the art is nowhere near as magnificent, but the tone, in the end, is the same. Wagner's music would doubtless have been familiar to many of *Duel*'s viewers, not to mention its scriptwriters, and I strongly suspect that *Tristan*'s climax played an important role in the creation of *Duel*'s quasi-operatic finale. In any case, the two endings resonate with the same archetypal meaning for the human soul: the union of dark and light, the eternal battle of the sexes, the irrationality of love, and its primacy even over death.

A Wagnerian flavor was far from present in Niven Busch's original 1944 novel, however. In the book, Pearl kills Lewt and goes on to marry Jesse, and the manner in which the climactic duel is described is anything but Romantic:

> They were together, they were in that country for an agonized instant as Pearl pulled the trigger. Lewt's body leaped toward her. It bounded several inches upward in an awful spasm of energy. It settled back, the eyes wide open, terrible, accusing, the hole in the chest small, black, and burned with particles of flesh and blood blown on the rock behind him. Falling on her knees she vomited, watching life fade out of his open eyes.[4]

A far cry indeed from Selznick's Love-Death. Busch, as it turns out, only sold the rights to his novel but had nothing to do with the crafting of the film's screenplay. Thus, the forces of Hollywood were able to take a grim, gritty original and remake it as Romantic operatic legend, seasoned with a certain amount of post–Expressionist luridness.

Ultimately, *Duel in the Sun* is often jaw-dropping, but also engaging and entertaining when taken on its own garish terms, featuring excellent production values and acting, and with a terrific climactic scene. Even though Jones and Gish received Oscar nominations, the most memorable performances in my view are delivered by Barrymore, Huston, and Peck, portraying the three most shameless male characters. Peck is particularly vivid in a role that is a dark distortion of the classic Western hero: a manly singing cowboy who faces down anyone in his way, breaks the meanest of wild horses without fear, lives by grit and audacity, and takes what he wants—yet, in the end, also a self-interested villain who commits horrible acts of rape, outlawry, and murder. Lewt is a living rebuke to the traditional cowboy ideal, and Peck embodies powerfully both his character's charisma and his violent menace.

In viewing *Duel*, one is alternately gripped by its audacity and stunned into disbelief by its excesses. The

Pearl (Jennifer Jones) at film's end: lover and avenging angel. *Duel in the Sun* (Selznick International, 1946).

final significance of the movie is that, following on the heels of *The Outlaw*, it helped to usher in a new era of unapologetic sexuality and psychodrama, one which would

The cowboy ideal gone wrong: Gregory Peck as Lewt McCanles. *Duel in the Sun* (Selznick International, 1946).

eventually supersede the naive, squeaky-clean romantic relationships and characterizations that had until then dominated the popular Western. The best Westerns—those aspiring to be mythic and artistic—had always been more daring and complex, of course, but *Duel in the Sun* helped to bring these qualities into the mainstream too. Ordinary Western products could now feature a more mature approach to sexuality and psychology (subject to the limitations of the Hays Code, of course), and even high-quality films far more subtle and nuanced than *Duel*—such as *Pursued* (1947, from a Niven Busch screenplay), *Yellow Sky* (1948, also featuring Gregory Peck), *Shane* (1953), and *The Searchers* (1956)—benefited from the greater sexual and psychological license that Hollywood was willing to take, and for which *Duel* helped to open the door.

The possibilities for the Western as a whole were widening in the 1940s, as very different films such as *The Ox-Bow Incident* (1942), *My Darling Clementine* (1946), and *Duel in the Sun* kept pushing the expressive boundaries outward. These limits would continue to expand throughout the decade of the 1950s until—just as with music after Wagner—the center could no longer hold, the edifice collapsed, and the genre would have to find new, non-canonical ways to rebuild and move on.

Tidbits and Trivia

- Providing an unnecessary moral framing at the outset of the movie is a flaw not limited to *Duel in the Sun*. A more recent and notable example of this is the otherwise wonderful Western *Tombstone* (1993), which features a gratuitously tacked-on scene at the beginning establishing the Cowboys as purely evil—when in fact, in the narrative proper they are portrayed more ambiguously (and interestingly), not light-years distant ethically from Wyatt Earp and Doc Holliday, at least at first. *Tombstone*, like *Duel*, would actually have been enhanced by omitting the early moralizing bits.
- Lillian Gish and Lionel Barrymore had appeared together in eighteen films (mostly shorts) between 1912 and 1914. Aside from the silent version of *Ben-Hur* (1925), in which they were both uncredited crowd extras in the chariot race scene, they would not do so again until *Duel in the Sun*, three decades later. After *Duel*, Barrymore would continue to appear in pictures for another ten years, and Gish for an astounding forty-one—but they never acted together on screen again.

Angel and the Badman
(1947)

February 7, 1947 (Baltimore, San Francisco)
USA—English
John Wayne Productions / Patnel Productions
100m—Mono—BW—1.37:1

Direction: James Edward Grant
Screenplay: James Edward Grant
Principal Cast: John Wayne (Quirt Evans), Gail Russell (Penelope Worth), Harry Carey (Marshal Wistful McClintock), Bruce Cabot (Laredo Stevens), Irene Rich (Mrs. Worth), Lee Dixon (Randy McCall), Stephen Grant (Johnny Worth), Tom Powers (Dr. Mangram), Paul Hurst (Frederick Carson), Olin Howland (Bradley), John Halloran (Thomas Worth), Joan Barton (Lila Neal), Craig Woods (Ward Withers), Marshall Reed (Nelson)
Production: John Wayne
Cinematography: Archie Stout
Editing: Harry Keller
Art Direction: Ernst Fegté
Music: Richard Hageman

Fade in on a hand holding a pistol against a desert backdrop. The revolver quickly fires four shots in four directions, and then the man holding it runs to a waiting horse, vaults acrobatically into the saddle, fires two more shots, and gallops away, chased by a gang of horsemen. The man is John Wayne's character Quirt Evans, and the movie is *Angel and the Badman* (1947), the first film that Wayne himself produced and the most atypical of his entire catalog. Wayne and his writer-director friend, James Edward Grant, would eventually collaborate on a dozen pictures, including blood-and-guts war flicks like *Sands of Iwo Jima* (1949) and *Flying Leathernecks* (1951), as well as the pro–HUAC, McCarthyite wet dream *Big Jim McLain* (1952). And yet, inexplicably, for their first outing together Wayne and Grant chose to make a pacifist Western about a tough killer who falls in love with a Quaker woman and renounces his guns. As it turns out, those six gunshots in the opening eight seconds are the only ones that Wayne's character will fire throughout the entire movie. (The actual person firing the gun was almost certainly a stunt double rather than Wayne, given the ensuing acrobatics.)

Angel and the Badman has never been beloved by typical mainstream Western fans, and it remains a genuine enigma in the career of John Wayne. Critics of the time were puzzled as well, although some appreciated it as an antidote to the burgeoning sensationalism fostered by movies like *Duel in the Sun* (1946). The *Time* reviewer, for example, called the picture "pleasantly unconventional," and wrote: "The film will probably convert few gunsters to the Society of Friends, and still fewer Friends to shooting-iron diplomacy. But in a season when horse operas are going stridently sexy, it is nice to see the great open spaces filled with something a little more edifying than heaving, half-bared bosoms."[1]

In general, the movie has been dismissed both then and now, which is a true shame, because it is wonderful in so many ways—my favorite from among Wayne's "minor" Westerns, well worth watching despite its B-movie ambience, some stilted acting from the supporting characters, and dialogue that veers frequently toward the pedantic. The movie's flaws are completely forgivable, and in return it offers a lovely parable about nonviolence, two engaging lead characters, a hero who evolves convincingly over the course of the movie, and no small amount of resonance with the materials of myth.

The first particularly nice touch occurs at the very beginning. After those jolting first gunshots, Quirt Evans runs toward his horse and leaps into the saddle, and the action seems ever so slightly sped up, like a silent-movie reel. The movie's title appears over the exciting pursuit in a dramatic font which evokes the flavor of Poverty Row; the credits continue to roll as Quirt gallops across the desert, kicking up clouds of dust, sometimes silhouetted against the sky; and the musical score blares forth its diminished-seventh chords (familiar to us from stereotypical silent movie piano accompaniments as well as the scores of 1930s B-Westerns). In other words, everything so far feels as if we are watching a silent Western (except for the sounds of the gunshots) with live musical accompaniment or an early Poverty Row talkie. This especially includes the camerawork. The scene's photographer, Archie Stout, made over seventy Westerns in the 1930s; he was certainly familiar with the visual style of the B-movie, having contributed to its evolution himself.

The montage of Quirt's escape across the landscape of Monument Valley continues while the credits roll. He finally eludes his pursuers and collapses, along with his horse, in front of the homestead of the Worths, a Quaker family. But over the course of these two minutes of screen time, both the visuals and the musical soundtrack have gradually morphed into a more contemporary style, that of the postwar Western. This change is so pronounced that I cannot believe it is anything other than intentional, as if the filmmakers were situating Quirt's ride from gunplay to Quaker pacifism metaphorically—a journey, perhaps, from naivety to wisdom, from the simplistic pre-war treatment of violence in the early Westerns to the more sophisticated understanding of the consequences of killing that arose inevitably in the aftermath of the bloodiest war in human history. The hero solving all his problems with his gun is B-movie kid stuff, the opening seems to be saying; we are older and wiser now, and no longer view the elements of "peacemaking" so simplistically. Knowing what I know about Grant and Wayne, I'm not quite sure how to support this claim, except to note that the entire movie's existence is equally difficult to explain without assuming a deliberate effort on behalf of writer/director and producer/star to exalt a philosophy of nonviolence. As I said, the film is an enigma.

There is perhaps a nod to *Parzival* in Quirt's arrival at the Worth homestead: he is heading past the house toward the telegraph office when his horse collapses and he falls to the ground. In that sense, then, the horse has brought Quirt unknowingly to the place which will ultimately be his salvation, in the same way that Parzival's horse took the hero to the Grail Castle after he let go of the reins. We think we steer our lives by intention, and yet often the most transformative events happen when we relinquish control and let Nature lead the way.

As the Quaker patriarch Tom Worth (John Halloran) rides over to help the fallen "badman," we discover that Quirt has been wounded by gunshot. He still must get to the telegraph office, however, so Worth offers to drive him there. This is the moment in which Quirt first sees Worth's daughter, Penelope (Gail Russell), and his aesthetic arrest as he beholds her, sitting in the wagon and framed against the sky, cannot help but evoke the analogous moment from William S. Hart as Blaze and Clara Williams as Faith in *Hell's Hinges* (1916)—"one who is evil, looking for the first time on that which is good." Like that film, *Angel and the Badman* will be the story of a man of violence redeemed through the love of a devout woman. Even the allegorical character names are similar: Blaze has now become Quirt (a rawhide whip), and Faith has become Penelope, bearing the mythic name of Odysseus's faithful wife. (The character of Penelope Worth even works with a skein of yarn in one scene, just as her Homeric namesake memorably worked her loom.)

Aesthetic arrest: Quirt Evans (John Wayne) beholds Penelope for the first time. *Angel and the Badman* (John Wayne Productions, 1947).

The telegraph operator Bradley (Olin Howland) enlightens Tom and Penelope Worth, as well as the viewing audience, about Quirt's character. Quirt was one of Wyatt Earp's deputies in Tombstone, we are told, but apparently with quite a sinful side—like Doc Holliday without the tuberculosis. "He's quite a man with the gals," says Bradley. "They say he's closed the eyes of many a man and opened the eyes of many a woman." Penelope is troubled by this, but it's too late—as Quirt collapses unconscious into her arms after sending the telegram, we see that she has already fallen in love with him, love at first sight. "Through the eyes love attains the heart: for the eyes are the scouts of the heart," as the troubadour Guiraut de Borneilh sang.[2]

The Worths take the gravely injured Quirt back home and he is placed under Penelope's tender care—now echoing the medieval legend of Tristan, the knight nursed back to health by the beautiful Iseult. The Worths are ardent pacifists, but never judgmental toward the people around them. Mrs. Worth shows genuine affection for the misanthropic atheist Dr. Mangram (Tom Powers), and Penelope similarly makes it clear to Quirt that her philosophy is a positive one, not a restrictive one, never browbeating or hectoring but simply living out her beliefs by example. Penelope's morality is presented as things you do because they spread happiness and make you a better person, rather than behaviors you avoid in order to escape divine wrath. The contrast between this humane ethos and Quirt's worldly cynicism is highlighted in a scene when he finds Penelope working in the barn on the Sabbath:

Quirt (John Wayne) collapses into the arms of the delighted Penelope Worth (Gail Russell). Russell would have a tragically short career, dying of liver damage caused by alcoholism at the age of thirty-six. *Angel and the Badman* (John Wayne Productions, 1947).

> QUIRT: Thought you weren't allowed to work on Sunday.
> PENELOPE: Oh, Quirt, there's nothing we're not allowed to do. It's just that we don't believe in doing what we know is wrong.
> QUIRT: Well, that makes it pretty much each fella's own guess.
> PENELOPE (*smiling*): But each fella knows, inside.
> QUIRT: Well, there's a lotta gents I wouldn't want to give that much leeway to.

Both characters are delighting in one another; they are aware of their philosophical differences, but we sense no judgment or false superiority coming from either side. Quirt bluntly acknowledges his own tendencies to the Worth family, and teases them good-naturedly from time to time, but it is clear that he is making the joke as much at his own expense as theirs. *Vive la différence!* Slowly, Quirt's perspectives on Quaker ways begin to change, and he starts moving toward an ethical middle ground somewhere between the extremes of brute force and pacifism. For example, in one of the film's more touching moments, Quirt convinces the mean-spirited neighbor Carson (Paul Hurst) to release some of the unneeded water on his property to flow once more into the valley and replenish the water supply of the Worths and others, but Quirt accomplishes this only through the fear that his name produces and thus the implicit threat of violence. (This is true to the *Hell's Hinges* paradigm too; in the earlier film, Hart's character Blaze may have moved from the dark to the light side, but he never became a milquetoast.) Nevertheless, Quirt shows no anger and commits no harm. In fact, he is respectful to the

Quirt (John Wayne) straps on his weapons to confront the villains at the film's climax. This one will be different from all the rest. *Angel and the Badman* (John Wayne Productions, 1947).

old crank, and this ultimately leads to a reconciliation and renewed friendship between Carson and the Worths.

Needless to say, Quirt's past is destined to catch up with him, in the form of the villainous Laredo Stevens (Bruce Cabot) and his henchmen, Quirt's pursuers from the beginning of the movie. True to B-Western form, the bad guys all look and talk like Eastern gangsters. There is a terrific scene in which Quirt bluffs them with a gun that only he and the Worths know is not loaded, but this only delays the inevitable. Beyond a doubt, the villains will return at the end and Quirt will have a choice to make: whether to honor his own manly code of retribution or the peaceful ways of the woman he has grown to love. Complicating things is the Javert-like stalking of Quirt by Marshal Wistful McClintock (Harry Carey), who is surface-level friendly with Quirt but also determined to see him, eventually, hung with "an old rope." Quirt's ultimate choice of life-path will not come easily, of course; he will struggle with Penelope's challenging conception of living, and rebel against it twice before the end. First, after a moving moment where he is embraced by the Quaker community, a disturbed Quirt, in a striking act of renunciation, roughly grabs the arm of one of Penelope's suitors and says, "You dim-witted nail-bender, marry that girl," before fleeing back to the world of cattle rustling and dance-hall chanteuses (who, true to the Law of Time, perform sultry songs in contemporary style rather than in the idioms of Old West folk music). Quirt will return, but afterwards, when he thinks that Laredo's actions have resulted in Penelope's imminent death, he straps on his gun once more and rides out seeking vengeance.

We are very familiar with the trope in which the Western hero, who has laid down his gun, reluctantly picks it up again to face down villainy—this is a major plot point in Westerns as diverse as *Destry Rides Again* (1939), *My Darling Clementine* (1946), *High Noon* (1952), *Rio Bravo* (1959), *Pale Rider* (1985), and *Tombstone* (1993). Because we have seen this device employed to dramatic effect so many times, it is almost shocking to see a Western hero—played by John Wayne, no less!—pick up his gun prior to the climax, but then put it down again. In the movie's view—mine as well—this is strength, not weakness. The way of nonviolence is the tougher road, the manlier way. The old marshal, having dispatched the villains himself, is disappointed at first.

> McCLINTOCK: I'm patient. It's only a matter of time before I hang you!
> QUIRT: Not me, mister. From now on, I'm a farmer.
> *Quirt rides off in the Worth family wagon.*
> BRADLEY: That Quirt!
> *They spot Quirt's abandoned gun on the ground; the marshal picks it up.*
> BRADLEY: Hey, Quirt might need that!
> McCLINTOCK (*smiling in realization*): No. Only a man who carries a gun ever needs one.
> BRADLEY: What are you going to do with it?
> McCLINTOCK (*joyfully*): Hang it on a wall in my office—with a new rope!

The gun, representing Quirt's former ways, must die by proxy so that he can live. It is the violence that deserves to be "hung," not the man.

Hate the sin, love the sinner—not a bad philosophy for any era.

Pursued
(1947)

March 5, 1947 (USA)
USA—English
Warner Bros.
101m—Mono—BW—1.37:1

Direction: Raoul Walsh
Screenplay: Niven Busch
Principal Cast: Teresa Wright (Thor), Robert Mitchum (Jeb), Judith Anderson (Mrs. Callum), Dean Jagger (Grant), Alan Hale (Jake Dingle), Harry Carey, Jr. (Prentice), John Rodney (Adam)
Production: Milton Sperling
Cinematography: James Wong Howe
Editing: Christian Nyby
Art Direction: Ted Smith
Music: Max Steiner

Pursued (1947) is not a great movie, but it is an important one. First of all, it was a significant moment in the careers of two of its up-and-coming actors. *Pursued* was Robert Mitchum's first lead role in an A-level Western, although he had acted in a string of B-Westerns prior to this, and it was also the first A-Western to feature Harry Carey, Jr., who would soon become a fixture in the genre. (Technically speaking, Carey Jr.'s first film appearance was as an infant in his father's 1921 silent picture *Western Trails*, directed by none other than John Ford. Two decades later, the younger Carey launched his adult acting career with a small role in the 1946 B-Western *Rolling Home*, then followed it with *Pursued* the next year.) Carey would go on to act in about eighty movies and a great many television series and TV movies. His last Hollywood Western, amazingly, was *Tombstone* in 1993, which also featured Mitchum's voice-over narration.

Beyond the careers that it furthered, *Pursued* also represented a milestone in itself. As the first significant Western that participated equally in three other genres—psychological drama, melodrama, and *film noir*—it demonstrated the latent potentialities of the Western to cross over and combine with other styles. The canvas of the Old West had always been a broad, open space full of artistic, mythic, stylistic, and narrative opportunities. However, filmmakers began to realize after *Pursued* that even the considerable freedom that they had already enjoyed while tucked safely within the borders of the traditional Western still did not represent the full range of possibilities. The West was wider, and wilder, than even John Ford had imagined.

Pursued as psychological drama. Arguably, the first significant psychological Western was *The Ox-Bow Incident* (1943), a masterpiece which, as discussed earlier, opened the door for broader explorations of the human psyche as well as a heretical questioning of the Western genre's canonical elements. In a way, *Ox-Bow* explored human psychology in a similar way to traditional stage dramas such as *Hamlet*—it was an unflinching look at humanity's darker side, but through a literary lens rather than a clinical (or pseudo-clinical) one.

However, as the postwar era progressed, mainstream movies—inspired in part by prewar Expressionism in literature, film, and the other arts—began to take more of an overt interest in Freudian psychology. Expressionist and Surrealist forays into filmmaking had already resulted in such Freudian masterpieces as Robert Wiene's *The Cabinet of Dr. Caligari* (1920), Jean Cocteau's *Blood of a Poet* (1932), and—perhaps most famously—the nightmarish Surrealist short *Un Chien Andalou* (1929) by Luis Buñuel and Salvador Dalí. After the war, Dalí would go on to make a major contribution to the mainstreaming of the psychological drama by creating the memorable dream sequence for Alfred Hitchcock's groundbreaking thriller *Spellbound* (1945), featuring Gregory Peck as a man who has suffered a mysterious childhood trauma and, as a result, has amnesia due to his repressed memories. *Spellbound* brought Freudian drama into the Hollywood mainstream, and almost certainly was an influence on *Pursued* two years later. In addition, the man who wrote *Pursued*, Niven Busch, had already amassed impressive credentials in the crafting of psychological drama, having written the screenplay for *The Postman Always Rings Twice* (1946) as well as the novel which was the basis for *Duel in the Sun* (1946). As a screenwriter, he focused on psychological drama so much during the postwar era that some wags called it the period of the "burning Busch."[1]

Like Gregory Peck's character in *Spellbound*, Robert Mitchum's Jeb Rand is a potentially strong man who has been weakened—partially emasculated—by a secret from his childhood that he cannot recall. Jeb has flashes of insight, but his task—like Peck's in the earlier film—is clearly to decode his own psychic symbolism, unlock the mystery of his own past, and thereby solve his current dilemma. The movie begins at its end, as the protagonist and his adopted sister and lover Thor Callum (Teresa Wright, Busch's wife at the time) meet at a ruined ranch where Jeb, while awaiting his pursuers, has only a short time to try and piece together clues to his desperate plight from his own cloudy past. The majority of the narrative, then, is told in flashback, with occasional voice-over narration from Jeb. There are twists and turns as, starting from mere moments after Jeb's mysterious childhood trauma, we see his past unfold—including, frustratingly, some things that he could not possibly have known or witnessed. Gradually, however, Jeb's backstory is revealed, allowing him to come to terms with his past.

In true Freudian fashion, the personal history that Jeb has subconsciously suppressed is sexual, familial, violent, and quasi-incestuous. Adding to the Oedipal flavor, it becomes more and more clear that Jeb's adoptive mother, Ma Callum (Judith Anderson), is somehow at the center of the mystery. Also, taking a page perhaps from Bartók's opera *Bluebeard's Castle*, the landscape of the drama itself represents the interior of Jeb's soul. The character even comments on this overtly after visiting (in flashback) the ruined ranch house and seeing a number of unmarked graves. "That house was myself," Jeb narrates in voice-over. "If that house was me, what part of me was buried in those graves?"

Pursued as melodrama. Hollywood melodramas tend to focus on private life, domestic relations, family dramas, romantic struggles, and dark pasts. Central characters are often women (here, *Pursued*'s Teresa Wright gets top billing), men attempting to live within the "female" space of the home (like Jeb), or orphans (Jeb again). Emotions

Tormented lovers Jeb Rand (Robert Mitchum) and Thor Callum (Teresa Wright), with Ma Callum (Judith Anderson), the mother figure at the center of the mystery. *Pursued* (Warner Bros., 1947).

and gestures are exaggerated, and characters often undergo atypical amounts of hardship and suffering.

In *Pursued*, Jeb's life is dominated by two women: Ma Callum and her daughter Thor, whom he will grow to love romantically. Most of the men in Jeb's life, by contrast, are his enemies: his adopted brother Adam (John Rodney); Thor's onetime suitor Prentice (Carey); and his unseen adversary, the one-armed Grant Callum (Dean Jagger).

Despite loving him, Thor dominates Jeb almost completely; he has very little agency in their relationship, just as he has little agency in his life as a whole. (This is signified most powerfully by two separate events in which Jeb's fate is decided by the flip of a coin.) One particularly telling scene between Thor and Jeb occurs when they agree to marry—but Thor sets the terms very clearly.

> THOR: I want you to come court me. I know that seems silly when we grew up together, but I want to pretend we didn't. That's why you've got to come sparkin' me. Do you mind? You can get dressed up real fashionable. So will I. I'll have two chairs out in the gallery. I'll bring out some lemonade. We'll sit there and talk. You can ask me if I'll let you smoke. I'll say yes. I'll have a piece of sewing.
>
> JEB: What'll we talk about?
>
> THOR: Oh, sort of parlor talk. The words'll be like stitches we're sewin', pullin' our lives together. After a while, you can hold my hand.
>
> *Jeb kisses her.*

THOR: You're not supposed to kiss me till you've bought a ring. Ah, Jeb, can you understand? Can you see it my way?

JEB: Thor, I've never belonged here. I don't know why. I always have the feeling something's after me. It's a bad feeling I can't explain. Lots of times I'm happy, but it's still there. Thor, I've got to be with you. We've got to have a chance. Let's get away before something happens. Please, sweetheart.

THOR: We're gonna get married, Jeb. We're not gonna spend the rest of our lives doin' crazy things because you think something's gonna happen. We're not gonna run away at night like a couple of stagecoach robbers. I love you, Jeb, but if we're gonna get married, can't it be the way I say? Please, sweetheart.

She embraces him, and he sighs.

JEB: I only hope it turns out that way.

Jeb has been outmaneuvered, trapped both figuratively by the situation and literally—visually—by Thor's claustrophobic embrace.

There had been Western melodramas prior to *Pursued*, of course—most notably, *The Squaw Man* (1914, 1918, and 1931). Nevertheless, during and after World War II melodrama took a quantum leap forward in Hollywood, and the Western was no exception. After *Pursued*, the stage was set for melodramatic Westerns to come, such as *The Furies* (1950), *Rancho Notorious* (1952), and the inimitable *Johnny Guitar* (1954).

Pursued as *film noir*. *Pursued* may have the narrative structure and content of a Freudian psychological drama, and the domestic focus and emotionality of a Hollywood melodrama, but it has the aesthetics of *film noir*. Mitchum had already made forays into the genre with entries such as *When Strangers Marry* (1944), *Undercurrent* (1946), and *The Locket* (1946), and of course he would go on to star in *noir* classics like the superb *Out of the Past* (1946) and *The Night of the Hunter* (1955). Mitchum's ability to portray menacing figures such as the unforgettable, murderous Rev. Harry Powell in the latter film—perhaps his greatest performance—is prefigured by his moments of genuine darkness in *Pursued*, as in the scene in which Jeb straps on his guns after the brutal fight

with his adopted brother Adam and then says to Thor, "Tomorrow I'm coming back, and you're coming with me. If he tries to stop me, I'll kill him." It's a masterful, chilling delivery, hinting at darker moments to come.

Director Raoul Walsh had also ventured into *noir* territory with films like *They Drive by Night* (1940), *High Sierra* (1941), *Manpower* (1941), and *The Man I Love* (1947), and, after *Pursued*, would go on to direct Jimmy Cagney in *White Heat* (1949) and co-direct (uncredited) Humphrey

Trapped, visually and metaphorically: Jeb (Robert Mitchum) in a claustrophobic clinch with his adopted sister Thor (Teresa Wright). *Pursued* (Warner Bros., 1947).

The look of noir: Harry Carey, Jr., as Prentice (top left), Robert Mitchum as Jeb (top right), and Teresa Wright as Thor (bottom row). *Pursued* **(Warner Bros., 1947).**

Bogart in *The Enforcer* (1951). Other critical creative contributors to *Pursued* also had and would continue to have *noir* credentials, including screenwriter Niven Busch (*The Postman Always Rings Twice*, 1946; *Moss Rose*, 1947; *The Capture*, 1950), cinematographer James Wong Howe (*Out of the Fog*, 1941; *Hangmen Also Die*, 1943; *Body and Soul*, 1947; *He Ran All the Way*, 1951; *Sweet Smell of Success*, 1957), art director Ted Smith (*High Sierra*, 1941; *The Mask of Dimitrios*, 1944; *Conflict*, 1945; *Three Strangers*, 1946; *The Verdict*, 1946; *Flaxy Martin*, 1949), and composer Max Steiner (*Mildred Pierce*, 1945; *The Big Sleep*, 1946; *The Man I Love*, 1947; *Key Largo*, 1948; *Flamingo Road*, 1949; *White Heat*, 1949; *Caged*, 1950; *This Woman Is Dangerous*, 1952; *Illegal*, 1955; and many, many others).

As a result, *Pursued* has the look, sound, and feel of *film noir*, from beginning to end. It is soaked in darkness and shadows, both visually and narratively, and often features the kind of hard-boiled, cynical dialogue characteristic of the genre. "We're alone, each of us, and each in a different way," says Ma Callum at one point. And then there is Jeb's wonderful voice-over line, addressed to Thor and referring to the two people she cared about that he has already killed in self-defense: "Right then I knew I had to have you. I'd have to climb across two graves to get to you, but nothing in the world would hold me back." Mitchum's broodiness suits the style perfectly, as does the flashback structure, the Expressionistic sets and lighting, and the dark, psychologically twisted relationship between Jeb and Thor.

To the movie's credit, it manages to blend all four of these flavors—Western, psychological drama, melodrama, and *film noir*—into a coherent whole. *Pursued* is stylistically consistent and sits comfortably within its own aesthetic and narrative world. It also features some excellent scenes—the lovers' conversation described above, the coin-toss moments, the fistfight between the brothers and its aftermath, and Jeb's confrontation with Prentice—as well as strong production values. There are some difficulties with the movie, however, that for me keep it from being all that it could have been. For one thing, the big mystery is not much of a surprise once revealed. The narrative also requires a great many suspensions of disbelief on the part of the audience. Why is Prentice so easily goaded into confronting Jeb, almost certainly condemning himself to death, over such a trivial matter? Can we truly believe the motivation of the villain Grant when his quest is, at base, a ridiculous one? And does it make sense that Grant could motivate so many other henchmen to risk their own lives and become killers just to assist him on his bizarre and pointless mission? Why would Jeb abandon his new wife on their wedding night when attackers show up at their house? Plus, what happens to all of the henchmen at the end? They literally disappear from all shots, their fate unknown. In short, the movie expects us to accept too many plot holes and irrational motivations. When coupled with the often clunky flashback structure (which, as I mentioned, has Jeb recounting things he couldn't have witnessed) and relatively stilted voice-over narration, this yields a movie with wonderful intentions and true artistry in its making that still falls short of the mark.

Nevertheless, *Pursued* has plenty of redeeming features and is well worth a look, not least for its historical importance to the Western genre. The movie opened up the possibilities of the Western to a degree not seen since *The Ox-Bow Incident*, and as a result, the genre was now free to mix itself with other styles. Not only did we now have the Freudian Western, the *noir* Western, and the Western melodrama on the table—all soon to be developed further in movies like *Yellow Sky* (1948), *The Gunfighter* (1950), *Rawhide* (1951), and the others mentioned above—but the path had also been cleared for the eventual development of additional crossover styles. Later in the twentieth century we would see such diverse and surprising possibilities as the fantasy Western, the horror Western, the rock-and-roll Western, the martial arts Western, the Communist Western, the acid Western, and the science fiction Western.

The latter hybrid, I should add, seems to have experienced a true flourishing in the postmodern era. For examples of the diverse possibilities (albeit varying widely in quality) afforded by crossing the two mythic genres of Westerns and science fiction, see *Westworld* (1973), *Battle Beyond the Stars* (1980), *Outland* (1981), *Back to the Future Part III* (1990), *Wild Wild West* (1999), *Serenity* (2005), *Cowboys & Aliens* (2011), and television series like *Cowboy Bebop* (1998), *Westworld* (2016), and *The Mandalorian* (2019)—not to mention the "Spectre of the Gun" episode of *Star Trek* (1968) that predated all of these, featuring Captain Kirk and crew playing the role of the Clantons in the shootout at the O.K. Corral!

Mythic, artistic, and narrative space to be explored—that is what the Western has always provided. *Pursued* showed that the genre could also cross-fertilize with other styles while still remaining coherent and true to its own vision. In 1932, a villainous rancher in *The Western Code* first uttered the now legendary line, "This town ain't big enough for the both of us"; but in 1947 people were beginning to realize that there was more room in both Western towns and Western movies than they had once thought.

The Treasure of the Sierra Madre (1948)

January 14, 1948 (Los Angeles)
USA / Mexico—English / Spanish
Warner Bros.
126m—Mono—BW—1.37:1

Direction: John Huston
Screenplay: John Huston, B. Traven (novel)
Principal Cast: Humphrey Bogart (Dobbs), Walter Huston (Howard), Tim Holt (Curtin), Bruce Bennett (Cody), Barton MacLane (McCormick), Alfonso Bedoya (Gold Hat)
Production: Henry Blanke
Cinematography: Ted D. McCord
Editing: Owen Marks
Art Direction: John Hughes
Music: Max Steiner
Awards: Oscar—Best Supporting Actor (Walter Huston), Oscar—Best Director (John Huston), Oscar—Best Screenplay (John Huston), Golden Globes—Best Picture (tie), Golden Globes—Best Director (John Huston), Golden Globes—Best Supporting Actor (Walter Huston), Faro Island Film Festival—Best Actor (Bogart), National Board of Review—Best Actor (Walter Huston), National Board of Review—Best Screenplay (John Huston), National Board of Review—Top Ten Films, National Film Registry, New York Film Critics Circle—Best Film, New York Film Critics Circle—Best Director (John Huston), Venice Film Festival—Best Score (Steiner), Writers Guild of America—Best Written American Western (John Huston)
Nominations: Oscar—Best Picture, BAFTA—Best Film from Any Source, Faro Island Film Festival—Audience Award, Best Actor (Bogart), Faro Island Film Festival—Audience Award, Best Film, Faro Island Film Festival—Best Film, New York Film Critics Circle—Best Actor (Walter Huston), Venice Film Festival—Grand International Award, Writers Guild of America—Best Written American Drama (John Huston)

I am going to write far less about *The Treasure of the Sierra Madre* (1948) than I should, not because it is anything less than magnificent, but simply because it is a movie that touches only tangentially on the boundaries of the Western genre without ever becoming a full-fledged Western. This, then, is just a brief interlude to acknowledge a canonical masterpiece which interacted with the mainstream Western in interesting ways, both in its creation and, especially, in its later impact. There are few Hollywood movies from this period that are so artistically and dramatically satisfying and yet also explore so powerfully concepts like greed, selfishness, honor, exploitation, free will, the darkness within the soul, and the futility of so many of our quixotic endeavors.

Somehow the three primary characters—Dobbs (Humphrey Bogart), Curtin (Tim Holt), and Howard (Walter Huston)—measure out, between them, a vast span of human ethical possibility, from Dobbs's self-serving avarice to Curtin's imperfect idealism to Howard's worldly pragmatism. Each is a three-dimensional character, fully realized. All three men will be tempted by the same things; what distinguishes them, in the end, is not the temptations they face but the choices that they make afterwards. *Treasure* is a movie that implicitly judges its characters by their actions, not their feelings.

The film features superb production values all the way across, and is expertly directed by the great John Huston, Walter's son. (The two would become the first father-son pair to win Oscars for the same movie.) Even though the unfolding of the plot has a certain grinding inexorability, it is still gripping, suspenseful, and moving throughout. Every time I watch, I catch new subtleties and masterstrokes.

The story is based on a 1927 novel by the reclusive novelist B. Traven, whose identity remains a mystery to this day. All that is known with any degree of confidence about the man behind the pseudonym is that he lived in Mexico for many years and was probably of German origin. The rest he kept hidden, submitting manuscripts only through agents or by post to protect his secrecy. "The creative person should have no other biography than his works," he believed.[1] The search for the real B. Traven has been as intriguing and perplexing as the search for gold that drives the plot of *The Treasure of the Sierra Madre*. One wonders if new advances in digital scholarship—such as the statistical analysis of texts—could shed some additional light on this elusive figure, or at least rule out some of the many names that have been suggested for Traven's true identity.

The film version of *The Treasure of the Sierra Madre* makes use of many elements

One cross-section of humanity: Dobbs (Humphrey Bogart), Curtin (Tim Holt), and Howard (Walter Huston). *The Treasure of the Sierra Madre* (Warner Bros., 1948).

common to the traditional Western: rugged, desert terrain; gunplay; barroom fights; grizzled prospectors; outlaws. Like *Pursued*, it is an early demonstration of how easily Western elements blend with other genres. However, *Treasure* is set not in the mythical Old West but rather in Mexico of the 1920s, featuring expatriate Americans down on their luck. True, the early Roy Rogers and Gene Autry Westerns were set around the same time, but they featured so many standard elements of the Western—cowboys, saloons, shootouts, ranches, horseback riding and stunts—that the contemporary setting did not move them far from the center of the genre. In contrast, *The Treasure of the Sierra Madre* plays as an all-out drama that just happens to be set in the Mexican wilds—a non–Western at heart, albeit one that nods frequently toward the genre. In truth the movie, whose journey is as much a psychological trip into the depths of the human soul as it is a geographical one, shares far more in common with Conrad's *Heart of Darkness* than it does with any Western prior to its time.

The true importance of *Treasure* to the Western, therefore, is not the ways in which it was inflected by the genre in its creation, but rather in the ways it would itself influence later Western movies. Its gritty, sweaty ambience and its all-too-human protagonists find echoes in a hundred subversive Westerns and anti–Westerns, including *Yellow Sky* (1948), *Vera Cruz* (1954), Leone's "Dollars Trilogy" (1964–66), *The Professionals* (1966), *Ulzana's Raid* (1972), and *Unforgiven* (1992), to name just a few. Perhaps most notably, *Treasure* was one of Sam Peckinpah's favorite films and a major influence on the director's groundbreaking masterpiece *The Wild Bunch* (1969). *Treasure* also helped to establish Mexico as a new frontier, a mythic landscape into which could be projected people and situations and conflicts and ethical questions when the possibilities of the tried-and-true Old West mining camps, ranches, homesteads, and boomtowns were becoming more and more exhausted. In Westerns from this period onward, as Richard Slotkin writes, Mexico—like the domain of the Indian—was able to provide "engagement with the world of the racial/ethnic Other as a utopian alternative to the corruption of American 'civilization' as well as the site of a potentially redemptive spiritual/sexual experience."[2]

One does not need a familiarity with the Golden Age Western to appreciate *The Treasure of the Sierra Madre*. Rather, and to the contrary, a viewing of John Huston's masterpiece—aside from being a cinematic delight in its own right—is also excellent preparation for understanding the development of stylistic elements that would become part and parcel of the revisionist Western in the decades to come.

Fort Apache
(1948)

March 27, 1948 (Phoenix)
USA—English / Spanish
Argosy Pictures
128m—Mono—BW—1.37:1

Direction: John Ford
Screenplay: Frank S. Nugent, James Warner Bellah (story "Massacre")
Principal Cast: John Wayne (Capt. Kirby York), Henry Fonda (Lt. Col. Owen Thursday), Shirley Temple (Philadelphia Thursday), Pedro Armendáriz (Sgt. Beaufort), Ward Bond (Sgt. Maj. Michael O'Rourke), George O'Brien (Capt. Sam Collingwood), Victor McLaglen (Sgt. Festus Mulcahy), Anna Lee (Mrs. Emily Collingwood), Irene Rich (Mrs. Mary O'Rourke), Dick Foran (Sgt. Quincannon), Guy Kibbee (Capt. Dr. Wilkens), Grant Withers (Silas Meacham), Jack Pennick (Sgt. Daniel Shattuck), Ray Hyke (Recruit), Movita (Guadalupe), Miguel Inclán (Cochise), Mary Gordon (Ma), Philip Kieffer (Cavalryman), Mae Marsh (Officer's Wife), Hank Worden (Southern Recruit), John Agar (2nd Lt. Michael Shannon O'Rourke)
Production: John Ford, Merian C. Cooper
Cinematography: Archie Stout
Editing: Jack Murray
Art Direction: James Basevi
Music: Richard Hageman
Awards: Locarno International Film Festival—Best Director (Ford), Locarno International Film Festival—Best Black-and-White Cinematography (Stout)
Nominations: Writers Guild of America—Best Written American Western (Nugent)

The Western pulp writer James Warner Bellah (active from the late 1920s through the 1950s) was, in the words of his own son, "a fascist, a racist, and a world-class bigot." With regard to the Native Americans about whom many of his stories revolved, Bellah wrote that "the smell of an Indian is resinous and salty and rancid. It is the wood smoke of his tepee and the fetidity of his breath that comes of eating body-hot animal entrails. It is his uncured tobacco and the sweat of his unwashed body." John Ford, who had met Bellah in India during World War II, did not share Bellah's politics or egregious racism, but the two men did have one thing in common: a reverence for the military.[1] Because of this, Ford became interested in filming adaptations of some of Bellah's *Saturday Evening Post* short stories, particularly those surrounding the exploits of the U.S. Cavalry. The result was Ford's so-called Cavalry Trilogy: *Fort Apache* (1948), *She Wore a Yellow Ribbon* (1949), and *Rio Grande* (1950), all based on Bellah's stories. Each one shows, with differing emphases, the cavalry fort as a microcosm of an idealized America, a place where people from widely varying origins—rich and poor, aristocratic and working class, native-born and immigrant, ex–Union and ex–Confederate, military and civilian, old and young, male and female—could come together and work side by side toward a common purpose.

For the first two of these adaptations, Ford engaged former *New York Times* film critic Frank S. Nugent, who was already a John Ford fan, having previously written glowing reviews of *Stagecoach* (1939) and *The Grapes of Wrath* (1940) before he left the *Times* to become a script doctor. Now a freelance writer, Nugent had recently met Ford on the Mexican set of *The Fugitive* (1947) while writing an article about the production of that movie, and *Fort Apache* would be the beginning of their long association, as well as Nugent's first screenplay. Nugent would go on to write for nine major Ford films outside of the Cavalry Trilogy: *3 Godfathers* (1948), *Wagon Master* (1950), *The Quiet Man* (1952), *Mister Roberts* (1955), *The Searchers* (1956), *The Rising of the Moon* (1957), *The Last Hurrah* (1958), *Two Rode Together* (1961), and *Donovan's Reef* (1963). Nugent's absence, however, would be keenly felt in the inferior third installment of the Cavalry Trilogy, *Rio Grande*. With so many other production elements—director, actors, crew—remaining the same, this shows just how important the writer's contributions are to the overall character of a film. (In fairness, *Rio Grande* was also not a film that Ford particularly wanted to make; he tossed it off quickly in order to get the green light for 1952's *The Quiet Man*.)[2]

About his enlistment for the *Fort Apache* project, Nugent later recalled: "I have often wondered why Ford chose me to write his cavalry films. I had been on a horse but once—and to our mutual humiliation. I had never seen an Indian."[3] In his typical demanding fashion, Ford set his screenwriter to reading everything he could find on the American Southwest. In Nugent's words, "After seven weeks of this I returned to Hollywood full of erudition, steeped in Indian lore and cavalry commands." Ford asked him if he was satisfied, and Nugent replied that he was. "Fine," Ford answered. "Now forget everything you've read and we'll start writing a story about the cavalry."[4]

Aside from bringing his outstanding screenwriting skills to the project, Nugent also jettisoned the loathsome racism that permeated Bellah's original text. A great deal of thought went into the portrayal of the Apache leader Cochise as Nugent and Ford began to develop the backstories for the film's major characters. (Ford was wont to do this in his pictures to make his characters more realistic, even when the backstories were never directly stated.) The movie's notes for Cochise describe him as "highly intelligent" and go on to say: "In our story his name will strike terror and dread into the hearts of men, but when we meet him, he will prove to be an impressive and dignified man, no mere vengeful fighter, but a man who has suffered much at the hands of the whites, and has, in fact, right on his side."[5] This radical (and much-needed) departure from Bellah's vile depiction of Indians as smelly vermin was not only the right choice from an ethical point of view; it also made for a much better movie—richer, subtler, more humane, and more complex.

Thousands of words have been written about the treatment of Native Americans in John Ford's Westerns. There is no simple assessment of this. On the plus side, Ford was far more progressive in his thinking than many other filmmakers of the time. In *Fort Apache*, for example, the true wrongdoers are not the natives but rather those white men who betray the Indians, are bigoted against them, or uncritically accept a simplistic view of the situation on the frontier. As Bosley Crowther wrote in a contemporary review, the movie presented a new and maturing viewpoint upon one aspect of the American Indian wars. For here it is not the "heathen Indian" who is the "heavy" of the piece but a hard-bitten Army colonel, blind through ignorance and a passion for revenge. And ranged alongside this willful white man is a venal government agent who exploits the innocence of the Indians while supposedly acting as their friend.[6]

Fort Apache portrays the Indians as adversaries, to be sure—but noble ones, just as classical myths, Arthurian legends, and Shake-

Cochise (Miguel Inclán), the noble adversary, reacts to having his honor impugned. *Fort Apache* (Argosy, 1948).

spearean dramas often did with their antagonists. It is not too much of a stretch, for example, to conclude that Ford (and Nugent) saw the Apaches in the same way that Homer saw the Trojans—that is, as honorable, worthy opponents who just happened to lose out, eventually, to the ancestors of those now telling the tale. Furthermore, Ford himself was compassionate toward the Native Americans he encountered in his life. Hundreds of Navajo Indians would joyfully participate as extras in a John Ford movie whenever he filmed in Monument Valley, and the director was generally "loved and admired" by them. In 1948, there were heavy snowstorms which blocked supply lines to the area, and Ford himself organized an airborne relief effort for the Navajo.[7]

On the other hand, one can deliver charity while still espousing a paternalistic viewpoint, and, as Michael Valdez Moses points out, the narrative of *Fort Apache* "ultimately depends for its moral and dramatic effect upon the questionable premise that the Apache would (and should) be perfectly content to live on the reservation, if only the federal government were a better steward of its wards."[8] In the classic Ford Western, Indians may certainly be noble and dignified, but there is, as yet, still no questioning of the belief in the rightness of American expansion from east to west.

I am inclined to forgive this paternalism in Ford; relative to his times, he was enlightened on the subject, and in his later career would become uncharacteristically apologetic about how his earlier works had depicted Native Americans (even though it can be argued, convincingly, that he had always remained ahead of the societal curve in this respect). Ford's last Western, 1964's *Cheyenne Autumn*, was described by the director as an attempt at reparation for his prior portrayals of Native Americans. "This will be the first picture ever made in which Indians are people," Ford would say, albeit inaccurately.[9]

In short, the relationship between John Ford and the figure of the Indian is a complicated one. In hindsight, from our privileged position, it is easy—too easy, in fact—to feel morally superior to Ford and to judge him from the vantage point of our contemporary perspective, which we would describe, perhaps arrogantly, as enlightened. But—setting aside the fact that future generations will probably judge us just as harshly—to do so would be to miss so much of the beauty, humanity, and perception that permeates the John Ford Western. *Fort Apache* is no more a white-supremacist document than the *Iliad* is an Achaean-supremacist one. Both works, to be sure, are part of a national mythology and situate their primary protagonists on one side of a conflict, but both also celebrate the valor and nobility of the opponents—whether Priam's Trojans or Cochise's Apaches. The Greek ideal of *kleos*—honor and glory earned in heroic exploits—obtains in both the *Iliad* and *Fort Apache*, applying equally to the warriors on each side of the conflict. In both works, primary characters speak openly of glory and its importance to them, and the adversaries of the main protagonists are shown as fully human, heroic, and noble. In *Fort Apache*, we see how important honor is to the men of the cavalry; we also see the outrage in the eyes of Cochise (Miguel Inclán) when the enraged cavalry commander, Lt. Col. Owen Thursday (Henry Fonda), says that he finds the chief without honor. We feel the sting of the moment ourselves—we admire and sympathize deeply with Cochise, just as we do with the *Iliad*'s Hector, and we grit our teeth at the frustrating character flaws so evident in the rigid Thursday, just as we do with those of the petulant Achilles.

The Cavalry Trilogy begins with a genuine fanfare, as a silhouetted cavalryman on horseback leaps into frame, blowing his bugle. We then see him in a longer shot with one of the Monument Valley monoliths in the background. As is typical in a Ford Western, epic vistas will dominate the action, providing "a landscape so immense in scale it both dwarfs men's accomplishments and sets them in a mythological framework," as Nancy Schoenberger expresses it.[10] This boisterous, exhilarating opening tells us that, come what may, the brave cavalrymen of Fort Apache will be celebrated by the film as the nineteenth-century equivalent of knights-errant. Watching *Fort Apache*, one finds it particularly apt that the words *cavalry* and *chivalry* descend from a common root.

The film's plot centers around the conflict in values between Colonel Thursday, the newly arrived, ramrod-straight, by-the-book commander of the titular outpost, and the seasoned, easygoing Captain Kirby York (John Wayne). Thursday is an obsessive, arrogant martinet, inflexible and bigoted against Indians (and others); his character arrives on the scene as a classist representative of East Coast aristocracy. In contrast, York is a true man of the West, essentially classless and self-made, a man of his word and a friend to the Indians.

And yet … none of the characters are quite that simple. The stiff, hidebound Thursday is difficult to like, especially because his dogmatism and prejudice lead to unmitigated disaster, but his affection for his daughter Philadelphia (Shirley Temple), however overprotective, is evident. He is also a widower, and a man of some military accomplishments who resents being, in his words, "shunted aside" against his will to this remote corner of the West, far from the civilization and the world that he has known. We can sympathize with this, which helps us notice the character's more redeeming qualities. One of my favorite lines in the picture comes when Thursday and some cavalrymen discover a cache of rotgut whiskey being sold to the Indians by the crooked Meacham (Grant Withers), hidden in boxes with deceptive labels. "'Bibles,' sir," Sgt. Quincannon (Dick Foran) observes ironically; but Thursday simply holds out a cup and says, "Sergeant, pour me some scripture." All of this allows us to see Thursday as a real person, more than just a cast-iron automaton, and to have some sympathy for him in spite of his

Philadelphia Thursday (Shirley Temple), Emily Collingwood (Anna Lee), and Mary O'Rourke (Irene Rich) watch the cavalrymen ride off to war. Each will lose someone they love before the day's end. *Fort Apache* (Argosy, 1948).

obvious flaws. John Wayne's Captain York, although more idealized, seems similarly real, a fleshed-out character, and Cochise is no typical Indian caricature either—he is honorable, yet also capable of unleashing cruel destruction upon his adversaries.

One of the true delights of *Fort Apache* is that it takes all the time it needs to present the inhabitants of the fort as real people—not just the leads, but colorful supporting characters like Philadelphia, her love interest Lt. O'Rourke (played by John Agar, Temple's husband at the time), the young man's parents (Ward Bond and Irene Rich), the veteran Collingwood (former John Ford star George O'Brien, now forty-eight) and his gentle wife (Anna Lee), the boisterous Irishman Mulcahy (Ford favorite Victor McLaglen), Sgt. Beaufort (Pedro Armendáriz), and others. We catch a glimpse of the intimate, everyday lives of these folks, trying their best to recreate a sense of civilization and continuity in this alien land. They gossip, form attachments, stage elegant dances and society functions, and generally carry on a semblance of a normal life within the wilderness. Ford's film lingers over these details. The movie cares about these people and is unwilling to simplify them down to cardboard cutouts or lose them in a flurry of action sequences, as is typically done in today's genre adventures. In fact, it is an hour in—halfway through the picture—before the first instance of conflict with the Indians occurs, which only makes the action scenes more dramatic when they come, because we have now grown to appreciate the cavalrymen and their families. These people are flawed, vulnerable, and human, just like all of us, and we are no more assured of their safety than they are. Anything could happen. Something real is at stake now.

As the action explodes at the one-hour mark, we are swept in the blink of an eye from the measured, lilting rhythm of the fort's genteel society into a bright, blazing, savage world of kinetic movement, filled with tracking shots of galloping horses and rushing stages. It slugs us in the gut; this is the mastery of *Fort Apache*. One of today's action flicks would already have had five gun battles by this point in its running time—while having spent perhaps thirty seconds on character development. *Fort Apache*'s way is the opposite of this, and it is exponentially more powerful. If only this lesson could be learned by today's filmmakers, it would go far toward redeeming the cinematic Waste Land that is postmodern Hollywood. Alas, I fear it will take a new generation of film creators—perhaps only children now—to discover and bring into the mainstream once more the beauty of nuance and imperfection in characters, and the enhanced power of hyper-dramatic moments when they don't come every ten minutes. Until that happens, there is little hope for quality in the factory-produced, market-driven Hollywood movies in which we currently drown.

As always, John Ford's two favorite actors—in their only featured appearance together in a Ford Western—are at the top of their game when working for the genre's master director. Wayne is inspiring, likeable, strong, and fully in his element as always; and Fonda, of course, is fantastic in the movie's most complex role. *Fort Apache*'s

An appointment with destiny: Capt. York (John Wayne), Lt. Col. Thursday (Henry Fonda), and Capt. Collingwood (George O'Brien, who starred in his first Ford Western, *The Iron Horse*, twenty-four years prior). *Fort Apache* (Argosy, 1948).

Colonel Thursday is a dark, driven man. As a clear George Armstrong Custer archetype, he represents a sort of waystation along Hollywood's Custer path, positioned somewhere in the middle of the scale from the noble patriot depicted in *The Plainsman* (1936) and *They Died with Their Boots On* (1941) to the murderous madman of *Little Big Man* (1970). The character also gives Fonda the opportunity to show once more a glimpse of what he would be capable of in even darker portrayals to come.

Fort Apache is unabashedly romantic, and elegiac as well, depicting an era long since passed, if it ever existed at all. Anticipating the "print the legend" perspective voiced in the last great Ford/Wayne Western, *The Man Who Shot Liberty Valance* (1962), *Fort Apache* blends fact and legend seamlessly, with complete self-awareness. As Frank Nugent wrote, "I suspect that when [Ford] starts thinking about a story, he calmly devotes himself to personal research, gets hold of the music of the period and, generally, comes to his office well provided with a mixture of facts and fancy."[11] Understanding John Ford's tendency to use history, but also to be willing to bend it for mythic or artistic effect—to "print the legend"—is the key to making sense of the troubling, enigmatic, endlessly debated ending of *Fort Apache.* Just what is more real, and more significant, in the final analysis—the history or the myth? The hero's archetypal adventure or the gritty facts of biography? The romantic ideal or the disenchanted reality? The symbol or the literal truth? York gives us his answer at the end, and it doesn't sit entirely comfortably with us; it's not supposed to. We live in a factual world, but one which we can often only make sense of, and face, through metaphor. Ford, since the beginning, has understood this, and embraced this ambiguity through the complexities of his stories and characters. This is why his movies resonate. This is why his heroes live.

What do we make of characters who fight and die for causes in which we can no longer believe? Unquestionably the desire for American expansion was not a just cause for war; neither was the abduction of Helen, as Homer makes all too clear. And yet, as both Homer and John Ford understood, allies and enemies may both be capable of committing heroic and noble acts—or, for that matter, atrocities.

One possible way forward as we encounter pieces of art (and *kleos*) like *Fort Apache*—and other martial works like the *Iliad, Le Morte d'Arthur, Henry V, The Three Musketeers, The Man Who Would Be King, The Four Feathers,* or *Beat to Quarters*—is to realize that the true worth of these is metaphorical, not literal. They are valuable stories to us not because of their comment on history and warfare, but because of what they tell us about facing struggles heroically in our own lives, and the ways in which they can inspire us to stand and confront our destinies with strength, courage, and self-sacrifice. In most cases, they also invite us to find the nobility and humanity even in those who are our enemies.

I will leave the last word about *Fort Apache*'s cavalry heroes—as well as their Apache antagonists, and all battlers in literature and legend from Troy to outer space—to the twentieth-century's greatest expositor of the Hero's Journey, Joseph Campbell:

> The hero sacrifices himself for something—that's the morality of it. Now, from another position, of course, you might say that the idea for which he sacrificed himself was something that should not have been respected. That's a judgment from the other side, but it doesn't destroy the intrinsic heroism of the deed performed.[12]

Red River
(1948)

August 26, 1948 (Texas, Oklahoma, Kansas)
USA—English / Spanish
Monterey Productions
133m—Mono—BW—1.37:1

Direction: Howard Hawks
Screenplay: Borden Chase (story "The Chisholm Trail" and screenplay), Charles Schnee
Principal Cast: John Wayne (Thomas Dunson), Montgomery Clift (Matt Garth), Joanne Dru (Tess Millay), Walter Brennan (Nadine Groot), Coleen Gray (Fen), Harry Carey (Mr. Melville), John Ireland (Cherry Valance), Noah Beery, Jr. (Buster McGee), Harry Carey, Jr. (Dan Latimer), Chief Yowlachie (Quo), Paul Fix (Teeler Yacey), Hank Worden (Simms Reeves), Mickey Kuhn (Matt as a boy), Ray Hyke (Walt Jergens), Hal Taliaferro (Old Leather)
Production: Howard Hawks
Cinematography: Russell Harlan
Editing: Christian Nyby, Francis D. Lyon (uncredited), Jack Murray (uncredited)
Art Direction: John Datu
Music: Dimitri Tiomkin
Awards: Faro Island Film Festival—Best Actor (Clift), Faro Island Film Festival—Outstanding Artistic Contribution (Donald Steward, Allen Q. Thompson, special effects), National Film Registry
Nominations: Oscar—Best Writing, Motion Picture Story (Chase), Oscar—Best Film Editing (Nyby), Directors Guild of America—Outstanding Directorial Achievement (Hawks), Faro Island Film Festival—Best Film, Writers Guild of America—Best Written American Western (Chase, Schnee)

The culture that we in the West have inherited is largely a Manichaean one. That is to say, our world is so often depicted by art, literature, and religion as dualistic, under constant tension between good and evil, light and dark, right and wrong. Eastern thought often involves the interplay of opposites as well, of course—in the notions of *yin* and *yang*, for example—but the tendency there is more frequently to seek an integration of the opposites, a unification, an understanding of the ways in which contrasting principles interact to form the world, and often a mystical realization of how, behind the scenes, the two apparent opposites are actually one. In the Manichaean West this is typically not the ideal. Instead, the goal is for good to overcome evil, the light to conquer the dark, right to win out over wrong. In today's polarized America, Manichaeism dominates, as the localized winning/losing dichotomy we recognize from team sports has been translated onto the larger cultural, geographical, and political stage. Now, in all arenas of life from great to small, the primary emphasis is not on working together productively and gaining strength through our differences but rather on doing whatever it takes to ensure that our team scores a total victory over the other team, whom we hate. "Us and Them": the essential principle behind a great deal of modern Western political and religious rhetoric.

However, some Occidental cultural products stray from this position and take on what we could think of as a more Eastern flavor. This is not necessarily to imply any direct influence, just an acknowledgment that some people westward of the Levant have also occasionally played around with nondualism, speculating about integrating opposites rather than forcing them into battle with one another. A notable early literary example of this approach is Wolfram von Eschenbach's *Parzival*. As mentioned previously, the hero of this marvelous medieval romance is a naive young fool, one who must ultimately learn to reject the dualistic thinking of his mother, father figure, and the church, and find instead his own integrative path between the pairs of opposites in order to achieve the Grail. Even the Grail itself in this version is nondualist, a stone brought to earth by the neutral angels who did not take either side in the heavenly war between God and Lucifer. *Parzival*, from beginning to end, upholds the virtues of the middle way, harmonizing in that sense very well with both Aristotle and the Buddha. Others in the West before and after Wolfram have also explored this realm, of course—the Gnostics, Plotinus, the Kabbalists, Eckhart, Pico della Mirandola, the Transcendentalists, Whitman, Nietzsche, Jung, Aldous Huxley, and beyond—but for me, *Parzival* remains nondualism's quintessential literary expression in the Occident.

The genre of the classical Western movie, with its heritage rooted in rich Judeo-Christian and European soil, is dominated by Manichaean stories resolved when one party wins through, dominating over its opposite. Cowboys and Indians, good guys and bad guys, railroads and farmers, ranchers and settlers will face off during these dramas, and the situation is total war: one side must win a full victory over the other (typically through violence) in order for peace and civilization to follow. The Manichaean template helped to inform the expectations that audiences had when they first encountered *Red River* in 1948—but this particular Western had surprises in store for them.

Both the story writer (and screenplay co-writer) Borden Chase and the director Howard Hawks had plenty of experience crafting dualistic dramas prior to *Red River*. Chase had already written for the World War II propaganda flicks *Destroyer* (1943), *The Fighting Seabees* (1944), and *This Man's Navy* (1945), and among the more than two dozen movies Hawks had directed before *Red River* are the war pictures *The Dawn Patrol* (1930), *The Road to Glory* (1936), *Sergeant York* (1941), and *Air Force* (1943), as well as crime dramas like *The Criminal Code* (1931), *Scarface* (1932), and *The Big Sleep* (1946). In other words, Hawks and Chase were no strangers to Manichaean drama. In addition, both were passionate political conservatives, Chase going so far as to become an active participant in Hollywood blacklisting during the McCarthy era.

Robert Sklar, in his excellent essay on *Red River*, points out that film critics of the time were overjoyed to proclaim the movie free from ideology, but that this was a misreading—there was actually quite a bit of ideological content there.[1] My own view is that this is true, but that it is subordinate to the greater scheme of the movie, which seeks to blend and integrate numerous contrasting perspectives, including but not limited to political ones. The film, therefore, avoids espousing any overt ideological stances. Despite his political commitments, Hawks generally preferred this neutral approach in his films, and Chase was happy as a writer (if not as a member of the Motion Picture Alliance for the Preservation of American Ideals) to eschew didacticism, explore ambiguity, and juxtapose contrasting perspectives with sympathy for both. This led both men to be capable of producing unconventional, surprising, idiosyncratic work, not least the magnificent *Red River*, which on the surface has all of the elements of the traditional Western and yet is unlike nearly all of its predecessors, rejecting a simplistic Manichaean dualism in favor of the interaction and ultimate integration of opposites.

At its heart, *Red River*, like so many Howard Hawks movies, centers around the relationship between two male characters who have both antipathy and love for one another. Hawks once called this paradigm "the greatest love story in all of the world. I don't mean sexual. I have always believed that a man can actually love and respect another man more so than he can a woman."[2] As might be expected, these two men— obsessively driven cattleman Tom Dunson (John Wayne) and his adopted son Matthew Garth (Montgomery Clift)—embody many of the contrasts that will ultimately be united and integrated by the film's end: old and young; authoritarian and democratic; individualistic and community-oriented; rigid and flexible; controlling and free-flowing; and even masculine and feminine. At first glance we might think that Dunson consistently represents the first in each of these pairs and Matt the second, but the reality is more subtle than that. In fact, the real problem with Dunson is that he is an extremist along all of these scales, whereas Matt has found a balance, a blend of both opposites. So, for example, Dunson is stubbornly rigid all the way, whereas Matt demonstrates a mixture of discipline and flexibility; likewise, Dunson is a firm authoritarian, whereas Matt, while he has an authoritarian side, tempers it with a more humane, egalitarian, communal outlook. As with *Parzival*, moderation and balance between opposites is the primary virtue, and dogmatically stubborn extremism is the primary vice.

In many ways the key to the whole picture is given, deftly disguised, in a very early scene. It is about fifteen years prior to the great cattle drive that is the main focus of the narrative. Dunson and his sidekick Nadine Groot (Walter Brennan) have decided to break off from the wagon train they have been accompanying and forge their own way into the wild, but first Dunson must say goodbye to the woman he loves, Fen (Coleen Gray). He believes, wrongly, that she will be safer remaining with the wagon train, and plans to send for her later. Before departing, Dunson gives Fen a bracelet, a circle that recalls the ancient ouroboros symbol, but with two protruding "heads." This is the union of opposites: two heads pointing in different directions, but united within the eternal circle—and the bracelet will recur at several strategic points during the narrative.

As Dunson holds Fen in his arms and bids her goodbye, she smiles confidently at him and delivers the following extraordinary speech:

> Hold me. Feel me in your arms. Do I feel weak, Tom? I don't, do I? Oh, you'll need me. You'll need a woman. You need what a woman can give you, to do what you have to do. Oh, listen to me, Tom. Listen to your head, and your heart too. The sun only shines half the time, Tom. The other half is night.

At face value, this seems straightforward, just a girl pleading with her man that he needs the comforts of a relationship with a good woman. And the bit about the day and the nighttime can be read simply as well: a man needs someone to cuddle up with after the sun goes down. But as I read the film, this all means something entirely different from its surface-level content. Dunson, as we will soon discover, is a man whose life is out of balance, so hypermasculine that he has never incorporated any "feminine" virtues into his psychology. A Jungian might say that all people are in a sense bisexual; we all contain both male and female, arising as we do from the coequal biological union of both. Men, therefore, still have their feminine side (*anima*), and integrating its strengths into the total personality rather than suppressing them is an important key to balance in one's life, just as integrating the *animus* is for a woman—although even here, according to Jung, balance and moderation are critical. Both masculine and feminine principles, in Jung's view, contain positive and negative potential, and so integration becomes both necessary and dangerous. Reconciling the two is not easy, and nearly always involves sacrifice.

Dunson's primary affliction in *Red River* is that he has not achieved this synthesis. In this light, it is easy to see Fen more as an incarnation of the *anima* than as a literal character. (Easier still because she only appears in one scene, with no opportunity for us to get to know her as a personality. Ethereal and abstract, Fen is the feminine principle made manifest; is her odd name in fact a contraction of "feminine"?) Rereading Fen's speech in this way—the submerged Jungian *anima* speaking to Dunson from his own subconscious—unlocks deeper layers hidden within the text. Fen is telling Dunson that he needs what his repressed feminine side can give him in order to balance his extremist masculinity; that his *anima* has a strength of its own, one that he will need to incorporate into his psyche to accomplish his ambitions. "Listen to your head (masculine side), and your heart (*anima*) too," Fen says. Unite the pairs of opposites, bring them together in accord. The sun only shines half the time; the other half is night. *Yang* and *yin*, light and dark, opposing principles brought into accord—this is the way of balance, the piercing of the valley between extremes that can lead Dunson and his cattle drive to their destiny, just as it led Parzival to the Grail. Fen's speech is more than just an argument for the virtues of companionship—it is an argument for integration within the individual psyche.

But Dunson stubbornly refuses to listen; he rides off with Groot, and within minutes of screen time his *anima* is dead. Nevertheless, the hero on the Hero's Adventure is always given the tools he needs to complete the quest. Before long, Dunson and Groot encounter Matthew Garth (Mickey Kuhn), a young boy who is the last survivor of a fearful Indian attack. Orphaned and dazed, Matt rambles incoherently to himself as he stumbles along across the open grassland, leading a cow. Dunson sees that Matt is hysterical and slaps him. Quick as a flash, the boy pulls a pistol out. Dunson acts as if to talk with him, but suddenly knocks Matt down and grabs the pistol. "Don't ever trust anybody till you know him," Dunson advises. "I won't, after this," the boy

Tom Dunson (John Wayne) bids farewell to his love—and *anima*—Fen (Coleen Gray) in an early scene that may hold the key to the entire movie. *Red River* (Monterey, 1948).

replies. "Thanks for tellin' me." Soon after, Dunson returns the gun and asks, "Well, are you gonna use it?" "No," answers Matt, "but don't ever try and take it away from me again." Dunson turns to Groot and says approvingly, "He'll do." Matt has satisfied Dunson's expectations for manhood, at least to all appearances, and Dunson adopts Matt (informally) as his own son and heir.

But things are not entirely as they seem, for Matt—as discussed earlier—has integrated both the masculine and feminine sides of his soul. He, rather than the dead Fen, will be the vehicle of *anima* for Dunson, a role made symbolically explicit by the fact that Matt is providing the cow to match Dunson's bull. From the progeny of this animal pair will arise the Red River D ranch. Dunson kneels down to sketch his idea for the brand in the dirt, a vertical pair of wavy lines representing the banks of the Red River, with a D to the left. Soon Dunson and Groot craft the corresponding branding iron and apply it to Dunson's bull.

> DUNSON: Well, there's the first one—the first Red River D.
> MATT (*protesting*): You gonna put that on my cow too?
> DUNSON: Why not?
> MATT: She's mine. I see a D for Dunson, but my name's Matthew.
> DUNSON: We'll talk about that later.
> MATT: I don't see any M on that brand.
> DUNSON: I'll put an M on it when you earn it.
> MATT (*considers*): That's fair enough. I'll earn it.

From this, the audience might infer that the movie will center around Matt's evolution, his journey toward earning his place on the brand. Matt certainly has his own character arc, but the most dramatic transformations will occur within Dunson. Dunson, even more than Matt, must show his true worth by the end.

Cut to fourteen years later: Dunson has built his ranch, but times are hard in post–Civil War Texas. Matthew Garth is now a grown man (beautifully played by Montgomery Clift), back from serving in the war and eager to help Dunson realize his dream of driving ten thousand cattle hundreds of miles north to Sedalia. As we know, Westerns involving journeys are about more than just geographical movement, and *Red River* is no exception.

One of the most memorable scenes in the movie is the depiction of the quiet, pre-dawn moments just before the cattle drive sets out. We linger on the faces of the men, and, over a hushed but intense musical accompaniment, the camera does a slow, nearly full-circle pan around the assembled cattle and cowboys, finishing on Dunson, who turns to his adopted son and says simply, "Take 'em to Missouri, Matt." The cowboys explode in delighted whoops and the drive is underway. The three-minute scene is a masterpiece of pregnant anticipation followed by joyous release.

Things on the drive start out smoothly enough—too smoothly, in fact, as noted by cowhand Simms (played by the delightfully idiosyncratic character actor Hank Worden), who is a "wise fool," a Parzival archetype all his own. Underscoring once again the movie's interest in a balance between opposites, Simms conveys his apprehension about how well things are going to his fellow cowhands, explaining, "Well, I don't like to see things go good or bad. I like 'em in-between." This might at first seem like just a throwaway line, but—as with Dunson's conversation with Fen—the moment is more thematically significant than it seems.

The drive may have been easy so far, but trouble soon comes in the form of a night-time stampede (preceded by an anticipatory sequence just as intense as its counterpart before the drive set out). The catastrophe, which will cost the young cowboy Latimer (Harry Carey, Jr.) his life, is triggered inadvertently by one of the hands, Bunk (Ivan Parry), who has been sneaking sugar habitually from the chuck wagon. This time, Bunk manages to knock over a bunch of pans, and the clatter pushes the already spooked cattle over the edge. After the chaos is finally brought under control and Latimer's body is found and buried, Dunson wants to tie Bunk to a wagon wheel and whip him. Bunk resists and starts to draw his gun; Matt is quicker, and shoots Bunk in the shoulder, knowing that if Dunson gets to Bunk first, he will kill him. This leads to an extraordinary moment when Matt helps tend to Bunk, who thanks Matt for shooting him. Matt then sends Bunk home, telling him to be sure and take along an extra horse. Here is another instance of the contrast between the two lead characters: Dunson is all "masculine," wanting solely to punish; whereas Matt is already a traveler on the Middle Way between *animus* and *anima*, still able to use violence (as in the gunshot to the shoulder), but tempered with humane compassion. And Matt is not alone: Nadine Groot, who also lives in the integrated middle (note his androgynous character name), is able to say quite bluntly to his boss after the incident, "You was wrong, Mr. Dunson."

The next major difficulty along the trail comes when three men try to desert the drive. They confront an unarmed Dunson with guns, but Groot tosses him a shotgun, and then he and Matt gun down the rebellious hands. Again we observe that Matt is not hesitant to use violence when necessary; his tough side is just as accessible to him as his gentle side is. Both means of interacting with others and the world are part of Matt's repertoire, whereas all Dunson knows is the stick. After the confrontation is over, Dunson says, "Well, there's quitters to be buried. I'll—I'll read over 'em in the morning." He walks off, and once again the wise fool Simms plays the role of Greek chorus, commenting: "Plantin' and readin', plantin' and readin'. Fill a man full o' lead, stick him in the ground, and then read words at him. Why, when you've killed a man, why try to read the Lord in as a partner on the job?" This prairie Parzival's wonderful speech occurs, significantly, at almost the exact midpoint of the film.

I should pause for a moment to acknowledge just how brilliantly all of this is played. Following its own lead, *Red River* never falls into the trap of Manichaean thinking. Matt clearly has the more enlightened viewpoint of the two main characters, but it is not as if Matt is "good" and Dunson is "evil." We see Matt's ability to be cold-blooded and violent, and we also understand and sympathize with Dunson's reactions—when, for example, he wants to whip the sugar thief, whose slinking skullduggery, after all, resulted in the death of a man; or when he enforces stern discipline on the men working under him, whose lives depend upon one another. In a movie with so much simmering, and occasionally erupting, conflict, it is amazing the degree to which we recognize bits of ourselves in every single one of the characters, on all sides. No one is a saint, and no one is an unredeemable villain; everyone is human in this great humanist Western.

Nevertheless, Matt is on the natural path from which Dunson has strayed, and the movie takes great advantage of symbolism to underscore this. Matt's ways are easy, relaxed, fluid, where Dunson is a tightly wound spring, clenched and controlling. If horses truly do symbolize Nature, it seems significant that Dunson, on multiple occasions, scolds other men who fail to "hold that horse!" Nature is to be conquered, tamed, broken, controlled—and so are men. But even Nature herself has a comment

Cherry Valance (John Ireland) and Matt Garth (Montgomery Clift) fondle each other's guns in a famous scene. Much has been written about the homosexual subtext here, and the observation is entirely apt. I have avoided discussing the scene at length only because so much ink has already been spilled over it. Nevertheless, it is yet another excellent example of the film showing Matt's character as an integrated balance of stereotypically "masculine" and "feminine" traits. *Red River* (Monterey, 1948).

to make about the two men's approaches: when the herd is preparing to cross the Red River, Dunson and Matt ride out into the water to scout for potential hazards. From the upstream side, Dunson calls: "Quicksand out in here, mark it! More of it in here!" But Matt reports from downstream, "Firm all the way!" Dunson has moved against the current and found quicksand; Matt, moving in the direction of the river's flow, finds solid footing.

The rift between the two men is inevitable, and it comes quickly when Dunson proposes to lynch two deserters that have been tracked down and brought back to camp. This is too much for Matt. The destined Oedipal moment has come, as Matt rebels against his tyrannical adopted father and takes control of the herd, intending now to drive it to Abilene rather than Sedalia. Dunson tries to stop him by force, but gunslinger-turned-cowboy Cherry Valance (John Ireland) shoots Dunson in the hand. The injury isn't significant, but enough to temporarily disable Dunson's ability to fight Matt. The gentle cowhand Buster (Noah Beery, Jr.) then shoots Dunson's dropped pistol away, and at this point, once again, we feel for the emasculated Dunson, even while recognizing that he is in the wrong. His bull-headed determination has turned to pathological obsession, and it now falls to Matt to lead the others and bring the herd in. Before

Matt (Montgomery Clift) assists the wounded Tess Millay (Joanne Dru) during the Indian attack. Note the phallic arrow motif we first encountered in *The Covered Wagon* (1923). *Red River* (Monterey, 1948).

leaving Dunson behind, Matt promises to do his best to get the cattle to Abilene, but Dunson offers a chilling reply:

> Cherry was right. You're soft. You shoulda let him kill me 'cause I'm gonna kill you. I'll catch up with you. I don't know when, but I'll catch up. Every time you turn around, expect to see me—'cause one time you'll turn around and I'll be there. I'll kill you, Matt.

We have no doubt that he means it, and this will set the tone for the rest of the movie, a tense drive to the finish with the dark specter of Dunson always trailing behind.

There is plenty more drama to come for Matt and his band: an encounter with a wagon train filled with gamblers and dance-hall girls, a battle with Indians, another *anima* representative in the form of Matt's love interest Tess Millay (Joanne Dru), and a last desperate drive to the promised land of Abilene. Although Tess has been semi-validly criticized as a character, she does fulfill some important functions to the plot—most especially in her excellent scene with Dunson when he encounters the wagon train a few days behind Matt's group. Tess offers to bear Dunson the son he wants if he will renounce his vendetta against Matt; Dunson ultimately refuses, though, recognizing her love for his disowned son. Once again the *anima* is rejected, although we wonder if, in doing so, Dunson becomes just a bit more human.

All of this leads inevitably to the gripping climax in Abilene, after Matt brings the herd in while knowing that Dunson is not far behind. The slow burn of the plot has finally brought things to a boil, and for me the final scene is a masterpiece. It is certainly gripping, exciting, and violent—but it resolves through reconciliation. The ending of *Red River* has divided critics since the beginning; many feel that it betrays the direction of the plot, but I believe this judgment depends upon a misreading of the movie's mythic content. The essential underlying theme of *Red River* is the integration of opposites into a higher-functioning unity—almost following the Hegelian dialectic model of thesis, antithesis, and synthesis. How could this be given its due if one of the two antagonists were simply to gun the other one down? (Also, how could such a trite, simplistic ending be aesthetically satisfying in this marvelously rich film?) I would maintain that many of those who are dissatisfied with the ending of *Red River* are trying to read it primarily in Oedipal terms, even if unconsciously. There are obviously Oedipal elements to the father-son conflict between Dunson and Matt, but the true model here partakes much more of Wolfram than it does of Sophocles. At its core, *Red River* is a story about moderating between the pairs of opposites; the movie features the garb of an Oedipal drama but not its heart. In true Eastern (or Wolfram-esque) fashion, the opposing forces must be brought together in unity, rather than one of them destroying the other. Were Matt simply to gun down Dunson, as many first-time viewers no doubt expected, then the son would simply become the father. Dunson would win by losing, in that his hoped-for son would be cast in his own image, and the sins of the father would endure into the next generation. Instead, we are presented with an ending that gives us the strength of both men and unites all of the oppositions: male and female, discipline and flexibility, violence and peacemaking, old and new, individual and community. It is deeply, intensely satisfying on that level, and the final shot of the movie is the perfect capstone: the new Red River brand traced in the sand by Dunson's fingers, with its wavy lines in the middle, a D on the left, and now a balancing M on the right.

Red River is a masterpiece, expertly made in all production values—story, screenplay, direction, cinematography, editing, and musical score—but in addition, it features outstanding acting from its entire cast, and especially from the two incomparable leads. Clift's first foray into Hollywood film in *Red River* was also his breakthrough role, as he knew it would be, even though—incredibly—he was personally dissatisfied with the film. (Clift wrote in a letter to James Jones: "I knew that I was going to be famous so I decided I would get drunk anonymously one last time.")[3] Whatever Clift may have thought of *Red River*, his performance is one for the ages, exquisitely real and nuanced. One of the greatest of Hollywood's first wave of Method actors, Clift would appear in only seventeen films before dying of a heart attack at forty-five—a movie career both tragically brief and astoundingly strong.

John Wayne matches Clift in intensity, however, showing the fierce, dark energy that he was capable of bringing to more sinister roles—later exploited by John Ford to perfection in *The Searchers* (1956). In fact, Ford famously commented to Hawks after seeing Wayne's performance in *Red River*, "I never knew the big son of a bitch could act"[4]—this after already having directed Wayne in *Stagecoach* (1939), *The Long Voyage Home* (1940), *They Were Expendable* (1945), and *Fort Apache* (1948). In *Red River*, Wayne also shows his ability to play convincingly characters of different ages, as the plot requires Dunson to move from young to middle-aged over the course of the narrative. Ford's *She Wore a Yellow Ribbon* (1949) would soon take advantage of this talent once

An unstoppable force of nature: Tom Dunson (John Wayne) walks straight toward his fateful encounter with Matt, never breaking stride. Even the cattle hasten out of his way. *Red River* (Monterey, 1948).

again, with Wayne at forty-one playing a cavalryman approaching retirement, artificially aged as he was in *Red River.*

It is disappointing to learn that, on set, the conservatives Wayne and Brennan did not get along well with the left-wing Clift. (Wayne later referred to Clift in an interview as "an arrogant little bastard.")[5] Unfortunately, in that sense at least, the main players may not have absorbed the philosophy at the true heart of the movie. Nevertheless, whatever their feelings for one another, they did work together to help craft an enduring masterpiece—a useful metaphor, perhaps, for our own troubled and polarized time.

Tidbits and Trivia

- There was a two-year delay between *Red River*'s filming and its release. As a result, *The Search* (1948) became, by a few months, the first Montgomery Clift picture to be released, even though *Red River* was the first Hollywood movie on which he worked.
- Interestingly, Dunson is killed in Borden Chase's original story, shot by Cherry Valance. His body is taken back to Texas by Matt and Tess, anticipating a plot point in the greatest cattle-drive Western since *Red River, Lonesome Dove* (1989)—which undoubtedly was an homage to the earlier Western in many ways.

All such stories are probably inspired, at least in part, by real-life cattleman Charles Goodnight, who famously brought his partner Oliver Loving's body from Fort Sumner, New Mexico, to Weatherford, Texas, for burial, in accordance with Loving's dying wish.

Yellow Sky
(1948)

December 25, 1948 (limited release)
USA—English
Twentieth Century–Fox
98m—Mono—BW—1.37:1

Direction: William A. Wellman
Screenplay: Lamar Trotti, W.R. Burnett (story)
Principal Cast: Gregory Peck (James "Stretch" Dawson), Anne Baxter (Constance Mae "Mike"), Richard Widmark (Dude), Robert Arthur (Bull Run), John Russell (Lengthy), Harry Morgan (Half Pint), James Barton (Grandpa), Charles Kemper (Walrus)
Production: Lamar Trotti
Cinematography: Joseph MacDonald
Editing: Harmon Jones
Art Direction: Lyle R. Wheeler, Albert Hogsett
Music: Alfred Newman
Awards: Locarno International Film Festival—Special Prize, Direction (Wellman), Writers Guild of America—Best Written American Western (Trotti)

A lot of the same talent that went into the creation of the wonderful anti–Western *The Ox-Bow Incident* (1942) was a part of *Yellow Sky* (1948) as well—director William A. Wellman, writer Lamar Trotti, set decorator Thomas Little, and actors Harry Morgan, Paul Hurst, and Victor Kilian—and it shows, starting from the first interior scene in *Yellow Sky*, which deliberately and obviously recapitulates the initial saloon scene from *Ox-Bow*. In both of these openers, the shooting location was the same town, and the exterior and interior of the bar look virtually identical too, with only minor cosmetic changes. The same seedy-looking character (Hurst) leans on a post outside the saloon, and the same barkeep (Kilian) serves the patrons inside. At the beginning of *Yellow Sky*, a rough group of men enter and sit on the stools, and—just like Henry Fonda and Harry Morgan in *Ox-Bow*—they gaze longingly at a titillating painting of a woman that hangs over the bar. True, the artworks are different ones, and the town is subtly different as well, but these contrasts are minor. The characters from the two movies seem cut from the same cloth—although it must be said that the men staring at the painting in *Yellow Sky*'s bar scene seem a shade more odious than Fonda and Morgan in *Ox-Bow*, as shown by their respective attitudes and remarks. Fonda's Gil Carter looks at the bar painting in aesthetic rapture, then notices the man in the background of the picture beholding the comely woman. "That guy's awful slow gettin' there," he says thoughtfully. "I got a feelin' she could do better." In contrast, *Yellow Sky*'s Lengthy leers at his painting—this time, a shapely woman strapped to a rearing horse—and says in an oily way, "I wonder if she's

265

got any plans after she gets through ridin' that horse." The other men snicker appreciatively, and the bartender looks on with more concern than he did with Gil.

The striking similarities between the openings of the two films suggest that they are, in today's terms, "set in the same universe." *Yellow Sky* gives us once again a grim, tough, cynical world full of hard-bitten men, where no one's heart is completely pure (even more so, arguably, than in *The Ox-Bow Incident*, which at least offered Sparks as a moral exemplar). All of this may lead us to anticipate that *Yellow Sky* will be just as challenging and subversive in its own way as *Ox-Bow*. This expectation will not be disappointed.

For *Yellow Sky*, Wellman and Trotti looked to an unpublished novel by W.R. Burnett (later revised and published in 1950 under the title *Stretch Dawson*) for their script's source material. The novel was a loose adaptation of Shakespeare's *The Tempest*, and the influence of the Bard's otherworldly play is felt in the movie as well. Like many mid-century psychological Westerns, from *The Ox-Bow Incident* to *3:10 to Yuma* (1957), the plot of *Yellow Sky* is relatively spare, with the emphasis being on exploring dark, interior elements of character and morality.

Two years after the close of the Civil War, six bandits (ex–Union soldiers) flee into the desert after a bank robbery. Chased by garrison troops and threatened by blinding sandstorms and impassable terrain, they have only one option for moving forward, and so the outlaws are swept along to the deserted, rubble-filled town of Yellow Sky, just as the mariners in *The Tempest* were helplessly shipwrecked on Prospero's Mediterranean isle. Yellow Sky's crumbling, fallen sign informs us it was once the "Fastest Growing Town in the Territory," but now it is a blasted wasteland with only two remaining inhabitants. The "Prospero" figure is old Grandpa (James Barton), a reclusive prospector concealing not magical powers but rather a stockpile of gold. "Miranda" is his granddaughter Constance Mae (Anne Baxter), whose nickname "Mike" accurately reflects her tomboy nature. Like her Shakespearean antecedent, Mike has little experience of men beyond her elderly guardian and the Apaches, stand-ins presumably for the wild and savage Caliban. Our six newly arrived fugitives, just like the shipwrecked nobles of *The Tempest*, are ethically tainted and ready to transgress again. After learning of Grandpa's hidden gold, they have no qualms about taking it from him and his granddaughter. They offer a fifty-fifty split with the old man, but most if not all of them are actually intending to make off with all the loot. Whereas in Shakespeare's fantasy Prospero will eventually forgive and reconcile with all of his enemies, the outcomes for each of the six bandits are not as neat and tidy. They will meet various ends, influenced in part by each man's actions and motivations—but even that is not as simple as it might seem.

The members of the gang of outlaws are: Stretch (Gregory Peck), the leader, a hard-boiled individualist who shows occasional, but infrequent, glimmers of compassion; Dude (Richard Widmark), an oily gambler, amoral, double-dealing, and greedy for gold; Lengthy (John Russell), a lustful, leering, cruel, capriciously violent man; Half Pint (Harry Morgan), tough and sometimes cheerfully immoral, but with a gentle side as well; Walrus (Charles Kemper), a hapless, alcoholic glutton who stupidly brings a canteen of whiskey with him into the desert instead of water; and Bull Run (Robert Arthur), a likeable and naive young kid with a heart, but a follower rather than a leader.

Early on, as these six men cross the brutal desert on their way to Yellow Sky, we get a brilliant scene that tells us a great deal about them in a very short time. Walrus, on

Lengthy (John Russell) is confronted by Half Pint (Harry Morgan) after impulsively killing a desert lizard. The characters of all six outlaws are revealed, at least partially, in this telling scene. *Yellow Sky* **(Twentieth Century–Fox, 1948).**

the verge of dying of thirst, tells his companions that he is going to need to trade some whiskey for some of their water, but they ignore him. The code of these outlaws is clearly "every man for himself," as Stretch makes clear when Dude indicates a desire to head back toward the town of the robbery and take his chances. "There's your share," Stretch says, pointing to a bag of loot on the ground, and then rides off, commanding the others to "Make your choice!" All, including Dude, opt to follow Stretch, soon having to walk their faltering horses across the miles and miles of burning, sinking sand. Even though Stretch (along with the others) has ignored the needs of the pitiful Walrus, he takes advantage of a moment's rest to give a water-dampened rag first to his own horse and then to Walrus's horse as well. Dude, leaning languidly against his mount, mocks Stretch:

> DUDE (*sneering*): Kinda noble, aren't you?
> STRETCH: A horse's a useful animal. No use lettin' him suffer just because he belongs to a jackass.
> DUDE: Looks like he's not the only jackass on this trip. I told you we'd never make it.
> STRETCH: Nobody said you had to come.
> LENGTHY: Ha! Old Walrus here's got nearly a thousand dollars in his pocket. Can't even buy hisself a drink of water. Don't that beat the devil?
> *Walrus looks miserable. Lengthy notices a lizard on the desert sand.*
> LENGTHY: Look at that old lizard there. He's better off than you, Walrus! Yessir. A heap better off. (*He is suddenly resentful.*) That ain't right.

Lengthy draws his gun and fires.
HALF PINT (*upset*): You got no call to do that!
LENGTHY: What's eatin' you? It's just a lizard.
HALF PINT: It wasn't doin' you no hurt. What'd you have to kill it for?
LENGTHY: Well, of all the—say, what's got into you anyhow? A lizard!
STRETCH (*to Lengthy*): Shut up!
Lengthy considers, then holsters his gun.
LENGTHY: All this fuss over one little lizard.
WALRUS (*panting*): If I don't get some water pretty soon, I'm just gonna fall down and die.
STRETCH (*unsympathetic*): Yeah, looks that way.
Stretch leads his horse off. Bull Run, who has been watching quietly the whole time, shakes his head thoughtfully and follows.

All six characters have been involved in this scene (including Bull Run's non-involvement), and we as viewers have learned critical things about each one in an economically compact amount of time. At this point, the passive Bull Run seems like the cleanest and noblest of the group; Dude and Lengthy seem the most villainous; and Stretch, Half Pint, and Walrus are somewhere in the middle, complex and multifaceted—yet all six of them are hard men, each (with the possible exception of Bull Run) more wicked at heart than anyone we met in *The Ox-Bow Incident*. As with earlier movies involving the possible rehabilitation of violent criminal gangs—including the two that cemented the paradigm, *3 Bad Men* (1926) and *Hell's Heroes* (1929)—we are drawn to ask: can any of these men redeem themselves? And if so, which ones?

Three-dimensional, nuanced characterization is an essential quality of any psychological drama, and this is one of many areas in which *Yellow Sky* excels. The characters do not just occupy fixed points on a simple ethical spectrum; like actual human beings, they have their better and worse moments. Each remains a coherent personality, but—again, like real people—they can also be unpredictable and inconsistent. In this sense, the film strikes me as an important precursor to *The Wild Bunch* (1969), another movie in which we are often startled by our own shifting perceptions of the characters. What makes both of these movies so effective (among many other virtues) is that this is also how we respond to people in our own lives. How many times have we felt like we had someone figured out, and then had to rethink our appraisal when we caught another facet of the personality? I find myself doing this often in watching *Yellow Sky*. Half Pint is indignant at Lengthy's casual killing of the desert lizard, but later he gleefully shoots at his former comrade Stretch, then changes his attitude yet again. Bull Run passively accepts the brutality of the others most of the time, but then boldly stands up to Lengthy in defense of Mike. Walrus seems weak and pitiful during the desert crossing but is resignedly stoic later when it looks like the gang is going to be killed by Apaches. "We're sure gonna be mighty rich corpses," he jokes. How refreshing all this is! In most of today's movies, in place of real characters we get embodied types, the psychological equivalent of mathematical functions: input a situation, and the little fixed personality machine processes it and outputs a reaction according to its pre-programming. Screenwriting by recipe—just add stock characters to situations and stir. Once again, the Law of Craft: *the most successful Westerns are far more sophisticated, nuanced, and perceptive than we give them credit for.*

No character in *Yellow Sky* is more nuanced and contradictory than Stretch. As the analogue to *The Tempest*'s Ferdinand and Mike's eventual love interest, he is the one

Tomboy Mike (Anne Baxter) has a less-than-pleasant first meeting with Stretch (Gregory Peck). *Yellow Sky* (Twentieth Century–Fox, 1948).

of the six outlaws we end up rooting for, but Stretch is certainly difficult to like at first and, throughout the movie, shows his dark side just as often as the light. This contradictory nature is most apparent in his stormy relationship with Mike. When the two first meet, she is holding a rifle on him. He seizes the opportunity to knock it away, but she punches him, hard, and he falls to the ground. Stretch rises up, outraged, and we can see he intends to strike her back. This is the moment at which Grandpa emerges from their house for the first time, pointing a pistol at Stretch. "I wouldn't go stirrin' up no trouble with that girl if I was you, young fella," he warns, but Stretch's ire has passed. He chuckles and then says appreciatively, "Quite a punch you got there, ma'am. Come in mighty handy when you get married." This response, even though it wasn't Stretch's original one, makes Grandpa warm to him. "You're right, son—she's as tough as a pine nut," he admits.

At this point we might expect the typical Hollywood romance arc—from dislike to appreciation to eventual love. But *Yellow Sky* is never that straightforward. The next time Stretch and Mike meet, it is night, and Stretch forces himself on her, pinning her to the ground and kissing her, even after she head-butts him violently—a difficult scene to watch today, but outrageous even in 1948, when movie "protagonists" would never treat a lady in such a way. Unlike very similar (and equally disturbing) scenes in later movies—*Goldfinger* (1964), for example—Mike never melts into the kiss but instead, once she realizes she can't overpower Stretch, just turns still and unresponsive. But now Stretch gets up, laughing and elated, and says, "Just wanted to show you how safe you'd be if I really wanted to get rough!" We don't buy this, however, and neither does Mike, who screams, "Didn't anybody ever tell you before that you smell bad?" She then retreats into the barn with her pistol, turns, and shoots Stretch from out of the darkness, grazing the top of his head and leaving him dazed. A complicated start to their relationship, and it will continue to be so, ambiguous and contradictory, until Stretch evolves as a human being, cleans himself up both literally and figuratively, and is able to call forth the compassionate side of his character that, until now, we have only seen exhibited toward horses.

One thing that does remain consistent about Stretch, and will eventually be the source of his redemption, is that he is always who he appears to be. For better or worse, he can be taken at face value, unlike the movie's primary villain Dude, who is deceptive and duplicitous. Even when Stretch is bad, at least he is honest about it. This may not seem like much of a virtue to build upon, but again *Yellow Sky* will show its capacity to surprise us. We discover to our shock that Stretch—as opposed to the other robbers—is true to his word; this is important to his image of himself. "I come from good people," he says to Grandpa and Mike. "When I give my word, I mean it." Looking at Stretch, we see a true example of the phrase "honor amongst thieves." His true moment of transformation comes when he realizes that Grandpa kept his word also; he could have turned Stretch and his gang over to the Apaches but didn't. Stretch says to the other outlaws: "The old man played it square, stuck to his bargain. If it hadn't been for that, we'd all be layin' around here dead right now. Whether you like it or not, we're givin' 'em their full share. If that don't suit you, you've got a fight on your hands, and you'd better get at it quick!" This instinctive response, in sympathetic vibration with Grandpa's honor and evoking at last the nobility hidden deep within Stretch's soul, is what finally tips him over, and also changes his perception of Mike. "You got yourself quite a granddaughter, mister," he says to Grandpa. "I know that," Grandpa replies. "It's her future that's worrying me."

Yellow Sky's approach to its characters is to assign great importance to the things that motivate them—not just *what* but *why*. For example, all eight of the primary characters are passionately interested in the gold—but for most, especially Dude, this is simply out of selfish greed. Grandpa wants it just as dearly, and of course he has earned it rather than just stealing it, but—as he voices to Stretch—it also matters why one wants the gold:

> Yes, mighty dangerous thing, if you want it out of plum greediness. I've seen it ruin many a man. Course, I had good reasons for wantin' it myself. Now Mike here—I, I'm the only one she's got. So you see, I, I wanted to see her took good care of before I died.

Grandpa also indicates his desire to use his riches to revitalize the town of Yellow Sky, to see it come to life again. Motivation matters in this world—in fact, it makes all the difference.

The two truly irredeemable characters in *Yellow Sky* are Dude and Lengthy, for this very reason. Their essential desires are stated quite plainly as they prepare to face down Stretch, Mike, and Grandpa.

> LENGTHY: Before anybody starts giving orders around here, let's get one thing settled. I got first call on that girl, understand?
> DUDE: Aw, who cares about her?
> LENGTHY: I do!
> DUDE: All right, go ahead and take her. All I want is that gold.

This is more psychologically significant than it may at first appear. *Yellow Sky* was made during a time when Freud was at the peak of his popularity in the public imagination. Whatever subtlety may have existed in Freud's original writings, the understanding of the common person in the street was unsubtle and reductionistic, that the primary element propelling the psychology of human beings was the sex drive. Running counter to this was another strong view, this time originating in Nietzsche, namely, that the main human motivation was the will to power. Others tried to moderate between these extreme positions—Alfred Adler, for example, who would describe the will to power as a neurosis that should be risen above through the cultivation of community feeling, empathy, and social connectedness; and Carl Jung, who sought to integrate both drives into a more complex system. In *Yellow Sky*, Lengthy certainly embodies the Freudian drive, and Dude the Nietzschean, but the movie rejects both, presenting a more complex view of the human personality in which functional people represent a blend of different, sometimes contradictory drives, and the goal is simply to be true and authentic to the nobler parts of human nature while still integrating the dark side rather than suppressing it. The problem with Dude and Lengthy is not that they are moved by these drives; so are all the characters, including Stretch. Instead, the problem with Dude and Lengthy is that they are *only* moved by these drives. Stretch, Mike, and Grandpa interact with life on a higher plane (eventually, in Stretch's case)—one that is holistic and multifaceted, not reductionist and dualistic. Once again, walking between the pairs of opposites, denying nothing human no matter how dark, but leaning toward the light—perhaps

Yellow Sky (Twentieth Century–Fox, 1948).

this is the best that we can hope for, and it is certainly the virtue espoused by *Yellow Sky*.

Another way in which this film is quite perceptive is in its acknowledgment of the powerful role that chance plays in our lives. The final alliance of the thieves—some with Stretch, Mike, and Grandpa, and some arrayed against them—is due as much to chance as anything else. This theme is reinforced dramatically in the movie's magnificent climax, a gripping three-way showdown between Stretch, Dude, and Lengthy, each now an enemy of the other two. Fittingly, this occurs in the darkened, wrecked town saloon, and the movie brilliantly chooses not to show us the gunfight itself. Instead, the camera remains outside, and we are given only the sounds of gunfire and flashes of light through the windows. Then comes an unforgettable masterstroke of cinematic art—the image of a slowly spinning Wheel of Fortune lying among the ruins. The meaning is clear. Who lives, and who dies? In the darkness of the room—like the impenetrable mystery amid which our lives unfold—no one can foretell. No one even knows whose bullet struck whom. (The other violent death in the movie, which occurs prior to this scene, is also a matter of accident.) This is consistent with the film's viewpoint on both violence and indeterminacy. The human will may be strong, but ultimately it is still at the mercy of chance. All we can do is fire blindly into the dark and hope for the best. When the battle is done, Mike rushes in and sees three bodies lying sprawled in the shadows. Is there life in any of them? Who lives, and who dies?

The Wheel of Fortune spins on, silent and unfathomable.

Yellow Sky is a truly great Western, which makes it doubly tragic that it is so little-known today. It anticipates the subversive moral ambiguity that would become such an essential part of the anti–Western during the Silver Age—in fact, it doesn't just anticipate it, it fully embodies it. Like *The Ox-Bow Incident*, *Yellow Sky* is tough, gritty, and realistic, packing a great deal of power into its lean ninety-eight minutes. The movie would be perfectly at home if it had been made in the late 1960s rather than the late 1940s. (Appropriately enough, *Yellow Sky* was indeed remade in South Africa in 1967 as *The Jackals*, starring Vincent Price in the Prospero role.)

I consider *Yellow Sky* a masterpiece, not only for its magnificent aesthetics and powerful drama but for its genuine psychological insights. The movie is well aware of the primitive, barbaric creature living within all of us, as well as the need to integrate rather than destroy it—taking its cue, perhaps, from Shakespeare's Prospero when he says of Caliban, "This thing of darkness I acknowledge mine."

Tidbits and Trivia

- I can't help but wonder if the makers of the early James Bond movies were influenced by *Yellow Sky*. Not only does the barn scene between Bond and Pussy Galore in *Goldfinger* echo the distressing one in *Yellow Sky* in which Stretch overpowers Mike, but *Yellow Sky* also has a scene later on in which Mike aims her gun at Stretch and we see him through the rifled barrel, an image remarkably similar to the iconic one that starts the Eon-produced Bond movies.

She Wore a Yellow Ribbon
(1949)

July 26, 1949 (Kansas City, Kansas)
USA—English
Argosy Pictures
104m—Mono—Technicolor—1.37:1

Direction: John Ford
Screenplay: Frank S. Nugent, Laurence Stallings, James Warner Bellah (stories "The Big Hunt" and "War Party")
Principal Cast: John Wayne (Capt. Nathan Cutting Brittles), Joanne Dru (Olivia Dandridge), John Agar (Lt. Flint Cohill), Ben Johnson (Sgt. Tyree), Harry Carey, Jr. (Second Lt. Ross Pennell), Victor McLaglen (Top Sgt. Quincannon), Mildred Natwick (Abby Allshard), George O'Brien (Maj. Mac Allshard), Arthur Shields (Dr. O'Laughlin), Michael Dugan (Sgt. Hochbauer), Chief John Big Tree (Chief Pony That Walks), Fred Graham (Sgt. Hench), George Sky Eagle (Chief Sky Eagle), Tom Tyler (Cpl. Mike Quayne), Noble Johnson (Chief Red Shirt)
Production: John Ford, Merian C. Cooper
Cinematography: Winton C. Hoch
Editing: James Murray
Art Direction: James Basevi
Music: Richard Hageman
Awards: Oscar—Best Color Cinematography (Hoch)
Nominations: Writers Guild of America—Best Written American Western (Nugent, Stallings)

What happens to heroes—that is to say, all of us—as age creeps in? As someone wrestling with the problems of middle age myself, art that explores the grand desires of aging heroes to accomplish even one more meritorious deed resonates deeply within my soul. I'm not sure that any creative artist ever explored this area more powerfully than Alfred, Lord Tennyson in his remarkable poem "Ulysses," narrated by the Trojan War veteran himself as he whiles away his time on Ithaca, ruminating on his advancing age:

> How dull it is to pause, to make an end,
> To rust unburnish'd, not to shine in use!
> As tho' to breathe were life. Life piled on life
> Were all too little, and of one to me
> Little remains: but every hour is saved
> From that eternal silence, something more,
> A bringer of new things; and vile it were
> For some three suns to store and hoard myself,
> And this grey spirit yearning in desire
> To follow knowledge, like a sinking star,
> Beyond the utmost bound of human thought.

But Ulysses has a solution, which he invokes to his mariners:

> Death closes all: but something ere the end,
> Some work of noble note, may yet be done,
> Not unbecoming men that strove with Gods.
> The lights begin to twinkle from the rocks:
> The long day wanes: the slow moon climbs: the deep
> Moans round with many voices. Come, my friends,
> 'Tis not too late to seek a newer world.
> Push off, and sitting well in order smite
> The sounding furrows; for my purpose holds
> To sail beyond the sunset, and the baths
> Of all the western stars, until I die.[1]

The aging hero facing obsolescence is a common theme in the narrative and mythic arts, from Tennyson's Ulysses to Malory's Launcelot to the Irish Fionn mac Cumhaill. And in American lore, no genre was better prepared to explore this theme than the elegiac Western.

Since I have already written at greater length about John Ford's Cavalry Trilogy in my essay on *Fort Apache* (1948), I will say far less than I could about its second installment, *She Wore a Yellow Ribbon* (1949)—which is a shame, really, because it is my favorite movie of the three, and certainly stronger than the mediocre third installment, *Rio Grande* (1950). Like the other two members of the loose trilogy, *She Wore a Yellow Ribbon* takes great pains to depict the everyday lives and culture of the inhabitants of the frontier cavalry outposts, to show all of these people—not just the leading characters— as real, personable, and colorful. But for me, the thing that sets *Yellow Ribbon* at the head of the Cavalry Trilogy is the wonderful central character of Nathan Brittles, perhaps the most likeable soul that John Wayne ever portrayed.

Brittles is an aging cavalry captain (played by an artificially aged Wayne) who is inching ever closer to mandatory retirement; we watch him, on several occasions, crossing off dates on a wall calendar as he approaches the critical day, circled in red. When that day arrives, he will draw a dramatic red line through it, tear off the calendar page, and place it in the fire. Over the course of the movie we grow to love Brittles, and not, as one might expect, for his courage and heroism, which are considerable, but rather for his vulnerability and his capacity to fail. Brittles is shown to be fully human, and that's what makes him one of the most compelling figures that Wayne ever played. As any outpost captain would be, Brittles is tough and disciplined, but the filmmakers—especially including the screenwriters and Wayne himself—surprise us by the depths of gentleness, kindliness, and even age-appropriate sentimentality that they evoke from this multifaceted character.

In the mainstream movies of today, Brittles is a character that would be difficult to sell; for one thing, the egos (and agents) of current megastars—and Wayne was indeed a megastar of his day—would likely not stand for such a realistically imperfect lead role. Furthermore, *She Wore a Yellow Ribbon* is a Western adventure whose hero never kills anyone! In fact, no cavalryman kills anyone during the entire movie; the heroic act here is not prevailing in conflict but rather in avoiding conflict altogether. The film is primarily concerned with the intimate lives of its inhabitants rather than sensationalism, horror, or lurid violence. All of this serves to make *She Wore a Yellow Ribbon* far too honest and real (psychologically) to be greenlit as a Hollywood production today. But take

Capt. Brittles (John Wayne) converses with his wife at her grave. One of Wayne's greatest moments as an actor. *She Wore a Yellow Ribbon* **(Argosy, 1949).**

heart, movie lovers—this pendulum will swing back one day. Independent cinema has proven itself to be so rich, so vibrant—it may ultimately provide the spark that revitalizes the industry. Mainstream assembly-line American movies, though, with few exceptions, have bottomed out in terms of emotional and psychological depth; from here, there's nowhere to go but up. (I hope.)

Among its many virtues, *She Wore a Yellow Ribbon* is a masterclass in the power of the individual scene to establish nuances of character and draw the audience in emotionally. Nearly every scene in this movie is a delight, but there are four in particular that stand out for me. Each is relatively static, in two different ways. First of all, there is very little actual physical motion or action in the scenes; they are still and inward-focused, emphasizing character and dialogue. Second, these scenes may advance the plot in some small way, but this does not seem to be their primary purpose. Rather, they are the cinematic equivalent of the traditional opera aria, whose dramatic purpose (as opposed to its musical purpose) is typically to linger in the feeling of a moment and connect us to the characters rather than to move the action rapidly forward.

In the cemetery. The first of these scenes occurs early in the film, when Captain Brittles walks out to the fort's graveyard in the red evening light and waters the flowers on his wife's grave. Sharp-eyed viewers will notice the graves of the captain's two daughters there as well, flanking Mary on either side. The death dates of all three are within a week of one another; although the film doesn't explain this, a backstory provided by

John Ford in a letter to James Warner Bellah indicates that they all died in a smallpox epidemic.[2] Mary would have been thirty-two when she died, nine years before the action of the film; Jane and Elizabeth were four and six. Brittles, we see, has suffered tragic losses, his entire family wiped out and no descendants left. And yet here he sits, watering his wife's flowers, and carrying on a conversation with her just as if they were sitting across from one another at the dinner table.

> Well, Mary, only six more days to go and your old Nathan will be out of the Army. Haven't decided what I'll do yet. Somehow I just can't picture myself back there on the banks of the Wabash rockin' in a front porch. No, I've been thinking I'd maybe push on west. New settlements, California. We had some sad news today, Mary. George Custer was killed, and his whole command—Miles Keogh among 'em. You remember Miles: happy-go-lucky Irishman—who used to waltz so well with you! Yeah, I know, I—I guess I was a little jealous. Never could waltz, myself. Well—take the troop out in the morning. Cheyennes around. I'm to pick up the patrols and drive 'em on back north. Probably be my last mission, Mary. Hard to believe, isn't it? Hard to believe.

There is no bitterness in his voice, just a gentle regret, but most of the time he is smiling lovingly. It is clear to us that these companionable "conversations" happen on a regular basis. Wayne's delivery here is pitch-perfect. His entire speech lasts about ninety seconds, with only three camera cuts, alternating between full and medium shots to bring us closer to the character for the more intimate statements. It is a masterful piece of acting, one of the finest of Wayne's career, and it reveals depths to Brittles that we would not otherwise have seen. Immediately afterwards, the impetuous young Olivia Dandridge (Joanne Dru) appears, apologizing for interrupting and carrying flowers for Mary's grave. Brittles is genuinely appreciative and unafraid to show it; this is the first scene of many that establishes his unfailing courtesy toward the women of his post. During this wonderful, static scene, which occupies about four minutes of screen time, the plot is not being advanced at all, but something far more valuable is provided to the audience: a character they can care about deeply.

The gun-runners. But Brittles is a well-rounded character, not to be summed up simply. He has his hard side too, as he must, both for dramatic purposes and for verisimilitude—we would not buy a veteran cavalry captain who couldn't be tough and firm when needed. Perhaps the best demonstration of this quality is in the second scene I would like to highlight. As William Indick points out, the writers of classic Westerns always assumed to be true what was actually a historical fallacy: that Custer's defeat at Little Bighorn was due to the fact that his cavalrymen carried single-fire rifles while the Sioux had repeating rifles.[3] Because of this, a consistent cardinal sin in the traditional Western is the selling of guns to Indians. In the scene in question, we watch Brittles, accompanied by Lieutenant Pennell (Harry Carey, Jr.) and Sergeant Tyree (Ben Johnson), sneaking up on a nighttime meeting between some sleazy gunrunners and a group of natives. The cavalrymen dismount and crouch down behind some thorny bushes, just in time to see the greedy white traders trying to put the squeeze on the Indians—insulting them and attempting to extort a high price for the weaponry. The enraged Indians cut the gunrunners down. Two of the traffickers are shot with arrows; a third is thrown repeatedly into the fire. The tortured man screams, and we cut back to the three cavalrymen watching from their safe vantage point. Brittles reaches toward Tyree. "Sergeant?" he prompts. Tyree, misunderstanding, starts to hand his captain a rifle. "It's cocked, sir," he says, but Brittles responds, "No, your knife." We hear more screams from offscreen

Brittles (John Wayne) in the Indian camp. *She Wore a Yellow Ribbon* **(Argosy, 1949).**

as the gunrunners continue to be butchered. Brittles takes Tyree's knife and calmly cuts himself a chaw of tobacco, offering the same to his companions; the three men watch the slaughter, doing nothing.

In the Indian camp. We have now seen Brittles's gentle side and his hard side. Yet another scene will powerfully demonstrate his enlightened side. In *Yellow Ribbon*, as in many of his Westerns, John Wayne's character is a friend to the Indians. While the local tribes (Apache, Cheyenne, Kiowa, and Comanche, we are told) unite and prepare to make war, Brittles and Tyree ride straight into the Indian camp to try and make peace. In the thick of his enemies, Brittles dismounts and says, "Were you ever scared, Tyree?" "Yes, sir," Tyree replies, "up to and includin' now." As Brittles draws near to the tribal elders, the firebrand warrior Chief Red Shirt (Noble Johnson) shoots an arrow contemptuously into the ground by Brittles's feet, but Brittles picks up the arrow, breaks it in half, spits on it, and hurls it back into Red Shirt's face. There he is, showing his steel once again. But then Brittles approaches his old friend, Chief Pony That Walks (Chief John Big Tree), who is opposed to the bloodthirstiness of the younger tribesmen spoiling for a fight. The two men exchange puffs on the pipe, and then Brittles gets to the point:

> BRITTLES: Pony That Walks, my heart is sad at what I see: your young men painted for war, their scalp knives red, the medicine drums talking! It is a bad thing! (*He spits on the ground.*)
>
> PONY THAT WALKS: A bad thing, Nathan. Many will die. My young men, your young men. No good, no good.
>
> BRITTLES: We must stop this war.

PONY THAT WALKS: Too late, Nathan. Young men do not listen to me. They listen to big medicine! Yellow Hair—Custer—dead! Buffalo come back. Great sign! Too late, Nathan. You will come with me, hunt buffalo together, smoke many pipes. We are too old for war.

BRITTLES (*nods*): Yes, we are too old for war. But old men should stop wars!

Despite his sympathy and reverence for Custer, the old soldier Brittles understands— perhaps better than any non-warrior could—the wisdom of peacemaking.

The silver watch. As much as I love these scenes, what springs to mind most frequently as I recall the character of Captain Brittles is just a wonderful little grace note in the latter part of the film. On the last day of his captaincy, Brittles prepares to leave the post and is greeted by his troop, assembled in formation on the field. They present him with a silver watch. He reads the sentiment engraved on the watch, deeply affected, and once again we are reminded of how unfair conventional wisdom has been about the quality of Wayne's acting. *To Captain Brittles from C Troop. Lest we forget.* I defy anyone to see Wayne's character accepting this gift and not be moved.

Previously in the film, we have seen Brittles marking time, literally, in days on his wall calendar. Now, the calendar has been replaced by a watch, which—aside from its value as an expression of love from C Troop—also symbolizes the last few hours of his service, ticking away. As Brittles (with his troop) undertakes what we assume will be his final task as a soldier, he proudly refers several times to the watch he has been given by his grateful band of cavalrymen.

BRITTLES: For the next four hours—accordin' to my brand-new silver watch and chain— I'm an officer in the United States Cavalry.

BRITTLES: Mr. Cohill, can you read the time by my brand-new silver watch?
COHILL (JOHN AGAR): Yes, sir. It's twelve minutes to midnight, sir.
BRITTLES (*sadly*): Yeah. Gentlemen. Bugler, sound the charge.

BRITTLES: Can you read what time it is by my brand-new silver watch?
COHILL: Two minutes past midnight, sir.
BRITTLES: Yeah. Been a civilian for two minutes. It's your army, Mr. Cohill! Good luck! (*He salutes and rides off.*)

It is a wonderful effect, not only because of the symbolism of the watch, but also because Brittles acts exactly as we would expect a warm-hearted old soldier to act when given a thoughtful retirement gift by the men who look up to him. He can't get enough of it; this simple gesture brings him so much joy. Subtle touches

Capt. Brittles (John Wayne) is moved by the gift of the "brand-new silver watch"—and, thanks to Wayne's performance, so are we. The glasses were Wayne's idea. *She Wore a Yellow Ribbon* (Argosy, 1949).

like these moments—and others too numerous to mention here—help to make Captain Nathan Brittles one of the most memorable characters in the history of the Western. We feel like we know him, and we are happier for having spent some time in his company.

In fact, this applies to so many of the characters in *She Wore a Yellow Ribbon*. I haven't even touched on the delights provided by the brawling Irishman Sgt. Quincannon (Victor McLaglen), the tough-skinned but lovable Abby "Iron Pants" Allshard (Mildred Natwick), and the soft-spoken southerner Tyree. By the end of the movie, we truly like these characters and others; they feel like old friends. The love triangle between Cohill, Pennell, and Olivia Dandridge is perhaps the least interesting subplot in and of itself, but it is still worthwhile because of the way in which it throws reflected light onto the character of Brittles, who seems even more seasoned and wise in comparison to the muddled romantics of the youngsters. It also gives Brittles a chance to deliver one of the funniest lines in the movie to Lt. Cohill: "Well, haul off and kiss her back, blast you! We haven't got all day!" The dialogue in the movie is sparkling and virtually perfect throughout, outdone perhaps only by the spectacular Technicolor cinematography by Winton C. Hoch, for which he won a well-deserved Academy Award. Inspired by classic Western paintings by Remington, Bierstadt, and others,[4] and featuring the grandeur of Monument Valley as it has never appeared before or since, Ford and Hoch deliver one of the most visually beautiful Westerns ever filmed.

This quiet movie—with its aging and fallible protagonist, few action sequences, and no cavalry battles—is not only the best of Ford's Cavalry Trilogy, not only the best movie about the cavalry ever made: it is also one of the greatest Westerns of all time.

"Beyond the sunset, and the baths of all the western stars"—ride on, Captain Brittles.

Tidbits and Trivia

- Ben Johnson was a stuntman and rodeo rider (Team Roping World Champion in 1953) who began Hollywood work as a wrangler for *The Outlaw* (1941). After stopping a stampede and probably saving lives on the set of *Fort Apache*, Johnson was given a small speaking part in Ford's *3 Godfathers* (1948). Nevertheless, *She Wore a Yellow Ribbon* was his first significant role. He would go on to be a wonderful fixture in Westerns over the years, playing memorable and important parts in *Wagon Master* (1950), *Shane* (1953), *One-Eyed Jacks* (1961), *The Wild Bunch* (1969), and dozens of other movies all the way up until his death in 1996. Although he famously preferred doing action scenes over dialogue, Johnson would eventually win a Supporting Actor Oscar (and many other awards) for his stunning portrayal of Sam the Lion in *The Last Picture Show* (1971).

Wagon Master
(1950)

AKA: *Wagonmaster*
April 19, 1950 (Oklahoma City)
USA—English / Navajo / Spanish
Argosy Pictures
86m—Mono—BW—1.37:1

Direction: John Ford
Screenplay: Frank S. Nugent, Patrick Ford, John Ford (story; uncredited)
Principal Cast: Ben Johnson (Travis Blue), Joanne Dru (Denver), Harry Carey, Jr. (Sandy), Ward Bond (Elder Wiggs), Charles Kemper (Uncle Shiloh Clegg), Alan Mowbray (Dr. A. Locksley Hall), Jane Darwell (Sister Ledyard), Ruth Clifford (Fleuretty Phyffe), Russell Simpson (Adam Perkins), Kathleen O'Malley (Prudence Perkins), James Arness (Floyd Clegg), Francis Ford (Mr. Peachtree), Fred Libby (Reese Clegg), Jim Thorpe (Navajo Indian), Mickey Simpson (Jesse Clegg), Cliff Lyons (Marshal of Crystal City), Hank Worden (Luke Clegg), Don Summers (Sam Jenkins), Movita (Young Navajo Indian)
Production: John Ford, Merian C. Cooper
Cinematography: Bert Glennon
Editing: Jack Murray, Barbara Ford (uncredited)
Art Direction: James Basevi
Music: Richard Hageman

If there is one overriding theme in the Westerns of John Ford, it is *community*. Time and again, these movies present, symbolically and in microcosm, idealistic examples of how people from different backgrounds and with different interests can come together to work toward the common good while also, along the way, participating in social rites—dances, church services, dinners, parades, funerals—as a varied community of equals. This democratic vision, tolerant of differences and even celebrating them, pervades the Ford Western, from *The Iron Horse* (1924) to *Stagecoach* (1939) to *My Darling Clementine* (1946) to the Cavalry Trilogy (1948–50) and on into the later works of the fifties and sixties. No film embodies this theme so directly and fully as *Wagon Master* (1950).

Wagon Master is, in many ways, the "odd film out" in Ford's Western *oeuvre*, a small, intimate movie featuring no big-name stars and a very simple plotline. If, as Orson Welles once observed, John Ford was poetry to Howard Hawks's prose,[1] then no Ford Western is more poetic than *Wagon Master*. The movie is not an epic poem like *My Darling Clementine* or *The Iron Horse*, to be sure, but more like an Elizabethan sonnet or a pastoral, one extolling the beauty of human connections amid the grandeur of nature's offerings. (*Wagon Master* even acknowledges its own poetic roots, subtly, by naming the medicine-show character, played by Alan Mowbray, after the Tennyson poem "Locksley

Hall.") Despite its modest scale, the film remained one of Ford's own favorites; he told filmmaker Peter Bogdanovich that "along with *The Fugitive* and *The Sun Shines Bright*, *Wagon Master* came closest to being what I wanted to achieve."[2] It is interesting that all three of these suffered box office losses—another example of the tension between what the artist hopes to give and what the public wants to receive.

Wagon Master has divided critics and viewers from its own time to ours. Some hail it as a masterpiece—Bogdanovich even considers it Ford's greatest Western,[3] and he is not the only one—while others consider it no more than a perfectly fine minor work. My own view is close to that of Fenin and Everson, who admired *Wagon Master* very much, calling it "a beautiful *little* film," while also maintaining that the European John Ford "cult" had overblown the merits of the movie. *Wagon Master*, in their view, "is as close to a genuine Western film-poem as we have ever come, but attempts by Ford's admirers to enlarge it beyond that do both it and Ford a disservice. [It] is a film that should be seen, felt, and, above all, *fairly* evaluated."[4] (All emphases theirs.) For me, *Wagon Master* is poetic and enjoyable, although I would not place it in my top tier of Ford Westerns— currently occupied by *3 Bad Men* (1926), *Stagecoach*, *My Darling Clementine*, *She Wore a Yellow Ribbon* (1949), and *The Searchers* (1956).

Ford first conceived the idea for *Wagon Master* while getting to know Mormon extras during the shooting of *She Wore a Yellow Ribbon*.[5] Out of this experience, plus what Ford had learned about the San Juan Expedition of 1879–80, grew the film's basic

The film's three protagonists, played—democratically—by character actors rather than leading men: Travis (Ben Johnson), Elder Wiggs (Ward Bond), and Sandy (Harry Carey, Jr.). *Wagon Master* (Argosy, 1950).

storyline about a pair of itinerant horse traders hired by a group of Mormons to guide their wagon train to the Promised Land. Along the way, the caravan encounters several other groups of people representing, in miniature, various segments of the American melting pot.

It is only appropriate that the most communitarian of John Ford's Westerns is a movie without a star in the usual sense. *Wagon Master* has no John Wayne, Henry Fonda, or equivalent figure on hand to over-dominate the proceedings; instead, the film features as its protagonists three of the Western genre's sturdiest character actors—Ben Johnson, Harry Carey, Jr., and Ward Bond—and divides the emotional and narrative weight pretty evenly between them. If we go into *Wagon Master* expecting the traditional larger-than-life Western hero, then at first the movie might seem like a body without a head; but in fact, this lack of star power is a feature, not a bug, bringing our attention as viewers to the larger (mobile) community of the movie rather than focusing it too tightly on any one individual.

Movies are cooperative endeavors to begin with, but the creation of *Wagon Master* seems to have been especially so. Joseph McBride describes the nineteen-day shoot as a "relaxed, communal effort with some of Ford's favorite actors, crew people, stuntmen, and extras."[6] The film included many contributions from Ford's extended family as well: his two children, two of his brothers, his nephew, and his brother-in-law. The most significant family contribution, other than that of John Ford himself, came from his son Patrick, who co-wrote the screenplay along with Frank Nugent—although the final result was still very much John Ford's creation, due to the director's notorious habit of heavily reworking screenplays himself during filming. At least Ford acknowledged this idiosyncrasy to his two writers this time, saying impishly, "I liked your script, boys. In fact, I actually shot a few pages of it."[7]

Wagon Master starts with a bang: a bank robbery committed by the Clegg family—scruffy, heavy-set Uncle Shiloh (Charles Kemper) and his simpleminded "boys" (James Arness, Fred Libby, Mickey Simpson, and Hank Worden)—before the opening credits run. As the thieves make their way out, a young teller grabs a pistol and fires out the door at them. Shiloh comes back in, clutching a wounded left arm, and says with deceptive gentleness, "I wish you wouldn't have done that." The young man pleads for his life and runs away, but Shiloh takes a shotgun and shoots him twice in the back. It is a tough, gripping beginning, one that imbues this otherwise gentle story with an undercurrent of suspense. The outlaws disappear from the narrative after this first scene, but we know they will return.

Soon afterward, we are introduced to the three charming leads: horse traders Travis (Johnson) and Sandy (Carey), soon to become wagon masters, and Elder Wiggs (Bond), the leader of the Mormon pioneers who employs the two young men to guide his band of migrants to the San Juan River country. Although devout now, Wiggs clearly has an earthier, non–Mormon past, as evidenced by his hot temper, knowledge of "secular" behavior, and comically frequent urge to swear. (Ward Bond would go on to portray a wagon master himself—Major Seth Adams—in 133 episodes of the NBC television series *Wagon Train* between 1957 and 1961. The series was inspired by this very movie; Bond was its star until his untimely death from a heart attack at fifty-seven, at which point his *Wagon Train* character was replaced without explanation.)

Ben Johnson, playing the gentle-hearted Travis, is real, solid, and likeable as always—perfect for a role not too far, one suspects, from his own personality. (As Johnson once said, "Everybody in town's a better actor than I am, but none of them can play Ben Johnson.")[8] Travis is no outsized hero, just a regular guy trying to make the best of a challenging lot. When the outlaw Clegg gang, now on the run, attach themselves to the wagon train, Travis appeases them at first rather than trying to confront them. "We hired out as wagon masters, not gunfighters," he explains to Sandy. No John Wayne hero would ever respond this way; this is one of the things that makes *Wagon Master* such a refreshing change. At one point, Uncle Shiloh asks Travis if he and Sandy ever draw their guns on anyone; Travis replies, "No, sir—just snakes." We recognize the mythological symbolism in this, even if Travis himself doesn't at the time: the Mormon settlers are seeking Paradise, but the Cleggs seem likely to become serpents in their Garden of Eden.

The second horse-trader-turned-guide is just as likeable as Travis. Harry Carey, Jr.'s Sandy is a rascally, exuberant youth, a sort of Huckleberry Finn of the Colorado Plateau. Open-hearted and friendly, and with a definite eye for a pretty face, Sandy can also be scrappy when riled. One of the movie's funniest moments is when he gets into an altercation with a young Mormon, Jackson (Chuck Hayward), with whom Sandy strikes up an initially friendly bit of small talk that goes sour right away:

> SANDY: Good morning; how are ya? By golly, I bet it's gonna be hotter than—
> JACKSON: Mind your language!
> SANDY: I wasn't cussin'!
> JACKSON: You were gonna say "hell"!
> SANDY: I was gonna say "Hades"! But "hell" ain't cussin'—it's geography!

This escalates into a scuffle between the two men, and Elder Wiggs comes over to break it up, resulting in yet another delightful moment, this time at Ward Bond's expense. There were a couple of dogs at the shooting location who were always fighting with one another, and Ford had the idea to throw them into the mix while Carey and Hayward were rolling around in the dirt, to add to the general belligerent atmosphere of the scene. However, instead of tussling with his opposite number, one of the dogs ripped Ward Bond's pants, and the result clearly shows in the scene. After Bond's character breaks up the fight, Jane Darwell (playing Sister Ledyard) reaches down and tugs at the rip running down the thigh of Bond's pants. You can see the actress's amusement clearly, and Bond wisely plays along, staying in character, pulling the torn flaps of fabric together indignantly and hobbling off. Ford liked the way the shot played and kept it in the film.[9]

Wagon Master was a leap forward in the careers of all three lead actors. As wonderful as they are in the picture, however, for me the most memorable performance comes from Charles Kemper as the villainous Uncle Shiloh. Old Clegg is an unforgettable character, sly, seedy, insinuating, and fearsome. When he and his gang, fleeing a posse, first meet up with the wagon train during one of their communal nighttime dances, the wounded Clegg pretends neighborly friendliness toward the settlers, despite the threatening presence of his well-armed kin.

> Evenin'. Me and the boys seen your fire. Scared at first you might be Navajo. Then I heard your mountain music. Said to Floyd here, "Wherever there's singin' and dancin', you can be sure there's Christian folks." Never did know a bad man that had any music in 'im!

Clegg speaks gently during his time with the Mormons, often using the words of a devout Christian—"God-fearing," "Providential," "He marks the sparrow's fall," and so

A wounded Uncle Shiloh Clegg (Charles Kemper) seeks refuge with the wagon train, flanked by his outlaw kinsmen Luke (Hank Worden) and Floyd (James Arness). *Wagon Master* (Argosy, 1950).

forth—yet he lives a life of unbridled greed and violence. Throughout the picture, Kemper's Clegg presents a spellbinding mixture of charisma, pathos, and menace. This villain is no cookie-cutter bad guy, and Kemper, with his decades of stage experience prior to his Hollywood career, brings the outlaw leader to life with great subtlety and realism. It is truly a masterful performance, made tragic by history: three weeks after *Wagon Master*'s release, Charles Kemper died in a car crash at the age of forty-nine.

True to Ford's democratic vision, the wagon train will become home to various diverse groups along its journey—the American melting pot in microcosm. We have the Mormon settlers, of course, representing communities of faith, and portrayed as real, likeable, and fallible people rather than caricatures, but the pilgrims are soon joined by the quite secular medicine-show troupe, and later some friendly Navajos and a posse in search of the Cleggs. All of these groups are portrayed sympathetically, and although there are some tensions between them, they tolerate one another, coexist peaceably, and even work together for a common purpose on occasion. The glaring exception to this collaborative spirit, of course, is the Cleggs, who have bullied their way into the wagon train by means of their intimidating reputation. These outlaws have no egalitarian idealism or desire to cooperate for the common good; aside from being murderers and thieves, they are the opponents of democracy, acting only out of self-interest and seeking to obtain what they want by force.

Travis and Sandy, psychologically and sociologically, occupy a space somewhere in the middle of these groups, partaking of many of their qualities while staying removed from the extremes. The two guides share the determination and forthrightness of the Mormons without being rigid; the secular, life-affirming *joie de vivre* of the medicine-show troupe without being hedonistic; the wide-ranging freedom of the Navajo while still staying in touch with their own culture; the righteousness of the posse while resisting vigilantism; and the toughness of the outlaws without being criminal. The two men serve as a human bridge between the various factions, sympathetic toward all (except the Cleggs) but not committed to any one system. This is what renders them so fit to guide the wagon train on its journey. By extension, one could read the movie as saying that the best guides for our own messy democracy along its bumpy path are those who can connect with people from varying walks of life while still remaining centered, objective, compassionate, freethinking, subscribing to no philosophy but their own, intolerant of criminality but tolerant of all other views. I would certainly welcome more leaders of this type in today's world.

At its heart, *Wagon Master* is a poetic depiction of the pioneer spirit and the dream of America. Along with *Rio Grande* from the same year—also featuring the landscape of Moab and the folk songs of the Sons of the Pioneers—*Wagon Master* arguably represents the end of Ford's optimistic portrayal of the West. From this hopeful place, Ford would soon move on to the grim darkness of *The Searchers* (1956), the elegiac wistfulness of *The Man Who Shot Liberty Valance* (1962), and the injustice of the government's treatment of the Native Americans in *Cheyenne Autumn* (1964).

But for now, with *Wagon Master*, we still abide in hope. The movie teems with images of the Promised Land, from the language and mission of the settlers themselves to the quasi-comical motif of Sister Ledyard blowing her enormous horn, recalling the Hebrew shofar and, by extension, the wanderings of the Israelites across the wilderness in search of the original "land flowing with milk and honey." But what, really, is the Promised Land that the Mormon settlers seek in *Wagon Master*? Well, prosaically, it is the southeastern region of Utah, a piece of fertile earth that the travelers hope to cultivate, but poetically, it is our communal future as a democracy, the optimistic vision of America for which we strive but have not yet reached.

Brilliantly, Ford underscores this with the movie's closing moments. Just as *Wagon Master*—unlike any other John Ford picture[10]—begins, pre-credits, with the action already in progress, so the film ends with the story still going. The poem was there before we arrived; it remains after we leave. The wagon train proceeds toward the Promised Land in montage, crossing a great valley, rolling onward and onward, while the people dance and romance and sing and live their lives. On the soundtrack, the Sons of the Pioneers sing:

> White-tops are a-rollin', rollin',
> The big wheels keep on turnin'.

The wagon train reaches a river crossing—Ford loved river crossings—and the final credits roll, directly over the action, horses and wagons still midstream. We leave the movie with the journey still underway, for the American democratic experiment is likewise unfinished. The story goes on.

The Gunfighter
(1950)

May 26, 1950 (Philadelphia)
USA—English
Twentieth Century–Fox
85m—Mono—BW—1.37:1

Direction: Henry King
Screenplay: William Bowers (story and screenplay), William Sellers (screenplay), André De Toth (story)
Principal Cast: Gregory Peck (Jimmy Ringo), Helen Westcott (Peggy Walsh), Millard Mitchell (Marshal Mark Strett), Jean Parker (Molly), Karl Malden (Mac), Skip Homeier (Hunt Bromley), Anthony Ross (Deputy Charlie Norris), Verna Felton (Mrs. August Pennyfeather), Ellen Corby (Mrs. Devlin), Richard Jaeckel (Eddie)
Production: Nunnally Johnson
Cinematography: Arthur C. Miller
Editing: Barbara McLean
Art Direction: Lyle R. Wheeler, Richard Irvine
Music: Alfred Newman
Nominations: Oscar—Best Writing, Motion Picture Story (Bowers, De Toth), Writers Guild of America—Best Written American Western (Bowers, Sellers)

Some pieces of music seem unfettered and loose in their construction (even if there is quite a rigorous structure beneath the apparent freedom): the wild, wide-ranging evocations of Richard Strauss, Toshiro Mayuzumi, and Joan Tower; the open, ever-varying forms of John Cage, Karlheinz Stockhausen, and Pauline Oliveros; or the free jazz improvisations of Ornette Coleman, Cecil Taylor, and Albert Ayler. Others, in contrast, are more obviously tightly composed, building a definite structure through the development and recombination of specific motifs, while remaining both architecturally and aesthetically beautiful: the fugues of J.S. Bach; the sonatas and symphonies of Johannes Brahms; the arch forms and process pieces of Béla Bartók. (Most of these composers, I should add, have shown their abilities to write pieces all across this spectrum; I do not mean to imply that a great composer cannot be free-form in one work and controlled in the next.)

Movies are like musical works in many ways. They unfold over time; they have contrasting sections and, often, discernible structure; they have motifs that recur, interact, and undergo transformations; their dramatic shape depends upon the building and releasing of tension; they have expositions, transitions, points of relative stability, development sections, climaxes, and denouements; and like music, their composition can reflect different responses to the tension between freedom and control—from the loose improvisational forms of John Cassavetes, Robert Altman, and Christopher Guest to the elegant, intricate constructions of Alfred Hitchcock, Stanley Kubrick, and Wes Anderson.

Within the Western genre, however, I know of no picture that is as deliberately composed and tightly controlled as Henry King's *The Gunfighter* (1950), which stars Gregory Peck as a world-weary pistoleer, sick of his celebrity and seeking to avoid the crowds he inevitably attracts: sycophants, bloodthirsty spectators, and young guns wanting to knock off the champ. Despite its dramatically subversive, myth-challenging nature, the movie is clean, economical, and classically proportioned, full of recurrent motifs and events juxtaposed and interacting in counterpoint with one another. Each scene has a definite, perceivable structure, like a Bach fugue or a Brahms piano trio, although on the large scale its formal model comes from theater, not music: *The Gunfighter* may be cloaked in the garb of the American Western, but it's a classical Greek tragedy at heart.

The plot of *The Gunfighter* is straightforward, spare, and simple: the title character, Jimmy Ringo (Gregory Peck), can find no peace due to the relentless efforts of young up-and-comers trying to knock him off the top of the pyramid. As Richard Slotkin writes about the gunfighter archetype in general, "he himself has been rendered isolated and vulnerable by the very things that have made him victorious in the past."[1] One night in a saloon, minding his own business, Ringo is confronted by the drunken young wannabe Eddie (Richard Jaeckel), who initiates a fight with him. Ringo is forced to kill the young man in self-defense, then leaves town, trailed by Eddie's three brothers (Alan

Gregory Peck as world-weary killer Jimmy Ringo. *The Gunfighter* (Twentieth Century–Fox, 1950).

Hale, Jr., David Clarke, and John Pickard). Ringo confronts the brothers out in the desert, disarms and "unhorses" them, and leaves them to make their way back to town on foot. Ringo whistles for his own horse, which, significantly, bears a white lightning bolt on his forehead—in ancient Greek iconography, Zeus's thunderbolt was a symbol of human punishment by the gods. Ringo rides onward to the little town of Cayenne, seeking his estranged wife Peggy (Helen Westcott) and young son Jimmie (B.G. Norman). Ringo hopes to give up his gunslinging ways and head for California to start a new life, bringing his family with him. Eddie's brothers, however, have other ideas.

Once in Cayenne, where the bulk of the narrative takes place, Ringo establishes himself in the Palace Bar and meets an old friend, Mark Strett (Millard Mitchell), a former fellow outlaw who has gone straight and is now the town marshal. The two men greet each other warmly, and although he has sworn to protect Peggy's anonymity even from Ringo, Strett agrees to carry a message to her on Ringo's behalf. Meanwhile, another hotheaded aspiring gunfighter, Hunt Bromley (Skip Homeier), learns of Ringo's presence in town and gets ideas of his own. From these bits of plot, the movie builds a complete Greek-style drama, with Ringo as the tragic hero struggling to escape his inevitable fate.

Greek tragedy, of course, was both supremely mythological (evolving as it did from Dionysian hymns and epic poems, among other sources) and also supremely psychological. It gifted the world with the quintessential, canonical versions of character-archetypes like Oedipus, Antigone, Orestes, Prometheus, Electra, Ajax, and Medea, all of whom have entered our cultural lexicon, and several of whom have become shorthand symbols for various elements of the human psyche (Oedipus, Electra, Prometheus, and Medea in particular). Greek tragedy also carried with it certain structural and stylistic conventions that had a profound effect on drama, from ancient times to ours. Much has been written about the form of the Greek tragedy, and our understanding of it has been shaped largely by Aristotle's *Poetics*—filtered through, among others, Italian Renaissance humanists and French neoclassical dramatists—and also by Nietzsche's *The Birth of Tragedy*. These analyses have yielded a very coherent picture of the elements that made up the classical Greek tragedy.

Narrative structure. On a strictly formal level, the typical structure of Greek tragedy—at least as exemplified by the works of its three great surviving representatives, Aeschylus, Sophocles, and Euripides—was straightforward: after a prologue and *parodos*, which provided the background to the narrative and introduced the characters, the primary story played out through a series of episodes (*epeisodia*) alternating with brief interludes (*stasima*) commenting on the action. After the narrative reached its conclusion, there was typically a short *exodus* that underscored the moral of the tragedy.

The Gunfighter exhibits these exact components in its own formal structure. The prologue and *parados* equivalents unfold during the first ten minutes, in discrete sections. The prologue is supplied by the opening credits, which show Ringo riding across the landscape, followed by a title paragraph introducing this lead character and establishing him as the deadliest gunfighter in the West. The *parados* delivers the first actual dramatic scenes of the movie: the showdown between Ringo and Eddie in the saloon; the subsequent confrontation between Ringo and Eddie's brothers; and Ringo riding off toward Cayenne. After these introductory scenes have set the stage, the central story, set entirely in Cayenne, unfolds in a series of episodes involving Ringo and his interactions with various characters. These episodes, which take place mainly in the Palace Bar, alternate with brief scenes featuring secondary characters (e.g., Strett, Peggy, Bromley, Karl Malden's barkeep Mac) in other locations outside of the saloon; these scenes serve as *stasima*, responding to and commenting on Ringo's situation through their own dialogue and action. There are ten episodes overall—more than one would have in a Greek tragedy, because the filmmakers wisely decided to take advantage of cinema's ability to cut between locations to interject more frequent *stasima*, thus heightening the suspense and increasing narrative momentum. (This also keeps *The Gunfighter* from seeming too "stagy," like a filmed play rather than a movie.) At the end of the picture, when Ringo has met his unavoidable fate, there is a three-minute *exodus* that wraps everything up, narratively and emotionally. This *exodus* is in two parts: first there is an intense confrontation in a barn immediately after the main action; and then, sometime later, the town comes together for Ringo's funeral.

Classical unities. Greek drama also famously exhibited the three so-called *Aristotelian unities* (although these were actually distilled from Aristotle's writings much later by Renaissance dramatists like Gian Giorgio Trissino and Lodovico Castelvetro): unity of action, unity of time, and unity of place. Following these principles, a Greek tragedy would focus specifically on one character's story, without side plots or subplots; it would take place during the daylight hours of one single day; and the action would unfold in one location.

In *The Gunfighter*, the primary action of the film—bookended between the opening prologue/*parados* and the brief *exodus* at the close—focuses completely on Ringo's situation and takes place during a single morning in the little town of Cayenne, and mostly in the town saloon, as mentioned above. Therefore, this main part of the drama, lasting for about seventy-two minutes, exhibits all three Aristotelian unities—action, time, and place; and these unities endow *The Gunfighter* with genuine dramatic power.

But why are the unities effective at all? Well, in this particular case, two of them—unity of action and unity of place—provide laser focus to the narrative, concentrating our attention tightly on the compelling personal drama unfolding on the screen. We are gripped from the very beginning, despite the fact that most scenes are dialogue scenes with very little action or even movement. We sweat and agonize along with Ringo as he tries to work out his own destiny and avoid the inevitable, and the fact that so much of the action takes place in one room gives the proceedings a claustrophobic feel that only adds to the intensity. Enhancing this effect is that, during establishing shots, Ringo is often filmed from a distance in the Palace Bar, off in a corner by himself. Despite his prowess with a gun, he is bound, confined, made small and vulnerable by his situation. Claustrophobic and imprisoning as it is, however, the saloon, with its ever-present crowd of curious onlookers hovering at a safe distance, also doubles as a theater. As Richard Slotkin notes, "its open board floor suggests a stage, and the action that occurs there could easily be transferred to a proscenium setting. Thus even when Ringo is just sitting at his table waiting for something to happen, he is still a celebrity, still 'on stage.'"[2]

And what of the third unity? It turns out that unity of time may be the most significant of all for this story; it certainly seems to have been for the filmmakers. In almost every scene with Ringo—and every single scene within the main barroom—we hear the wall clock ticking away, not only measuring out the drama in real time but also representing the slow but relentless draining away of Ringo's chances to escape his fate. Characters are constantly, anxiously checking the clock or a watch—time is of the essence,

Ringo (Gregory Peck) in the Palace Bar. Directly over him, symbolically, is the Otto F. Becker lithograph "Custer's Last Fight," which was actually widely seen in saloons of the era. To the left is a picture of a stag at bay; to the right, the endlessly ticking clock. *The Gunfighter* (Twentieth Century–Fox, 1950).

since we know, along with Ringo, that his pursuers are just a couple hours away. The degree to which this tightens the suspense of the drama is considerable, and the impact is heightened by the fact that, for most of the instances where we are made aware of the ticking clock, the movie denies us a look at its face. We often see the pendulum moving back and forth—sometimes even with a conversation occurring directly beneath it— but the clock face is usually out of shot. In one scene, we see the clock across the room, pendulum in full swing, but the face is blocked—frustratingly and very selectively—by a decorative protrusion on a wooden post. How much time has elapsed? How close are Ringo's pursuers? Everyone is worried about the time, but we don't (usually) get to see what the clock actually reads, making the tension even more relentless.

Those readers familiar with *High Noon* (1952) may be wondering if the main sequence of the narrative in *The Gunfighter* unfolds in real time. It does—almost. There are a few missing minutes of travel time—for example, when Strett makes his way to the schoolhouse to meet Peggy, or when Ringo sneaks up to the upper floor of the rooming house to confront the older gentleman Jerry (Cliff Clark) who means to ambush him— but besides those, the action flows as it would in the real world. The gap between screen time and narrative time is very small as a result. The two times when we are actually allowed to see the saloon clock face, it shows first 8:50 a.m. and then 9:57 a.m.—an interval of sixty-seven minutes, while fifty-one minutes of screen time have actually elapsed.

(I suspect, although I do not know, that the movie was first shot and assembled to occur in real time, and then some edits were made that caused the slight discrepancy, presumably to keep the dramatic momentum going.)

In any case, the complete action of the movie between the opening and closing frames occurs within the space of less than two hours on a school-day morning in Cayenne. This gives *The Gunfighter*, so still and composed on the surface, a taut, hushed energy that builds and builds until the fated climax. The realistic flow of time also adds to the tragedy; we realize in retrospect that we have been witnessing, in intimate detail, the last seventy minutes or so of a man's life, and they have been filled with so much humanity: his friendships, his love, his family, his weariness, his anger, his guilt, his nobility, and his heartbreakingly idealistic hopes for a better future.

Catharsis. Catharsis originally was a medical term, meaning a purgation, cleansing, or purification. In the *Poetics*, Aristotle adopts the word as a metaphor for the potential of tragedy to effect an analogous purging of the emotions through the depiction of drama that evokes pity and terror in the spectator. Scholars have debated just what the end results of this purification are meant to be; many argue that Aristotle's ultimate ideal was the moderation of the emotions and restoration of equilibrium, while others think he was suggesting a sort of clarification of the intellect. Whatever Aristotle's argument, there is no doubt both that catharsis became an integral part of tragedy, from the Greeks to the Elizabethans to today, and that there are demonstrated psychological benefits resulting from the cathartic release of emotion, properly employed.

Aristotle turns time and time again to these two poles, pity and terror, as the agents of catharsis, but, as James Joyce has Stephen Dedalus note in *A Portrait of the Artist as a Young Man*, the great philosopher never defines those two terms. Joyce's Dedalus does, however, in a passage that is justly famous and has greatly impacted our modern understanding of tragedy: "Pity is the feeling which arrests the mind in the presence of whatsoever is grave and constant in human sufferings and unites it with the human sufferer. Terror is the feeling which arrests the mind in the presence of whatsoever is grave and constant in human sufferings and unites it with the secret cause."[3] Both arrest the mind, and Joyce—speaking through his avatar Dedalus—is quite clear that true aesthetic arrest is only accomplished through artistic and formal beauty rather than "kinetic" appeals to desire or revulsion. (More on this in a later essay.) The difference, then, between the complementary evocations of pity and terror is that the former elicits our compassion for the tragic hero as a human being, whereas the latter elicits our mindful awareness of the "grave and constant" tragic elements that are part and parcel of the human experience, and in which we all share. I interpret this to mean that pity is aroused by the particular and terror by the universal; we pity individuals, whereas we are terrified by the more general existential horrors of human life.

In the case of *The Gunfighter*, it is not difficult to pity Ringo. We are moved to compassion for his character right away. Even in his very first scene, when he kills Eddie in the bar, we feel for him, not Eddie. He is just trying to enjoy a quiet drink by himself, but as always, his fame catches up to him. Eddie is obnoxious and belligerent, a direct contrast to Ringo's cool, withdrawn stillness. (The moment of Eddie's demise is a masterpiece of cinematic editing which I won't spoil here; it needs to be experienced.) Eddie's reaction to Ringo sets up a great deal of the rest of the film; we now understand why, even in the emptiness of the Palace Bar in Cayenne, if we look hard enough we can see reflected in mirrors the scores of people, mostly children skipping school, constantly peering in from outside to catch a glimpse of the great killer. Their presence provides a subtle, recurrent commentary on Ringo's stature in a way perhaps analogous to the chorus in a Greek drama.

All of this establishes Ringo as a man who wants only peace, but who is hounded by his own celebrity. Even though he can be frightful and imposing, we see his genuinely warm friendship with Strett, his deep concern for his wife and child, and—perhaps most movingly of all—his dreams for a better life ahead. One of the most amazing grace notes in a film filled with them is the brief interlude when a young rancher[4] comes into the saloon, unaware of Ringo's identity. He sits down next to Ringo and Mac the bartender and begins a friendly conversation. As the man describes the little ordinary details of his family and life on the ranch, we see how much it means to Ringo. This man is living the simple life that Ringo desires. We also see how much of a relief it is for Ringo to be carrying on a pleasant conversation with a nice fellow, one that has nothing to do with his own past or reputation. It is difficult to describe it here, but the scene is almost overwhelmingly touching, despite being brief, subtle, and understated. It has nothing to do with advancing the plot, but everything to do with who Ringo is and who he aspires to be. Touches like these make us truly care for Ringo; we do pity him, and so his tragedy is all that more powerful.

But what about terror? What is "grave and constant in human sufferings" that connects to Joyce's "secret cause"? In the case of *The Gunfighter,* a number of deeper, horrific human truths that Ringo's story embodies resonate with me. First of all, there is the terrible mystery of the forces that govern our lives—for example, the seemingly unsolvable tension between determinism and free will. The movie deliberately embraces this awful paradox, and—just like philosophy—refuses to resolve it. Seen from one perspective, *The Gunfighter* is strikingly fatalistic. From the very beginning, there is a feeling of inexorability to Ringo's story arc; his ultimate demise seems predestined, set in motion by his past and as inevitable as the sunset. In this sense, Ringo very much recalls the doomed heroes of the Greek tragedies, from Oedipus to Antigone, who stood at the mercy of Fate. In Greek mythology, Fate was personified in the three Moirai, the female incarnations of destiny (*moira*) who controlled the threads of each human life. They were more powerful even than the gods: "To Fate the might of Zeus must bow," wrote the Greek epic poet Quintus Smyrnaeus in *The Fall of Troy.*[5] I believe that Fate is personified in *The Gunfighter* as well, in the person of Ringo's old friend Molly. (The name "Molly" comes from a Hebrew root meaning "bitter" and of course also might suggest the Greek "Moira.") Interestingly, although the character of Molly clearly has an affectionate friendship with Ringo, in terms of the narrative she is always the force which keeps Ringo in Cayenne, where his destiny awaits. On two separate occasions Ringo is about to leave Cayenne, and each time, at the critical last moment, he is stopped by Molly's call, and lingers. At the climax of the picture, Molly is also tasked with checking to see if the alleyway outside the saloon is safe before Ringo departs for good, but her survey of the surroundings is incredibly perfunctory. I am convinced that the filmmakers intended the character of Molly to be an instrument of the Fates themselves (whether wittingly or not); she is the constantly recurring motif within the narrative that gently nudges Ringo, just enough to keep him on his path toward annihilation. And consider Molly's role in the last few seconds of Ringo's life. Ringo doesn't die cradled in the arms of his wife—she has fled with their son. Instead, his head lies in the lap of Fate— Molly's lap. And although our attention is riveted on him, try watching Molly after the gunfighter's life has trickled away. Her face goes through a series of the most curious, twitching, detached expressions. She doesn't act quite as we would expect a dear old friend to act in this moment; instead, she seems almost otherworldly, bizarre, unfathomable—perhaps like a manifestation of an ultimately impersonal, unknowable cosmic force.

And yet, scholars also remind us of the ambivalence that the humanistic Greeks had toward fatalism. The grinding away of the Fates figures prominently in Greek drama, but, as the Irish classicist E.R. Dodds points out in his aptly titled essay "On Misunderstanding the *Oedipus Rex*," there is just as much evidence in these plays of the workings of the human will. "What fascinates us" about *Oedipus*, he writes, "is the spectacle of a man freely choosing, from the highest motives, a series of actions which lead to his own ruin."[6] The same is true of Ringo. Despite Molly's well-timed promptings, there is nothing truly holding Ringo in Cayenne, where his destiny awaits, other than his own determination. He has plenty of warnings about the risk he runs by remaining, but he stubbornly stays, exhibiting the pride (*hubris*) featured in classical Greek dramas by setting his will against the wiser counsels of the "oracle," represented both by Strett and the endlessly ticking clock. All Ringo has to do to be safe is listen to his best friend's advice and ride on. He intends to, eventually—but the clock keeps ticking, ticking, and Ringo lingers on.

Greek goddesses in the Old West: Ringo's Muse Peggy (Helen Westcott) and the embodiment of Fate, Molly (Jean Parker). "Why don't you see him, if only for a few minutes?" Molly asks, once again serving to delay Ringo's departure. *The Gunfighter* (Twentieth Century–Fox, 1950).

This is the other, paradoxical element to Ringo's "grave and constant" human sufferings. Yes, he dies because of Fate, but he also dies because of his freely willed choices. This resonates with all of us; we know, all too well, how we can never fully escape our pasts, despite our best intentions. The choices we make can never be undone after the fact, and even when we try to make up for them, there is no guarantee that unexpected threats cannot still emerge, growing out of the soil that we ourselves have planted, to threaten our happiness or our very existence. We are prisoners both of our Fate and our Will, and each leads ultimately to our destruction. When the end comes, we will be able to see both the inexorable grinding away of human destiny, in which all lives are lost, and also the ways in which our own specific choices led directly to our demise. As the only animal who foresees its own inevitable death, the human being bears an existential knowledge that is "grave and constant" indeed.

The Gunfighter is filled with masterful touches even beyond those provided by its classical structure. Clichés are studiously avoided; Hollywood tropes (two friends on opposite sides of the law, a band of brothers riding on a vendetta quest, looming street showdowns) are deliberately teased only to have their typical outcomes subverted; and the narrative is filled with surprises. (Ironically, however, the film may have actually served to solidify the Western archetype of the gunfighter that it presumably sought to deconstruct.) Peck is superb in the lead role, but there is also great supporting work from the other cast members, most especially Millard Mitchell as Strett and Skip Homeier as the loathsome Bromley. The two actors provide one of the most unforgettably riveting scenes in the picture near the end, after Ringo has died. In the opening of the *exodus*, Strett takes Bromley into a barn and, in an explosion of violence, provides the audience with a heart-pounding release after all of the emotional tension that the film has built up—a catharsis of a different kind than the classical one of the primary narrative, but in some ways one that is even more complex. Ringo's dark vengeance has already been ordained for Bromley at this point, but even so, Strett's more direct and immediate punishment is almost guiltily enjoyable—at least at first. But Bromley's bloody writhing is also one of the most horrific, graphic images from the Golden Age Hollywood Western—and our savage satisfaction soon turns to something more troubling. As human beings, we have our ambitious side as well; we also are capable of dreaming of shortcuts to greatness while ignoring the potential cost to our souls. It doesn't take too much effort to recognize something of ourselves in the hideous, disfigured Bromley. Once again, we are confronted with that which is grave and constant. *This thing of darkness....*

Henry King's direction of the film is just as superb as its acting. When watching it, I feel I am in directorial hands as masterful as those of Hitchcock, Welles, or Renoir. Every shot is composed, every scene crafted for maximum impact. The pacing and editing reinforce the slow-burn intensity of the picture, and the photography and art direction are pitch-perfect throughout. Meanwhile, what may be the most easily overlooked and yet powerful production element is the music—or, more accurately, the lack thereof. In direct contrast to its Greek dramatic antecedents, The Gunfighter shuns the use of any music to enhance the action. Even Ringo's long-delayed romantic reunion with Peggy, not to mention his climactic appointment with Fate, occurs with only the natural sounds of the surroundings as accompaniment. Throughout, the film's aesthetic is one of gritty anti-sentimentality, avoiding all of the artifice typical of the Hollywood drama of the era; and just as the story's real-time pacing draws us powerfully into the realistic world of the picture, so also the absence of any music other than diegetic ("source" music that is part of the setting, produced and heard by the people in the drama) adds to the verisimilitude. There is a fully scored orchestral introduction that plays over the opening credits, but it fades away on an unresolved half-cadence as the initial montage ends (about two minutes in), succeeded by the tinny piano of the Gem Saloon playing Foster's "Beautiful Dreamer." This too ends on an unresolved chord, as the piano player seeks safety when Eddie confronts Ringo. Then that's it: the next music we hear of any sort is at Ringo's funeral, the last two minutes of the movie, with the church organ playing "Rock of Ages." As we dissolve into the image of a lone horseman silhouetted against the sunset (Ringo? Bromley?), the orchestra reappears, joining for the last two phrases of the hymn, and the movie is over. Two minutes of music frame the picture on either end, but the rest is silence.

The Gunfighter is one of the greatest Westerns that relatively few people know, a masterpiece of aesthetics, form, and power. The movie somehow manages to be both classical Greek tragedy and an *avant-garde* deconstruction of the American Western myth. For me, *The Gunfighter* completes the magnificent triad of subversive pieces from the first half of the Western's Golden Age, along with *The Ox-Bow Incident* (1942) and *Yellow Sky* (1948). All three movies even use the same town for exterior location shots; for the creators of *The Gunfighter*, this must have been a deliberate choice, connecting the later film with its two most obvious spiritual predecessors.

In their time, these three films—each, in its own way, very compact, contained, economical, and tightly structured—offered a different path, one possible direction forward for the Western creators (and audiences) for whom the old orthodox mythology no longer rang true. There were over-the-top, wild, free-form ways to be heretical as well, of course—as movies such as *Johnny Guitar* (1954) and *Vera Cruz* (1954) would soon show—but these three initial groundbreaking masterpieces demonstrated that economical, carefully crafted, quasi-classical forms could also carry within them the seeds of revolution.

Winchester '73
(1950)

June 1, 1950 (New Haven, Connecticut)
USA—English
Universal International Pictures
92m—Mono—BW—1.37:1

Direction: Anthony Mann
Screenplay: Robert L. Richards, Borden Chase, Stuart N. Lake (story)
Principal Cast: James Stewart (Lin McAdam), Shelley Winters (Lola Manners), Dan Duryea (Waco Johnny Dean), Stephen McNally (Dutch Henry Brown), Millard Mitchell (High-Spade), Charles Drake (Steve Miller), John McIntire (Joe Lamont), Will Geer (Wyatt Earp), Jay C. Flippen (Sgt. Wilkes), Rock Hudson (Young Bull), John Alexander (Jack Riker), Steve Brodie (Wesley), James Millican (Wheeler), Abner Biberman (Latigo Means)
Production: Aaron Rosenberg
Cinematography: William H. Daniels
Editing: Edward Curtiss
Art Direction: Bernard Herzbrun, Nathan Juran
Music: Daniele Amfitheatrof (uncredited), Charles Previn (uncredited), Milton Rosen (uncredited), Hans J. Salter (uncredited), Paul Sawtell (uncredited), Walter Scharf (uncredited), Frank Skinner (uncredited), Leith Stevens (uncredited)
Awards: National Film Registry
Nominations: Writers Guild of America—Best Written American Western (Richards, Chase)

In the years just prior to America's entry into World War II, Jimmy Stewart had arrived as a Hollywood leading man, starring in films such as *Vivacious Lady* (1938), *You Can't Take It with You* (1938), *Mr. Smith Goes to Washington* (1939), *Destry Rides Again* (1939), *The Shop Around the Corner* (1940), and *The Philadelphia Story* (1940). When war broke out, he enlisted in the Army Air Corps and went to Europe, serving heroically as a bomber pilot, earning the Distinguished Flying Cross and the Croix de Guerre, and advancing to the rank of colonel in just four years. After the war, Stewart returned to Hollywood and resumed his career as a leading man with *It's a Wonderful Life* (1946). This movie later became a perennial Christmas favorite, of course, but at the time it did not make much of a splash. In fact, Stewart struggled to revive his career throughout the latter half of the 1940s: out of the eight features he made during this period, only two—*Call Northside 777* (1948) and *The Stratton Story* (1949)—were both critically and commercially successful. Stewart needed to regain his traction as a star, but in order to do so he would have to move in new directions.

The rehabilitation of Stewart's career truly began with his return to the Western, after eleven years away from the genre, in a film called *Winchester '73* (1950), the first of five great Westerns Stewart would make with the director Anthony Mann over the next five years. These movies—*Winchester '73, Bend of the River* (1952), *The Naked Spur* (1953), *The Far Country* (1954), and *The Man from Laramie* (1955)—helped to solidify the actor's new persona and ushered in the next phase of his career. No longer was Stewart simply typecast as the soft-spoken, affable idealist; instead, he showed that he could excel in portraying complex characters with traumatic pasts, hidden dark sides, obsessions,

The new Jimmy Stewart: Lin McAdam smashes Waco Johnny (Dan Duryea). *Winchester '73* (Universal International, 1950).

and (often) the capacity for rage and violence. Stewart would eventually go on to a career peak—in his late forties and early fifties, no less—with masterpieces such as *Rear Window* (1954), *Vertigo* (1958), and *Anatomy of a Murder* (1959). But he might never have gotten there without *Winchester '73*.

It's easy for us to see in retrospect how perfect Stewart is for this lead role, one that required the layers of complexity and dark shadings that Stewart communicated so effectively, but audiences of the time hadn't seen this side of the actor yet; they still associated him with wholesome, gentle roles, and in fact, according to the screenwriter Borden Chase, at one of the sneak previews "there had been some titters in the audience at seeing Stewart's name in the opening titles of a Western." This soon changed, however—most notably in the gasp-inducing scene where Stewart's character slams the face of Waco Johnny (a brilliant Dan Duryea) down onto a saloon bar, twisting his adversary's body painfully while mad obsession plays across his face. Stewart performs this scene frighteningly well. "Once he smashed Duryea in the bar," Chase noted, "there was no more snickering."[1] Jimmy Stewart was back, but different now as he began this new phase of his career, and the Mann Westerns were the primary key to his renaissance. As Scott Eyman observes, this period marked "the definitive emergence of the postwar Stewart, in which he integrated the emotional upheaval of his war experiences with the tenacity that audiences had grown to love before the war."[2]

Borden Chase, best known at this point for Westerns and war movies, penned this first collaboration between Stewart and Mann along with Robert L. Richards, who most recently had been working in the generally more politically progressive genre of *film noir*. (Significantly, the right-wing Chase would go on to be a member of Hollywood's anti–Communist Motion Picture Alliance for the Preservation of American Ideals, while the left-wing Richards would eventually be blacklisted, effectively ending his Hollywood career.) The two writers, proceeding from a story by Stuart N. Lake, avoided overt politics in their script, crafting instead a twentieth-century American version of a literary form that originated over two centuries earlier in Britain: the so-called "novel of circulation," which follows a particular object—an article of clothing, a piece of furniture, a coin, a dish, a toy, or a pet, for example—as it circulates from person to person. This genre still appears from time to time; in fact, it experienced a burst of popularity in the late 1990s with E. Annie Proulx's novel *Accordion Crimes* (1996), Don DeLillo's novel *Underworld* (1997), and the movie *The Red Violin* (1998).

Obviously, the object of circulation in *Winchester '73* is the titular firearm, a rare ("one of a thousand") rifle that serves as a prize for a Dodge City shooting competition on the date of the American Centennial: July 4, 1876. The gun is presented by Wyatt Earp (Will Geer) himself, fairly won by the protagonist Lin McAdam (Stewart) but passing through five other pairs of hands before returning to its rightful owner. Despite (or perhaps because of) the rifle's unmatched quality as a weapon, everyone who claims it, rightly or wrongly, will suffer—all but one, in fact, in the worst possible way.

The movie features a rich cast of supporting characters, types—and archetypes—drawn from Western lore, and all played beautifully, including the faithful, stolidly philosophical sidekick High-Spade (Millard Mitchell); Lola, the dance-hall girl with the heart of gold (Shelley Winters); the tinhorn gambler (John McIntyre); the good-hearted, dignified, older cavalryman (Jay C. Flippen); the ineffectual man turned coward by the demands of the West (Charles Drake); and the "noble savage" Indian antagonist (Rock Hudson). There are two striking new developments in the villain category, however: first, the aforementioned Waco Johnny, who goes several steps beyond villainy into sheer psychosis; and second, the primary antagonist Dutch Henry (Stephen McNally), who is a nasty piece of work in his own right, but made even more horrific when we discover that he is actually protagonist McAdam's brother and the murderer of their father.

Winchester '73 is an excellent film, one which packs a lot of interest, excitement, and impact into its economical ninety-two minutes. Like all great movies, it is filled with subtle touches that make each repeat viewing filled with new discoveries. This time through, I genuinely appreciated nuances like Will Geer's delightfully genial Wyatt Earp, and the soft-pedaled but comical reaction from McAdam and High-Spade when they learn his identity; the breathtaking tracking shot when Steve the coward and his then-girlfriend Lola flee in an open wagon away from a band of pursuing Indians and toward the cavalry encampment; the understated moment when the kindly cavalry sergeant learns that McAdam and High-Spade were with him at the Battle of Bull Run—on the other side; the infamous face-smashing scene, of course; and the continuously perfect dialogue.

As much as any of these elements, though, on my most recent viewing I especially appreciated the character of High-Spade, as brought to life by Millard Mitchell. Mitchell had been a prolific stage and radio actor in the earlier part of his career, and prior to this movie had become a steady supporting player in a series of mostly unremarkable Hollywood films. In the late forties, however, he truly came into his own as a character actor, playing military officers in *A Foreign Affair* (1948) and *Twelve O'Clock High* (1949), and then doing a fantastic turn as Marshal Strett in *The Gunfighter* (1950). Not long after *Winchester '73*, Mitchell would win a Golden Globe for his work in *My Six Convicts* (1952), then famously play the movie studio mogul in *Singin' in the Rain* (1952) and a grizzled old prospector in the great Mann/Stewart Western *The Naked Spur* (1953). Tragically, Mitchell died of lung cancer in 1953, much too young at the age of fifty.

Waco Johnny (a magnificently loathsome Dan Duryea) menaces dance-hall girl Lola Manners (an equally excellent Shelley Winters). Winters later quipped: "I don't know what the hell I was doing in that picture.... There were all these guys running around trying to get their hands on this goddam rifle who should've been trying to get their hands on me.... In the end, nobody remembers me being in it." [Grant and Hodgkiss, *Renegade Westerns*, 43.] *Winchester '73* (Universal International, 1950).

There are many great scenes featuring Mitchell to choose from, but my favorite is a low-key one, when High-Spade and McAdam, trailing Dutch Henry, have stopped to rest for the night in the quiet desert. It's a scene that provides glimpses into parts of each man that we haven't yet seen; it also culminates in the closest thing to a tender moment that the film contains, as the two men, without a trace of soppiness, acknowledge the affection they have for one another. It starts when High-Spade asks McAdam about his father, for whom both men once worked:

HIGH-SPADE: You ever wonder what he'd think about you huntin' down Dutch Henry?
McADAM: He'd understand. He taught me to hunt.
HIGH-SPADE: Not men. Hunting for food, that's all right. Hunting a man to kill him? You're beginnin' to like it!
McADAM: Now that's where you're wrong. I don't like it. Some things a man has to do, so he does 'em.
HIGH-SPADE: What happens when the hunt is over? Then what?
McADAM: Well, hadn't given it much thought. Maybe we could get the ranch back together again, round up the strays, then we.... Hadn't given it much thought.
HIGH-SPADE: Now might be a good time, on account of we're comin' pretty close to the end of the trail.

MCADAM: Yeah, I guess maybe you're right. You been real fine people, High-Spade, ridin' along with me.

HIGH-SPADE: That's what friends is for, isn't it? Leastways, that's the way your dad always said.

MCADAM: Yeah, he did, didn't he? He said if a man had one friend, he was rich. I'm rich.

The words are simple, but this is one of those scenes that sparkle in the hands of accomplished performers. It's also the moment that I first realized, upon my initial viewing of this movie years ago, just how much I cared about what was going to happen to both of these characters.

Complementing the varied and colorful cast in *Winchester '73* is an abundance of different Western settings and situations, made possible by the circuitous wandering of the rifle that provides a skeleton for the narrative. Over the course of the movie, we have a town festival, a shooting contest, raucous saloons, a pitched battle between Indians and entrenched cavalry, a band of outlaws under siege (Billy the Kid-style) in a homestead, a rigged card game with references to the "dead man's hand," a botched bank robbery, a chase across miles of rugged wilderness, a final showdown, and even the initiating presence of Wyatt Earp—"the point where myth and history meet," as William Indick notes.[3] It is as if every Western trope is here, but in a new and original configuration. As Mann himself once said about the film, "the gun which passed from hand to hand allowed me to embrace a whole epoch, a whole atmosphere. I really believe that it contains all the ingredients of the Western, and that it summarizes them."[4] The way in which these elements are combined and employed, however, is not what we might expect at first, because the movie that results is no mere eclectic homage or derivative pastiche. Instead, the familiar touchstones from Western lore serve as a filter through which passes a deeper, more universal mythic story. The archetypes have been personalized, fitted to a particular idiom whose cultural shorthand allows the story to be conveyed directly, concisely, and coherently. Part of the answer to how and why this works so well lies, perhaps surprisingly, in anthropology.

Adolf Bastian (1826–1905) was a German ethnographer and anthropologist who, among other things, addressed himself to the problem of the "constants" and the "variables" in human myths. Bastian concluded that there were certain "elementary ideas" (*Elementargedanken*) shared across cultures simply because of the basic mental and biological framework that all human beings hold in common. However, like the Platonic ideals, these are never experienced in pure form, but only as filtered through (and elaborated by) the cultural idiosyncrasies of the local groups. These varied, specific societal colorations of universal archetypes were termed "folk ideas" (*Völkergedanken*) by Bastian.[5] To take a simple and well-known example, the elementary idea of a primordial flood, perhaps symbolizing the universal human longing for spiritual cleansing and psychological rebirth, appears in numerous ancient mythologies—Chinese, Hindu, Mesopotamian, Greek, Levantine, Norse, Celtic, Native American, South American, African, and Australian—but always inflected in particular, individual, and unique ways by each separate culture. Bastian's framework can help to explain how mythic constants are found all over the world, especially in remote cases where the simple diffusion of stories is not a feasible explanation for the striking similarities. Furthermore, the universality of these elementary ideas explains in part why mythologically rich stories and artworks from a variety of cultures and time periods still have the potential to move us in powerful, impactful ways.

This recalls what I have called the Law of Variation in Westerns, which was partially inspired by Bastian's thinking: "What's interesting is not the Western tropes themselves, but how the creators build upon them, interpret them, combine them, and sometimes subvert them, in order to fashion ever-varying works of art." One implication here is that the *interest* in a Western narrative arises largely from the curation, combination, and variation of the "folk" ideas that come from the genre's stylistic conceits, but that the *power* of a Western comes from the elementary ideas that underlie and are filtered through the local story (in combination, I would argue, with the aesthetic content, the sheer beauty of the acting, dialogue, visuals, music, and so forth—although even these aesthetic elements may have both "elementary" and "folk" components). Putting all of this together and oversimplifying, it is possible to model the impact of a Western (or indeed, any work of art) by analogy as a motor: the local "folk" ideas (and aesthetic elements) are the moving parts, and the universal "elementary" ideas (and aesthetic constants) are the fuel that drives the engine.

In the case of *Winchester '73*, it is not difficult to track the local stylistic elements that are present in such abundance, but what are the universal mythic ideas that power the movie? Most obviously, the narrative centers around the conflict between two antagonists who are also brothers. This is mythically significant. In the late 1950s, the anthropologist Clyde Kluckhohn and his team looked at fifty separate cultures from six geographic regions spread all over the world, and they found a number of frequently appearing mythological themes—flood myths, creation myths, monster killing, incest, castration, and androgynous deities, for example. But one of the most common motifs was that of the antagonism between siblings, often ending in fratricide, which occurred in thirty-two of the fifty cultures, and in all six continental zones.[6] It doesn't take long, even just scanning through our own cultural knowledge and the commonly known myths and legends of the world, for us to recall numerous examples of brotherly conflict in these stories: Isaac and Ishmael, Jacob and Esau, Absalom and Amnon, Eteocles and Polyneices, Romulus and Remus, Karna and Arjuna, Hodr and Baldur, Set and Osiris, Balin and Balan, Parzival and Feirifiz. These conflicts are resolved within these stories in different ways. Sometimes the brothers reconcile, as with Isaac and Ishmael or Parzival and Feirifiz (both being sets of half-brothers, interestingly, and associated with different races). In other cases, like Malory's Balin and Balan, the two destroy each other accidentally, each unaware of his brother's identity until it's too late. Perhaps most commonly, though, one brother will kill the other deliberately. The paradigmatic example of that outcome in the Judeo-Christian tradition, of course, is that of Cain and Abel. It is worth noticing at this point that the main character's last name in *Winchester '73* is McAdam—that is, "son of Adam." Only, in this version of the archetypal fratricide myth, Abel must kill Cain instead—for the murder of Adam.

In mythic fraternal conflicts, the brothers can symbolize many things, from large-scale to small: great and unfathomable cosmic forces, as with Set/Osiris; nations, races, or tribes, as with Parzival/Feirefiz and Ishmael/Isaac; foundational energies of society, as with Romulus/Remus; aspects of the Oedipal familial drama, as with Eteocles/Polyneices; or internal elements of the individual psyche, as with, ultimately, all of these. After all, the different sides of ourselves can be seen as siblings, in the sense that we are "parent" to them both. It is this interior, psychological dimension that is the most significant, in my mind, to the story of *Winchester '73*. The movie is part of a long storytelling tradition in which the protagonist and antagonist share a great deal in

High-Spade (Millard Mitchell), Lin (James Stewart), and Lola (Shelley Winters) at the end. The title gun, like Excalibur, now hangs at the side of its rightful owner—but at what cost? *Winchester '73* (Universal International, 1950).

common—either literal bloodlines, as with these fraternal connections or other family relationships (parent/child, brother/sister, uncle/nephew), or figurative ones, made clear usually when the villain points out that he and the hero actually have a great deal in common. (My favorite expression through dialogue of the figurative rather than literal brotherly connection between hero and villain in American pop culture is the line Belloq delivers to Indiana Jones in *Raiders of the Lost Ark*, 1981: "You and I are very much alike. Archaeology is our religion, yet we have both fallen from the pure faith. Our methods have not differed as much as you pretend. I am a shadowy reflection of you. It would take only a nudge to make you like me, to push you out of the light."), In *Winchester '73*, it could not be clearer that actual brothers Lin McAdam and Dutch Henry are shadowy reflections of one another—symbolized, among other things, by the way in which they shoot identical patterns in the opening contest for the rifle. Both men are grim, driven, and occasionally violent, the primary ethical difference being that McAdam acts out of his sense of justice rather than self-interest. However, this sense of justice includes a burning desire to avenge his father's death. As Slotkin points out, McAdam's "obsession with revenge and the fetishization of the rifle that is its symbol suggest that he may be driven by a madness akin to his brother's malice and that only by slaying his dark brother can he be free of it."[7]

In enemy sibling myths, renewal of the individual, familial, social, or cosmic order is achieved by the resolution of the conflict, but, as mentioned above, this can take different forms. When stories like *Parzival* end in reconciliation between the siblings, it indicates the value of external peacemaking and internal personality integration. When other stories (Balin and Balan, for example) have the two siblings slay each other accidentally, then we are in the realms of tragedy and the "secret cause" that we discussed earlier in relation to *The Gunfighter*. But many tales, like this one, require the death of one sibling at the hands of the other. This can be read in a Judeo-Christian, Manichaean way—good must destroy evil, whether in the outside world or inside the soul—but I don't believe that this is the perspective of *Winchester '73*. McAdam clearly has his own negative side; it seems significant that he wears a white hat which nevertheless bears noticeable dark stains. We do indeed sense that "only a nudge" might push him "out of the light." McAdam's solution is to kill the darkness, in the person of his evil brother, rather than integrate it; but the moment he does so, we see him slump forward, head bowed in sadness and resignation. From then until the end of the movie, the character never utters another word. McAdam did what had to be done, but in doing so, may have lost a critical part of himself. Whether he will ever be able to reclaim it, the movie does not tell.

Broken Arrow
(1950)

July 20, 1950 (New York City)
USA—English / Apache languages
Twentieth Century–Fox
93m—Mono—Technicolor—1.37:1

Direction: Delmer Daves
Screenplay: Albert Maltz, Elliott Arnold (novel *Blood Brother*)
Principal Cast: James Stewart (Tom Jeffords), Jeff Chandler (Cochise), Debra Paget (Son-seeahray), Basil Ruysdael (Gen. Oliver Howard), Will Geer (Ben Slade), Joyce Mackenzie (Terry), Arthur Hunnicutt (Milt Duffield)
Production: Julian Blaustein
Cinematography: Ernest Palmer
Editing: J. Watson Webb, Jr.
Art Direction: Lyle R. Wheeler, Albert Hogsett
Music: Hugo Friedhofer
Awards: Golden Globe—Best Film Promoting International Understanding, Writers Guild of America—Best Written American Western (Maltz, as Michael Blankfort)
Nominations: Oscar—Best Supporting Actor (Chandler), Oscar—Best Screenplay (Maltz, as Michael Blankfort), Oscar—Best Color Cinematography (Palmer), Golden Globe—Best Color Cinematography (Palmer), Picturegoer Award—Best Actor (Chandler), Writers Guild of America—Robert Meltzer Award (Maltz, as Michael Blankfort)

Thomas Jefferson Jeffords (1832–1914) was an Army scout, prospector, and mail superintendent who became famous for his friendship with the Apache chief Cochise (1805–74) and his brokering of a peace treaty (1872) between Cochise and the United States. When Cochise died, Jeffords was the only person outside of the tribe to know where he was buried, a secret Jeffords never revealed. In 1947, the novelist Elliott Arnold published a fictionalized account of the inspiring friendship between these two men, *Blood Brother*, wherein, among other additions, he created a love interest for Jeffords in the person of the Apache woman Sonseeahray ("Morning Star"). Postwar America was ready for a novel that stood firmly against bigotry and racism, having just survived a catastrophic global conflict in which people of all ethnicities had united to defeat a dictator who preached a monstrous doctrine of racial superiority. *Blood Brother* became a bestseller and is still read today.

Creative types in Hollywood during the postwar years were eager to make socially conscious movies, and the Western genre once again showed its versatility in this regard. A movie based on *Blood Brother* would have the potential to deconstruct a myth that needed to be deconstructed, thereby addressing more honestly the historical wrong that was done to Native Americans specifically, but it could also say something more broadly about rights and justice in a divided nation. In speaking out against the racist practices of the United States in the nineteenth century—from a safer temporal distance, so to speak—the movie could serve, more directly, as a commentary on contemporary race relations as well. This recalls once again the principle of the Law of Time: *At their heart, Westerns are about the era in which they are made, not the time in which they are set.*

Broken Arrow, filmed in 1949 and released in 1950, was adapted from Arnold's novel by Albert Maltz, although Maltz's friend Michael Blankfort was fronted as the screenwriter for the credits because Maltz was under blacklist at the time of the film's creation and release. (Maltz's credit for *Broken Arrow* was officially recognized by the Writers Guild in 1991, six years after his death. Recent video editions have restored his name in the credits.) Upon its release, the movie Maltz wrote—starring James Stewart as Jeffords, Jeff Chandler as Cochise, and a teenaged Debra Paget as Sonseeahray—became a smash hit, the highest grossing Western of 1950. Again, the country was ready for this, or at least large segments of it were.

It's a tricky thing, making a "political" work of art, whether a social novel, protest painting, or "message movie." At some point, the creative artist(s) must decide what the balance will be between aesthetic value and persuasive political content. But must it always be a trade-off? Can't a play, movie, song, or sculpture be *both* an artistic masterpiece *and* the conveyor of a powerful message, one that can change people's minds and get them to think in a new way about their society? Or does foregrounding political content, even for a moment, take something away, in some slight measure at least, from the aesthetic impact of a work of art?

I'll speak for myself first, and then let two others far better equipped than I am tackle the question—one of the thorniest in the arts, especially today. Personally, I cannot think of a single moment where political content or ethical messaging became overt in a work of dramatic art in which its aesthetic power, at the same moment, was also heightened for me. Persuasive content, no matter how noble, when it occurs in a play, movie, or novel, always has the same effect on my connection to the artwork's deeper beauty as would receiving a text message or a cell phone call in the middle of my viewing or reading. It's not a bad thing *per se*, but it does switch my brain over from "apprehension of art" mode to "digesting, analyzing, and evaluating content" mode. I've just gone from poetry to journalism, and the two of those, for me, do not coexist simultaneously. Perhaps this is just a weakness of my non-multitasking brain, which apparently can be awestruck in

James Stewart as Tom Jeffords. *Broken Arrow* (Twentieth Century–Fox, 1950).

aesthetic arrest or persuaded by a political argument but cannot do both at the same time.

I feel somewhat vindicated in this shortcoming by the position of James Joyce, not only one of the greatest writers of the twentieth century but also, in my opinion, one of its most profound aesthetic philosophers. The key to Joyce's aesthetics—which has been largely ignored by professional philosophers, while so many people in the arts find it ringing true—may lie in one short passage in *A Portrait of the Artist as a Young Man*. Here Joyce, speaking through Stephen Dedalus, lays out the core of a powerful aesthetic theory:

> The feelings excited by improper art are kinetic, desire or loathing. Desire urges us to possess, to go to something; loathing urges us to abandon, to go from something. The arts which excite them, pornographical or didactic, are therefore improper arts. The esthetic emotion … is therefore static. The mind is arrested and raised above desire and loathing.[1]

The greatest art, then, induces a timeless feeling of stasis in the apprehender, who is neither drawn toward what is depicted through desire (pornographic art) nor repelled by what is depicted through loathing (didactic art). This is an almost Buddhist philosophy of aesthetics—just as the Buddha achieved enlightenment by being moved neither by desire nor fear, so it is with the human getting at least a taste of Nirvana through beholding "proper art." Joyce's philosophy, it seems to me, has a great deal to say to our own time, an era in which nearly all of the art we experience is carefully crafted to jerk on our psyches (kinetically) at all times, to play constantly on our fears and desires in order to provoke a strong emotional reaction that, with any luck, we might mistake for an artistic response.

There is so much to like about Joyce's aesthetic; not only does it put cheaply manipulative art firmly in its place, but it does the same for that other nauseating product of contemporary life in which we are likewise being drowned, advertising. As a ubiquitous aspect of culture—it's estimated that we encounter as many as 10,000 advertisements *per day*—whose sole purpose is to elicit feelings of desire for the object being depicted, advertising is pure pornography in Joyce's terms. Like porn, it may serve a very specific purpose, but let's don't ever mistake it for art or assume that its ultimate purpose has anything to do with beauty.

Amazingly, Albert Maltz expressed his own views about kinetic art (especially of the didactic variety) a few years before his movie, and as it turns out, his thoughts aligned very closely with Joyce's. In fact, Maltz incensed his fellow leftists with a 1946 essay in the American Marxist magazine *The New Masses*, in which he criticized writers of the time for prioritizing polemical value over artistic value. Maltz bemoaned the fact that the motto "art is a weapon" had been interpreted by many on the contemporary left to mean that "*unless* art is a weapon like a leaflet, serving immediate political ends, necessities and programs, it is worthless or escapist or vicious." He argued that the demands of creating art of "immediate political utility" resulted in art that was shallow, vulgar, and untrue to the qualities of human character and behavior.

> The pitfall of the socially conscious writer who uses his art in a shallow manner is that his goal all too often subtly demands the annihilation of certain characters, the gilding of others. It is very, very difficult for him *not* to handle characters in black and white since his objective is to prove a proposition, not to reveal men in motion as they are.
> Consequently, it is more than likely that he will "angle" character and events to achieve his

point. He may not wish to do this. But he is led to it by his goal—led into idealistic conceptions of character, led into wearing rose-colored glasses which will permit him to see in life that which he *wishes* to find in order to prove his thesis—led into the portrayal of life, not as it is, but as he would like it to be. And this is not only inferior art but shallow politics as well.

Maltz summarized: "When the artist misuses his art, when he practices journalism instead of art—however decent his purposes—the result is neither the best journalism, nor the best art, nor the best politics."[2]

Setting aside the gendered language of Maltz's era, this may seem reasonably harmless to us today, whether we agree with it or not (and I do); however, in 1946 the true believers were not about to tolerate the heresy of prioritizing artistic values over political ones. Maltz was excoriated by the American Communist Party and forced into writing a rebuttal of his own article in the *Daily Worker* so as not to lose his standing with the Party. In the final humiliation, he was coerced into denouncing himself publicly, on stage, in front of a room full of Marxist writers.[3] Whether on the left or the right, has it ever been a good thing when an entire side of the political spectrum was compelled to march in lockstep, with ideological purity strictly enforced, artists toeing the party line, and no dissenting views tolerated? This is one way of ensuring unanimity and concentrating political impact, of course—the only cost being the death of the arts, the wrecking of lives, and the annihilation of the free human spirit.

So how did Maltz respond to this humiliation by his compatriots on the left? Ultimately, as it turns out, with courage and principle. A year after the *New Masses* debacle, Maltz was confronted by the House Un-American Activities Committee. This time he stuck to his guns, refusing to answer questions before HUAC and publicly challenging the constitutionality of the proceedings. As a result, he was named one of the "Hollywood Ten" and jailed for sticking to his leftist principles—a sacrifice, tellingly, that his former critics did not themselves find it convenient to make for the cause. Then Maltz went on to write *Broken Arrow*, which changed, forever and for the better, the way that Native Americans were depicted on the American screen. In short, Maltz—at great risk to his own well-being and career—set a heroic example by continuing to work for the good even while being attacked by both his opposition and his supposed allies. His case underscores a timeless truth: there are those who talk, and there are those who do. Progress is made, ultimately, not by the sanctimonious but by the courageous; not by the forces of suppression but by the voices of freedom.

As strong as Maltz's efforts were on *Broken Arrow*, the film's success is due to the contributions of many people, not least the wonderful cast. Jimmy Stewart, of course, turns in an outstanding performance, and Debra Paget (fifteen years old at the time of filming, a quarter-century younger than Stewart!) is enchanting as the Indian maiden Sonseeahray. Nevertheless, the true star of the movie is Jeff Chandler, rightly lauded (and Oscar-nominated) for his magnificent portrayal of Cochise. As played by Chandler, the Apache chieftain is a noble man, to be sure—wise, charismatic, and compassionate—but also proud, and capable of violence without quarter in his war to defend his people.

This speaks to a key strength of *Broken Arrow* on a more general level: the Native Americans in the film are shown as real and often quite admirable human beings who have been treated poorly, but they are not over-idealized (with the possible exception of Sonseeahray). In Maltz's own terms, they have not been "gilded" or had their characters "angled" to strengthen a political argument—at least not to an extreme, beyond the norms of Hollywood at the time. They still commit the atrocities of war, torture prisoners, and kill women and children just like the whites do. Similarly, the whites are neither saints nor devils—Jeffords has fought against the natives in the past, and we even understand the motivations of the treacherous Ben Slade (Will Geer), whose wife has been killed in an Apache attack, while still not condoning his vile actions. In short, our sympathies lie entirely with Cochise, but not because any character, on the right or wrong side of history (and ethics), has been reduced down to a simplistic caricature. It would have been easier to drive home the political point if the Apache characters had all been saintly and pure, or if Slade were portrayed as a soulless monster, and indeed this is an approach that many later, well-intentioned movies dealing with the plight of Native Americans would take. Even Western epics like *Little Big Man* (1970) and *Dances with Wolves* (1990)—as magnificent as they are—present the Native Americans through quite a bit of sentimental haze, and there is an artistic sacrifice that this entails. In *Broken Arrow*, the natives are human beings of equal intrinsic worth to all others, but who have been terribly wronged; in *Little Big Man* and *Dances with Wolves*, they are essentially a nobler, superior brand of human being altogether. Again, I adore these latter two films, but their more romanticized approach toward the Native Americans entails a certain artistic trade-off. Paradoxically, and as Maltz noted in his essay, it can even weaken the political statement as well; it's easy to argue against the persecution of a people who are uniformly noble and idealized, but how well does that argument work in real life, when any group of people whose persecution one wishes to condemn is necessarily made up of all-too-human beings, warts and all? I suspect this is why the filmmakers—especially Maltz and director Delmer Daves—took such pains to show the Apaches as fully human, aside from any aesthetic considerations about avoiding didacticism. No group of people should be asked to exhibit superior worth or perfection just in order to be afforded the same basic rights that we all share. Just being human should be enough.

It's hard to please everyone when making a highly politicized work of art, and *Broken Arrow* has certainly garnered its share of criticism, during its time and afterward. Grant and Hodgkiss call it "one of the most divisive westerns ever made."[4] For some, it was too political; for others, not political enough. Slotkin writes, "Its formulas permitted the audience to indulge, and congratulate itself on, a 'liberal' attitude toward non–Whites without having to abandon the fundamental assurance of their own superiority."[5] Corkin echoes this sentiment when discussing *Broken Arrow* and other Westerns of the era that looked skeptically on violence and expansionism: "This approach, while certainly an important commentary of the national mood and typically connected to positions identified with Cold War liberalism, allows for an airing of national anxieties regarding war, both actual and potential, without facing historical conditions head-on."[6]

The fact remains, however, that *Broken Arrow* was the first significant pro–Native American Western to be greenlit under the Hays Code, a watershed moment and an inflection point for the genre as a whole. After its release, and the opening of the similarly themed *Devil's Doorway* (1950) two months later, it became more and more difficult for any Western to go back to the stale old formulas, with the rightness of Manifest Destiny as a given and Indians as merely generic, disposable antagonists. Indeed, *Time* magazine, which had praised pro-expansionist Westerns regularly in the relatively recent past, was, by the end of 1950, criticizing John Ford's *Rio Grande* for its "shoddy taste in material" in its treatment of the Indians[7]—a change in perspective that must have been wrought, in part, by the impact of *Broken Arrow*. In addition, socially conscious movies like this one, both inside and outside of the Western genre, would play a role, however incrementally, in softening up the broader cultural ground during the 1950s, helping to set the stage for the flowering of the civil rights era in the 1960s and beyond.

Another criticism made about the film is the fact that the character of Sonseeahray is killed at the end, which many felt to be a capitulation to contemporary white fears of miscegenation. Michael Walker writes:

> I feel that Sonseeahray died because she presented too much of a problem for the film. At the end of her penultimate scene, she says to Jeffords: "In time to come we will see our children ride white horses, maybe." Poignant though this comment is in retrospect, it also draws attention to an issue even trickier than miscegenation: mixed race children. Quite simply, the film could not handle it.[8]

However, it should be noted that in Arnold's original novel—which was presumably not bound by considerations like the Hays Code or the pressures of movie-mogul executives—the character also died. Thinking only in artistic terms, one can see that there are good narrative, dramatic, and mythic reasons for Sonseeahray's death. In the movie, it also affords the character of Cochise to show once more his wisdom and enlightenment when he says harshly to the anguished Jeffords now longing for vengeance, "Are you a child that you thought peace would come easily? You who taught me so well? Is it my brother who asks me to spit on my word?" There is a dark, horrible, and magnificent truth here, made manifest in the words of Cochise, which are in turn made possible by the death of Sonseeahray. The struggle for peace has always required the martyrdom of heroes. Perhaps it always will.

The most lasting criticism of *Broken Arrow*, though, is the movie's avoidance of casting any actual Native American in a major role. (The most significant part assigned to a Native American actor is probably Geronimo, played by an uncredited Jay Silverheels, but even his character has only a handful of lines.) Today it would certainly be unthinkable to create a movie about Native Americans that casts only white actors made up as Indians for the most important characters—but what about in 1950? Without wishing to excuse too much on the part of the makers of *Broken Arrow*, I do wish to note in fairness that at the time of its creation—and due, without question, to the systemic racism of the era—there was not a substantial pool of experienced Native American actors in Hollywood to fill these roles. Although pains were taken to try and show Apache culture authentically, and hundreds of Apaches were in fact given small parts or served as extras in the film, the primary roles presented more of a challenge. As Grant and Hodgkiss write, "The fact remains that there were no Indian actors of sufficient experience (and box-office caliber) to stand toe-to-toe with James Stewart."[9] Of course this perspective would not convince us today—we have seen marvelous debut performances by Native American actors who had no difficulty in assuming meaty roles and carrying them off splendidly—but what Grant and Hodgkiss are describing would certainly capture the viewpoints of filmmakers in the mid-twentieth century.

But even this argument doesn't convey all of the complexity and nuance of the problem. For example, Iron Eyes Cody—who played a minor Indian role in *Broken Arrow*—once said in regard to this controversy: "Indians have no tradition of acting

Innocents in Eden: Sonseeahray (Debra Paget) and Tom Jeffords (James Stewart). *Broken Arrow* (Twentieth Century–Fox, 1950).

or plays. Our culture consists more of ceremonial. There were very few Indian actors because we weren't conditioned to it."[10] This might sound at first like a pretty convincing

"To talk of peace is not hard. To live it is very hard." Jeff Chandler as the magnificent Cochise. *Broken Arrow* (Twentieth Century–Fox, 1950).

argument that lets Hollywood filmmakers partially off the hook, especially considering its source—until one learns that "Iron Eyes Cody" was actually born Espera Oscar de Corti, of Sicilian and southern Italian descent, and with no known Native American blood whatsoever. His ability, then, to speak to the subtleties of Native American cultures—much less their dramatic capabilities—is suspect, to say the least. (Cody would go on to become famous as the "Native American" shedding a tear about pollution in the television PSA for "Keep America Beautiful," first introduced on Earth Day in 1971.)

All of this is just to note that these are difficult and complex problems to attempt to untangle, and it seems unlikely that any stance can be taken on completely solid ground. The fact is that America in the mid-twentieth century was in a mess from a civil rights perspective, and most attempts to make things better were therefore doomed to be correspondingly messy, awkward, and imperfect. It would take the arrival of Rosa Parks, Dr. King, the Freedom Riders, and other heroes to show us how to advance the cause of justice in a better way. This doesn't mean that prior efforts, clumsy though they may have been, were not critically needed, however. There is no doubt in my mind that the makers of *Broken Arrow* had the right intentions, and that the work they made did indeed connect and resonate with audiences in a powerful and important way. The legacy of the film is one of which its creators could rightly be proud.

My own criticisms of *Broken Arrow*, compared to those voiced above, are relatively mild, and are more about aesthetics than politics. Overall, I find the film engaging and moving, with excellent production values and acting—if not a great movie, at least a very good one. Chandler, Stewart, and Paget are all excellent, and the last eight minutes are as gripping and gut-wrenching as any Western climax has a right to be. Despite its power, though, *Broken Arrow* in its very nature must be didactic to a certain extent, by Joyce's (and Maltz's) reckoning. The screenwriter himself may have struggled somewhat to find the sweet spot that he described in his 1946 essay; true, his characters are not terribly over-romanticized, but Jeffords's life among the Indians is. In many ways, his sojourn among the Apache with Sonseeahray evokes images of Adam and Eve in Eden. The couple cavorts in a lush, green Paradise that stands in stark contrast to the harsher conditions of "civilization." While this imagery can certainly resonate with us on a mythological level, it also does precisely what Maltz decried in his earlier essay: "angling" elements of the story to serve a rhetorical purpose. Again, I say this with the deepest respect for everyone involved in the making of *Broken Arrow*: it is a beautiful and affecting film, and one completely necessary for its times, with something important to say not only about tolerance and justice but also, arguably, the importance of reconciliation with nature—both internal and external. Nevertheless, the movie clearly has artistic aspirations just as high as its pedagogical ones, and I still remain skeptical that a work of art can ever be a masterpiece in both areas simultaneously. Something, somewhere, must always be sacrificed.

In the case of *Broken Arrow*, I think the filmmakers made the right choice. Yes, we need artistic masterworks in our lives, but we also need powerful ethical statements that use the tools of art to hold us to account, as individuals and as a nation, for the choices that we make, and to call us, as *Broken Arrow*'s Cochise does, to something better.

Devil's Doorway
(1950)

September 15, 1950
USA—English
Metro-Goldwyn-Mayer
84m—Mono—BW—1.37:1

Direction: Anthony Mann
Screenplay: Guy Trosper
Principal Cast: Robert Taylor (Lance Poole), Louis Calhern (Verne Coolan), Paula Raymond (Orrie Masters), Marshall Thompson (Rod MacDougall), James Mitchell (Red Rock), Edgar Buchanan (Zeke Carmody), Rhys Williams (Scotty MacDougall), Spring Byington (Mrs. Masters), James Millican (Ike Stapleton)
Production: Nicholas Nayfack
Cinematography: John Alton
Editing: Conrad A. Nervig
Art Direction: Cedric Gibbons, Leonid Vasian
Music: Daniele Amfitheatrof
Nominations: New York Film Critics Circle—Best Film, Writers Guild of America—Best Written American Western (Trosper)

For Anthony Mann, 1950 was an eventful year. Not only did he arrive as an A-picture director at that time, but he also gave the public the first of several fruitful collaborations with Jimmy Stewart in *Winchester '73*, presented a daring blend of *noir* and Western melodrama with the Barbara Stanwyck vehicle *The Furies*, and released *Devil's Doorway*, a powerful and fitting companion piece to Delmer Daves's *Broken Arrow*, which came out just two months earlier.

Broken Arrow and *Devil's Doorway* are milestones, the first heralds of a sea change in the way that Hollywood would treat Native Americans in the Western from this point forward. There are interesting differences between the two 1950 films, however. *Broken Arrow*, filmed in Technicolor, features big-budget production values, has as its hero a white man who is sympathetic to the Apaches, and is both lyrical and classically tragic. *Devil's Doorway*, on the other hand, is stark and brutal, rough rather than polished, and filmed in an uncompromising black-and-white. The movie is tragic like *Broken Arrow*, but several shades bleaker and more pessimistic. Most importantly, its hero, with whom we are called to identify, is a full-blooded Shoshone rather than a well-meaning white man; at the time, this challenged white audiences to take their sympathies a step further than they were asked to do with *Broken Arrow*.

Devil's Doorway was actually previewed for audiences several weeks before *Broken Arrow*'s release, but its grimness did not play well with the crowd. As a result, the studio delayed its release until after Daves's movie had come out in a strong opening.[1] Even then,

A joyous homecoming: Sgt. Major Lance Poole (Robert Taylor) reunites with his friends, Marshal Zeke Carmody (Edgar Buchanan) and bartender Bob (Tom Fadden). *Devil's Door-way* (MGM, 1950).

Devil's Doorway saw a limited release and failed to turn any significant profit. From the beginning it was overshadowed by its counterpart, and today, sadly, the movie is almost forgotten. It may not be a masterwork, but it is a powerful statement nonetheless, one that stays with the viewer and features at least one absolutely unforgettable scene.

We saw earlier how *Broken Arrow* was ostensibly about the treatment of Native Americans by white expansionism but also had much broader things to say, subtly, about the treatment of all American minorities on the eve of the civil rights era. However, there is nothing subtle about *Devil's Doorway* in this regard; it puts its cards on the table early on.

The protagonist of the movie is Lance Poole (Robert Taylor), whom we meet as he returns to his hometown of Medicine Bow, Wyoming, after serving as a cavalryman in the U.S. Army during the Civil War. Poole is a veteran of Mechanicsville, Antietam, and Gettysburg who was awarded the Congressional Medal of Honor for his valor and service to the Union. However, as we soon learn, Poole is also Broken Lance, a full-blooded son of the local Shoshones who live and work on a vast, beautiful swath of land called Sweet Meadows. Upon Lance's return, he is greeted with warmth and affection by many of the locals who knew him in his youth, including the sympathetic Marshal Zeke (Edgar Buchanan). Nevertheless, in the local tavern, he is sneered at by the film's chief villain, lawyer Verne Coolan (Louis Calhern), who says after Lance's departure, "Did you notice how sour the air got? You can always smell 'em."

Lance leaves for Sweet Meadows with his old, sick father, played by Shakespearean actor Fritz Leiber in his final film role before his death. (Leiber's son, Fritz Leiber, Jr., was an actor like his father before becoming one of the giants of fantasy and science fiction.) The old Shoshone is skeptical about the reception that his war-hero son is about to experience, but Lance has faith in his fellow townsfolk. Their conversation speaks not only to the world of the post–Civil War frontier but also to the post–World War II culture of 1950s America. *At their heart, Westerns are about the era in which they are made, not the time in which they are set.* To his father—and to the viewers in the postwar audience—Poole articulates the central problem of the film (echoing the perspective of *The Vanishing American* a quarter century earlier) when he says, too optimistically:

> The war's over—all the wars, even yours. The country's growing up! They gave me these [sergeant major's] stripes without testing my blood. I led a squad of white men, slept in the same blankets with 'em, ate out of the same pan, held their heads when they died. Why should it be any different now?

Why indeed? This was in fact the question that America was being forced at long last to ask itself, as soldiers of all races had been demobilized and were returning to society after having fought against racial purists in the bloodiest conflict the world had ever known. How could anyone justify not giving these brave soldiers—and by extension, all Americans of all races—their due? But the old sage has seen far too much to be that hopeful. "You are home," Lance's father answers flatly. "You are again an Indian." Sadly, he is right.

But *Devil's Doorway* spends far less time working on our sympathies than it does stoking our righteous outrage. There are so many infuriating injustices, from Coolan's underhanded trickery in stealing the well-earned cattle-raising land from the Shoshones to the town doctor's unwillingness to interrupt his cribbage game so he can ride out to Sweet Meadows and tend to Lance's dying father. By far the most gut-wrenching scene is in the saloon, when the lowlife Ike (James Millican), goaded by Coolan, picks a fight with Lance after his father has died. Lance and his friend Red Rock (James Mitchell) enter the bar, only to find a new sign in crude lettering pinned over the bar: "No liquor allowed for Indians." Zeke, who put up the sign, is apologetic to Lance, but this is the new territorial law. "Civilization's a great thing," the marshal mutters cynically before walking out in disgust. The bartender, Bob (Tom Fadden), tries to help out his friend, saying, "No law says I can't buy you a drink, Lance," but Lance, seeking to avoid conflict with the others in the bar, orders soda water for himself and Red Rock. Coolan and Ike are still not pleased, however, so Coolan begins to tell Ike, pointedly and loud enough for all to hear, about the new laws that essentially give homesteaders the rights to Indian lands. "You've never seen Sweet Meadows, have you?" he asks Ike. "It's like the laugh of a beautiful woman. You ride through the Devil's Doorway and the wind is cold. Then you see Sweet Meadows. Somehow the sky is a deeper shade of blue and the grass is greener. Oh, it's the—it's the dream all men have when they ache for home."

This lyricism soon changes to violence, however, as Ike indicates his plan to stake a claim for Sweet Meadows, then turns to its current inhabitant Lance and sneers, "That all right with you, Injun?" Soon he has drawn his six-shooter, saying, "I don't even think it's right for an Indian to stand at the same bar with a white man." (This clearly must have evoked images of mid-century segregated establishments for the film's original audiences.) Ike then blasts the glasses in front of Lance and Red Rock, shoots Lance's hat off, and wings his hand, foot, and shoulder. But the unarmed Lance stands calmly, counting bullets, and when the sixth shot has fired, he charges.

The fistfight that follows is one of the most brutal and non-romanticized examples of its kind in the history of the Western. There is no music, no Hollywood-style resonant punch sounds, no graceful choreography. The two men roll around in the dust, their punches land with sickeningly dull thuds, and

Broken Lance (Robert Taylor) near the end; little remains of Sgt. Major Lance Poole. *Devil's Doorway* **(MGM, 1950).**

the fight goes on and on, a battle of attrition. (The entire scene lasts five minutes, with the fight occupying about two, but it seems much longer.) The scene is disturbing on many levels, not only for the racism and injustice that ignites it but also from the primitive emotions that it evokes in the viewer. Perhaps the most troubling aspect of all is the almost lasciviously voyeuristic way in which the other bar patrons watch the fight, not uttering a sound. (The camera cuts to and lingers on the hungrily rapt faces of the onlookers six separate times during the scene.) We feel disgust at these men, then—in true Hitchcockian fashion—recognize ourselves in them, as we too respond viscerally to the violence on screen. Despite my pacific leanings, I truly wanted Lance to kill Ike in this scene; that's how powerfully it is handled, how masterfully it stirs our anger. These brutal, horrific five minutes are a masterpiece of cinematic craft. The next action scene is about twenty-five minutes away, which is fortunate, as the audience needs at least that long to recover.

Devil's Doorway is certainly grim, a darker and more pessimistic take on race relations than *Broken Arrow*, and yet I don't read it as ultimately despairing of the ability of the races to live together harmoniously. True, this particular tale doesn't end well for the indigenous people, but there are still glimmers of hope for the future: in the farsighted wisdom of the tribe; in the willingness of sympathetic whites like the lawyer Orrie (Paula Raymond), her mother (Spring Byington), and Zeke to despise, challenge, and overturn unjust laws; and in the striking reverence for the land that is so clearly present in members of both races. Even the villain Coolan waxes lyrical about the land, as quoted above. This is reflected more eloquently by Lance himself when he says to Orrie:

> It's hard to explain, how an Indian feels about the earth. It's the pumping of our blood, it's the love we've got to have. My father said the earth is our mother. I was raised in this valley. Now I'm part of it, like—like the mountains and the hills, the deer, the pine trees and the wind.

Reverence for the earth has the capacity to help bind us together, as do the other things we hold in common. The film consistently shows whites and Indians holding similar values, expressing themselves in similar ways. After all, as human beings we have vastly more commonalities than differences, and compassion is not limited to any one group of people. *Devil's Doorway* recognizes this. For example, the settlers who will eventually fight Lance for the Shoshone land are sympathetic characters. Their representative Rod MacDougall (Marshall Thompson) is essentially kind-hearted; he recognizes the legitimacy of Lance's claim, while also aware of the harsh reality that he and his colleagues will starve if they can't find land on which to raise their sheep. Rod's first instinct is to talk with Lance, to try and reach some sort of compromise. Significantly, we begin to realize that it is not the settlers who are the villains here, as narratively easy as that would have been. Instead, the evil arises primarily from two sources: unjust laws, and the greedy, inhumane scoundrels who seek only to profit by fomenting strife. The moral is clear, resonating authentically from the film's day down to our own: *make the laws just, and stop giving credence to those voices who seek only to get rich by stirring up hatred and setting us against one another.* This is every bit as important a lesson today as it was in 1950.

As bleak and tragic as it is on the surface, it seems to me that *Devil's Doorway*, deep down, is also about unrealized possibilities. This is symbolized most strongly in the closest thing the film has to a love scene. Lance and Orrie have grown fond of one another, and in the final standoff between Lance's Shoshone and the whites (including, ironically, the U.S. Cavalry whose uniform Lance once wore), Orrie is sent in to try to negotiate the peace by persuading Lance to surrender to the Federal troops and move his people to a reservation. She expresses her fears for the fate of the tribal women and children who will surely die if Lance continues to resist.

> ORRIE: Who are you to ordain who shall live and who won't?
> LANCE (*bitterly*): It's good to have advice. Just what I needed, especially now. Nothing an Indian needs like a speech from a lawyer telling him to give up! Well, now you've made it. Your conscience is clear.
> ORRIE (*directly*): It's much more than conscience, Lance—and it's more than the women and children.
> LANCE: If you're trying to say it's feeling for me, then I don't believe you. The color of my hide means just as much to you as it does to them out there. When you found out I could be lonely for a woman like any other man, you stayed on the safe side of the fence. How much does my life mean to you, Orrie? What would you give to see me live? (*He grabs her in a tight embrace.*) Would you let an Indian put his arms around you? Would your conscience say it's worth kissing me?

At this point Orrie's head is tilted upward, her lips an inch away from Lance's, waiting. But then Lance turns away. The kiss cannot happen—not in the 1860s, and not in America of 1950 either. *Broken Arrow* could have an interracial marriage, but there it was the man who was white, not the woman. Mid-century white filmgoers were not yet ready for the same scenario with the sexes reversed. The filmmakers knew this and used the film itself—and particularly this scene—to comment on this hypocrisy. "You better go back now," Lance says sadly. "What are you going to do?" Orrie asks. After a pause, Lance's voice hardens again. "Tell the Lieutenant he'll have to come and get us."

Five years before the Civil War, abolitionist poet John Greenleaf Whittier wrote: "For of all sad words of tongue or pen, / The saddest are these: 'It might have been!'"[2] Lance and Orrie embody the tragedy of what might have been, not only in their roles as potential lovers kept apart by their unenlightened time but also as metaphors for the races of humanity, continually thwarted from coming together in love and compassion by the forces of hatred, bigotry, and division.

A great man once said, "The arc of the moral universe is long, but it bends toward justice."[3] In *Devil's Doorway*, Lance anticipates a portion of this idea when, after the scene just described, he becomes tender with Orrie one last time, attempting to comfort her in the face of failure, defeat, and death. "Don't cry, Orrie," Lance says with a gentle smile. "A hundred years from now it might have worked."

The kiss that never happens: Orrie (Paula Raymond) and Lance (Robert Taylor). *Devil's Doorway* (MGM, 1950).

In post–Civil War Wyoming, it didn't work for Lance. But screenwriter Guy Trosper and the makers of *Devil's Doorway* expressed, through Lance's words, the hope that things might change in post–World War II America—as indeed they did, even if still incrementally, insufficiently, incompletely.

"*A hundred years from now....*" Prescient words. A hundred years, almost to the month, after the Battle of Gettysburg in which Lance fought (and fifteen years after *Devil's Doorway*), Dr. Martin Luther King, Jr., stood in front of the Lincoln Memorial and delivered the greatest American speech of the twentieth century in front of a quarter of a million people, calling us all to share in his revolutionary dream. We haven't reached the Promised Land yet, but on the scale of the arc of the moral universe, perhaps we can hope, like Lance, that it might still work one day.

Rawhide
(1951)

AKA: *Desperate Siege*
March 25, 1951 (USA)
USA—English
Twentieth Century–Fox
89m—Mono—BW—1.37:1

Direction: Henry Hathaway
Screenplay: Dudley Nichols
Principal Cast: Tyrone Power (Tom Owens), Susan Hayward (Vinnie Holt), Hugh Marlowe (Rafe Zimmerman), Dean Jagger (Yancy), Edgar Buchanan (Sam Todd), Jack Elam (Tevis), George Tobias (Gratz), Jeff Corey (Luke Davis), James Millican (Tex Squires), Louis Jean Heydt (Fickert)
Production: Samuel G. Engel
Cinematography: Milton R. Krasner
Editing: Robert L. Simpson
Art Direction: Lyle R. Wheeler, George W. Davis
Music: Sol Kaplan
Awards: Bambi Award—Best International Actor (Power, shared with *The Black Rose*)

When we think of myths and legends, we tend to picture the great, larger-than-life heroes and heroines who populate them: Achilles, Heracles, Odysseus, Atalanta, Beowulf, Brunhild, Launcelot, Robin Hood. These characters have human virtues expanded to a nearly superhuman degree: strength, intelligence, invincibility, speed, skill with arms, physical beauty. Many have been ordained by the gods themselves for greatness. Each, in a way, represents through archetype a human virtue distilled down to its essence and then magnified. This is why these myths, centered around impossibly accomplished superhumans, still speak to everyday people—because the heroes represent the potentialities of various aspects of the human spirit that we all possess, even if imperfectly. Inside the mildest, meekest office worker beats the heart of an Achilles; the ordinary flesh and garb of the shopkeeper may cover an Atalanta, or a Circe, or a Cassandra—perhaps even all three, and much more.

And yet there are also myths that, very specifically and intentionally, center on ordinary people with ordinary abilities who have been thrust into extraordinary situations. I think of Baucis and Philemon, a poor couple living in Phrygia who happened to be the only people in their village to offer food, drink, and lodging to two strangers—Zeus and Hermes in disguise. As a result, the gods blessed the couple, spared them from their divine wrath when they flooded the rest of the town, and later transformed them into an intertwining pair of trees when they died of old age. This myth celebrates the everyday virtue of hospitality, not any super-heroic deeds or abilities. Baucis and

318

Philemon do what any of us are capable of doing: they are kind. Because of this, they are immortalized. We need myths like this too, stories that celebrate what ordinary folk can accomplish through compassion, perseverance, or noble ideals. Most of us will never be a Hector or a Hippolyta, even if these archetypes still live in our souls, but any of us may face situations (without the divine or epic trappings) analogous to those that Baucis and Philemon faced, or Penelope, or Job, or Gawain against the Green Knight—situations that test our characters rather than our abilities.

Heroes of great natural (or supernatural) ability versus heroes of ordinary ability but great character: we see this dichotomy in our contemporary "myths" as well, sometimes even within the same story. Luke Skywalker is the gifted Jedi savant who must learn to develop his mystical powers further, whereas Han Solo has no superhuman skills—he must pass the test of character instead. Gandalf is a wizard of extraordinary wisdom and magical power, and Aragorn is a prophesied warrior-king, but the hobbits are just ordinary village folk, the furthest thing from "larger-than-life" both literally and figuratively, who must nevertheless show steadfast will and perseverance to get the job done. All the great bodies of mythic literature give us both of these types of heroes and heroines, as do many of the fantasies from modern popular culture—Tolkien, Le Guin, *Star Trek*, *Star Wars*, Neil Gaiman, and others. Perhaps this will help these contemporary myths to endure and survive, although stories without that humanizing balance may not be as fortunate. In fact, one of the (many) criticisms I would level against the current flood of comic-book movies is that they tend to celebrate only heroes with extraordinary gifts or abilities, while ignoring the other kind. One can certainly argue that comic-book superheroes are equivalents to the extraordinarily gifted figures from the Greek myths, but the difference is that the classical heroes, as mentioned above, have abilities that reflect aspects of the human psyche, whereas this is true less consistently in modern superheroes. It's not hard to see how strength, swiftness, cleverness, or skill at arms translate metaphorically into our own lives; but what in the world is supposed to be symbolized by shooting laser beams from one's eyes, or the ability to teleport, or a suite of futuristic technological gadgetry? What element of human psychology do retractable, unbreakable, razor-sharp claws represent, other than teenage wish-fulfillment fantasy?

As you might guess, my claim is that the dichotomy between superhuman and ordinary protagonists in myths and legends informs the hero-making of Western movies as well. On the one hand, for example, we have the preternaturally gifted gunfighters, whether drawn from actual history (Doc Holliday, Wild Bill), embellished from legend (Billy the Kid, "Jimmy" Ringo), or entirely fictional (Shane). These men must win through by virtue of their extraordinary abilities; they must literally outgun their opposition. But throughout its history the Western has also, quite consistently, presented the other type of hero (and heroine), the more ordinary, relatable one whose challenges are those of character and morality rather than skill. We have already encountered some of this type in these pages: Sally Cameron (Mae Marsh) in *The Battle of Elderbush Gulch* (1913); Jim Carston (Dustin Farnum) in *The Squaw Man* (1914); Will Banion (J. Warren Kerrigan) in *The Covered Wagon* (1923); Bob Sangster (Charles Bickford) in *Hell's Heroes* (1929); Mollie Monahan (Barbara Stanwyck) in *Union Pacific* (1939); Gil Carter (Henry Fonda) and Sparks (Leigh Whipper) in *The Ox-Bow Incident* (1942); Jeb Rand (Robert Mitchum) in *Pursued* (1947); Travis (Ben Johnson) and Sandy (Harry

Carey, Jr.) in *Wagon Master* (1950); and Tom Jeffords (James Stewart) in *Broken Arrow* (1950).

Of course—and problematically—there may always be found an abundance of "ordinary heroes" among the female love interests of the classic Westerns, even (or perhaps especially) in the movies that feature prodigiously skilled male protagonists. Wyatt Earp and Billy the Kid and Jimmy Ringo may be wizards of gunplay, but they are often accompanied and supported by reliable, faithful, persevering women who excel in character rather than capability. In such cases, the female is almost invariably overshadowed by the male; her role is a supporting one (in both senses), but her man is the star.

This is why Henry Hathaway's *Rawhide* (1951), another nearly forgotten movie today, marks such a refreshing moment in the history of the Western. It gives us a balanced pair of protagonists, female and male, simply regular people living regular lives who get swept up in a situation beyond their control and must do their best to carry on and survive despite their own fears, flaws, and errors. This may have been particularly relevant to the time in which the film was made, after a war effort in which so many "everyday" folks—farmers, schoolteachers, factory workers, accountants, nurses—were called upon to become heroes, and were now being called yet again for the next war. In addition to its engaging and relatable protagonists, *Rawhide* is also taut, gripping, and impeccably made, a true nail-biter that recalls some of the "Everyman" thrillers of Hitchcock and also anticipates the style of the gritty Boetticher/Scott "Ranown Cycle" Westerns of the later fifties, especially *The Tall T* (1957).

Tom Owens (Tyrone Power) is a young man who is learning his father's business—running the Rawhide stagecoach station along the mail route. The father is elsewhere, but the wise old stationmaster Sam (Edgar Buchanan) is around to give Tom some assistance. A stage arrives carrying several passengers, including an assertive and independent young woman named Vinnie Holt (Susan Hayward), traveling with a toddler whom we take at first to be her own child but who is actually the daughter of Vinnie's deceased sister. Eventually news arrives that four convicts have broken out of a nearby prison and robbed a stagecoach, and also that a major gold shipment is expected to be passing through the area, a likely target for the escaped criminals. Cavalrymen hustle the passengers away, escorting them to safety, but the rules of the mail company say that their stages are not allowed to carry children into

Rafe Zimmerman (Hugh Marlowe), leader of the criminals. "What kind of a man are you, Zimmerman?" Tom asks him. "Anybody can see that you're educated, that you've had a good background." "Do as you're told and nobody'll get hurt," Rafe replies curtly. *Rawhide* (Twentieth Century–Fox, 1951).

Jack Elam as the despicable Tevis. *Rawhide* (Twentieth Century–Fox, 1951).

dangerous situations. For this reason, Vinnie and her niece must remain overnight at the station house with Tom and Sam.

Soon a man showing a deputy sheriff's badge arrives, ostensibly in search of the fugitives, but he is actually their leader, Rafe Zimmerman (Hugh Marlowe), a clever and educated criminal. Rafe will soon be joined by his three fellow escapees: simple-minded and gentle-hearted Yancy (Dean Jagger); steady and reliable Gratz (George Tobias); and the worst of the lot, slimy and leering Tevis, played by up-and-coming character actor Jack Elam, who would go on to enjoy an illustrious five-decade career in Westerns playing both despicable villains and lovably crusty sidekicks. Tevis and Gratz soon gun down old Sam as he makes a desperate attempt to flee, then drag the old man's corpse unceremoniously through the dirt in a scene that would be fully at home in the Silver Age anti–Westerns of the following decade.

Rafe assumes, incorrectly, that Tom and Vinnie are a married couple with their only child, but he needs Tom alive and cooperative (for now) in order to meet the evening stage without raising suspicions that would prevent the gold-laden transport from arriving, ripe for the plucking, the following day. At this point the movie becomes a tense hostage drama, with Tom and Vinnie struggling just to stay alive and protect the young child while imprisoned in the station house.

There is so much to like about *Rawhide*. It plays like a Western crossed with *noir* crossed with Hitchcock, a psychological and suspenseful slow burn with a satisfying payoff. None of the characters, not even the villains, are cardboard cutouts. Rafe is very compelling, both loathsome and perversely likeable—a direct forerunner of the fantastic charismatic villain played by Richard Boone in *The Tall T*—and he is matched in intensity by the freakishly monstrous Tevis, who clearly longs to force himself on Vinnie and at one point fires shots from a distance at the crying toddler. Like in a Hitchcock film, we are both horrified by the villains and attracted to them; we want their plan to fail, but perversely, we don't want that to happen too soon. Why do I feel relieved when Rafe's true identity isn't discovered by the passengers on the first stagecoach to pass through? One of them almost recognizes him, and I feel the same sense of suspense on his behalf that I do when, on the other side, Tom drops his hastily scrawled rescue note in the dirt and it is almost discovered by one of the villains. *Dial M for Murder* (1954) was still three years away; I can't help but wonder if Alfred Hitchcock ever saw *Rawhide*.

One of the best parts of the movie is the interaction of the two lead characters. Tom and Vinnie don't know each other at all in the beginning, and in fact when they do meet, they don't seem to like each other very much. She is brash and slightly abrasive, paying him scant attention; he is just an unremarkable stagecoach station employee in her eyes. Events throw them together, however, and they must learn to rely on each other and on their own imperfect resourcefulness. Since Rafe needs Tom's cooperation, the two hostages agree to pose as the husband and wife Rafe takes them to be, to better protect Vinnie and the child. At this point in the narrative, we may be bracing ourselves for the inevitable Hollywood romantic clichés to come a-rolling—but in fact they never do. This may or may not be the dawning of a romantic relationship, but that is not a particular concern of the movie or its two lead characters, who are simply struggling, realistically, to stay alive. The interest here is not in Tom and Vinnie as a potential couple, but rather as two individuals we grow to care about as they work together to survive a terrifying situation.

All the assumptions we've inherited from the Western tradition—especially the gender-based ones—are thrown out the window in *Rawhide*. Tom is no fearless, masterful hero, and Vinnie is neither a meekly supporting helpmate nor a shrew. When the time comes, it won't be Tom who single-handedly saves the day while Vinnie waits to rush into his arms. These are two real people who will work as equal partners to escape their desperate situation, and over the course of the movie the pair will move (in our eyes) from being a nondescript milquetoast and a hard-edged frontier girl to two people we genuinely like and with whom we want to spend more time. In order to get there, Tom doesn't have to learn to stand tall and become a John Wayne (or an Achilles); nor does Vinnie need to soften up or learn "the error of her ways" from Tom. They are who they are, and that's exactly what they need to be.

It's hard to describe, but one of the most delightful things about these two characters, what truly endears them to me, is that they continually make mistakes, miss opportunities, botch their plans—and yet there are no recriminations between them. Once trouble starts, they are a team. Like real people in such a situation, they don't execute a flawless plan. They stumble and improvise and do the best they can, both frightened but always supporting each other and working together. The filmmakers could have added to the emotional intensity of these scenes by having the two characters start to snap at one another—"How could you lose that note?"; "Why did you force that knife into the rock so hard it got stuck?"—but this would have dampened our growing affection for both of them and lessened our emotional investment in their plight. The movie resists the easy temptation of cheap manipulation in favor of something more subtle and humanistic, and as a result, perhaps paradoxically, adds far more emotional power to the drama than would have ever been possible the other, easier way. Another lesson for today's filmmakers.

In a 2000 essay, William Goldman tells the story of the time he was chatting with a retired New York City firefighter and asked him about the greatest and most heroic colleague he had ever known—the "Willie Mays of firemen," as Goldman put it. The old veteran

"Ordinary" heroes Tom (Tyrone Power) and Vinnie (Susan Hayward) pool their efforts in a desperate struggle to survive. *Rawhide* (Twentieth Century–Fox, 1951).

thought for a bit, then recalled a time that he and a partner were getting out of a burning building that was about to collapse, when the other man suddenly thought he heard the cry of a baby from inside. The partner charged back into the building, kicking through several doors while shielding himself from the blaze with another door he had kicked off its hinges, finally to find and rescue the infant girl who was trapped inside. "Bravest thing I ever saw," recalled the old man. In his essay, Goldman heartily agrees, but then (using references appropriate to the time) drops his bombshell, which he describes as "among the saddest and most important things" he had to learn as a Hollywood screenwriter:

> That incredible act of heroism the Willie Mays of firemen did? That is what Sylvester Stallone does in an action picture before the opening credits start to roll. That is what Arnold Schwarzenegger does in an action picture before breakfast. That is what Harrison Ford and Mel Gibson do in their action pictures before they've brushed their teeth![1]

The movies have so overinflated our understanding of what constitutes a heroic act that the bravest real-life feat a veteran urban firefighter ever saw over a decades-long career isn't enough to qualify for even the first act of one of today's action pictures or comic-book blockbusters. The popcorn-flick "arms race" of spectacle has led us to a point which is unsustainable; our heroes now have to perform acts so ridiculously unrealistic that they have absolutely zero chance of ever happening in the real world, simply to hold our attention and keep us hanging on until the next action sequence.

What a breath of fresh air it is, then, to encounter a rare picture like *Rawhide*, one that features real and believable people facing difficult situations imperfectly, with fear and vulnerability, and in a human rather than a superhuman way. This brings the significance of the drama back home where it belongs, inside of us. We can populate our movies with characters who shoot laser beams from their eyes or walk through walls if we wish; but we can also fill them with characters that resemble the people we actually know, even people we have a chance of being, or becoming. This is mythic too; for as Joseph Campbell reminds us, "The latest incarnation of Oedipus, the continued romance of Beauty and the Beast, stand this afternoon on the corner of Forty-second Street and Fifth Avenue, waiting for the light to change."[2]

Along the Great Divide
(1951)

May 16, 1951 (New York City)
USA—English / Spanish
Warner Bros.
88m—Mono—BW—1.37:1

Direction: Raoul Walsh
Screenplay: Walter Doniger (story and screenplay), Lewis Meltzer (screenplay)
Principal Cast: Kirk Douglas (Marshal Len Merrick), Virginia Mayo (Ann Keith), John Agar (Billy Shear), Walter Brennan (Timothy "Pop" Keith), Ray Teal (Deputy Lou Gray), Hugh Sanders (Frank Newcombe), Morris Ankrum (Ed Roden), James Anderson (Dan Roden), Charles Meredith (Judge Marlowe)
Production: Anthony Veiller
Cinematography: Sidney Hickox
Editing: Thomas Reilly
Art Direction: Edward Carrere
Music: David Buttolph

When Kirk Douglas, fresh from his triumph as the amoral boxer in *Champion* (1950), was slated to make his first Western, he was reportedly less than thrilled,[1] yet he delivered a powerful performance as haunted peace officer Len Merrick in Raoul Walsh's *Along the Great Divide* (1951) and began a long and fruitful relationship with the genre. Douglas would go on to star in seven more Westerns over the next decade (seventeen more over the course of his career), while also creating classic roles in great films like *Lust for Life* (1956), *Paths of Glory* (1957), and *Spartacus* (1960).

Along the Great Divide is one of a number of Western stories from the fifties, both in feature films and on the small screen, that present a group of people escorting a prisoner to justice over the course of a long and difficult journey while facing ethical dilemmas and interpersonal conflicts along the way.[2] In each case, the protagonist must hold true to his mission and resist numerous temptations (including pressure from others less strong-willed than he is) to take the easy way out. Although I have no proof of this, I cannot help but wonder if this new thematic focus stemmed in part from America's experiences during and after the Second World War, still fresh in the national memory. In many ways, the Allied victory over the Axis had been a matter of endurance—having the will as a united group of nations, civilians, and (most of all) combatants to grind it out, slowly and steadfastly, day after day, year after year, in order to attain victory. Hitler began actively losing the war as early as 1941 with his invasion of the Soviet Union, and this was augmented by the entry of the United States into the war less than six months later, yet the Allies still had to see it through to the bitter end, resisting the temptation to take the superficially easier path of half-measures and mediocre commitment. This lesson certainly wasn't lost on postwar America, especially as it soon faced the invasion of South Korea by North Korea, an intensifying Cold War with the Soviet Union, and domestic issues around civil rights, labor, and the economy. All of these, as in the struggle against the Axis, were long-term challenges that suggested, in various ways, the need for patience, perseverance, and a commitment to ideals. History

"An obsession with the law": Kirk Douglas as Marshal Len Merrick. *Along the Great Divide* (Warner Bros., 1951).

can judge how well the United States actually responded to these crises, but certainly the desire of the writers of the time to celebrate the virtues of grit and steadfastness is understandable.

The best of the "prisoner's journey" Westerns is the Mann/Stewart vehicle *The Naked Spur* (1953), but *Along the Great Divide* is a worthy runner-up. The film's already interesting material (though presented with jarringly awkward editing at times) is elevated dramatically by powerful acting, most especially from Douglas in the lead role of Merrick. At first, his character seems to be the stereotypical hard-as-nails lawman, a John Wayne–style iconic tough guy, but as the movie proceeds, we begin to see signs of Merrick's relatable humanity—his pain, his vulnerability, his fallibility. The marshal starts the film as a larger-than-life cipher, but he ends it as one of us. It's a terrific performance from Douglas, supported wonderfully by Walter Brennan as the sly but charismatic prisoner Pop Keith and Virginia Mayo as Pop's cynical daughter.

The first thing we notice about Merrick himself is his obsessive devotion to the law. In his opening scene, he prevents the lynching of his eventual prisoner by the old rancher Ed Roden (Morris Ankrum), who is convinced that Pop murdered his son. Merrick won't let the summary execution happen; he and his men face down Roden, his surviving son Dan (James Anderson), and the other ranch hands.

> RODEN: Who are you?
> MERRICK: My name's Merrick. I'm United States Marshal here.
> DAN (*dismissively*): You're new in the territory.
> MERRICK (*smiling with mock sweetness*): The law isn't.
> DAN: We're the law!
> RODEN (*pointing*): This man's a killer! He killed my son.
> MERRICK: Then he'll hang by *government* rope.

Merrick is so devoted to the principles of due process that, in this confrontation, he offers up his own life in sacrifice for it. Douglas himself recognized this almost fanatical determination as one of the keys to his character and to the drama, as we see from the script notes that he wrote and sent along to Warner Brothers prior to filming:

> To dramatize Merrick's inner conflict, to achieve the point of this story, Merrick *must* go to the other extreme before he is straightened out. His determination to deliver his prisoner must be *more* than that of a good law officer. It must be an *obsession*—an obsession with the law, manifested by absolute *refusal* on his part to concern himself in any way prior to the start of his transformation, with guilt *or* innocence, in other words, *justice*.[3]

These are the words of an actor who is attacking head-on the challenge of how to inhabit his character to most effectively serve the drama. How many other Western stars of the day—or Hollywood stars in general—were digging so deeply and intelligently into their roles? Douglas delivers on this thoughtful analysis consistently throughout the film; we truly feel it when Pop asks Merrick if he thinks he is truly a murderer, and Merrick responds, "I don't think about it, one way or the other." What matters to Merrick is not Pop's guilt or innocence; the marshal's religion is the law and its proper application.

Even though the West, as depicted here, is far wilder and more anarchic than 1950s America, in the film's view the best lawmen are still the ones who stand rigorously behind the law and leave the administration of justice to the courts. This is distant indeed from what portrayals of officers would later become in Hollywood films, from *Dirty Harry* (1971) to the present day, in which cop protagonists are typically loose cannons prepared and encouraged to act as judge, jury, and executioner. At this writing, police violence against American citizens—especially people of color—is at the forefront of the nation's consciousness, and one cannot help but wonder to what degree modern Hollywood's constant and irresponsible portrayal of police officers as one-man murder machines has warped both public and police understandings of what their proper role should be, and contributed to the problem now crying out (and being decried) so dramatically on our nation's streets.

As I mentioned, Merrick's character—or at least our understanding of it—is not static. We see him first just as a hard-driven marshal with a difficult job to do, but as the film progresses, his inner pain and vulnerability start to reveal themselves. This gradual shift in tone is echoed by the structure of the movie itself, which comes in like an action picture but gradually morphs into a very Freudian psychological Western, closer to the feel of director Walsh's earlier *Pursued* (1947). Merrick, we

Merrick (Kirk Douglas) has his weaknesses probed by his enigmatic prisoner Pop Keith (Walter Brennan). *Along the Great Divide* (Warner Bros., 1951).

begin to realize, is not only addressing himself to the problem at hand but also working out a past family trauma in his own life. The trek along the great divide, already symbolizing the virtue of sustained ethical commitment on a cultural level, also becomes an exterior metaphor for Merrick's inner journey from pain to redemption.

This is the advantage of featuring characters with realistic flaws and weaknesses as the heroes of movies: it can speak directly to all of us in a true, honest, and human way. Who among us has not had their own trek along the great divide to undergo, tempted and challenged constantly by the voices of others to take a simpler, easier, less ethically committed, more self-centered path? When we watch Merrick struggling with his own demons—and Douglas projecting an almost childlike fear and vulnerability—we see ourselves in this character, in a way that we will never be able to with the one-dimensional wish-fulfillment heroes that gradually began to take over Hollywood a few decades ago and that have gained almost complete ascendancy in the new millennium. These plastic fashion-plate characters are an insult to our intelligence; even their supposed "flaws," sprinkled on top in a desperate attempt to make them more than cardboard cutouts, are market-tested sexy ones—nothing so icky or unattractive as actual human fear, weakness, or indecision.

This lamentable sea change, unfortunately, was already underway in Hollywood at the time of *Along the Great Divide*. Even just four years after this movie's release, the great film critic Pauline Kael observed, when comparing typical American movies with European ones:

> The creation of a simple hero is a problem that doesn't come up often in European films, where the effort is to create characters who move us by their humanity—their weaknesses, their wisdom, their complexity—rather than by their heroic dimensions. Our films, however, deny the human weaknesses and complexities that Europeans insist upon. It's as if we refused to accept the human condition: we don't want to see the image of ourselves in those cheats and cuckolds and cowards. We want heroes, and Hollywood produces them by simple fiat.... Real heroism is too dangerous a subject for Hollywood—for there is no heroism without failure risked or faced, and failure, which is at the heart of drama, is an unpopular subject in America.[4]

Kael was certainly no knee-jerk, Eurocentric, high-culture snob when it came to evaluating movies—as her famous (and delightfully titled) essay "The Come-Dressed-As-the-Sick-Soul-of-Europe Parties" demonstrates—but she was very cognizant of the dramatic power that multi-dimensional and imperfect protagonists could bring to a movie, and the degree to which such human heroes were rapidly disappearing from American filmmaking.

But flawed heroes aren't relevant only because we as ordinary people (and audiences for the films) are flawed too; they are relevant because *heroes* in real life are imperfect, a lesson that we seem to have forgotten today, both in our moviemaking and in our disillusionment with past historical figures who do not live up to our standards of purity. (May we not be judged as harshly by history as we currently judge our forerunners!) And yet there is another, perhaps more profound reason why imperfect protagonists resonate with us, one that shines through in Kael's observation but that was also realized beautifully by the great German writer Thomas Mann a half century earlier—the principle of *erotic irony*.

In recent years I have taken to posting, on the inside of my office door, a collage of the faces of people throughout history that I take to be my personal heroes, the people who, as I describe it to myself, have left something behind that has made my life better. Since my door is usually open when I meet with students and colleagues, this little homemade poster is typically something that only I see; it's not meant for anyone else, but just serves as a source of momentary inspiration for me when I start to feel despondent or hopeless or overwhelmed. It reminds me what even fallible people like myself have managed to accomplish in the past. It also reminds me that every single one of us has a hero inside, waiting to be born.

The collage started small, a single sheet of paper with printed images of some of my personal heroes, but then I kept adding to the list: more and more people from the last three millennia, spanning ethnicities and nationalities and religions and genders—musicians, scientists, writers, artists, medical workers, philosophers, poets, playwrights, dancers, comics, filmmakers, public servants, agents of social change, and on and on. Now I am up to several pages splattered across my door: nearly three hundred faces, and still growing. The biographies of some of these people, especially from the ancient world, are cloudy at best, but for most, we actually know a great deal about them—they are historical figures whose lives and actions and beliefs are relatively well documented. As I peruse them now, I am struck by the one thing which all of these individuals—from such disparate backgrounds, eras, places, and identities—hold in common: they are imperfect. They have feet of clay, every single one. In that sense, they are just like the rest of us.

This is the great truth that is reinforced every time we encounter a Len Merrick, or a Sethe, or a Holden Caulfield, or an Emma Woodhouse, or a Parzival. We need protagonists that reflect our own flawed humanity back at us, not only because true heroes are flawed just like us, or because we all are heroic in our own way, but because of an even deeper truth underlying all of this: that our imperfect humanity is itself heroic, and serves as the ultimate source of both our inspiration and our redemption. This is the erotic irony that Thomas Mann celebrated, the fact that people are lovable not in spite of their defects but because of them. As the character Tonio Kröger writes in Mann's 1903 novella of the same name:

> I admire those proud, cold beings who adventure upon the paths of great and dæmonic beauty and despise "mankind"; but I do not envy them. For if anything is capable of making a poet of a literary man, it is my *bourgeois* love of the human, the living and usual. It is the source of all warmth, goodness, and humour.[5]

Joseph Campbell describes Mann's erotic irony in a somewhat different way, one that throws light on the mythic value of characters like Len Merrick—but may also have something broader to say about puritanical sanctimony and judgmentalism in our own era:

> [Erotic irony] is the posture of an artist not afraid to see what is before him in its truth, its frailty, its inadequacy to the ideal, and whose heart then goes out to it in affirmation of this frailty, as of its life. For it is according to its imperfection that each existence moves, acts, and becomes, perfection being not of this earth. Consequently, it is in naming its imperfection that the artist gives to each its life, its possibility.[6]

If only today's Hollywood—and today's America—had ears to hear.

Bend of the River
(1952)

AKA: *Where the River Bends*
January 23, 1952 (Portland, Oregon)
USA—English
Universal International Pictures
91m—Mono—Technicolor—1.37:1

Direction: Anthony Mann
Screenplay: Borden Chase, William Gulick (novel *Bend of the Snake*)
Principal Cast: James Stewart (Glyn McLyntock), Arthur Kennedy (Emerson Cole), Julie
  Adams (Laura Baile), Rock Hudson (Trey Wilson), Lori Nelson (Marjie Baile), Jay C.
  Flippen (Jeremy Baile), Chubby Johnson (Cap'n Mello), Harry Morgan (Shorty), Royal
  Dano (Long Tom), Frances Bavier (Mrs. Prentiss), Howard Petrie (Tom Hendricks),
  Stepin Fetchit (Adam)
Production: Aaron Rosenberg
Cinematography: Irving Glassberg
Editing: Russell F. Schoengarth
Art Direction: Bernard Herzbrun, Nathan Juran
Music: Hans J. Salter

As readers may have noticed throughout this book, there are some words—like Art
and Beauty—that I find it very difficult not to capitalize, even though technically they
are not proper nouns. My guess is that this impulse on my part is similar to that of a
devout Christian who uses He and Him and His in connection with Jesus—the capi-
talization is an indication of the spiritual reverence that one feels toward the subject.
Another word that has that effect on me is Nature.

Nature, of course, is a powerful player in many Western narratives, both as a plot
element and as a metaphor. In the classic Western, Nature provides a mythic backdrop,
an appropriately grand stage on which the action can unfold. Nature throws up obstacles that our heroes must overcome—dangerous river crossings, avalanches and sandstorms, treacherous mountain passes, parched deserts—but also bestows its boons at
the end—lush green valleys, crystal clear lakes, and the fruits of the fertile soil. Nature
is the space in which the Western journey, outer and inner, takes place; but more than
that, the natural world is also an active space, one which facilitates and participates in
the hero's arc.

In the beginning, Western feature films were often centered around a journey of
some sort, as we have seen: westward settlement under the doctrine of Manifest Destiny in *The Battle of Elderbush Gulch* (1913), *The Covered Wagon* (1923), *The Iron Horse*
(1924), *The Big Trail* (1930), *Union Pacific* (1939), and *Wagon Master* (1950); rushes for

land or gold in *Tumbleweeds* (1925), *Cimarron* (1931), and *The Treasure of the Sierra Madre* (1948); cattle drives in *Red River* (1948) and its many imitators; or individual journeys with more personal objectives, such as those undertaken by Jim Carston in *The Squaw Man* (1914), the three outlaws in *Hell's Heroes* (1929), Ruggles in *Ruggles of Red Gap* (1935), the travelers to Lordsburg in *Stagecoach* (1939), and Lin McAdam in *Winchester '73* (1950).

The pilgrims in these movies found perils along the way, both internal and external—and of the latter type, "Indians" were the most frequently appearing threat to the protagonists in the earlier Westerns. As time went on, however, vilifying Native Americans on screen was increasingly recognized as wrong, especially after the Second World War. Western filmmakers rightly sought ways to steer the genre away from this damaging practice. Some, in pictures like *Broken Arrow* (1950) and *Devil's Doorway* (1950), sought to tackle the problem of the treatment of indigenous peoples head-on. Others made Westerns that were more stationary, fixing the main action of the drama in one place, often the town or the ranch, with Native Americans absent or playing only minor roles in the narrative: see, for example, *My Darling Clementine* (1946), *Duel in the Sun* (1946), *Yellow Sky* (1948), *The Gunfighter* (1950), and *Rawhide* (1951).

Still others, however, were not willing to let go of the powerful metaphor of the journey, and so resuscitated it in ways more acceptable to the changing mores of the postwar era (and to our own sensibilities as well). We have already seen this in *Along the Great Divide* (1951), for example, and it would be a common device throughout the fifties and beyond. This is not to suggest that these movies were suddenly ethically blameless in their treatment of Native Americans; many of the plots, especially in the early fifties, still featured Indians as occasional antagonists, as the changes wrought by *Broken Arrow* and *Devil's Doorway* took time to be incorporated into the mainstream. Nevertheless, in prestige Westerns at least, the days of creating easy and disposable villains just by slapping Hollywood's version of war paint onto white actors and turning them loose were gradually, and mercifully, drawing to a close. Audiences just couldn't buy it anymore.

So what did filmmakers do if they still wanted to take advantage of the kinetic, scenic, and metaphoric possibilities of the Western trek in their dramas, while avoiding using Indians as (at least primary) antagonists? One obvious solution was to set their protagonists against white villains roaming the frontier; sometimes these were just enemies encountered along the way, while at other times they were demons from the hero's past, generating the "vendetta" or "vengeance-quest" Western. (This sub-genre would soon come fully into its own in the Silver Age.) A second solution, often accompanying the first, was to pit the heroes against the challenges of the natural world as they traversed the wilderness; and a third option was to make the journey as much an interior one as an exterior one, as we have just seen demonstrated in *Along the Great Divide*.

All three of these approaches come together harmoniously in the second of the great Western collaborations between director Anthony Mann and actor James Stewart: 1952's *Bend of the River*. Here, Nature rises to the forefront; not only does its splendor burst forth from the screen magnificently, but it is also woven tightly into the story, serving narrative, emotional, psychological, and metaphorical functions. Never in a Western have the developments of the plot and the inner states of the characters been more intimately connected with and reflected by the external world than they are in *Bend of the River*. As a result, the Hero's Trail as a metaphor has now been resurrected and concretized in an unprecedented way.

The story setup of *Bend of the River* is simple. Glyn McLyntock (Stewart) is the quintessential "man with a past," a onetime Missouri border raider who is trying to reform. His current work is escorting a small wagon train of settlers, led by Jeremy Baile (Jay C. Flippen), to their new home in the Oregon Territory. McLyntock is well liked by the pilgrims, and likes them in return, especially Baile's daughters Laura (Julie Adams) and precocious Marjie (Lori Nelson), whom he affectionately calls "funny face." Old Baile

Glyn McLyntock (James Stewart) happens upon a lynching. The scarf around his neck is significant. *Bend of the River* (Universal International, 1952).

is a very upright man, kind and attached to his daughters, if prone to moralizing. The patriarch believes in the straight and narrow, and is of the opinion, expressed vocally many times, that once a man strays from the righteous path he will not return. Baile, of course, does not know about McLyntock's own checkered past, and McLyntock is in no hurry to tell him.

The action opens with the settlers far along the trail, already in Oregon and in sight of the actual Mount Hood, rising majestically before them. Their goal is to get to Portland, purchase supplies for the settlement, and then make their way upriver to the Promised Land. One day, McLyntock is riding through the lush, green country scouting when he stops short. Suddenly, the camera does a startling swish-pan to a close-up of Emerson Cole (Arthur Kennedy) with a rope around his neck, about to be lynched by a small group of vigilantes. McLyntock nervously, and significantly, tugs at his own bandanna; this moment provides us with the whole core of the plot, entirely visually, in a matter of mere seconds, although we may not realize it until later. McLyntock rescues Cole and drives off the vigilantes, and then the two men ride to the camp, already becoming friends. Soon we discover that Cole is also a former border raider; it turns out that each man knows the other very well by reputation. However, Cole strikes us as just a shade more cynical, a shade less reformed than McLyntock is. The men are clearly two sides of the same coin, only a few whiskers apart morally. This makes the drama work: we can believe the pair both as friends and as enemies, and we see them as both. We also like them both.

I should stop for a moment to observe that the performances of the two lead actors are spectacular in this movie. Stewart is wonderful as always, although the most fascinating character is Cole, played brilliantly by Kennedy. Emerson Cole is in fact one of the most memorable antagonists in the history of the Western. Yes, technically he is the villain of the piece, but he is incredibly charismatic, a foreshadowing of later indelible characters like Burt Lancaster's villain in *Vera Cruz* (1954) or Richard Boone's in *The*

"I never pick the same star": Laura Baile (Julie Adams) listens, charmed, as Emerson Cole (Arthur Kennedy) describes his own moral compass. *Bend of the River* (Universal International, 1952).

Tall T (1957)—and, it must be noted, no worse than the amoral drifters that would later become the *protagonists* of Westerns during the coming subversive Silver Age.

After his rescue, the grateful Cole decides to ride along with the wagons for a while. He meets and charms the lovely Laura (to McLyntock's dismay), and then everyone prepares to bed down for the night. At this point the metaphorical significance of the natural world is made explicit when McLyntock reorients the tongue of the Baile wagon and advises Laura, "Always point this toward the North Star…. Then, come morning, we'll know where we're going." It's clear that this represents McLyntock's own moral compass, not just a geographical one. Laura immediately turns to Cole and asks, "Is that the way you travel?" "Always," Cole answers. "But I never pick the same star."

Soon afterward, we gasp in shock as an arrow suddenly whistles through the air and pierces Laura's breast, once again echoing the phallic rape motif previously seen in *The Covered Wagon* (1923) and *Red River* (1948). As it turns out, there are only a handful of natives hidden in the surrounding woods, so McLyntock and Cole venture out into the night and dispatch the attackers one by one. This is the only significant appearance of Indians in the film, a holdover from pre–*Broken Arrow* days. Since it is jarring to the modern viewer to see Native Americans treated once again as faceless antagonists, even in only one short sequence, it is worth asking what purpose this bit serves. My answer is fourfold: narratively, it requires that Laura will now have to recuperate in Portland once she arrives there, which becomes significant to the plot; emotionally, it invests us deeper in the friendship between McLyntock and Cole, as the two work bravely together and save each other's lives in the process; psychologically, it allows the shadowy, dimly seen Indian assailants to represent the demons that lie dormant in the inner lives of the two men, waiting to spring forth unexpectedly at any time—or remain hidden; and metaphorically, it binds both men to the natural world, as they crawl along the earth and through the underbrush, ease through streams on their bellies, crouch behind fallen trees, and imitate bird calls. Even though it is nighttime, the vibrant green of the foliage pops out in Technicolor, and the excellent musical score by Hans J. Salter (who studied under Alban Berg in Vienna, among others) is an unexpected highlight here: despite the danger of the situation, Salter's music alternates more traditionally tense, dissonant passages with serene, timbre-centered phrases featuring open major harmonies and luscious added seconds and sixths, reminiscent of the Nature evocations of Wagner or Mahler or Debussy. It's a strange choice, and yet it works so well. Once more we find ourselves in thrall to Nature, even in the middle of an action scene. Nevertheless, to our modern eyes the battle with the Indians is troubling, especially just two years after Stewart's own *Broken Arrow*. Surely there could have been other devices that would have achieved these ends. The sequence remains one of the few false notes in an otherwise masterful movie. (Others include the trite, platitude-spewing Baile and—most especially—the cringe-inducing walking stereotype of the buffoonish captain's assistant Adam, played by vaudeville veteran Stepin Fetchit, whose anachronistic minstrel-show persona was rapidly losing its appeal for audiences of the time.)

As the travelers near their destination, Baile comments on the quality of the land itself to McLyntock. "Let's hope we can keep it this way. Missouri and Kansas was like this when I first saw 'em. Good, clean. It was the men who came in to steal and kill that changed things. We mustn't let it happen here." This is yet another role that Nature will play in this drama: a proving ground for human character. However, it is worth observing that Nature is never an enemy in *Bend of the River*. It tests, hones, refines human souls through its obstacles—and the journey of the pioneers is certainly never an easy one. Nevertheless, unlike many other Westerns immersed in the natural world, there are no storms or stampedes or rockslides or floods or droughts; ultimately Nature is an ally to the pilgrims, providing just the right amount of challenge to build character but also buoying their spirits, presumably, by the sheer grandeur and beauty of the surroundings. (The hardships of the journey also claim no lives—a far cry from the brutal reality of westward migration in the nineteenth century.)

There are two main things that the characters in *Bend of the River* hope to take from the earth: food and gold. This is where the movie places an ethical dividing line. The noble settlers are seeking a place to farm, a piece of land to cultivate. The prospectors, on the other hand, are there for another purpose altogether, and their effect is devastating. Portland becomes a completely different place between the two times that McLyntock visits it, and the difference is made by the advent of the gold rush and the multitudes of greedy opportunists who come along with it.

Of course, the movie is in no way about farming vs. prospecting; that perspective accounts for neither the passion of the narrative or the impact that it has. The power of the contrast between the bounties of the earth here is a metaphorical one. The earth—Nature—is also a human life, and in the film's view, what matters is what you hope, primarily, to take from life: material riches (gold) or spiritual nourishment (crops).

This leads us to the title metaphor of the river itself. Rivers of course can represent a number of things: the flow of life; the passage of time; sustenance; cleansing; renewal; fertility; and the boundary between one (metaphorical) realm or state and another. We speak of "swimming upstream" in our lives; people who have died are said to have "crossed over" to the other side; Christians are baptized in the river, and of course the Bible speaks of justice rolling like a river, righteousness like a mighty stream. What all these have in common is *change*. Heraclitus knew the power of this metaphor twenty-five hundred years ago when he observed that one can never step into the same river twice. Even a second later, it is different water washing over your feet. And this is the thematic centerpiece of *Bend of the River* as well: change, flux, metamorphosis. Old Jeremy Baile expresses his anti–Heraclitean philosophy clearly to McLyntock when he says, about Cole, "His kind never change!" But McLyntock replies, with feeling, "I hope you're wrong, Jeremy. I sure hope you're wrong." And it's not Cole he's thinking about.

Even though the film sets up McLyntock and Cole as two men cut from the same cloth, with only a little bit of daylight between them, the filmmakers still manage to fit another character into that tiny interstitial space: the gambler Trey Wilson, played by a young Rock Hudson shortly before his rise from supporting player to leading man. And how do the makers of *Bend of the River* split that difference? By making Wilson amoral rather than immoral. McLyntock is a tough customer who is faced with the

McLyntock (James Stewart), Wilson (Rock Hudson), and Cole (Arthur Kennedy)—a visual moral spectrum. *Bend of the River* (Universal International, 1952).

choice between self-giving and self-interest, and purposefully leans toward the former. Cole sees the same options and favors the latter. Wilson isn't even aware that he has the choice; he moves primarily out of self-interest, like Cole, but only because he's never really given the matter any thought. He simply doesn't know that there is another alternative.

All this is illustrated vividly through one of the film's most artful visual metaphors, in a nighttime scene where the settlers are being pursued by the villainous Hendricks (Howard Petrie) and his henchmen. McLyntock, Cole, and Wilson, knowing that the attack is coming, purposefully send the wagons into a box canyon, then perch in the surrounding high ground and prepare to surprise their own pursuers. Their ruse works, and they begin to rain death down upon the attackers, firing repeatedly at them until the survivors turn tail and retreat. Cole and Wilson continue to shoot at the fleeing men, but McLyntock yells, "All right, they've had it, let 'em go!" Still Cole keeps firing, a sadistic grin on his face. "Why?" he shouts defiantly. Wilson stops shooting, turns to McLyntock, and echoes Cole—"Why?"—but he is not defiant, just genuinely puzzled. "Well, if you don't know, I can't tell you," says McLyntock resignedly, and at this moment we realize that we are seeing a literal moral spectrum manifested before our eyes: McLyntock on one side, Cole on the other, and Wilson—of course—in the middle.

Despite Wilson's mediation, the two main characters separated by a hair's breadth—the two men who are really just opposite poles of the forceful human spirit, the noble side and the shadow—must inevitably come into deadly conflict. We know this from the very beginning. More importantly, though, the filmmakers know that we know, and so they continue to set us up. Time and again, McLyntock and Cole find themselves on potentially opposite sides of a situation, with McLyntock in peril. Each time, Cole stands on a razor's edge. Which way will he fall? Will he support his friend or take the selfish way out? One of the most thrilling of these scenes occurs in the big Portland gambling house and saloon where McLyntock first confronts the crooked Hendricks. (This is prior to the attack described above.) Hendricks is trying to cheat the desperate settlers out of the supplies that they have bought and paid for, and which they will need to survive. It is an awkward situation, because at this point Cole and his now-girlfriend Laura are working for Hendricks, so we wait for Cole to finally line up against McLyntock. Instead, Cole tosses his friend a gun and the two men fight their way out, soon joined by Wilson. It's one of the most elating spectacles in a movie full of them, and this keeps happening: more and more situations arise that have the potential to tempt Cole away from McLyntock, and every single time Cole defies our expectations and stands steadfastly beside his friend—until, finally, he doesn't.

The fatal moment happens in a setting brimming with natural/metaphorical implications—how else? It is in a high, snowy mountain pass, the last obstacle facing McLyntock as he, Baile, Laura, Cole, Wilson, and some untrustworthy lowlifes collected along the way bring provisions back to the desperate settlers. The farmers need the supplies to survive, but the party encounters a group of miners who—anxious not to abandon their claim and vast riches by returning to Portland for food—offer to pay McLyntock's party a hundred thousand dollars for the contents of their wagons. Cole smiles and says, casually, "Hey, that's a lot of money." "Yeah," McLyntock replies warily. "That's a lot of money." The miners are sent away, and once more Cole comes to his friend's aid when the lowlifes rebel. He doesn't want to see McLyntock hurt—but Cole's observation still hangs out there, unresolved. *That's a lot of money.* The trail forks. One path, the more

Light and shadow allied, at least for the moment: McLyntock (James Stewart) and Cole (Arthur Kennedy) fight their way out of the den of thieves. *Bend of the River* (Universal International, 1952).

difficult one, leads to the farmstead; the other is an easy trek down the mountainside to the already visible mining camp. The die is cast.

In the final act, McLyntock—left to the mercies of the wilderness by Cole—becomes a force of Nature himself. His last words to Cole before his abandonment are a grim, chilling parody of Tom Joad's famous speech from *The Grapes of Wrath*: "You'll be seeing me. You'll be seeing me. Every time you bed down for the night, you'll look back into the darkness and wonder if I'm there. And some night I will be. You'll be seeing me." And yet we don't see McLyntock, nor does Cole. He disappears from the screen for a full eleven minutes—and yet the lowlifes begin to be picked off, one by one, out in the wild, as if Nature itself were exacting revenge for the betrayal. (Nature gets an assist from Laura as well, who covertly looses one of the horses from the caravan for McLyntock to use in his pursuit.)

The climactic conflict between the two men—that is, between the two sides of McLyntock's soul, light and shadow—occurs, as it is destined to, at the bend, within the torrent of the raging river itself. The two who are actually one, and almost visually indistinguishable in their final encounter, will both be engulfed in the flood. One will emerge cleansed; the other will disappear, washed away to the sea.

High Noon
(1952)

May 1, 1952 (London)
USA—English / Spanish
Stanley Kramer Productions
85m—Mono—BW—1.37:1

Direction: Fred Zinnemann
Screenplay: Carl Foreman, John W. Cunningham (story "The Tin Star")
Principal Cast: Gary Cooper (Marshal Will Kane), Thomas Mitchell (Mayor Jonas Henderson), Lloyd Bridges (Deputy Marshal Harvey Pell), Katy Jurado (Helen Ramírez), Grace Kelly (Amy Fowler Kane), Otto Kruger (Judge Percy Mettrick), Lon Chaney, Jr. (Martin Howe), Harry Morgan (Sam Fuller), Ian MacDonald (Frank Miller), Eve McVeagh (Mildred Fuller), Morgan Farley (Dr. Mahin), Harry Shannon (Cooper), Lee Van Cleef (Jack Colby), Robert J. Wilke (Jim Pierce), Sheb Wooley (Ben Miller)
Production: Stanley Kramer
Cinematography: Floyd Crosby
Editing: Elmo Williams
Art Direction: Ben Hayne
Music: Dimitri Tiomkin
Awards: Oscar—Best Actor in a Leading Role (Cooper), Oscar—Best Film Editing (Williams, Harry Gerstad), Oscar—Best Original Song (Tiomkin, Ned Washington for "High Noon"), Oscar—Best Scoring of a Dramatic or Comedy Picture (Tiomkin), Golden Globes—Best Actor: Drama (Cooper), Golden Globes—Best Supporting Actress (Jurado), Golden Globes—Best Original Score (Tiomkin), Golden Globes—Best Black-and-White Cinematography (Crosby), Bodil Awards—Best American Film, Cinema Writers Circle Awards (Spain)—Best Foreign Film, National Board of Review—Top Ten Films, National Film Registry, New York Film Critics Circle—Best Film, New York Film Critics Circle—Best Director (Zinnemann), Photoplay—Most Popular Male Star (Cooper), Writers Guild of America—Best Written American Drama (Foreman)
Nominations: Oscar—Best Picture, Oscar—Best Director (Zinnemann), Oscar—Best Screenplay (Foreman), Golden Globes—Best Motion Picture: Drama, Golden Globes—Most Promising Female Newcomer (Jurado), Golden Globes—Best Screenplay (Foreman), Directors Guild of America—Outstanding Directorial Achievement (Zinnemann)

Few Westerns have had more written about them than Fred Zinnemann's 1952 classic *High Noon*. For many, it is the quintessential picture from the Golden Age of the Western. For others—new fans of the genre, or non-fans, or more modern-minded fans—it may be the earliest Western they have ever seen or the first one they think of when someone mentions "old" Westerns, despite the fact that *High Noon*, of course, stands at the end of fifty years of myth-building and genre-making, and is in fact part of the culmination of a rich golden era, the classical Western in full flower.

Even casual Western fans know something of the aspects of *High Noon* that have sparked discussion, criticism, and analysis over the years: the fact that the drama, in

Greek fashion, unfolds in real time over one morning in one little town; the film's allegorical subtext as a commentary on the Hollywood blacklist; the divided and politically complex reception it has received (Presidents Eisenhower, Reagan, and Clinton were great fans, whereas John Wayne called it "the most un–American thing I've ever seen in my whole life")[1]; and the enormous influence it has had on subsequent films, both inside and outside the Western genre.

Therefore, rather than trying to recapitulate or even just redundantly summarize any portion of the excellent commentary that already exists around *High Noon*, my plan is to set aside all that others have written about this monolith and try to approach it new, with fresh eyes and from a personal perspective. (For readers interested in learning more about the historical background, making, cultural and political context, and reception of the film, I highly recommend Glenn Frankel's excellent 2017 book *High Noon: The Hollywood Blacklist and the Making of an American Classic*.)

Everyone knows the story: on the morning of his wedding to the peace-loving Quaker Amy Fowler (Grace Kelly), retiring Hadleyville lawman Will Kane (Gary Cooper) learns that the vicious Frank Miller (Ian MacDonald), whom Kane originally put away, has been released from prison and is on a train bound for the town to meet up with his three henchmen and wreak his revenge on Kane. The new marshal, Kane's replacement, is not due yet, and so Kane is faced with a choice: leave Hadleyville quickly with his new bride and thus avoid the showdown (for the time being); or stay and face it out. Amy wants him to decide to leave, and so do many of the townsfolk, either out of sympathy with the Miller gang (who brought anarchic "fun" and activity to the town) or, more frequently, because they don't want to take part; they want the conflict to occur someplace else, at a safe distance. Kane, however, decides that it is his duty to stay and confront the four gunmen, and he spends most of the time between his wedding and the train's arrival (at high noon) trying to drum up assistance from the "upright" members of the town. In the end, however, he finds himself standing all alone in a silent, empty street, awaiting his fate.

High Noon is a superb film, an impeccably crafted film, a film that justly earned its status as a classic. But when one tries to pinpoint just exactly what qualities make it such a cultural touchstone—the most iconic Western from the genre's first half century—the answers can be a little elusive at first. It is unquestionably suspenseful and gripping; its acting, direction, photography, and production values are first rate; it has an almost claustrophobic intensity, focused as it is on events unfolding within the span of a few morning hours, in real time, within a single small Western town; and the main character is a tremendously compelling one who immediately earns our respect and sympathy, a laconic but troubled man trying to come to grips with the violent fate that awaits him. But these elements are also present in the equally brilliant Western *The Gunfighter* (1950)—Aristotelian unities, slow-burn suspense, claustrophobic tension, and a gripping hero undergoing a crisis of conscience. And so, the question once again: why has *High Noon* become part of our cultural DNA, while *The Gunfighter* is almost forgotten today?

I don't think it is because of *High Noon*'s anti-blacklisting context; that element is subtle to begin with, and in fact the overall political stance of the movie, especially as it strikes the modern viewer, is not so clear-cut. Yes, the scriptwriter Carl Foreman had something to say about McCarthyism when he wrote *High Noon*, and the movie contains other elements that we would consider "progressive" by today's standards—most particularly the strong and sympathetic character of Kane's former love interest, Helen Ramírez (Katy Jurado in a fantastic performance). On the other hand, the film also espouses the right-wing critique of legal due process that is so common in male-oriented action pictures from *High Noon* to today, that American courts are too lenient (read "liberal"), turning murderers loose from prison left and right so they can prey again. Similarly, Kane's "duty," as he sees it, is to assume to himself the powers of the judicial side of the system in addition to those of

Gary Cooper as Will Kane. *High Noon* (Stanley Kramer, 1952).

the enforcement side; he appoints himself, unilaterally, as extra-judicial executioner. (It should be noted that, until the actual showdown itself, Frank Miller has done nothing illegal; he was released from prison legitimately and, so far, has done nothing more than board a train bound for the town in which he used to live.) Also, in the character of Amy Kane (*née* Fowler), the movie provides us once again with the trope of the peace-loving woman who needs to learn the error of her ways and come around to her strong husband's way of thinking—which, of course, she eventually does, in dramatic fashion. To be clear, I'm not criticizing any of this, just noting that in today's political terms, *High Noon* is a little bit hard to pin down. And that's fine, because in spite of the politically charged atmosphere in which it was created, and which fueled Foreman's writing, at its core *High Noon* is not a political film; didactic content is not a primary factor in its iconic status or lasting appeal. For that, we must look elsewhere, and as you might expect, I will argue that the secret to the movie's cultural impact may be found in the complementary areas of aesthetics and mythology. *High Noon* succeeds, and endures, because of its artistry and its mythic meaning.

The Art of High Noon

High Noon grips us from its very first frame. The opening shot is of a beautiful hilltop amid rolling, rocky grassland. Silhouetted against the sky is a lone gunman seated on a rock between two spreading trees, his horse off to one side. We see the man is waiting, just waiting. A medium shot soon reveals the lean, scarred, stubbled face of Jack Colby (Lee Van Cleef, whose iconic visage would later be immortalized in Leone's spaghetti Westerns). Colby stands up, having spotted movement on the horizon. As the opening credits roll, we soon see him joined by the two other members of Frank Miller's gang of ruffians, Ben Miller (Sheb Wooley) and Jim Pierce (Robert J. Wilke), who come galloping from different directions. The men, reunited, now ride off together, side by side, toward the fateful town.

The poetic grandeur of the landscape, the pacing of the scene, the grim countenances of the three men, and the ways in which, without words, the film conveys their sinister menace all combine to create a powerful opening. But what lifts the scene from powerful to unforgettable is an aesthetic masterstroke: throughout all of this, the only sound on the soundtrack is Tex Ritter singing the film's theme song, "The Ballad of High Noon," accompanied by nothing more than strummed guitar, accordion, and a soft, simple percussive *ostinato* (played on an electronic instrument, the Novachord). We hear no outdoor noises, no galloping hooves, no ambient sound at all, only the gentle throbbing of the theme song from what sounds like an enclosed studio setting. Visually, we are in the resplendent outdoors, but aurally, we are in a small, intimate, almost claustrophobic space. There is a contradiction here in which the scene revels. The three killers seem almost unreal, like phantoms, and amidst all this vastness the sound makes us feel cut off, hemmed in, alone—a feeling we will soon share with the movie's protagonist.

The song itself helps draw us into the story by giving voice to what will become Kane's inner crisis:

> Do not forsake me, oh my darlin',
> On this our weddin' day.
> Do not forsake me, oh my darlin'.
> Wait, wait along.
> The noonday train will bring Frank Miller;
> If I'm a man, I must be brave,
> And I must face that deadly killer
> Or lie a coward, a craven coward—
> Or lie a coward in my grave.

Another Western released just weeks before *High Noon*, Fritz Lang's *Rancho Notorious* (featuring Marlene Dietrich and Arthur Kennedy), had tried a similar device but with much less success. Its over-the-top recurring song, with deep male voices intoning "hate, murder, and revenge" multiple times, matched the campy, stylized nature of the movie, but only at the cost of coming across as immediate self-parody. *High Noon* avoids this mistake; the tune is an unobtrusively perfect counterpoint to the action, and when it recurs throughout the movie, it does so not with ham-fisted cries of "hate, murder, and revenge," but rather as a flickering instrumental *leitmotif*, barely registered, hovering just on the edge of our awareness while it subtly knits the film together.

When the opening credits sequence of a movie is already a masterclass in scene-making, that's both startlingly unexpected and a tough act to follow; nevertheless, *High Noon* does not disappoint. Every scene to follow in the film is just as artful, just as brilliant in its execution. I would not necessarily rank *High Noon* any higher than some of the other masterpieces discussed in this collection, and I do acknowledge that (and understand why) the movie has divided critics and connoisseurs over the years. (William Goldman famously wrote: "At the risk of a sweeping statement, the single most irritating performance in the history of world cinema is Grace Kelly's in *High Noon*.")[2] However, I will say that, for me, *High Noon* belongs to that rare category of impeccably crafted films—including, surprisingly, two others featuring Kelly herself, *Dial M for Murder* and *Rear Window* (both 1954)—about which I find it exceedingly difficult to find anything to criticize. I don't know any change I could suggest for any one of these movies that wouldn't make it worse. I understand Goldman's complaint—that we as the audience want to see Gary Cooper go out there and triumph, and resent Kelly's character for hampering that and, at least at first, deserting her husband in his hour

The Four Horsemen: Ben Miller (Sheb Wooley), Frank Miller (Ian MacDonald), Jack Colby (Lee Van Cleef), and Jim Pierce (Robert J. Wilke). *High Noon* (Stanley Kramer, 1952).

of need—but I would maintain that the character of Amy Kane serves a very necessary function to both the plot and the artistry of *High Noon*, and that the movie would be diminished without her. (More on this in a moment.)

The silent threat of the three villains, and the most fearsome fourth that will join them at noon, is an undercurrent that runs through the entire picture. The idea of a band of killers in a longstanding feud with the hero is one of the most frequently employed tropes in Hollywood, used as a mundane plot device in countless Westerns and action pictures, and on occasion exploited expertly, as in *Stagecoach* (1939). However, in *High Noon* this cliché becomes something greater than itself. From the very beginning, these antagonists are treated with mythic significance. As Frank Miller's henchmen ride into Hadleyville at the opening, over the tolling of church bells (the first diegetic sound we get in the movie), the townsfolk look on in horror. A shawled Mexican woman crosses herself; a blacksmith freezes in his work, then runs into his shop. Gradually it becomes clear: this is more than just the typical handful of nasty thugs who will take on the hero in a standard Western. Joined by Frank Miller at the film's climax, they have become the forces of darkness personified—the Four Horsemen of the Apocalypse.

There is too much that is great in *High Noon* to go through scene by scene, but I would like to highlight a few spectacular elements:

Gary Cooper. Of course. His portrayal of Will Kane is perfect, now indelibly imprinted on the American psyche. The laconic actor could say more with a tightening

The two women in Kane's life: the one he just married, Amy Fowler Kane (Grace Kelly), and his true kindred spirit, Helen Ramírez (Katy Jurado). *High Noon* (Stanley Kramer, 1952).

of his lips and a couple of exquisitely inflected words than most actors could convey in an extended monologue. This role was the triumph of his already distinguished career.

Katy Jurado. As Kane's ex-lover Helen Ramírez, Jurado—who reportedly put in numerous hours of study to learn English for the role—delivers an extraordinary performance. As played by Jurado, Helen is perhaps the film's most nuanced character, seemingly contradictory and yet real and believable. She is both passionate and cool-reasoning; free-spirited and sensible; ambitious and ethical; compassionate and tough-as-nails. We can easily see her as the onetime beloved of both Kane and the callow deputy Harvey Pell (Lloyd Bridges), just as we can believe that her strength of character enables her to deal on an even footing with the town's white male business elite, who treat her with respect. Helen is both the perfect foil to the mousy, uptight Amy and—we clearly see—a much better romantic match for Kane than the woman he has just married. The two seem to be kindred spirits, which adds to the sense of weary defeat that surrounds Kane at the end of the film, even after he has triumphed over his enemies, as he rides away in silence with his new bride.

The other supporting characters. The townsfolk come across as real people, not just part of the scenery, and of course they play an integral role in the plot as each one of them, for different reasons, finds a way to fail to help Kane in the moment of crisis. The supporting players become a virtual catalog of the excuses that people give—to others, and to themselves—for not standing up to injustice. For the people in the bar, the town was more fun when the Miller gang was in charge. Others are afraid for their own skins. Still others are simply all talk and no action; or are just looking out for their own self-interest; or are too cynical to think that there's any way to win. When Kane interrupts the morning worship service looking for help, the preacher scolds him. ("You don't come to this church very often, Marshal, and when you got married today, you didn't see fit to be married here!") Meanwhile, the congregants soon lose themselves in bureaucratic committee discussions that lead nowhere. The mayor (Thomas Mitchell) seems sympathetic to Kane's cause at first, but then says, "We gotta think about the business interests who won't like what they hear about this town. We can't have a shoot-'em-up here." Later, when Kane pleads with retired officer Martin Howe (Lon Chaney, Jr.), saying, "You've been a lawman all your life," the old veteran responds bitterly: "Yeah, all my life. It's a great life. You risk your skin catchin' killers, and the juries turn 'em loose so they can come back and shoot at you again. If you're honest, you're poor your whole life. And in the end, you wind up dyin' all alone on some dirty street. For what? For nothin'. For a tin star." The poor old man is already defeated; he has been beaten down by life's disappointments, has failed to rise above them. "It's all for nothin', Will. It's all for nothin'," he finishes, nihilistically—but Will has already left the room.

The most gut-wrenching betrayal comes from the deputy, Harvey Pell, who resents being passed over as Will Kane's successor and losing the beautiful Helen, the only person in the town—other than an idealistic fourteen year old (Ralph Reed)—whose sympathies stay unwaveringly with Kane. When Pell finally confronts Kane in the livery stable, the brutal fistfight that ensues is just as intense and emotionally exhausting, if not more so, than the climactic showdown still to come. There is a deeper truth being reflected here, that times of crisis often spark treachery even from one's own putative allies the moment they sense blood in the water, and thus the hero must enter the final battle already weakened by cowardly attacks coming from those supposedly on his own side. This is a phenomenon that I suspect we all have experienced. It was recognized at least as far back as the ancient Greeks who, in their legend of the Golden Fleece, told of an army sprung forth from dragon's teeth sown into the soil; when Jason tossed a stone into their midst, the magical warriors promptly fell upon each other and destroyed themselves. There may be something archetypal, then, in the battle between Kane and Pell. Whatever the reason, the scene packs perhaps the most powerful wallop in the film.

The long, slow burn. *High Noon* starts suspensefully and only continues to pile it on, minute by minute, little bit by little bit, until the intensity is nearly unbearable. For a quintessential Western, there is surprisingly little action until the last third of the movie, but the prolonged sense of taut anticipation would have been ruined by any gratuitous, extraneous action sequences. In order to deliver its payoff, *High Noon* relies on the long, slow build-up. The relentless ticking of the real-time clock, accentuated by Dimitri Tiomkin's often synchronically pulsating musical score, drives gradually and irresistibly toward the film's climax.

One major key to this effect, of course, is editing. (Elmo Williams is one of the most deserving Oscar winners in the history of the Academy.) Perhaps the most brilliant example of this occurs in the last moments before the final showdown, when everyone is just waiting in hushed expectation for what is coming next. Here Williams gives us a series of cuts, unfolding in real time, and weaving back and forth between the various players in the drama. Within just two minutes, and with absolutely no dialogue, we see in sequence:

- Kane loading his gun;
- The Miller gang, at the depot, loading their guns;
- Kane making out his Last Will and Testament;
- The swinging pendulum of the ticking clock;
- The gang looking down the empty railroad track, receding into the distance;
- The congregants in the church praying;
- The sweaty, worried face of the mayor sitting in his pew, not praying;
- Another congregant bowing his head in despair;
- The nervous patrons in the bar;
- The ticking clock again;
- Kane and the will again;
- Various shots of the town's empty streets and, once more, the empty railroad track;
- The gang again;
- Anxious townsfolk peering towards the horizon, or looking at each other guiltily from the safety of their homes;
- The stoic face of Helen Ramírez;
- The worried face of Amy Kane;
- The clock face at the hotel where Amy waits showing a minute to noon, and its pendulum swinging directly toward us, dominating the screen;
- The sweaty trio of henchmen in close-up;
- Kane again, also in close-up;
- His clock again, now just seconds before the deadly strike;
- A tracking shot closing in on the empty chair from which Frank Miller originally swore his revenge.

As the scene progresses, the cuts in general get shorter and shorter, while all the time the musical score has been ticking the seconds away, beat after beat after beat, louder and louder, hammering away at a dissonant version of the theme song until the ticking becomes a pounding. Suddenly the music stops, at the blaring sound of a train whistle. We see Amy react to the noise in alarm, and then, out on the horizon where the rails seem to converge, a distant puff of smoke....

Two minutes of screen time—and an eternity.

The Mythic Meaning of High Noon

Like *The Gunfighter, High Noon* is a very psychological movie, focusing in on the inner turmoil of its protagonist as his inevitable destiny approaches, second by agonizing second. Will Kane, just like the earlier film's Jimmy Ringo, is unreservedly human. He is imperfect. He has fears, insecurities, self-doubts. He is seduced at first by the tempting notion of running from the Miller gang; in fact, he is already miles from town, riding away with his beautiful young bride, before he manages to steel himself, turning at last to meet his fate head-on. Here is yet another example of a mainstream Hollywood Western acknowledging that true bravery is not fearlessness but rather facing one's very present fears and overcoming them.

Many disagreed. Howard Hawks and John Wayne, who would later make *Rio Bravo* (1959) together as a response to *High Noon*, hated Will Kane's doubts, his rescue at the hands of his wife during the climactic showdown, and most especially his desperate attempts to enlist the aid of his fellow townspeople in confronting the Miller gang. Hawks later said, "I didn't think a good sheriff [*sic*] was going to go running around town like a chicken with his head off asking for help, and finally his Quaker wife had to save him. That isn't my idea of a good western sheriff."[3] While many lawmen undoubtedly saw *High Noon*, and may have had similar reactions to those of Hawks and Wayne, the vast majority of the movie's audience connected with Kane not as an officer but simply as a fellow human being who, like all of us, must face both external threats and internal fears. Will Kane is most relevant not as a model of law enforcement but as a relatable character representing all of us as we confront challenges in our lives. And the great thing about Kane is that he does so while still getting on with the familiar parts of life—marrying, planning for the future, making out a will. He is a real person living a real life, not just a one-dimensional bad-guy eliminator. One of my favorite moments in the movie is a completely gratuitous one, from a plot standpoint, when Kane—after the nerve-shattering scene described above just prior to the final gunfight—still pauses to rouse the town drunk (Jack Elam) and let him out of his jail cell before going off to face the Four Horsemen in the dusty streets of Hadleyville. "Hey, Charlie, you can go home now," he says, revealing nothing to the man about the drama about to unfold. Life goes on.

When Kane does step out into the street, he is passed by a wagon carrying Amy and Helen to the train station, both (ostensibly) leaving town, leaving Kane to his fate. Amy stares resolutely ahead, but Helen turns back to look at Kane in pity and, in a tracking shot from her point of view, we see him standing alone, deserted, receding further and further into the distance, becoming smaller and smaller on the screen amidst the empty town streets as the wagon leaves him behind. This is one of the loneliest shots in the history of cinema.

As we know, Amy will return and assist Kane in his struggle. She rushes back into town on foot, soon—to her horror—coming across the body of the first gunman to die at Kane's hand. Behind her, we see the office of the Justice of the Peace where she was married less than two hours before; but the sign shows "Justice" clearly, whereas "Peace" is obscured by an intervening lantern. In a movie this carefully crafted, shot by shot, this cannot be an accident. Peace, in the film's view, must be partially sacrificed in the interests of (frontier) justice. And while John Wayne and Howard Hawks would presumably have approved of that sentiment, soon comes the moment that particularly alienated them, when Amy dispatches one of the villains herself. But this is not stylistically inapt; in fact, it is an essential part of the unity of the artwork. Kane's aloneness, his desertion by all the people he thought he could count on, is integral to the conception of *High Noon*. All of his allies, being true to their own natures, have left him, including Amy. Out of love and pity for Kane, she eventually reconsiders and rises to his aid, but after she shoots down the gunman, we see her sag in despair. This is a defeat, not a victory. A crucial part of Amy's own soul has had to die in order that Kane can live. She has become his ally, but only by killing her own values. Amy loves Kane, as do his two other supporters, Helen and Johnny the teenager. But like Amy, neither one can help Kane without sacrificing who they are. Kane understands this: he refuses Johnny's offer of assistance, nor does he ask help from Helen or Amy. The people who care about Kane can't help him without mortally wounding themselves, and the people who should help him don't care about him enough. From the film's perspective, this is the insoluble problem. The narrative requires the apathy and cowardice of the townsfolk in order to look at one side of this conundrum, but it also needs the counterpoint of Amy, Helen, and Johnny to explore the other side.

High Noon ends as it began, in silence. After the battle is over, there are no more lines of dialogue, and the movie concludes with a rapidity of which even William Goldman must have approved. The townspeople rush out onto the streets, relieved, but Kane has no warmth left for them—only young Johnny, at whom he smiles briefly. Amy, now lost, climbs silently into the wagon, and Kane takes off his tin star, dropping it unceremoniously in the dirt. Although this gesture has been imitated many times since, this is no angry condemnation of the justice system as it is in, say, *Dirty Harry* (1971). Rather, in *High Noon* the badge is a symbol of service to a community, a community that Kane now realizes is an illusion.

Loneliness, our seemingly insurmountable isolation from one another, is a pervasive theme in mythology, literature, poetry, drama, visual art, and film. No matter how close we may think that we become to those whom we love, ultimately we are all prisoners in our own heads, with direct access only to our own experiences, thoughts, and feelings. No one can ever fully understand the subjective experience of another. This is a profoundly disturbing truth and an apt subject for mythic treatment.

I remember so many times over the last eleven years, as my young children have been growing up, when I have held one of them in my arms, snuggling our heads up against one another, and then been struck with a poignant realization. Here I am, embracing a person whom I love more than I love my own life. And our brains, the seats of our all of our conscious experiences, the organs that, more than any others, make us who we are, are literally just inches apart. Yet, as tightly as I hold this child, as much as I want to feel our souls merging as one, I won't ever be able to bridge that gap. I'll never know what it is truly like to look at the world through my son's eyes or hear the world through my daughter's ears. I'll never think their thoughts, feel their feelings, or experience what it is like to be them. Their minds are their own universes in which they move, just as my mind is mine. I can travel through physical space to the other side of the globe. Theoretically, I can voyage to the moon, to the stars—but I cannot ever traverse this tiny little spatial gap between my consciousness and my child's. Less than two inches away—and yet more than a universe away.

The myths that endure do so because they touch upon universal human constants such as this. However, the greatest ones don't do this pedantically, spelling everything out in literalistic prose. Rather, the grand myths present their themes metaphorically and poetically. This symbiosis between aesthetic and mythic elements is the point; all the mythic content in the world doesn't provide any impact if it is not delivered with artistry. Movies like *Zardoz* (1974), *Star Trek V* (1989), and the Matrix trilogy (1999–2003) may be brimming over with genuine mythological, psychological, or humanistic insights, but in these cases and others such content can be weakened (if not negated) by artistic choices and/or execution that are less than ideal or inconsistent at best, ham-fisted or catastrophic at worst.

High Noon does not suffer from this difficulty, representing as it does a beautifully executed synthesis of the mythic and the aesthetic. Nevertheless, it is not, at its core, a didactic film. I'm not sure that we emerge from a viewing of it with any knowledge we

High Noon (Stanley Kramer, 1952).

did not already possess. It doesn't instruct us at all; to the contrary, it resonates with us because we recognize in it a reality that we already understand, even if we rarely admit it to ourselves. Watching *High Noon*, we already understand that this feeling of isolation is an inescapable part of the human condition, experienced by everyone. Thus, the film anchors a large part of its emotional impact on a deep, paradoxical realization—namely, that it is possible to have an illusory feeling of community by contemplating just how isolated we are, but comforting ourselves by recognizing that we also share this in common with one another. "Alone together," as we say nowadays.

High Noon stands as one of the pinnacles of the Western genre. It continues to survive and connect with audiences because it employs superlative cinematic/artistic technique and raw emotional power while also commiserating with us in our understanding of this dark truth: that despite all illusions of community and connection, each one of us is finally, absolutely, and irrevocably alone.

The Naked Spur
(1953)

January 30, 1953 (Washington, D.C.)
USA—English
Metro-Goldwyn-Mayer
91m—Mono—Technicolor—1.37:1

Direction: Anthony Mann
Screenplay: Sam Rolfe, Harold Jack Bloom
Principal Cast: James Stewart (Howard Kemp), Janet Leigh (Lina Patch), Robert Ryan (Ben Vandergroat), Ralph Meeker (Roy Anderson), Millard Mitchell (Jesse Tate)
Production: William H. Wright
Cinematography: William C. Mellor
Editing: George White
Art Direction: Cedric Gibbons, Malcolm Brown
Music: Bronislau Kaper
Awards: National Film Registry
Nominations: Oscar—Best Story and Screenplay (Rolfe, Bloom)

What are the needs and desires that move us to action, the engines that propel us forward in our lives? And are they the same in all of us but present in different proportions, or do they vary widely from individual to individual? Psychology has had many things to say about human motivations over the years, of course, and we've already touched briefly upon some of these—for example, the psychosexual elements of Freudian psychology or the aggressive will to power (including the acquisitive impulse) described by Adler. Those familiar with Maslow's hierarchy of needs will also remember the fundamental physiological demands of survival that sit at the foundational level. Survival, sex, acquisition, power—are these the bases of all human desires, needs, and actions?

Certainly not as Maslow saw it, nor others who likewise postulated a hierarchy of motivational forces. Obviously essential needs—food, water, warmth, personal safety—must be met before a person can seek to fulfill higher-order desires, but taking a reductionist approach by claiming that all human behavior boils down to a handful of simple biological urges has proved neither accurate nor helpful.

Among the earliest thinkers to probe the nuances of human motivational hierarchies were the writers of the Upanishads some three thousand years ago, and one of the most far-reaching concepts emerging from these Vedic texts was that of Kuṇḍalinī. In Hindu spiritual practice, Kuṇḍalinī is a form of concentrated energy believed to live at the base of the human spine. ("Kuṇḍalini" is a Sanskrit word for the "coiled snake" to which this energy is likened.) Through the discipline of yogic meditation, the Kuṇḍalinī may uncoil and work its way gradually upwards through the spinal column, passing (potentially) through various stations along the way, described as lotuses or wheels (*chakras*, sometimes rendered as *cakras*). Great practitioners are able to bring the Kuṇḍalinī energy all the way to the seventh *chakra* at the crown of the head (*Sahasrāra*, the "thousand-petaled lotus"), thus merging with the transcendent, erasing all distinctions between subject and object, and losing the self in the Self—although most will not be able to progress that far.

Setting aside Kuṇḍalinī yoga as a spiritual practice, and disregarding any questions of literal truth, many—including Carl Jung and Joseph Campbell—have found the mythic imagery of Kuṇḍalinī to be psychologically meaningful. Each *chakra* has its own character corresponding to various human drives, behaviors, and experiences, and the seven *chakras* are ordered in a clear hierarchy, with the more spiritually elevated qualities literally higher on the spinal column. Interpreted metaphorically then (how else?), the system of *chakras* in Kuṇḍalinī yoga can be seen, among other things, as a distillation of ancient insights into the variety of human psychological drives—beating Maslow to the punch by untold centuries.

The first and lowest *chakra* is where the Kuṇḍalinī serpent normally sits in repose, at the base of the spine. Joseph Campbell describes the character of human psychology at this level by bringing a Western image into this Eastern mythology:

> At this point the serpent is like a dragon. We all know the character of dragons—at least, Western dragons: they live in caves, and they have a gold hoard in the cave, and they have a beautiful girl whom they have captured in the cave. They can't do anything with either treasure or maiden, but they simply want *to hold on*. Dragons, like people whose lives are centered around the first *cakra*, are based around gripping, holding on to power, holding on to a life that is no life at all because there is no animation in it, no joy in it, no vitality in it, but just grim, dogged existence.[1]

Above this starting point we find the second *chakra* at the level of the genitals, and there the emphasis is obviously on the sex drive. The third *chakra*, at belly level, focuses on consumption, and therefore is the home of avarice and the will to power.

These three can be seen to represent the "lower" human impulses—selfishness, lust, greed. But at the level of the heart and the fourth *chakra*, things begin to change. This is where the aesthetic experience comes in, the appreciation of the beauty of life and the world around us—the point at which the crude matter of humanity first touches the spiritually transcendent.

From here on up, things get only more spiritual: there is an ascetic purgation of self at the fifth *chakra* (throat level), a beholding of the divine at the sixth level, and self-dissolving unity with the divine at the seventh and highest level.

The distinctions between the upper three *chakras* and their esoteric nature may be difficult to translate to Western non–Hindus (myself included); people in the West may be more likely, for example, to prize the "self-actualization" that sits at the top of Maslow's hierarchy over the Nirvanic annihilation of self represented by the top three *chakras* of the Kuṇḍalinī system. These are entirely contradictory spiritual goals. Nevertheless, there is a general hierarchy of needs (and therefore motivations) implied by this system overall that I find both generalizable and insightful, even as a Westerner. It might be summarized, crudely, in the following fashion, with the qualities listed from most to least elevated:

- The needs of the spirit (*chakras* 5–7)
- The aesthetic impulse (*chakra* 4)
- The drive for acquisition, consumption, and power (*chakra* 3)
- The sex drive (*chakra* 2)
- Mere survival (*chakra* 1)

A hierarchy like this can be expressed through a mytho-philosophical system like Kuṇḍalinī, of course, but it may also be conveyed (consciously or unconsciously) by art—perhaps, even, by a Western movie.

Howard Kemp (James Stewart) is a would-be rancher who left his fiancée in possession of his property while he went off to fight in the Civil War. The faithless woman, however, sold the ranch and ran off with another man, and so Howie returned home from preserving the Union only to find all of his personal dreams shattered. Now he spends his days as a bounty hunter, tracking a former acquaintance and killer with a price on his head, Ben Vandergroat (Robert Ryan), in order to raise enough money to buy back his spread. Howie soon takes on two helpers: one by choice, old prospector Jesse Tate (Millard Mitchell); and one grudgingly, the sociopathic ex-soldier Roy Anderson (Ralph Meeker). Together the three men capture Ben in the Colorado Rockies, along with his loyal and subservient companion, Lina Patch (Janet Leigh), and begin to transport the wanted man across the wilderness to his presumed hanging in Abilene, Kansas.

The movie is *The Naked Spur* (1953), the middle and greatest of the five Mann/Stewart Westerns. It is a "journey Western," in the same general subgenre as *Along the Great Divide* (1951) but with a very different flavor. The Technicolor scenery in *The Naked Spur* is lush, evocative, and sublime, but the action, in contrast, is very concentrated, stripped down to bare essentials. The film begins in the wilderness and ends in the wilderness; there is never a town or even a building to be seen. The five parts mentioned above are the only speaking roles, and the drama is far more interior than exterior, even if the psychological journey undergone by all of the characters (and especially Howie) is reflected by the natural elements and obstacles of the landscape: valleys, cliffs, crags, rockslides, thick forests, dark caves, treacherous mountain passes, and raging rivers. The resultant film is an intimate, gripping, starkly minimalist slow-burn masterpiece that is as emotionally intense as it is visually beautiful.

One of the many elements that combine to make *The Naked Spur* such a stunning success is its outstanding screenplay, which justly earned an Oscar nomination for its two writers, Sam Rolfe and Harold Jack Bloom, neither of whom had written a movie script before. Rolfe would eventually create what is arguably the best Western television series ever made, *Have Gun—Will Travel*, and also co-created the groundbreaking espionage show *The Man from U.N.C.L.E.* Bloom likewise spent most of his writing career in television, working mainly on spy thrillers, military adventures, detective shows, and Westerns, and creating medical dramas like *Emergency!* Neither man, as far as I know, had any particular connection to the Upanishads or to yoga, and yet the Western they wrote together exemplifies the (metaphorically interpreted) Kuṇḍalinī yoga perspective on human psychology to an extraordinary degree. As I said about *Destry Rides Again* (1939) with its Taoist elements, I would never claim that this Eastern resonance was intended overtly. Rather, in each case I believe that both the individual artwork and the ancient belief system are tapping into the same deep well of universal human constants—Bastian's *Elementargedanke*—but then inflecting them as *Völkergedanke* in different, culturally colored ways.

In any event, the correspondence between the Kuṇḍalinī system and the five characters in *The Naked Spur* is a striking one. Each character seems to embody a different *chakra*, in terms of both personality and motivation. All are fiercely driven, sometimes to an obsessive degree, by the burning desires that they take (erroneously) to be their primary needs. Only Lina starts the movie with what are eventually revealed to be the purest motivations, but even these are misapplied at first. Before film's end, each character will have been stripped naked psychologically, all vulnerabilities and frustrated desires exposed to our view. The *chakra* hierarchy provides a good framework for examining these five memorable characters one at a time.

First *chakra* (*mūlādhāra*)—Ben Vandergroat. Robert Ryan is extraordinary as Ben, an unrepentant narcissist with absolutely no concern for any other human being, despite the fact that he always seems to be smiling, laughing, and trying to ingratiate himself with his captors. We in the audience know better, of course. Ben knows how to talk the talk of decent folk, but his sentences strike us as entirely empty, like those of a person sounding out words phonetically in a language not his own. Everything Ben says or does is for one purpose only, his mere survival. Paradoxically, however, this habitual liar acting purely out of self-interest often becomes the only person speaking most truly and relevantly to the ethics of the situation.

It is this complexity that makes the despicable Ben the most compelling character in *The Naked Spur*. Yes, he is a complete sociopath, motivated entirely by lowest-*chakra* survivalism. Like Campbell's dragon, he hoards the trappings of life without appreciating any of the qualities that make life worth living. Even the beautiful, good-hearted, and devoted Lina only matters to him as a means to an end. He has no love for her—not even lust, as far as we can tell. She is like the princess held captive to whom the dragon clings, even when he is no position to enjoy the boons she offers. This is "grim, dogged existence" indeed, and yet Ben still knows how to ape the mannerisms of people who can appreciate life's joys. (This is apparently true of real-life sociopaths—they are often compelling and charismatic on the surface and able to "pass" for ordinary people, which is why their true nature is often difficult to detect.)[2]

Nevertheless, because of Ben's very single-minded urge to survive by escaping his captors, he occasionally resorts to the unvarnished truth when such truth suits his purposes better than a lie would. And Ben does have the capability of honesty, as demonstrated by the fact that he is at least honest with himself, more than

The sociopath with charisma: Ben Vandergroat (Robert Ryan). *The Naked Spur* (MGM, 1953).

any other character in the movie. At one point, Ben pretends to ruminate on his own nature for the benefit of his listeners. "Maybe if I'd seen what was ahead when I was younger, I wouldn't be in this fix." But then, to our surprise, he chuckles and admits the actual truth. "Aw, course I would. Some of the things…. Nope. Nope, I wouldn'a done nothin' no different."

When people write about *The Naked Spur*, they tend to quote one of Ben's lines more often than any other from the film, when he says to Howie, "Choosin' a way to die, what's the difference? Choosin' a way to live—that's the hard part." It's a great line, but none of the commentaries I have read go on to quote Ben's next sentence, which is the real crux: "That's what's eatin' you, ain't it, Howie?" Although Ben is the most morally stunted member of the party, he is also the only one (at this point) perceptive enough to pick up on Howie's inner conflict, the ways in which his captor is not being true to his own values as Ben is true to his, warped though they may be. As is common in Mann Westerns, the hero and antagonist are reflections of one another, and in many ways know each other better than anyone else does. Throughout the film, Ben makes several observations about Howie's character that hit home: "I calculated some horse-thieving scum would want the price on my hide—but not you, Howie!"

Ben's most honest and incisive comment happens within an intense, eleven-minute scene as the party takes shelter from the rain in a dark cave. Ben waits for his chance, then tries to escape by crawling through a narrow passage in the back, but his attempt is thwarted. (This itself seems mythical: Ben, from his dragon's cave, is unable to pass through the dark canal and thus be "reborn"—that is, to become fully human.) Howie—furious because his own attention was distracted by Lina—jams a gun into Ben's waistband and attempts to goad him into a quick draw. Howie goes through the motions of honorability, giving Ben the opportunity to draw first, but Ben knows he is outmatched no matter what. "I ain't got a prayer against you," says Ben truthfully, "and you know it." "It's your first move," Howie responds grimly, crouched and ready. This is to be a summary execution disguised as a fair fight, as is plain to everyone, but only Ben puts it into words. "If you're going to murder me, Howie," he says, "don't try to make it look like somethin' else."

Ben's deepest pain, very likely, is his helplessness in the face of his own unreasonable and unsatisfiable covetousness, which he takes as justification for his misdeeds. "Man needs what he likes," he tells Lina bluntly. The flip side of this, of course, is that these needs can never be satisfied. The dragon can never hoard enough gold or capture enough virgins; even what he already possesses can never bring him joy. Ben understands this deep down, knows that he is doomed to be a prisoner of his unslakable thirsts. Late in the film, after he brutally murders Jesse, Ben is baffled by Lina's horror at the act, because from his point of view his victim has been freed from the trap from which Ben cannot free himself. "I swear, he ain't half as worried over it as you are!" he exclaims to Lina. "Look at him! Lyin' there, peaceful in the sun. Ain't never gonna be hungry again. Never want anything he can't have. That's more'n we can say!"

Second *chakra* (*svādhishṭhāna*)—Roy Anderson. Roy is an ex-military man whose dishonorable discharge describes him as "morally unstable." ("The army never did understand me," he explains.) He certainly exhibits third-*chakra* greed throughout the story, but Roy's most obvious moral failing is his second-*chakra* lust. He relentlessly bombards the disgusted Lina with leering sexual insinuations, but this behavior is clearly not limited to her, as he is also being hunted by a band of Blackfoot Indians due to the same character flaw. As Roy explains, "Seems this chief's daughter fell into some trouble with a handsome young Army lieutenant and—well, you know how it is." But this was clearly something much darker than just a hedonistic dalliance. When the Indians catch up to the party, Jesse asks Roy, "This chief's daughter you was holdin' hands with—was she willin'?" "Never mind the sermon," Roy snaps back. "We've got a fight on our hands!" So it was rape. "This is your fight, not ours," says Howie in disgust, and he soon tries to make peace with the pur-

The men in the middle: Howie Kemp (James Stewart), Jesse Tate (Millard Mitchell), and Roy Anderson (Ralph Meeker). *The Naked Spur* (MGM, 1953).

suing band, raising his arm toward them in a gesture of friendship. But Roy—now regressed to first-*chakra* concerns—makes peace impossible when, in the movie's most horrifying sequence, he betrays Howie's intentions by concealing himself and shooting down the Indians from behind.

Third *chakra* (*maṇipūra*)—Jesse Tate. The grizzled prospector Jesse is played by Millard Mitchell in his last Western appearance. (As mentioned earlier, this wonderful character actor died tragically at the age of fifty, less than nine months after *The Naked Spur*'s premiere.) Jesse is sympathetic and likeable—certainly driven by the acquisitive impulse, as evidenced by his lifelong (and mostly vain) pursuit of gold, but showing flickers of humanity as well; after all, in Kuṇḍalinī terms, he at least functions on a higher level than either Ben or Roy. Lust doesn't seem to be a part of his consciousness, but neither does any positive consideration toward women; Jesse speaks harshly and disrespectfully to Lina on multiple occasions. His greed binds him to Howie, who purchases his services for (at first) a mere twenty dollars, but there is no real loyalty there. Later the gullible prospector will sell out all of his companions for a chance at the nonexistent gold promised by Ben, a mistake for which he will pay a terrible price.

We learn a great deal about both Jesse and Ben in an earlier exchange, when Jesse talks about his life scratching for gold, and Ben feigns companionable sympathy. "Never hit it, huh, Jesse?" he asks. "Nothin' worth the mention," Jesse answers. "Seems I've been lookin' all my life. All my life. That's a long time to look for somethin'." As viewers, the proper response to this springs immediately to mind: *maybe you've been looking for the wrong thing, Jesse.* But instead, Ben remarks suggestively, "Maybe you been lookin' in the wrong places." In this moment, Jesse's fate is sealed.

Fourth *chakra* (*anāhata*), lapsed—Howard Kemp. The protagonist is a man who, before his fall from grace, was clearly moved by Beauty. However, we first get to know Howie as a hard, harsh, cynical man, seemingly motivated only by the bounty on Ben's head. Although Howie is first mistaken for a lawman by Jesse, he has absolutely no interest in justice. When Ben reminds him of their former acquaintanceship, Howie explodes bitterly. "Aw, quit actin' like we was friends! You—Maybe we sat down at the same card game once or twice, but that don't mean dirt to me now. You shot a man in the back and I'm takin' you in to hang for it." Lina protests, "It wasn't Ben that killed that man," but Howie responds simply, "It's him they're payin' the reward on." At this point, Howie is keeping Jesse company at the third *chakra*.

But we soon see that Howie naturally belongs on a different moral level than his three male companions. When he finally opens up to Lina about his dreams for his ranch, his eyes light up and his words ring with a sense of aesthetic rapture, as the tune of Stephen Foster's "Beautiful Dreamer" weaves its way through the accompanying soundtrack. We may at first associate this with Lina, herself a beautiful dreamer who longs for a new life in California, but the music is telling us something about Howie as well. Here it is his dreams that are beautiful, and they speak to him at the level of the heart, at the level of *anāhata*.

In his nighttime conversation with Lina at the mouth of the cave, we catch yet another glimpse of Howie's aesthetic nature, as well as the first hint of a sense of humor. The party has set their tinware out in the rain to be washed clean, and the drops striking the cups and plates sound like a kind of natural gamelan. Lina remarks on this.

> LINA: It's, uh, makin' music.
> HOWIE: Yeah, there's a sour one someplace.
> *He picks up one of the cups, dumps a little water out, and holds it up, smiling wryly.*
> HOWIE: Roy's. At that, it sounds better than some fiddlers I've heard.
> LINA *(warming)*: Is dancing hard to learn?
> HOWIE: Nope, not the way I do it.

Scenes like this humanize Howie, giving us a sense of the man that he once was and perhaps could be again.

But Howie has been pulled down to the lower levels by his own cynicism after having had his dreams betrayed by his former fiancée. One of the reasons why he is so drawn to Lina, we realize, is that she is exceptionally loyal to Ben. Howie may loathe Ben, but he sees in Lina a level of commitment and devotion that he didn't get from his faithless former love. Once upon a time, a woman, motivated by the lower-level concerns of greed and sexual desire, dragged Howie's own consciousness downward. The question now is: can a woman of higher character, Lina, help him rise back up again? This may seem secondary, but it isn't; in fact, Ben's interior journey is the core of the drama. This is made especially clear late in the film when the primary antagonist is already dead and we suddenly realize, to our surprise, that the true emotional climax hasn't even happened yet. The moment of truth is still to come, and when it does come it is almost devastatingly cathartic.

Howie has a difficult journey to make—both physically, along the arduous trail with all of its human and natural obstacles, and psychologically, as events continually pull his psyche downward in contradiction to his true character. For Howie, as we have seen, the external world mirrors his inner reality, and at no point is this clearer than in what is perhaps his darkest moment, when Roy initiates the slaughter of the small Indian band. As noted above, Howie wanted to make peace, and in fact sympathized with the Indians in their pursuit of the cowardly rapist. His flat statement to Roy—"This is your fight, not ours"—was the spur to Roy's temporary departure from the group, but since Roy has chosen to attack the Indians in the same place that they are parleying with Howie, Howie's choices are gone. Against his will, he is now an enemy to the

Blackfoot band, and can either join in the fight on Roy's side or be killed. Once the shooting starts, Howie has hit rock bottom, the first *chakra*. His only motivation is to survive, which he does in the only way open to him, by joining in the massacre. He is wounded in the battle, which will eventually bring delirium and delay the progress of the party, but his spiritual wound runs even deeper. After the killing stops, Howie sits on his horse, looking down on the sprawled corpses of the Indians, and we witness the agony and bleak despair in his body. He has been crippled in both body and mind; is there any coming back from this dark place?

From doormat to Grail maiden: Lina Patch (Janet Leigh). *The Naked Spur* (MGM, 1953).

Fifth *chakra* (*viśuddha*)—Lina Patch. As the yogi's Kuṇḍalinī crosses the heart and ascends to the top three spiritual levels, the first waystation—the fifth *chakra*—is a site of asceticism, purgation, renunciation. This seems to be the level at which Lina Patch lives most of her life. Like a yogi, she has begun to purge her sense of self, losing it in the service to another person who, unfortunately, does not merit such devotion. Soon, however, her selflessness will take on a more universal and appropriately directed character. Lina seems simple at first, largely because of this apparently blind allegiance to Ben, but we gradually discover that she is the true conscience of the group, both more ethical and more compassionate than any of the other characters.

Initially Lina resents Howie as the man who aims to transport the object of her devotion to a waiting noose. Once, while railing at Roy after he manhandles her— "You're a big man for beatin' up women, ain't ya?"—Lina then turns her wrath unexpectedly on Howie, who has been watching passively: "And you're no better!" But after Howie is wounded in the battle with the Indians, her heart goes out to him, and she comforts him in his delirium when he takes her for the woman who deserted him, reliving a conversation from before he left to fight in the Civil War. "When I get back, it'll be just like we talked about last night. You understand, Mary? You remember what you said?" Lina responds kindly, from her heart, as Mary: "I remember. I—I said, 'I'll wait for you.'" And Howie is eased gently back into sleep.

We genuinely do not know if Howie is salvageable, if he will be capable of rising above the lower impulses to which his life circumstances have driven him—but if anyone can help him in his ascent, it will be Lina.

The Naked Spur is a grim, dark morality play that plumbs the depths of human nature over the course of its short running time, yet also offers some slight hope of redemption. It stands as one of the greatest Westerns of the 1950s, not only for its relentless intensity, gripping performances, and outstanding production values, but most especially for its incredible, mythic ending. The final fifteen minutes, in terms of artistry and emotional impact, are unlike anything else I have ever seen in the classical Western, and the very last dialogue scene is the most heartbreakingly beautiful of all.

In the final image of the movie, two people ride slowly across a grand but desolate landscape, fallen trees strewn across the emptiness. It is both bleak and gorgeous at the same time—the Waste Land, perhaps, but with great towering peaks in the background suggesting at least the possibility of a new and better life beyond them. As we know from the Grail legends, the compassion of noble hearts can heal both the Waste Land and the wounded soul. Will Lina and Howie be able to find their own healing? The movie leaves the question hanging, unresolved, in the clear mountain air.

Shane
(1953)

AKA: *George Stevens' Production of Shane*
April 23, 1953 (New York City)
USA—English
Paramount Pictures
118m—Mono [Stereo version later created]—Technicolor—1.37:1

Direction: George Stevens
Screenplay: A.B. Guthrie, Jr., Jack Sher (additional dialogue), Jack Schaefer (novel)
Principal Cast: Alan Ladd (Shane), Jean Arthur (Marian Starrett), Van Heflin (Joe Starrett), Brandon De Wilde (Joey Starrett), Jack Palance (Jack Wilson), Ben Johnson (Chris Calloway), Edgar Buchanan (Fred Lewis), Emile Meyer (Rufus Ryker), Elisha Cook, Jr. (Stonewall Torrey), Douglas Spencer (Axel "Swede" Shipstead), John Dierkes (Morgan Ryker), Ellen Corby (Liz Torrey), Paul McVey (Sam Grafton), John Miller (Will Atkey), Edith Evanson (Mrs. Shipstead), Leonard Strong (Ernie Wright), Ray Spiker (Axel Johnson), Janice Carroll (Susan Lewis), Martin Mason (Ed Howells), Helen Brown (Martha Lewis), Nancy Kulp (Mrs. Howells)
Production: George Stevens
Cinematography: Loyal Griggs
Editing: William Hornbeck, Tom McAdoo
Art Direction: Hal Pereira, Walter H. Tyler
Music: Victor Young
Awards: Oscar—Best Color Cinematography (Griggs), National Board of Review—Best Director (Stevens), National Board of Review—Top Ten Films, National Film Registry
Nominations: Oscar—Best Picture, Oscar—Best Actor in a Supporting Role (De Wilde), Oscar—Best Actor in a Supporting Role (Palance), Oscar—Best Director (Stevens), Oscar—Best Screenplay (Guthrie), BAFTA—Best Film from Any Source, BAFTA—Best Foreign Actor (Heflin), Directors Guild of America—Outstanding Directorial Achievement (Stevens), New York Film Critics Circle—Best Director (Stevens), Writers Guild of America—Best Written American Drama (Guthrie, Sher)

The American Western movie turned a half-century old in 1953. At this point, the genre was at its peak: in the early 1950s, around a hundred Western feature films were being produced in Hollywood each year,[1] and although that number would begin to gradually decline as the decade wore on, it was counterbalanced by a staggering increase in Western television shows. By decade's end, there would be 48 Western series on the air,[2] including such classics as *The Life and Legend of Wyatt Earp, Gunsmoke, Have Gun—Will Travel, Maverick, The Rifleman, Bonanza, Rawhide,* and *Wagon Train.*

Nevertheless, on the cinematic side, change was in the air as the Golden Age neared its apotheosis. Western filmmakers had spent the last fifty years building up a grand, coherent, and relatively consistent mythic edifice. Construction was now complete, and as is true of all successful mythologies, the tropes had been fully absorbed in the culture. The orthodox Western had given the world the summative, culminating artistry of movies like *My Darling Clementine* (1946), *Red River* (1948), *She Wore a Yellow Ribbon* (1949), and *High Noon* (1952)—masterpieces all, to be sure, but where did one go from here? In simple terms, it must have seemed to the Western's creators that there were essentially two ways open now: continue to repeat and recycle the familiar formulas, or dig deeper into the heretical, deconstructive possibilities already suggested by subversive classic-era movies like *The Ox-Bow Incident* (1943), *Yellow Sky* (1948), and *The Gunfighter* (1950). The parallel coexistence (and interaction) of these two general types, the orthodox neoclassical Western and the revisionist anti–Western, would be perhaps the defining characteristic of the coming Silver Age.

But first, in the genre's fiftieth year, the American Western had one more classical masterpiece to give to the world. It would become the most financially successful Western of the 1950s,[3] and part of the nation's consciousness—and even identity—for decades to come. Most poignantly, it also seemed to know that it was the last great instance of its kind. While summing up its era, it also deliberately provided the tools for its successors to begin the undoing of its own mythology.

In 1949, Jack Schaefer published his first novel, *Shane*, adapted and expanded from his three-part story "Rider from Nowhere," which had appeared in the pulp magazine *Argosy* in 1946. The novel tells the story of a mysterious, wandering gunslinger who rides into the lives of a family of homesteaders, the Starretts, eventually helping them and their fellow farmers stand up to a crooked rancher intent on driving them all off their land. His mission accomplished, the eponymous hero then departs as quickly as he came, vanishing back into nowhere. As the boy Bob Starrett—eleven years old at the time of the story's action—narrates in the novel's last sentence: "He was the man who rode into our little valley out of the heart of the great glowing West and when his work was done rode back whence he had come and he was Shane."[4]

The 1953 movie version, directed by George Stevens and starring Alan Ladd in the title role, also proceeds largely (though not entirely) from the perspective of the Starrett boy, here named Joey and played by Brandon De Wilde in a performance that earned the child actor an Oscar nomination. Joey is the only character to see both Shane's arrival and his departure, and also witnesses Shane's two battles against the gang working for rancher Ryker (Emile Meyer)—the first fought with fists, the second with guns.

Shane is a beautiful film to look at, thanks not only to the magnificent Technicolor photography of Loyal Griggs but also to the vision of George Stevens, one of the few film directors of his era to have started as a cinematographer himself. Griggs and Stevens give us a screen filled with lush colors, artfully composed frames, and striking contrasts between day and night, outdoors and indoors, fair weather and foul, verdant landscapes and muddy streets. The backdrop of the Grand Tetons is stunning, made even more so by Stevens's decision to use telephoto lenses for many of the outdoor shots so that the mountains would loom even larger in the background.[5]

Stevens recognized early on the possibilities of a film that Paramount saw as just another ordinary Western, even a B-picture. He was both meticulous and extravagant in his creation of *Shane*, blowing past his budget and the original shooting schedule, then spending nearly two years in post-production cutting the final product together. Filming on *Shane* wrapped in the autumn of 1951, but the movie was not released until

1953, nearly a full year after *High Noon*, which was shot at the same time. Paramount—now quite pleased with Stevens's result, seeing its potential as one of the flagship movies of the year—decided to release the completed *Shane* in "flat widescreen" format, a 1.66:1 aspect ratio achieved, unfortunately, by simply projecting the movie as it was onto a larger, more rectangular screen, thus cropping out the top and bottom of the frame. All of the careful shot compositions that Griggs and Stevens had crafted were undone by marketing whizzes who assumed (rightly) that the widescreen format would be a big audience draw. Today, luckily, the original 1.37:1 aspect ratio is still available on disc; this version is vastly superior to the other, despite the smaller acreage it takes up on the screen.

Shane opens with its hero riding down into the valley where lies the Starrett homestead. Joey is outside, hiding in the bushes, taking pretend aim with his small, unloaded rifle at a great antlered deer who stands framed by the magnificent mountains behind, drinking regally from a pure pool of water. Already we are in the realms of Arthurian legend, where great adventures were often sparked by the sighting and pursuit of a mystical stag in the wilderness, often at a watering place. In this case, the stag's appearance heralds the arrival of Shane the knight-errant, which we witness through Joey's eyes. Shane himself, like his Arthurian forebears, is courtly, genteel, and aristocratic in bearing, despite his grim profession. As Schaefer explained about his novel:

> *Shane* began as a study of the basic legend of the West, the man with a gun using it to right wrongs, in a sense the American version of a knight on horseback. I deliberately presented the story through the eyes of a boy so that the man himself, seen thus, could be thrown up larger than life, more heroic, without the tale degenerating into outright overblown melodrama.[6]

Here, the author clearly acknowledges the debt owed by both the Western in general and his own novel in particular to the genre's chivalric ancestry, as well as the childlike wonder that these legends can evoke. Like other high Westerns, *Shane* springs from the same fertile soil that once gave the world the writings of Chrétien, Gottfried, Malory, and Wolfram, although many of the movie's own descendants, such as the Clint Eastwood films *High Plains Drifter* (1973) and *Pale Rider* (1985), would take this archetypal figure—the mysterious savior who rides out of the mist, sets things right, and then disappears—one step further, endowing him with supernatural qualities on top of his more worldly abilities. Shane himself, in contrast, remains a fully human character—a knight certainly, but not a ghost.

Joey looks up to Shane in the same way that children of countless generations have worshipped the knights of old, but there is another Arthurian element in *Shane* to which the young boy is, thankfully, oblivious—namely, the love triangle between the three significant adults in his life: his idol Shane, his father Joe (Van Heflin), and his mother Marian (Jean Arthur in her last movie role). We see that all three adults love each other, and we also see that all three recognize this—and the whole thing is conveyed without a single word being spoken about it. This subtle, distant echo of Launcelot, Arthur, and Guinevere is one of the most remarkable aspects of a remarkable film. Today, a Hollywood picture featuring such a triangle would have its characters spell everything out aloud, for each other and for the audience. We would hear endless speeches unlike anything ever said by actual human beings, just so the screenwriters could assure themselves that they had provided a proper exposition to match what they perceive to be our

Joe (Van Heflin) and Marian (Jean Arthur) celebrate their anniversary on the Fourth of July, as Shane (Alan Ladd) and Joey (Brandon De Wilde) look on. *Shane* (Paramount, 1953).

limited intelligences and attention spans. But in *Shane*, it's all done silently, visually. By nothing more than a look here, a look there, a slight lingering on a moment, a certain framing of the scene by the camera, we see everything. We see the great affection that all three characters have for one another, just like their Arthurian counterparts did. Also like the members of the Camelot love triangle, each character is fully aware of how the other two feel.

Early on, as Marian's own feelings for Shane are clearly beginning to blossom, she says to Joey, "Don't get to likin' Shane too much," but we know that she is really talking to herself. The only verbal acknowledgment that we ever hear of the whole situation is in one of Joe Starrett's finest moments, when he believes he will be riding off to his own death. He addresses his worried wife frankly and compassionately:

> I, I've been thinkin' a lot, and I know I, I'm kinda slow sometimes, Marian, but I see things. And I know that if, if anything happened to me, that you'd be took care of. You'd be took care of better than I could do it myself. Never thought I'd live to hear myself say that, but—guess now's a pretty good time to lay things bare.

Even now, no one comes right out and says it. This is as close as anyone will ever get, and it's beautiful. The love triangle in *Shane* is handled with such grace and subtlety and compassion for each of the characters that the movie flies in the face of the hackneyed notion that classic Westerns were nothing more than pedestrian, oversimplistic shoot-'em-ups. The Law of Craft is in play once again; *Shane* and other ambitious and artistic Westerns of the time were in fact tremendously nuanced and featured truly powerful insights about what it means to be human.

The friendship between Joe Starrett and Shane is a key element to the triangle, making it far more poignant and impactful than it might have been. Reportedly, Alan Ladd and Van Heflin became genuine friends on the set, and that chemistry pours forth

The famous slow dissolve: Wilson (Jack Palance) enters the drama. *Shane* **(Paramount, 1953).**

from the screen in every scene they have together, starting from the delightful moment in which they both take axes to the stubborn tree stump in the Starretts' yard. Toward the end of the film, when Shane has to fight and overcome Joe to keep him from going into town and suicidally taking on Ryker's hired gun Wilson (Jack Palance), we experience firsthand the boy Joey's horror as he watches these two noble friends locked in fierce combat, paradoxically moved to violence out of love for one another. This is so painful to watch because we, like Marian and Joey, have come to love both of these men. Perhaps the most tragic part of *Shane*, realized after the fact, is that this is the last interaction the two friends will ever have.

The warmth that we as viewers feel toward Shane and the Starrett family is counterbalanced by the dread and terror that Wilson inspires. Jack Palance is perfect as the loathsome killer, clad in black like the Angel of Death with a grinning skull for a face. When Wilson first walks into Grafton's, the town saloon and general store where all of the film's violence occurs, there is a striking "lap dissolve" in which Wilson moves from door to bar without traversing the intervening space; for a moment, we see him in both places at once. I have no idea what inspired Stevens, Griggs, or editors Hornbeck and McAdoo to perform this famous dissolve—it's certainly not out of the standard filmmaker's playbook—but it is an effect whose chilling power is difficult to describe or explain. It simply works, on a seemingly primal psychological level. Shane may be flesh and blood, but Wilson seems like a menacing wraith from the underworld: grotesque, soulless, and deceptively still. The contrast with Shane could not be starker, nor their coming conflict more inevitable. Whereas *High Plains Drifter* and *Pale Rider* give us supernatural protagonists wreaking divine (or demonic) justice upon human wrongdoers, *Shane* provides just the opposite: a proficient but very human hero going up against Death itself.

The most famous part of *Shane*, of course, is the ending. His work accomplished, the wounded Shane has a last conversation with Joey in which he delivers classic lines that people today recognize even if they haven't seen the movie. "A man has to be what he is, Joey. You can't break the mold." "Joey, there's no living with—with a killing. There's no going back from it." "Now you run on home to your mother and tell her—tell her everything's all right. There aren't any more guns in the valley." "You go home to your mother and your father and grow up to be strong and straight. Joey, take care of them—both of them."

All of this dialogue is adapted pretty faithfully from Schaefer's novel, but the immortal finishing touch comes straight from the film's screenwriter, A.B. Guthrie, Jr., one of the greatest Western novelists in his own right. (Guthrie's six-book Western sequence beginning with *The Big Sky* in 1947 received numerous accolades, including a Pulitzer Prize for its second installment, 1949's *The Way West*.) In Guthrie's adaptation, Shane rides off into the night, toward the distant hills, and young Joey calls after him, his pleading voice ringing across the valley: "Pa's got things for you to do! And Mother wants you! I know she does! Shane! Shane! Come back!" Finally we see Shane on his horse, now miles away, as Joey's final, distant cry echoes through the night. The last shot is of Shane in silhouette, slumped slightly in his saddle, riding through a hilltop graveyard, the great mountains still towering in the distance. In the darkness, cresting the hill and then descending, the shadowy figure seems to sink into the ground as the picture fades.

Today an ambiguous ending like this would spark endless internet debates and fan theories. (Given *Shane*'s financial success, it would most probably also spark the idea for *Shane II* in some studio executive's head.) But in 1953, the point was not whether Shane was alive or dead at the end; the point was the ambiguity itself. I like to think that not even Guthrie, or Schaefer, or Stevens knew Shane's ultimate fate. That's the beauty of it. Over the course of the movie, we have come to care for Shane, and yet he remains an enigma to the very end. We don't know why he rode into the valley. We don't know where he came from. We don't know how he became a gunfighter. We don't even know if Shane is his first or last name. It is only fitting, then, that his departure is as mysterious as his arrival.

Despite being, in so many ways, the culmination of the Golden Age Western—a moment at which the ideals of the classical Western were fully realized—*Shane* also, as mentioned above, carried within it hints of the Silver Age that would eventually supplant it. The most obvious of these elements is the treatment of violence.

George Stevens was a veteran of World War II, and as a result he had no desire to trivialize killing. Prior to *Shane*, most Westerns had bloodless gun deaths. The victim of a mortal bullet wound would clutch his chest and then slump slowly, quietly, gently to the ground. Stevens was having none of this. As he recalled in an interview:

> In most westerns, everybody shoots and nobody gets hurt. One thing we tried to do in *Shane* was reorient the audience to the horror of a pistol. We used gunplay only as a last resort of extreme violence. There's no shooting in *Shane* except to define a gun shot, which for our purposes is a holocaust. It's not a gesture of bravado, it's death. When guns are used, they're deadly. Our characters have an abhorrence of violence and a knowledge of the responsibility of taking a life that doesn't exist in most westerns.[7]

Stevens had witnessed firsthand what happens when bodies are struck by bullets, and to recreate this, he had the victims of gunfire in *Shane* rigged so that they could be pulled

Herald of the coming Silver Age: the body of Stonewall Torrey (Elisha Cook, Jr.) is thrown violently backward as Wilson (Jack Palance) brutally guns him down. Violence in Westerns would never be the same. *Shane* **(Paramount, 1953).**

backward sharply to simulate the impact of the bullet.[8] The most horrifying example of this is the death of the plucky Southern farmer Stonewall (Elisha Cook, Jr.) at the hands of Wilson. The sinister killer, standing on the wooden walkway outside of Grafton's, goads Stonewall into a showdown, but the poor man is much too slow. Wilson whips out his pistol before Stonewall can even clear his holster. Stonewall freezes and Wilson, gun drawn, looks at him for a long moment before coldly shooting him down. Stonewall's body jerks violently backward and sprawls in the mud, while the Angel of Death grins down upon his inert body.

This moment changed everything. Meant to deromanticize the inflicting of violence, the brutal depiction of Stonewall's death—and, later, Wilson's at the hands of Shane—actually carried a visceral, emotional, *aesthetic* impact commensurate with the physical impact depicted on screen. As film writer Howard Hughes notes, "the action, when it comes, is startling in its ferocity. In *Shane*'s fairytale frontier setting, the action sequences anticipate the 'mud and rags' treatment of the west over a decade later."[9] Filmmakers were quick to pick up on the power of this more graphic approach, and as the influence of the Hays Code began to wane and movies became more explicit, the trend toward a more realistic depiction of violence only grew stronger. Ironically, then, this lyrical Golden Age Western, experienced through the eyes of an innocent child, heralded the birth of graphic, deromanticized violence in Westerns. The culmination of this trend in the Silver Age may have been the films of Sam Peckinpah, including ultra-violent Westerns like *The Wild Bunch* (1969) and *Pat Garrett and Billy the Kid* (1973). We can take Peckinpah's observation as straight from the horse's mouth, then: "When Jack Palance shot Elisha Cook Jr., in *Shane*, things started to change."[10]

"Shane! Come back!" Has the innocence of youth ever been so perfectly and poignantly captured in a Hollywood Western? And yet *Shane* is about so much more than lost innocence. It's about family, and friendship, and loyalty, and bravery, and community, and the gentle pain of loving. Perhaps just as importantly, *Shane* is a wistful, poignant homage to the early Westerns—those idealized, romanticized

The end of an era: Alan Ladd as Shane. *Shane* (Paramount, 1953).

dreams featuring chivalrous, knightly heroes who truly were "strong and straight," and which undoubtedly fired the imaginations of *Shane*'s creators when they first watched them as children. (Guthrie was born in 1901, Stevens in 1904, Schaefer in 1907.) It is not hard, therefore, to see Joey as their stand-in, and ours. His adoring eyes, gazing upon Shane, are theirs, and ours. Through Joey, we relive the experience of what it was like to have true heroes, as we did once; and we catch a glimpse of how the great classic Westerns were able to speak to this experience in a resonant way.

The character of Shane, seen in this light, is the classical American Western itself— filmic shorthand, a symbol of all of those wonderful movies that thrilled and moved and transformed generations of people, adults and children, giving them a mythology that spoke to their own culture, their own time. But a new wind was already blowing, as the makers of *Shane* knew well; the old myths of spotless heroes and grand historical destinies and divinely ordained expansion would not long survive in a country still reeling from a world war, and beginning to face up at last to the issues of race and civil rights that had been so long denied and neglected. This is the secret to *Shane*'s enduring beauty. Just as the knowledge of our own mortality only makes human life more precious and more beautiful, so *Shane*'s unspoken acknowledgment that the Golden Age was drawing to a close gives the movie a grand valedictory power. It knows that its day has come, that it is time to move on from childlike, comforting assurances and into the ambiguities and complexities of adulthood, both as filmgoers and as a culture. Like Joey, America was growing up, and Shane was not coming back.

And yet, perhaps the final word on the mythology of *Shane*—and on the classical Western itself—belongs to Marian as she is portrayed in Schaefer's original novel. Here, after Shane's departure, Joe has become, in his own words, "sick of the sight of this valley," ready for the family to pull up stakes and head to Montana. But Marian chastises him: "So you'd run out on Shane just when he's really here to stay!" A puzzled Joe protests, insisting that his wife doesn't understand, reminding her that Shane is gone for good.

In her wisdom, however, Marian knows the truth, both about Shane and about the mythology that he represents. "He's not gone," she answers her husband. "He's here, in this place, in this place he gave us. He's all around us and in us, and he always will be."[11]

Conclusion

Sir Gawain of the Round Table was a knight under a curious enchantment. His prowess as a warrior was tied to the sun; it waxed and waned with the golden orb's arc across the dome of the sky. Gawain's knightly powers were at their zenith at noontime, but after that he would grow progressively weaker as the sun sank lower and lower toward the horizon.

There is an intriguing phenomenon captured in this legend, one that applies to far more than mythical chivalric combat. Any enterprise that experiences a peak, a heyday, also experiences a bittersweet and unavoidable paradox: the moment of greatest success is also the precise moment at which the decline begins. The sun reaches its highest point in the sky at noon; a millisecond later, it has already begun to diminish.

The noontime of the Western was, appropriately enough, the era of *High Noon* (1952). This film, along with *Shane* (1953), showed the classical Golden Age Western at the height of its power—but the corollary to this, as both movies seemed to understand and subtly acknowledge, was that from this point on the shadows would start to lengthen. Colors would deepen into evening, darkness would begin to predominate, and eventually night would fall. That dark night—the Silver Age—would have a life and energy and interest of its own, of course. Like that of a vibrant city, the nightlife of the Western would be fun and wild and dangerous and unfettered in its debauchery. But after *High Noon* and *Shane*, energy began to drain from the formulas and motifs and moral certainties of the pure classical Western. Like the hero Shane himself, something had ridden away, never to fully return, although glints and fragments and nostalgic reminiscences of it would continue to crop up from time to time, sometimes in the oddest places.

Vietnam and Watergate are often cited as watershed moments, the turning points when America "lost its innocence." But in fact, the process started well before the era of Kennedy, Johnson, and Nixon. Western movies, always a barometer of American culture, were already showing societal mores beginning to come apart at the seams by the middle of the 1950s. The whitewashed, flag-waving mythologies of previous generations were no longer believable or tenable. More importantly, they no longer served well the needs of new generations of Americans growing up within a rapidly changing culture. It was becoming increasingly difficult for Westerns to cling to the old values; and even just a few years after *Shane* gave the Golden Age Western its last great pure incarnation, movies that continued to try and cling to the old values—*The Alamo* (1960) and *How the West Was Won* (1962), for example—seemed archaic, naive, dated, out of step.

With the death of the old mythology—focused on the Nation and, thereby, on notions like Manifest Destiny and American exceptionalism—a vacuum was left to be filled by a new perspective, one which was skeptical of the nationalistic, jingoistic, and moralistic claims of true believers. The heroes—antiheroes—of the new Westerns would be individuals, careless of societal norms, making their own way in a violent and unpredictable world. They shunned all ideologies except their own; like the Vulgate Grail knights, they entered the forest "wherever they saw it thickest and wherever path or track was absent."[1] The new Western protagonist had abandoned the well-established Hero's Trail for a way of his—or her—own making.

This change, of course, didn't happen in an instant; it wasn't brought about by a single movie at a particular time. And although the revisionist Western truly came into its own in the 1960s and 1970s, we can see the seeds of the transformation well before that. In little ways and big ones, movies such as *Hell's Heroes* (1929), *Billy the Kid* (1930), *The Ox-Bow Incident* (1942), *Yellow Sky* (1948), *The Gunfighter* (1950), *Broken Arrow* (1950), and *The Naked Spur* (1953) had already begun laying the groundwork. So, in a different way, did the body of Elisha Cook, Jr., lying in the mud in *Shane*.

Within a few years, as the fifties waned and the revolution of the sixties got underway, the old edifice would begin to crumble in earnest. The countercultural Westerns of the sixties and seventies would not just replace the old mythology: they would dynamite it.

A great, mythic age was drawing to a close—while another, far more heretical but equally magnificent, was dawning. No one could have known it during this transitional time of upheaval, but truly wonderful things still lay in wait beyond the horizon: films like *Vera Cruz* (1954); *The Searchers* (1956); *The Tall T* (1957); *3:10 to Yuma* (1957); *The Magnificent Seven* (1960); *Ride the High Country* (1962); *The Professionals* (1966); *The Good, the Bad and the Ugly* (1966); *Hour of the Gun* (1967); *Will Penny* (1967); *The Wild Bunch* (1969); *Butch Cassidy and the Sundance Kid* (1969); *Little Big Man* (1970); *The Outlaw Josey Wales* (1976); *Lonesome Dove* (1989); *Dances with Wolves* (1990); *Unforgiven* (1992); *Tombstone* (1993); *Lone Star* (1996); *Smoke Signals* (1998); and the radically reconsidered Westerns of the twenty-first century.

The Golden Age of Westerns had been a wild ride, but over time the territory had become more familiar, more settled, the paths more well-worn. In order for the Western to continue as a relevant genre, it had to venture out beyond its own fences and find new ways. Shane, the last great exemplar of the classic Western protagonist, had ridden across that dark hilltop cemetery and vanished, into the earth or beyond the distant mountains.

The era of the Hero's Trail was over.

The era of the Wild Frontier was just beginning.

Appendix:
A Western Viewing List,
1903–1953

Following are the Western features and shorts from 1903 to 1953 that I watched specifically for the preparation of this book (in addition to the Westerns I've been watching all my life), listed in order of release date. Directors' names and year of release are given in parentheses, and the top-billed actor/actress is shown after the dash. If the movie has a corresponding essay in this book, it is listed in boldface type.

The quality of these films varies, but watching through them does provide an amazingly thorough history of the American Western movie, as well as an interesting slice of American culture as it evolved over five tumultuous decades. I learned something from every one of these pictures, from mundane to masterpiece.

All of these, as of this writing, are easily obtainable via streaming services or DVD, and most of the earlier ones are in the public domain and can be viewed online for free. Websites of the Library of Congress and the American Film Institute are particularly helpful in this area.

The Great Train Robbery (Edwin S. Porter, 1903)
The Battle of Elderbush Gulch (D.W. Griffith, 1913)—Lillian Gish
The Squaw Man (Oscar Apfel, Cecil B. DeMille, 1914)—Dustin Farnum
The Bargain (Reginald Barker, 1914)—William S. Hart
Knight of the Trail (William S. Hart, 1915)—William S. Hart
Keno Bates, Liar (William S. Hart, 1915)—William S. Hart
Hell's Hinges (Charles Swickard, 1916)—William S. Hart
The Heart of Texas Ryan (E.A. Martin, 1917)—Tom Mix
The Covered Wagon (James Cruze, 1923)—J. Warren Kerrigan
Hustlin' Hank (Scott Pembroke, 1923)—Will Rogers
The Iron Horse (John Ford, 1924)—George O'Brien
The Vanishing American (George B. Seitz, 1925)—Richard Dix
Tumbleweeds (King Baggot, 1925)—William S. Hart
3 Bad Men (John Ford, 1926)—George O'Brien
Two-Gun of the Tumbleweed (Leo D. Maloney, 1927)—Leo D. Maloney
In Old Arizona (Irving Cummings, 1928)—Warner Baxter
The Virginian (Victor Fleming, 1929)—Gary Cooper
Hell's Heroes (William Wyler, 1929)—Charles Bickford
The Big Trail (Raoul Walsh, 1930)—John Wayne

Billy the Kid (King Vidor, 1930)—Johnny Mack Brown
Cimarron (Wesley Ruggles, 1931)—Richard Dix
The Squaw Man (Cecil B. DeMille, 1931)—Warner Baxter
The Texan (Clifford Smith, 1932)—Jay Wilsey
Come on Danger! (Robert F. Hill, 1932)—Tom Keene
The Man from Monterey (Mack V. Wright, 1933)—John Wayne
Riders of Destiny (Robert N. Bradbury, 1933)—John Wayne
The Lucky Texan (Robert N. Bradbury, 1934)—John Wayne
Viva Villa! (Jack Conway, 1934)—Wallace Beery
Randy Rides Alone (Harry L. Fraser, 1934)—John Wayne
The Trail Beyond (Robert N. Bradbury, 1934)—John Wayne
In Old Santa Fe (David Howard, 1934)—Ken Maynard
Ruggles of Red Gap (Leo McCarey, 1935)—Charles Laughton
The Ivory-Handled Gun (Ray Taylor, 1935)—Buck Jones
Rose-Marie (W.S. Van Dyke, 1936)—Jeanette MacDonald
Three Godfathers (Richard Boleslawski, 1936)—Chester Morris
The Plainsman (Cecil B. DeMille, 1936)—Gary Cooper
Way Out West (James W. Horne, 1937)—Stan Laurel
Black Aces (Buck Jones, 1937)—Buck Jones
Under Western Stars (Joseph Kane, 1938)—Roy Rogers
Jesse James (Henry King, 1939)—Tyrone Power
Stagecoach (John Ford, 1939)—Claire Trevor
Dodge City (Michael Curtiz, 1939)—Errol Flynn
Union Pacific (Cecil B. DeMille, 1939)—Barbara Stanwyck
Frontier Marshal (Allan Dwan, 1939)—Randolph Scott
Drums Along the Mohawk (John Ford, 1939)—Claudette Colbert
Destry Rides Again (George Marshall, 1939)—Marlene Dietrich
The Westerner (William Wyler, 1940)—Gary Cooper
Melody Ranch (Joseph Santley, 1940)—Gene Autry
Western Union (Fritz Lang, 1941)—Robert Young
They Died with Their Boots On (Raoul Walsh, 1941)—Errol Flynn
The Ox-Bow Incident (William A. Wellman, 1942)—Henry Fonda
The Outlaw (Howard Hughes, 1943)—Jack Buetel
Along Came Jones (Stuart Heisler, 1945)—Gary Cooper
My Darling Clementine (John Ford, 1946)—Henry Fonda
Duel in the Sun (King Vidor, 1946)—Jennifer Jones
Angel and the Badman (James Edward Grant, 1947)—John Wayne
Pursued (Raoul Walsh, 1947)—Teresa Wright
The Treasure of the Sierra Madre (John Huston, 1948)—Humphrey Bogart
Fort Apache (John Ford, 1948)—Henry Fonda
Red River (Howard Hawks, 1948)—John Wayne
3 Godfathers (John Ford, 1948)—John Wayne
Yellow Sky (William A. Wellman, 1948)—Gregory Peck
She Wore a Yellow Ribbon (John Ford, 1949)—John Wayne
Wagon Master (John Ford, 1950)—Ben Johnson
The Gunfighter (Henry King, 1950)—Gregory Peck
Winchester '73 (Anthony Mann, 1950)—James Stewart

Broken Arrow (Delmer Daves, 1950)—James Stewart
The Furies (Anthony Mann, 1950)—Barbara Stanwyck
Devil's Doorway (Anthony Mann, 1950)—Robert Taylor
Rio Grande (John Ford, 1950)—John Wayne
Rawhide (Henry Hathaway, 1951)—Tyrone Power
Along the Great Divide (Raoul Walsh, 1951)—Kirk Douglas
Bend of the River (Anthony Mann, 1952)—James Stewart
Rancho Notorious (Fritz Lang, 1952)—Marlene Dietrich
High Noon (Fred Zinnemann, 1952)—Gary Cooper
The Big Sky (Howard Hawks, 1952)—Kirk Douglas
The Lusty Men (Nicholas Ray, 1952)—Susan Hayward
The Naked Spur (Anthony Mann, 1953)—James Stewart
Shane (George Stevens, 1953)—Alan Ladd

Notes

Introduction

1. Campbell discusses these four functions in many places; one of the best summaries may be found in the "Conclusion" of *Occidental Mythology*, 518–23.
2. May, *The Cry for Myth*, 15.
3. Picasso, "Picasso Speaks," 315.
4. Slotkin, *Gunfighter Nation*, 658–59.
5. Ebert, *Questions*, 270 (italics mine). This quote (which Ebert himself called "Ebert's Law" in this source) exists in a number of places in Ebert's writings, sometimes slightly varied.

Part One

The Great Train Robbery (1903)

1. Jay Hyams, *Life and Times*, 18.
2. Hyams, 15.

The Battle of Elderbush Gulch (1913)

1. The 19th-century anthropologist Adolf Bastian's concepts of the *elementary idea* and the *folk idea* will be discussed in more detail later in the essay on *Winchester '73* (1950).
2. Campbell, *Hero*, 117.
3. Wolfram, *Parzival*, 369.

The Bargain (1914)

1. The lovers' names are rendered variously among medieval versions of their tale: Tristan, Tristran, Tristram, etc.; and Iseult, Yseult, Isolt, Isoud, Isolde, etc.
2. Procter, *Poems*, 213–14.

Hell's Hinges (1916)

1. Wolfram, *Parzival*, 401–6.
2. Fenin and Everson, *The Western*, 91. Tellingly, they also write: "All the red meat was there, free of any murky undertones." (*Ibid.* 83.)
3. Wilmington, "Cowboy Pioneer," 262.
4. Fenin and Everson, 91.

The Covered Wagon (1923)

1. Hyams, *Life and Times*, 33.
2. Malory, *Le Morte d'Arthur*, vol. 2, 530.

3. Quote reprinted in "Close-Ups," 61.
4. Hyams, 34.

The Iron Horse (1924)

1. Hyams, *Life and Times*, 34.
2. "Brief Descriptions and Expanded Essays of National Film Registry Titles," Library of Congress, accessed October 7, 2019, loc.gov/programs/national-film-preservation-board/film-registry/descriptions-and-essays/.

The Vanishing American (1925)

1. Different releases of this movie have slightly varying names for four of the characters, as I have shown in the cast list. The version I own, unlike the original release, follows Grey's spellings for Marian and Ramsdell, but for some reason changes Gekin Yashi to Gekin Yasha and Shoie to Tolie.
2. Grey, *The Vanishing American*, Chapter XXII.
3. Grey, *The Vanishing American*, Chapter XXIII.
4. "'Vanishing American,'" 2257.
5. Brownlow, *War*, 345.
6. Wilson had been a schoolteacher in real life, prior to her Hollywood career.
7. Pauly, *Zane Grey*, 278.
8. Godwin, *The Last Rainbow*, 466–67.

Tumbleweeds (1925)

1. Goldman, *Adventures*, 125.
2. Goldman, 117.
3. Fenin and Everson, *The Western*, 102.

3 Bad Men (1926)

1. Whitaker, *Over the Border*, 7.

Part Two

In Old Arizona (1928)

1. All quotes from Henry, "The Caballero's Way," 86–93.

The Virginian (1929)

1. Corkin, *Cowboys as Cold Warriors*, 22.
2. Wister, *The Virginian*, 480–81.

Hell's Heroes (1929)

1. Kyne, *The Three Godfathers*, 544.
2. Slesin, *American Masters*.

The Big Trail (1930)

1. Schoenberger, *Wayne and Ford*, 25.
2. Indick, *Psychology of the Western*, 75.

Billy the Kid (1930)

1. Fenin and Everson, *The Western*, 200.

Cimarron (1931)

1. "Cimarron (1960)," Rotten Tomatoes, accessed October 28, 2020, https://www.rottentomatoes.com/m/1004177-cimarron.
2. Ferber, *Cimarron*, 206.

Viva Villa! (1934)

1. Buscombe, *BFI Companion*, 427–28.
2. Davis, *Duke*, 57.

Ruggles of Red Gap (1935)

1. Laughton, "Role I Liked Best," 102.
2. Laughton, 102.
3. White and White, *Subtreasury of American Humor*, xvii.

The Plainsman (1936)

1. Presley and Vieira, *Cecil B. DeMille*, 173–174. Presley is DeMille's granddaughter.
2. Nicholson, "Happy Jack," 222.
3. Presley and Vieira, 173.

Jesse James (1939)

1. "Top Grossing Movies of 1939," Ultimate Movie Rankings, accessed November 19, 2019, ultimatemovierankings.com/top-grossing-movies-of-1939/.
2. Indick, *Psychology of the Western*, 178.

Part Three

Stagecoach (1939)

1. Emerson, *Essential Writings*, 150.
2. From *Faust, Part Two*, Act I, Scene 5, wherein Faust proclaims, "Das Schaudern ist der Menschheit bestes Theil." The English rendering I used, done by Thornton Wilder, seems to be the most common today, and is reasonably faithful to the original. George Madison Priest's rhymed translation, widely read in earlier generations, is: "And yet in torpor there's no gain for me; / *The thrill of awe is man's best quality.* / Although the world may stifle every sense, / Enthralled, man deeply senses the Immense." However translated, a noble truth indeed.

3. Pippin, *Hollywood Westerns*, 4.
4. Welles, "Playboy Interview," 58.

Dodge City (1939)

1. Slotkin, *Gunfighter Nation*, 289–90.

Union Pacific (1939)

1. Stravinsky, *Poetics of Music*, 68.

Destry Rides Again (1939)

1. All quotes from the *Tao Te Ching* taken from *Tao Te Ching: A New English Version*, translated by Stephen Mitchell (1992). Mitchell's translation is a beautiful one, although English versions vary widely in their interpretation of this continually elusive and subtle text. To interested readers I would highly recommend, in addition to Mitchell's, the excellent translations done by James Legge (1891), Hua-Ching Ni (1979), Victor H. Mair (1990), Roger T. Ames and David L. Hall (2003), David Hinton (2013), and most especially Ursula K. Le Guin (1997). For those of us unable to read the *Tao Te Ching* in its original language, comparing different English versions may be the best way to get a deeper sense of the mysterious original.
2. For an excellent discussion of the latter element, please see: McGee, *From Shane to Kill Bill*, 40–50.
3. About the film, Fenin and Everson write, "Here is one case where nostalgia for the past has not worked its magic on the celluloid image." (*The Western*, 253.) McGee calls it "one of the strangest Westerns ever made." (*From Shane to Kill Bill*, 40.) The great (and not easy to please) Pauline Kael, however, seems to have been a fan, based on her brief notes on the film provided in her anthology *Kiss Kiss Bang Bang*, 317–18.

The Westerner (1940)

1. Coyne, *The Crowded Prairie*, 27.
2. Bandy and Stoehr, *Ride, Boldly Ride*, 120.
3. Aristotle, "Nicomachean Ethics," 406.
4. Bruce Eder, "Walter Brennan," on All Movie website, accessed January 29, 2020, allmovie.com/artist/walter-brennan-p8313.
5. Hawthorne, *Twice-Told Tales*, 257.

Melody Ranch (1940)

1. Crowther, "At the Criterion," 7.

The Ox-Bow Incident (1942)

1. Eyman, *Hank & Jim*, 12, 110.
2. For a great discussion of the film's approach to ethics and how it can be interpreted via Martha Nussbaum's neo–Aristotelian responses to Kant, please see Hada, "Cost of the Code," 187–201. Despite the headiness of the subject matter, the chapter is both fascinating and very readable (at least to this layperson).

3. "The Ox-Bow Incident," on IMDb website, accessed February 14, 2020, imdb.com/title/tt0036244/trivia?ref_=tt_trv_trv.

My Darling Clementine (1946)

1. "John Ford—True to Hollywood," on True West website, accessed June 3, 2020, truewestmagazine.com/true-to-hollywood.
2. Hughes, *Stagecoach to Tombstone*, 11.
3. Hughes, 12.
4. Eyman, *Print the Legend*, 294.
5. In Buscombe, *BFI Companion*, 286.
6. Campbell, *The Power of Myth*, 129.
7. Eyman, *Print the Legend*, 295.
8. Indick, *Psychology of the Western*, 28–29.
9. Thomas, "Victor Mature Hits Stride," D15.
10. Hughes, 13.
11. Pippin, *Hollywood Westerns*, 143.
12. Indick, 152.
13. Corkin, *Cowboys as Cold Warriors*, 25.

Duel in the Sun (1946)

1. Hyams, *Life and Times*, 66.
2. Coyne, *The Crowded Prairie*, 42.
3. This is my favorite translation of the text, although as yet I have been unable to find the name of the translator. Everywhere I have seen it—online, in program booklets and liner notes—it is uncredited.
4. Busch, *Duel in the Sun*, chapter 37.

Angel and the Badman (1947)

1. "The New Pictures," 111.
2. Quoted in Campbell, *Power of Myth*, 185.

Pursued (1947)

1. Hyams, *Life and Times*, 66.

The Treasure of the Sierra Madre (1948)

1. Pateman, *The Man Nobody Knows*, viii. The words in quotation marks are often attributed to Traven, but Pateman provides them as a summary of Traven's views, without quotes.
2. Slotkin, *Gunfighter Nation*, 417–18.

Fort Apache (1948)

1. Eyman, *Print the Legend*, 307–8.
2. Eyman, *Print the Legend*, 367–78, 371.
3. "Frank S. Nugent," 21.
4. Eyman, *Print the Legend*, 274.
5. Eyman, *Print the Legend*, 311.
6. Crowther, "Fort Apache," 26.
7. Moses, "Savage Nations," 288–89.
8. Moses, 270.
9. Hyams, *Life and Times*, 148.
10. Schoenberger, *Wayne and Ford*, 69–70.
11. Bandy and Stoehr, *Ride, Boldly Ride*, 287.
12. Campbell, *The Power of Myth*, 127.

Red River (1948)

1. Sklar, "*Red River*," 14–19.
2. "Borden Chase—Writer," Film Reference website, accessed April 2, 2020, filmreference.com/Writers-and-Production-Artists-Ch-De/Chase-Borden.html.
3. Capua, *Montgomery Clift*, 46.
4. Frankel, *The Searchers*, 239.
5. Bosworth, *Montgomery Clift*, 121.

She Wore a Yellow Ribbon (1949)

1. Tennyson, *Works*, 162–63.
2. Eyman, *Print the Legend*, 330.
3. Indick, *Psychology of the Western*, 159.
4. Bandy and Stoehr, *Ride, Boldly Ride*, 285.

Wagon Master (1950)

1. Peter Bogdanovich, "I'm Hard to Get, John T.," Observer website, accessed May 1, 2020, observer.com/2007/07/im-hard-to-get-john-t/2/.
2. Bogdanovich, *John Ford*, 88.
3. Lim, "A Second Look," D14.
4. Fenin and Everson, *The Western*, 250–51.
5. McBride, *Searching for John Ford*, 497.
6. McBride, 496.
7. McBride, 497.
8. Indick, *Psychology of the Western*, 164.
9. There are different versions of this story that vary slightly in details, although the essentials remain the same. Harry Carey, Jr.'s own recollection of the moment can be found in Eyman, *Print the Legend*, 344–45. Carey, however, reports (incorrectly) that he was fighting with Don Summers, not Chuck Hayward, and remembers the tear being in the seat of Bond's pants rather than the leg.
10. Eyman, *Print the Legend*, 345.

The Gunfighter (1950)

1. Slotkin, *Gunfighter Nation*, 390.
2. Slotkin, 387.
3. Joyce, *Portrait of the Artist*, 148.
4. Try as I might, I have been unable to discover the name of the uncredited actor who plays Tommy the rancher.
5. Smyrnaeus, *The Fall of Troy*, 567.
6. Dodds, "On Misunderstanding," 43.

Winchester '73 (1950)

1. Eyman, *Hank and Jim*, 203.
2. Eyman, *Hank and Jim*, 203.
3. Indick, *Psychology of the Western*, 119.
4. Maddrey, *Quick*, 59.
5. See Campbell, *Primitive Mythology*, for an excellent introduction to Bastian's thought.
6. Kluckhohn, "Recurrent Themes," 268–79.
7. Slotkin, *Gunfighter Nation*, 382.

Broken Arrow (1950)

1. Joyce, *Portrait of the Artist*, 149.
2. Maltz, "What Shall We Ask," 19–22.
3. Ron Capshaw, "The Recantation of Albert Maltz," Tablet website, accessed May 16, 2020, tabletmag.com/sections/news/articles/recantation-of-albert-maltz.
4. Grant and Hodgkiss, *Renegade Westerns*, 29.
5. Slotkin, *Gunfighter Nation*, 377.
6. Corkin, *Cowboys as Cold Warriors*, 95.
7. Coyne, *The Crowded Prairie*, 46.
8. Walker, "Westerns of Delmer Daves," 128–29.
9. Grant and Hodgkiss, *Renegade Westerns*, 30.
10. Walker, "Westerns of Delmer Daves," 124–25.

Devil's Doorway (1950)

1. Slotkin, *Gunfighter Nation*, 367.
2. Whittier, "Maud Muller" (1856). Full text at bartleby.com/102/76.html.
3. This quote, frequently ascribed to Dr. King, actually has a complicated history. The earliest example I know of Dr. King's use of this idea is in his 1956 "Statement on Ending the [Montgomery] Bus Boycott." His earliest printed version may be in the February 8, 1958 issue of *The Gospel Messenger*, p. 14, but Dr. King places the statement in quotation marks, suggesting that it is a preexisting aphorism. In fact, Quote Investigator has traced it back to an 1853 collection of sermons by Unitarian abolitionist Theodore Parker, who wrote: "I do not pretend to understand the moral universe, the arc is a long one, my eye reaches but little ways. I cannot calculate the curve and complete the figure by the experience of sight; I can divine it by conscience. But from what I see I am sure it bends towards justice." See quoteinvestigator.com/2012/11/15/arc-of-universe/#note-4794–8.

Rawhide (1951)

1. Goldman, *Which Lie*, 81–83.
2. Campbell, *Hero*, 2.

Along the Great Divide (1951)

1. Maddrey, *Quick*, 62.
2. See Newman, *Wild West Movies*, 49.
3. Maddrey, *Quick*, 62.
4. Kael, *I Lost It*, 47–48.
5. Mann, *Stories of Three Decades*, 132.
6. Campbell, *Creative Mythology*, 329.

High Noon (1952)

1. Frankel, *High Noon*, 282. This quote comes originally from Wayne's infamous *Playboy* interview of May 1971, in which the actor sets forth his controversial views on the Vietnam War, race, blacklisting, the counterculture, and other matters.
2. Goldman, *Adventures*, 470.
3. McBride, *Hawks on Hawks*, 163.

The Naked Spur (1953)

1. Campbell, *Myths of Light*, 29.
2. See, for example, Stout, *The Sociopath Next Door*.

Shane (1953)

1. Buscombe, *BFI Companion*, 426.
2. Buscombe, *BFI Companion*, 428.
3. Hughes, *Stagecoach to Tombstone*, 51.
4. Schaefer, *Shane*, 149.
5. Hughes, *Stagecoach to Tombstone*, 46.
6. McVeigh, *The American Western*, 50.
7. Hyams (Joe), "Making *Shane*," 11.
8. Hyams (Jay), *Life and Times*, 96.
9. Hughes, *Stagecoach to Tombstone*, 47.
10. Hyams (Jay), *Life and Times*, 96.
11. Schaefer, *Shane*, 146.

Conclusion

1. Radice, *Quest*, 53.

Bibliography

Aristotle. "Nicomachean Ethics." Trans. W. D. Ross. In *The Works of Aristotle, Volume II*. Chicago: Encyclopædia Brittanica, 1952.

_____. "On Poetics." Trans. Ingram Bywater. In *The Works of Aristotle, Volume II*. Chicago: Encyclopædia Brittanica, 1952.

Arnold, Elliott. *Blood Brother*. Lincoln, NE: University of Nebraska Press, 1947.

Bandy, Mary Lea, and Kevin Stoehr. *Ride, Boldly Ride: The Evolution of the American Western*. Berkeley: University of California Press, 2012.

Bogdanovich, Peter. *John Ford*. Revised and enlarged edition. Berkeley: University of California Press, 1978.

Bosworth, Patricia. *Montgomery Clift: A Biography*. New York: Harcourt Brace Jovanovich, 1978.

Brownlow, Kevin. *The War, the West, and the Wilderness*. New York: Alfred A. Knopf, 1978.

Busch, Niven. *Duel in the Sun*. New York: Hampton Publishing, 1944.

Buscombe, Edward, ed. *The BFI Companion to the Western*. New York: Da Capo Press, 1988.

Cameron, Ian, and Douglas Pye, eds. *The Book of Westerns*. New York: Continuum Publishing, 1996.

Campbell, Joseph. *The Hero with a Thousand Faces*. 3rd ed. Novato, CA: New World Library, 2008. [Originally published by Pantheon Books, 1949.]

_____. *The Masks of God: Creative Mythology*. New York: Penguin Arkana, 1991. [Originally published by Viking Penguin, 1968.]

_____. *The Masks of God: Occidental Mythology*. New York: Penguin, 1976. [Originally published by Viking Penguin, 1964.]

_____. *The Masks of God: Oriental Mythology*. New York: Penguin, 1976. [Originally published by Viking Penguin, 1962.]

_____. *The Masks of God: Primitive Mythology*. New York: Penguin Arkana, 1991. [Originally published by Viking Penguin, 1959.]

_____. *Myths of Light: Eastern Metaphors of the Eternal*. Novato, CA: New World Library, 2003.

_____. *The Power of Myth*. New York: Doubleday, 1988.

Capua, Michelangelo. *Montgomery Clift: A Biography*. Jefferson, NC: McFarland, 2002.

Carter, Matthew. *Myth of the Western: New Perspectives on Hollywood's Frontier Narrative*. Edinburgh: Edinburgh University Press, 2014.

"Close-Ups: Editorial Expression and Timely Comment." *Photoplay Magazine*. Aug. 1917, 61–63.

Corkin, Stanley. *Cowboys as Cold Warriors: The Western and U.S. History*. Philadelphia: Temple University Press, 2004.

Coyne, Michael. *The Crowded Prairie: American National Identity in the Hollywood Western*. London: I.B. Tauris, 1997.

Crowther, Bosley R. "At the Criterion." *The New York Times*. June 25, 1938, 7.

_____. "'Fort Apache,' RKO Western, with Fonda, Wayne and Temple." *The New York Times*. June 25, 1948, 26.

Davis, Ronald L. *Duke: The Life and Image of John Wayne*. Norman: University of Oklahoma Press, 1998.

Ebert, Roger. *Questions for the Movie Answer Man*. Kansas City: Andrews McMeel, 1997.

Emerson, Ralph Waldo. *The Essential Writings of Ralph Waldo Emerson*. Brooks Atkinson, ed. New York: The Modern Library, 2000.

Eyman, Scott. *Hank & Jim: The Fifty-Year Friendship of Henry Fonda and James Stewart*. New York: Simon & Schuster, 2017.

_____. *Print the Legend: The Life and Times of John Ford*. New York: Simon & Schuster, 1999.

Fenin, George N., and William K. Everson. *The Western: From Silents to the Seventies*. Reprint of Grossman revised edition. Harmondsworth, UK: Penguin Books, 1977.

Ferber, Edna. *Cimarron*. New York: Vintage Books, 2014.

"Frank S. Nugent, Screen Writer and Former Film Critic, Dead." *The New York Times*. December 31, 1965, 21.

Frankel, Glenn. *High Noon: The Hollywood Blacklist and the Making of an American Classic*. New York: Bloomsbury, 2017.

_____. *The Searchers: The Making of an American Legend*. New York: Bloomsbury, 2013.

French, Peter A. *Cowboy Metaphysics: Ethics and Death in Westerns*. Lanham, MD: Rowman & Littlefield Publishers, 1997.

Godwin, Parke. *The Last Rainbow*. New York: Avon Books, 1995. [Originally published in 1985.]

Goldman, William. *Adventures in the Screen Trade: A Personal View of Hollywood and Screenwriting*. New York: Warner Books, 1983.

_____. *Which Lie Did I Tell?: More Adventures*

in the Screen Trade. New York: Vintage Books, 2000.

Grandin, Greg. *The End of the Myth: From the Frontier to the Border Wall in the Mind of America.* New York: Metropolitan Books, 2019.

Grant, Kevin, and Clark Hodgkiss. *Renegade Westerns: Movies That Shot Down Frontier Myths.* Godalming, UK: FAB Press, 2018.

Grey, Zane. *The Vanishing American.* Kindle edition. Victoria, BC: Reading Essentials, 2019. [Originally published by Harper & Brothers in 1925.]

Hada, Ken. "The Cost of the Code: Ethical Consequences in *High Noon* and *The Ox-Bow Incident.*" In *The Philosophy of the Western,* edited by Jennifer L. McMahon and B. Steve Csaki, 187–201. Lexington: The University Press of Kentucky, 2010.

Hardy, Phil. *The Aurum Film Encyclopedia: The Western.* 2nd ed. London: Aurum Press, 1995.

Hawthorne, Nathaniel. *Twice-Told Tales.* Boston: Houghton-Mifflin, 1882.

Henry, O. "The Caballero's Way." *Everybody's Magazine.* July 1907, 86–93.

Hughes, Howard. *Stagecoach to Tombstone: The Filmgoers' Guide to the Great Westerns.* London: I. B. Tauris, 2008.

Hyams, Jay. *The Life and Times of the Western Movie.* New York: Gallery Books, 1983.

Hyams, Joe. "Making *Shane.*" In *George Stevens: Interviews,* 10–12. Ed. Paul Cronin. Jackson: University Press of Mississippi, 2004.

Indick, William. *The Psychology of the Western: How the American Psyche Plays Out on Screen.* Jefferson, NC: McFarland, 2008.

Joyce, James. *A Portrait of the Artist as a Young Man.* Unabridged republication of the original B. W. Huebsch edition text of 1916. Mineola, NY: Dover, 1994.

Kael, Pauline. *I Lost It at the Movies.* New York: Marion Boyars, 2002. [Originally published by Little, Brown and Company in 1965.]

_____. *Kiss Kiss Bang Bang.* New York: Bantam Books, 1969.

Kitses, Jim, and Gregg Rickman, eds. *The Western Reader.* New York: Limelight Editions, 1998.

Kluckhohn, Clyde. "Recurrent Themes in Myths and Mythmaking." *Daedalus.* Spr 1959, 268–79.

Kyne, Peter B. *The Three Godfathers.* Illus. ed. New York: Cosmopolitan Book Corporation, 1922.

Lake, Stuart N. *Wyatt Earp: Frontier Marshal.* New York: Houghton Mifflin Company, 1931.

Lao Tzu. *Tao Te Ching: A Book About the Way and the Power of the Way.* Trans. Ursula K. Le Guin. Boulder: Shambala, 1997.

_____. *Tao Te Ching: A New English Version.* Trans. Stephen Mitchell. New York: HarperPerennial, 1992.

Laughton, Charles. "The Role I Liked Best…" *Saturday Evening Post.* May 28, 1949.

Lim, Dennis. "A Second Look; 'Wagon Master' Rolls On." *Los Angeles Times.* September 20, 2009.

Maddrey, Joseph. *The Quick, the Dead and the Revived: The Many Lives of the Western Film.* Jefferson, NC: McFarland, 2016.

Malory, Thomas. *Le Morte d'Arthur.* 2 vols. Harmondsworth, UK: Penguin Books, 1969.

Maltz, Albert. "What Shall We Ask of Writers?" *The New Masses.* February 12, 1946, 19–22.

Mann, Thomas. *Stories of Three Decades.* Translated by H. T. Lowe-Porter. New York: Alfred A. Knopf, 1936.

May, Rollo. *The Cry for Myth.* New York: Delta, 1991.

McBride, Joseph. *Hawks on Hawks.* Lexington: University Press of Kentucky, 2013. [First published in 1982 by the University of California Press.]

_____. *Searching for John Ford.* Jackson: University Press of Mississippi, 2011.

McGee, Patrick. *From Shane to Kill Bill: Rethinking the Western.* Malden, MA: Blackwell Publishing, 2007.

McVeigh, Stephen. *The American Western.* Edinburgh: Edinburgh University Press, 2007.

Moses, Michael Valdez. "Savage Nations: Native Americans and the Western." In *The Philosophy of the Western,* edited by Jennifer L. McMahon and B. Steve Csaki, 261–90. Lexington: The University Press of Kentucky, 2010.

Myrsiades, Kostas. "Reading *The Gunfighter* as Homeric Epic." *College Literature.* Spring 2007.

"The New Pictures." *Time.* April 24, 1947.

Newman, Kim. *Wild West Movies: How the West Was Found, Won, Lost, Lied About, Filmed and Forgotten.* London: Bloombury Publishing, 1990.

Nicholson, Jack. "Happy Jack." Interview by Nancy Collins. *Vanity Fair.* April 1992.

Nietzsche, Friedrich. "The Birth of Tragedy." Trans. Walter Kaufmann. In *Basic Writings of Nietzsche.* New York: The Modern Library, 2000.

Pateman, Roy. *The Man Nobody Knows: The Life and Legacy of B. Traven.* Lanham, MD: University Press of America, 2005.

Pauly, Thomas H. *Zane Grey: His Life, His Adventures, His Women.* Urbana: University of Illinois Press, 2005.

Picasso, Pablo. "Picasso Speaks: A Statement by the Artist." *The Arts.* May 1923, 315–29.

Pippin, Robert B. *Hollywood Westerns and American Myth: The Importance of Howard Hawks and John Ford for Political Philosophy.* New Haven, CT: Yale University Press, 2010.

Presley, Cecilia de Mille, and Mark A. Vieira. *Cecil B. DeMille: The Art of the Hollywood Epic.* Philadelphia: Running Press, 2014.

Procter, Adelaide A. *The Poems of Adelaide A. Procter.* Complete ed. New York: Frank F. Lovell, 1885.

Radice, Betty, ed. *The Quest of the Holy Grail.* Trans. P[auline] M. Matarasso. Harmondsworth, UK: Penguin Books, 1969.

Schaefer, Jack. *Shane.* Albuquerque: University of New Mexico Press, 2017. [Originally published in *Argosy* magazine, 1946, and as a novel by Houghton Mifflin, 1949.]

Schoenberger, Nancy. *Wayne and Ford: The Films, the Friendship, and the Forging of an American Hero.* New York: Doubleday, 2017.

Sklar, Robert. "*Red River:* Empire to the West." *Cineaste.* Fall 1978.

Slesin, Aviva. *American Masters.* Season 2, episode 2, "Directed by William Wyler." Aired May 1, 1986, on PBS.

Slotkin, Richard. *The Fatal Environment: The Myth of the Frontier in the Age of Industrialization, 1800–1890.* New York: Atheneum, 1985.

_____. *Gunfighter Nation: The Myth of the Frontier in Twentieth-Century America.* Reprint of 1992 Atheneum edition. Norman: University of Oklahoma Press, 1998.

_____. *Regeneration Through Violence: The Mythology of the American Frontier, 1600–1860.* Middletown, CT: Wesleyan University Press, 1973.

Smyrnaeus, Quintus. *The Fall of Troy.* Trans. Arthur S. Way. London: William Heinemann, 1913.

Stout, Martha. *The Sociopath Next Door.* New York: Broadway Books, 2005.

Stravinsky, Igor. *Poetics of Music in the Form of Six Lessons.* New York: Vintage Books, 1956.

Tennyson, Alfred Lord. *The Works of Alfred Lord Tennyson.* London: Wordsworth Editions, 2008.

Thomas, Kevin. "Victor Mature Hits Stride." *Los Angeles Times.* December 7, 1966.

Tompkins, Jane. *West of Everything: The Inner Life of Westerns.* Oxford: Oxford University Press, 1992.

"'Vanishing American' Set For Feb. 15." *Motion Picture News.* November 14, 1925, 2257.

Walker, Michael. "The Westerns of Delmer Daves." In Cameron, Ian, and Douglas Pye, eds. *The Book of Westerns,* edited by Ian Cameron and Douglas Pye, 123–60. New York: Continuum Publishing, 1996.

Welles, Orson. "Playboy Interview." Interview by Kenneth Tynan. *Playboy.* March 1967.

Whitaker, Herman. *Over the Border.* New York: Grosset & Dunlap, 1917.

White, E. B., and Katharine S. White, eds. *A Subtreasury of American Humor.* New York: Coward-McCann, 1941.

Wilmington, Michael. "Cowboy Pioneer." *Chicago Tribune.* September 1, 1994.

Wister, Owen. *The Virginian: A Horseman of the Plains.* London: Macmillan and Company, 1902.

Wolfram von Eschenbach. *Parzival.* Trans. A. T. Hatto. London: Penguin Books, 1980.

Wright, Will. *Sixguns & Society: A Structural Study of the Western.* Berkeley: University of California Press, 1975.

Index

Numbers in **bold italics** indicate pages with illustrations

Lighton, Louis D. 99
Lillian Russell 181
Lincoln, Abraham 63–64, *65*,
  67–68, 138, 142–43, 146
Lincoln, Mary Todd 142
Lincoln County, New Mexico
  117–18, 120
Lincoln Memorial 317
Lindley, Bert 180
Litel, John 167, 204, 206
literalism 2, 7–12, 14, 17–18, 141,
  163, 172–73, 198, 225, 253, 257,
  347, 350; *see also* metaphor
literature 8–9, 14, 18–19, 43, 44,
  87, 95, 111, 139, 239, 253, 254–55,
  298, 329, 347; *see also specific
  authors and titles*
Little, Cleavon 140
Little, Thomas 265
Little Big Man 27, 140, 143, 253,
  308, 367
Little Bighorn 32, 204–6, 276
"Little Joe, the Wrangler" (song)
  186
Littlefield, Lucien 78, 80
Locarno International Film
  Festival Awards 247, 265
The Locket 241
Lockhart, Gene 204
"Locksley Hall" (poem) 281
Loeffler, Louis R. 94, 111
Loesser, Frank 186
"La Loma de los Vientos" (ranch)
  85
London 193, 338
London, Jack 87
London, Tom 22
Lone Star 367
Lone Star Productions 129
loneliness *see* isolation
Lonely Are the Brave 27
Lonesome Dove (miniseries) 27,
  30, 102–3, 198, 263, 367
The Lonesome Trail 45
Long, Hal 149
The Long Riders 152, 154
The Long Voyage Home 262
Lord, Robert 167
The Lord of the Rings (book/film
  series) 10, 111, 162–63, 172, 319
Lordsburg, New Mexico 156,
  162–65
Los Angeles 92, 94, 111, 220, 225,
  244
Losch, Tilly 225
The Lost Patrol 92
love triangles 46, 59, 61, 96, 103,
  113, 175, 177, 202, 218, 220, 228,
  279, 360–61
Loveridge, Leslie 28, *29*
Lovering, Otho 156
Loving, Oliver 264
Lowe, Edmund 94, 96
Lucas, George 10, 148, 162, 172,
  189, 319
The Lucky Texan 129, 370
Lundigan, William 167
Lust for Life 325

Lust in the Dust (nickname and
  eventual film) 226
The Lusty Men 371
Lynch, Helen *95*
lynching 100, 103, 169, 209–15,
  260, 326, *332*; *see also* frontier
  justice; law
Lyon, Francis D. 254
Lyons, Cliff 280

MacArthur, Charles 117
MacDonald, Ian 338–39, *342*
MacDonald, J. Farrell 63, 69, 86,
  87, 88, *89*, 91, 98, 217. *224*
MacDonald, Jeanette 370
MacDonald, Joseph 217, 265
MacGregor, Malcolm 71
Mack, Willard 117
Mackay, John Victor 201
MacKenzie, Æneas 204
Mackenzie, Joyce 304
MacLane, Barton 201, 244
MacPherson, Jeanie 141
Madero, Francisco I. 128, *132*,
  133–34
The Magnificent Seven 367
Magrill, George 71
Mahler, Gustav 334
Mailes, Charles Hill 28
Malden, Karl 286, 289
Maloney, Leo D. 369
Malory, Thomas 7, 12, 41, 53,
  61–62, 86, 88, 97, 253, 274, 301,
  303, 360; *see also* Arthurian
  romances
Maltz, Albert 304–8, 311
The Man from Laramie 211, 297
The Man from Monterey 129–31,
  370
The Man from U.N.C.L.E. (TV
  series) 351
The Man I Love 241–42
*The Man Who Shot Liberty
  Valance* 114, 253, 285
The Man Who Would Be King 253
Man with No Name (film trilogy)
  27, 95, 246; *see also specific titles*
The Mandalorian (TV series) 243
Mandell, Daniel 193
Manichaeism 254–56, 259, 303
Manifest Destiny 10, 12, 28–29,
  34, 60, 64, 69, 71, 114, 125, 142,
  146, 197, 249, 253, 308, 313, 330,
  365, 366
Mann, Anthony 186, 191, 211,
  296–98, 300, 312, 326, 330–31,
  349, 351, 353, 370–71
Mann, Thomas 15, 328–29
Manpower 241
Marble, Scott 22
"Marching Through Georgia"
  (song) 171
Marcus, James A. 63, 117
Marion, George F. 78
Marked Men 105
Marker, Harry 104
Marks, Owen 244
Marlowe, Hugh 318, *320*, 321

"La Marseillaise" (song) 170–71
Marsh, Mae 28, *29*, 30, 32, 247,
  319
Marshall, George 184, 370
Marshall, Herbert 225
Marshall, Tully 59, 111
Martin, Chris-Pin 117, 209
Martin, E.A. 56, 369
Marvin, Lee 140
Marx Brothers 138
Marxism *see* Communism
masculinity in Westerns 3–4,
  30–31, 99, 101–2, 130, 144, 170,
  186, 189–90, 197, 210, 215–16,
  228–30, 236, 239, 247–48, 256–
  60, 262, 320, 340, 343
The Mask of Dimitrios 242
The Masks of God (book series)
  185
Maslow, Abraham 349–50
Mason, James 83
Mason, Martin 358
mass shootings *see* guns
"Massacre" (story) 247
Masterson, Bat 180
The Matrix (trilogy) 347
Mature, Victor 183, 217, 219–20
Maverick (TV series) 358
Maxwell, Charles 179
May, Rollo 9
Mayall, Herschel 48
Maynard, Ken 95, 129, 201, 370
Mayo, Virginia 325–26
Mays, Willie 323
Mayuzumi, Toshiro 286
McAdoo, Tom 358, 362
McBride, Joseph 282
McCall, Jack 141, 147
McCarey, Leo 136, 138, 370
McCarthyism 232, 255, 339
McClaury, Frank 179
McClaury, Tom 179
McCord, Ted D. 244
McCrea, Joel 174, *175–76*, 177
McDaniel, Hattie 204
McDermott, Joseph 28, *29*
McDonald, Francis 174
McDowell, Nelson 117
McGee, Patrick 1
McGlynn, Frank, Sr. 142
McGuinness, James Kevin 128
McHugh, Frank 167
McIntire, John 296, 298
McKay, Scott 225
McKim, Robert 51
McKinley, William 96
McLaglen, Victor 247, 251, 273,
  279
McLean, Barbara 149, 286
McMahon, Horace 201
McNally, Stephen 296, 298
McNeil, Allen 209
McQueen, Butterfly 225, 227
McSween, Alexander 119
McVeagh, Eve 338
McVey, Paul 358
McWade, Robert 122
Medicine Bow, Wyoming 313